America's
Other
Children

University of Oklahoma Press : Norman

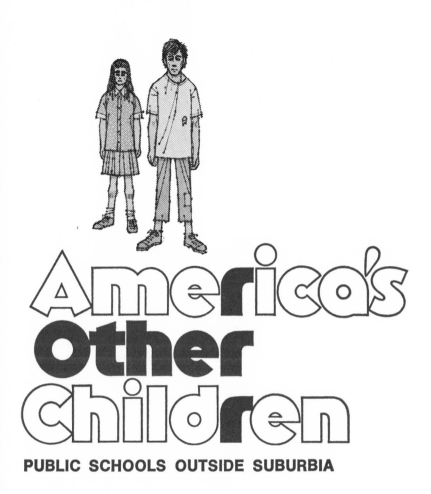

America's Other Children

PUBLIC SCHOOLS OUTSIDE SUBURBIA

Edited by GEORGE HENDERSON

By George Henderson

Foundations of American Education (with William B. Ragan) (New
York, 1970)
Teachers Should Care (with Robert F. Bibens) (New York, 1970)
America's Other Children: Public Schools Outside Suburbia (editor)
(Norman, 1971)

International Standard Book Number: 0–8061–0946–7

Library of Congress Catalog Card Number: 76–145500

Copyright 1971 by the University of Oklahoma Press, Publishing Division
of the University. Composed and printed at Norman, Oklahoma, U.S.A.,
by the University of Oklahoma Press. First edition.

To the Special People in My Life

Preface

FEW social institutions in America have received as much criticism as the urban public schools. While the critics vary greatly in terms of their academic disciplines, there is consensus in their dominant themes: The urban public schools are poorly educating most students, and the quality of urban school education is getting progressively worse. This indictment is found in such works as James Conant's *Slums and Suburbs* (1961), Charles Silberman's *Crisis in Black and White* (1964), Kenneth Clark's *Dark Ghetto* (1965), Bel Kaufman's *Up the Down Staircase* (1965), Jonathan Kozol's *Death at an Early Age* (1967), and the U.S. Commission on Civil Rights' *Racial Isolation in the Public Schools* (1967). If the detailed analyses in these and other books are only partly true, our urban elementary and secondary public schools are confronted with some of the major social problems and challenges of the twentieth century.

Within the past ten years, the focus on education has shifted almost exclusively to urban schools. In neglecting rural schools, we are neglecting one-fourth of our population nationally and upwards of two-thirds of the population in some states. Many student teachers still practice teach in small schools and, upon graduation, begin their careers in rural communities. Others must deal with students who through urbanization have been uprooted from their rural homes and are trying to adjust to the new set of values and attitudes they find in the city. For these reasons, I have attempted to write a book that would be of particular benefit to the many students who will never teach in an urban community, as well as those who will teach in big city schools which are also being affected by the influx of migrants from rural areas. In short, I have tried to bridge the gap between rural education on the one hand and urban education on the other hand.

Writers who cling unyieldingly to urban-rural dichotomies fail to notice the interdependence of town and country. This book is a study focusing on rural schools and small communities undergoing the process of urbanization. Therefore, our emphasis is on both similarities and differences between rural and urban school communities. It is my hope that students in educational problems and rural sociology courses will find this book to be of great use to them as they try to understand the effects of urbanization on rural community institutions, especially the family and the school.

Whatever value this book has as a tool for learning, I owe to the authors and publishers who granted permission to reprint their articles. Finally, special thanks go to the students at the University of Oklahoma who turned the attention of this urban educator to the problems of rural schools. From them, I received much more than I gave.

GEORGE HENDERSON

Norman, Oklahoma
February 1, 1971

Contents

1. Overview

AT the turn of the century, social scientists were paraphrasing the lyrics to a popular World War I song: "How're you gonna keep 'em down on the farm, after they have seen the city?" The life-style of man has undergone many changes throughout his remarkable history. Though still predominantly rural, human inhabitants of the world are becoming increasingly urban in residence and urbanized in characteristics.

Technically, *urbanization* refers to concentration of population, while *urbanism* connotes the social perspectives and life-styles of city dwellers. The urbanization of America is without a doubt bringing about an urbanism of rural institutions. Currently, over thirty definitions of urban populations are in use, but none is totally adequate for use on an international scale. However, by any measure being used, the United States is one of the most highly urbanized nations in the world.

By the middle of the twentieth century, it was evident that America would never again be a predominantly rural nation. The United States Census Bureau defines an urban place as any settlement of twenty-five hundred or more population. At the end of this past decade, 1970, we have completed our first half century of life as an urban nation. Over 70 per cent of Americans now live in urban places. In addition, few rural areas or people remain untouched by this change.

It should be stated at the outset that the words "urban" and "rural" represent a continuum along which types of communities are not always clearly distinguished. Villages are much like towns, towns shade into cities, and cities into metropolitan regions. Rural isolation and its concomitant social characteristics that were found in abundance at the beginning of the nineteenth century have all but disappeared. There are still semi-isolated rural communities (most of them marked by extreme poverty) but, as a whole, urban and rural

3

communities do not represent totally different localities. In a real
sense, the entire American population is "urban."

Urban-rural
dichotomies Rural people can be divided into two groups: those living in the
open country and those living in villages. Farmers who live on and
produce from the land make up the bulk of the open-country (rural-
farm) group. Also included in this category are nonfarming people
—ministers, livestock truckers, creamery operators—whose primary
social and business associations are with farmers and village residents. Villagers provide the necessary business and service institutions for the surrounding farms. Even though some villages may
have small manufacturing plants, their major source of wealth can
be traced to an interdependent relationship with the farming periphery. There are no completely independent communties.

Romantic conceptionalizations assign different values to rural
and urban communities. There are those who maintain idyllic
thoughts of rural life. "Rural" conjures up "the smell of freshly mown
meadows, herds of cattle, fields of crops, a country store, farmers
in overalls and wives in house gingham."[1] From this perspective, the
farmer is the prototype of the sturdy, independent man in a natural,
unspoiled environment. Conversely, urban life is viewed as unnatural and, indeed, bad. To support their position, critics of the city
cite the high incidence of physical and mental illnesses in urban
communities. And, these critics continue, the creator of this havoc
is none other than the "city slicker." Cities are said to be crowded,
dirty, and centers of crime. Oscar Lewis observed that many descriptions of the modern city read like an updated version of the fall of
man.[2]

On the other hand, there are those who view the city as the center
of civilization, the epitome of progress and the good life. From this
perspective, the urban dweller is the true prototype of civilized man.
Unlike Rousseau who viewed rural people as "noble savages," critics
of rural life label rural people "hicks" and "country bumpkins" who
do not share in the richness of culture found in urban areas. The
farmer, therefore, is viewed as a person of much brawn but little
brain or cultural refinement.

Somewhere between these extreme views is a more accurate picture of rural and urban life. To state that America is an urban nation

1 Gordon E. Erickson, *Urban Behavior* (New York, Macmillan, 1954), 86.
2 Oscar Lewis, "The Folk-Urban Ideal Types: Further Observations on the Folk-
Urban Continuum and Urbanization with Special Reference to Mexico City," in Philip M.
Hauser and Leo F. Schnore (eds.), *The Study of Urbanization* (New York, John Wiley
and Sons, 1965), 497.

is to overstate the obvious.[3] While it is true we are becoming increasingly more urban, one-fourth of the nation still resides in rural communities. In addition, the trend toward suburban living may cause a stabilization if not a return to rural areas.

The criterion of size—less than twenty-five hundred people—is hardly an adequate indication of what life is like in a rural community. Urban-rural comparisons of population growth, education and health facilities, housing conditions, and average family income suggest consistent disparities between "rural" and "urban" America, with rural America in the disadvantaged position. Thus books and programs which focus exclusively on "the urban crisis" neglect our disadvantaged rural citizens.

In terms of life-styles, there is much similarity between the so-called city slickers and country bumpkins. Both share and are influenced by the products of urbanization. Both have been enculturated in a country that has a strong rural bias against cities. Both have been educated in schools taught by teachers who have markedly similar professional training. Now we shall discuss some specific similarities and differences between urban and rural communities.

In rural communities people are surrounded by nature and are more likely to work out of doors, with animals and machines.[4] Children play freely with natural play materials, such as earth, flowers, rocks, and branches of trees. In addition, they can run, climb, jump, and swim without constantly being stopped by fences, buildings, and traffic. City dwellers are surrounded by man-made objects, such as houses, automobiles, and fences. They are hampered in their movements by crowds of people and signs designating restricted areas.

Community differences and similarities

Furthermore, in rural communities the dominant style of life is outdoors-indoors. Rural children can roam in and out of the house and easily make contact with adults. The world of the urban child is divided by walls, doors, elevators, and vertical distances. However, differences in socialization are diminishing because urban and rural children are being socialized by the same television programs, newspaper articles, and teaching materials.

The extension of commercial farming based on profit, along with the introduction of improved machinery, has greatly influenced the social organization of rural communities. The introduction of com-

3 See Advisory Commission on Intergovernmental Relations, *Urban and Rural America* (Washington, D.C., U.S. Government Printing Office, 1968).
4 See Ase Grude Skard, *What Happens to Children in the Transition From a Predominantly Rural Economy to Modern Industrialization?* (Washington, D.C., National Education Association, 1968).

mercialization and mechanization into agriculture has meant that the urban ways of life have crept into rural culture. Today the farmer typically produces goods for a wider market than surrounding villages, utilizes the money economy of urban society, and takes part in a larger political arena by paying taxes, voting, and sending his children to intercommunity or consolidated schools.

Before the introduction of rapid transportation and mass communication, along with the other intrusions of urban culture into rural communities, the small towns and villages were isolated very much like Washington Irving's Sleepy Hollow. Contact for the most part was face to face. There was an overriding sense of independence, on the one hand, and a rural solidarity, on the other. The range of interaction was restricted mostly to the rural community. This resulted in community efforts to keep the status quo and, concurrently, prejudice against outsiders, new ideas and practices. Contact with the outside world was slow coming but once established through newspapers, schools, and churches it altered forever the life-styles of rural communities.

An affluent elderly farmer looking around, wishing for the "good old days" is likely to notice that he has

> . . . the same modern plumbing as his city cousin; his wife uses an electric clothes washer; and her kitchen is equipped with an electric dishwasher. The children do not attend the little red schoolhouse but a large, centrally located consolidated school. The family shops at a chain supermarket, not a "cracker-barrel" general store. It reads metropolitan newspapers, listens to the same television programs as do city dwellers. . . . There are more cars, more places to go, and young folks, like their city cousins, go to drive-in movies. . . . There is more business to seek and more competition to meet. Our nostalgic man, looking back, remembers that everybody used to be warm and friendly. Probably this was not entirely the case even then, but if he returned to his childhood home today he would find some of the hardness, the conflict, the cruelty that one can find in the city.[5]

Farm people have the same appetite as city residents for telephones, newspapers, television sets, cars, and other consumer goods. Politically, rural communities have never been separate and independent governments. They derive their political and educational power from state government. In these and many other ways, it is clear that rural communities in America have no autonomous exis-

5 David Dressler, *Sociology: The Study of Human Interaction,* (New York, Alfred A. Knopf), 415.

tence of their own. Differences are blurred even more as rural people migrate to urban areas in search of better economic opportunity.

In 1790, 95 per cent of the United States population lived in rural areas; by 1860, the proportion was down to 80 per cent; and by 1900, it was 60 per cent. However, it was not until 1920 that the urban population outnumbered the rural population, 51 per cent to 49 per cent. Today approximately 25 per cent of Americans live in rural areas and less than one-fourth of them earn their livelihood from agriculture. Over three-fourths of the rural residents have nonfarm employment—a tenth of the United States labor force produces all of the country's food. **Population shifts**

When viewed from regional perspectives, rural areas show both decreases and increases in population. Between 1950 and 1970, approximately half the counties in the nation lost population and most of these were rural counties. Regions of heavy decline included (1) the interior coastal plain of the lower South from Georgia through Texas; (2) the continuous area of the Great Plains; (3) the Allegheny Plateau; (4) most of the Ozarks; and (5) other upland counties of Arkansas, Oklahoma, and Missouri.

Increases in rural populations were in California, Florida, Nevada, and in several of the outlying areas of large industrial centers of the lower Great Lakes and Atlantic seaboard. These increases did not reflect a revival of agriculture but instead increases in manufacturing and commuting to urban employment. Many urban workers desire the higher income of urban-based industries and the physical amenities of rural living. There does, consequently, appear to be a slight shift back to rural areas for housing but not for employment and entertainment.

The average successful farm represents an investment of more than fifty thousand dollars in land, buildings, and machinery. Lacking this kind of money for investment, one-fourth of the farmers are small, marginal businessmen who gross less than five thousand dollars per year. Three-fifths of the farm poor are too old, too inadequately educated, or too handicapped to transfer to other occupations, even if provided job retraining. As they retire or move away, their lands are added to other farms. This accounts for the fact that each year the number of farmers decreases, while the average size of farms increases.

Both central cities and rural areas share the distinction of having the highest proportions of males fourteen years or over in the labor force, and also the highest unemployment rates. It would appear that moving from the farm to the central city merely changes the location of the unemployment. Although they usually migrate to urban communities in hopes of improving their economic condition, most rural people return to their rural place of origin, not because they have saved enough money to buy a small farm but because they are broke.

Having strong family and kinship ties, rural migrants engage in voluntary segregation in their urban places of residence. The frequent presence of relatives sharing single dwelling units reflects kinship cohesiveness that shields newcomers from the cold, impersonal qualities of the city. "Home" is likely to be the migrants' place of rural origin. In addition, "home folks" are those of similar rural origin. In urban apartment buildings it is not uncommon to find entire buildings or floors occupied by home folks, i.e., "Tennessee," "Kentucky," "Alabama," or "Georgia" buildings or floors. As a whole, urban housing is better than rural housing.

Housing conditions Rural areas lag behind urban areas in structural adequacy of housing. In 1969, over 80 per cent of the urban residents lived in structurally sound houses with complete plumbing, while less than 60 per cent of the rural residents had equally good housing. Even though rural areas accounted for approximately 30 per cent of all housing units, nearly half the units lacked structural soundness or complete plumbing. Thirty per cent of the rural homes had complete baths compared with 97 per cent of the urban homes. Over 20 per cent of the rural homes did not have running water, while only 1 per cent of the urban homes lacked running water. Nearly one out of every five rural families did not have both hot and cold running water compared with nineteen out of twenty urban families that had both.

Other housing disparities can be found in the number of consumer goods—televisions, telephones, and automobiles—owned by rural and urban residents. Although lack of certain consumer goods, such as televisions and automobiles does not mean families are impoverished, it does indicate that most rural families have not achieved a level of living comparable to most urban families.

Poverty In a strict sense, poverty is the same no matter where it is found, and rural and urban poor have many traits in common—poor health, low levels of educational and occupational aspirations. Upon closer analysis, rural poverty is different from urban poverty in two ways. It is greater proportionately. It tends to be hidden because it is not near the main thoroughfares.

America seems to bear out the quotation in the Bible: "The poor ye shall have ever with you." Although it accounts for less than 30 per cent of the total population, rural America has almost as many poor people as urban America.[6] There are five urban poor persons for every three rural poor. There are more than two white poor persons for every nonwhite poor person. Yet poverty remains a dominant characteristic of nonwhite people, 41 per cent of whom are poor compared to 12 per cent of the whites. But to talk about poverty as either a racial or an urban problem is to miss its significance: poverty is not a phenomenon unique to any racial group or community.

Geographically, the rural poor are concentrated in portions of twelve states: the Appalachian regions; the Ozark and Ouachita Mountain areas of Missouri, Arkansas, and Oklahoma; the northern counties of Minnesota, Wisconsin, and Michigan; rural northern New England; and the Delta and Piedmont area in the South.

Both the urban and the rural poor are even more disadvantaged if characterized by one or both of the following conditions: (1) nonwhite families with female heads of households or (2) aged families. However, rural poor families with these conditions are in a more adverse position than urban poor families of similar conditions. While the per capita farm income has been increasing, it does not approximate that of nonfarm groups. Farm incomes are approximately 65 per cent of nonfarm incomes. But farm people must spend as high a proportion of their income on food and housing as do nonfarm dwellers. In addition, clothing, transportation, and medical care accounts for a higher proportion of farm than nonfarm family income.

High birth rate, limited occupational opportunities, a shrinking local population, and a declining tax base all combine to create large and small pockets of poverty in both central cities and rural communities. The children of the poor, often showing the physical signs of their hard lives, age quicker than their affluent counterparts. Socially, they become little old "men" and "women" before reaching chronological maturity. This condition is compounded by the fact that these children are but the continuation of generations of hope-

---

6 We shall use the same definition of poverty as the Social Security Administration in 1965: Costing a nutritionally adequate economy food budget for families of various compositions regarding number, age, and sex of members, and multiplying that food cost by three. Poverty threshold for farm families is 85 per cent of the money income of the relevant nonfarm family. The range of poverty threshold incomes is: nonfarm, $1,580 for one-person family under age sixty-fixe to $5,090 for family of seven or more persons; farm, $1,340 for one-person family under age 65 to $4,325 for family of seven or more persons. Of course, these figures only represent minimum subsistence.

lessness. They are born into families characterized by *not enough*. Vincent Siragusa described poverty as follows:

> To be in a poverty situation is like being locked in a little room with a window which is locked from the outside and cannot be broken. From the window they (the residents of the room) can see the affluence of America—new cars, big homes, prestige jobs, money, and opportunities which the affluent enjoy for themselves and pass on to their children. They can see dignity, the ability to control one's destiny, direct one's life because there are choices which "having enough" gives.
>
> Beyond the room, out there in middle-classness, life is perceived as real. Being a member of this class—the recipient of all the good things, both material and psychic that go along with affluence—yields the definition of the self for those in the room. Separated from a self so defined brings isolation, loneliness, and a sense of despair. In time the unreachable self crumbles along with dreams and hopes and the future, there is left a searing experience of nonself, of failure, a belief that no one cares, that your worth is nothing and that if death comes, no one will be the less for your passing.
>
> In the room there is the *now* only. There is no tomorrow worth anything. Pleasure, intense life, and often violence is all there is. Affluent society's rules, laws, or morals are of little importance, especially for those who receive some education and are the young among the hopeless. There is the ever-present realization that in the room, becoming more crowded year after year, there is not enough. Through the window there is the ever-present view of abundance. In the room there is not enough money, food, good jobs, prestige, clothes, hope, and love.
>
> Frustrations pile up in the room and tensions, stresses, and strains twist the spirit, and there is mental suffering.[7]

The poor have become a nagging conscience for America. As long as large numbers of Americans are poverty-stricken, our bragging about world excellence rings hollow. In our affluence there is a bitter irony. We are the nation that has been able to send the first men to the moon, build the world's largest airplane, produce the most automobiles, send more children to college, but fail to abate poverty. We have a better record of helping the poor throughout the world than here at home. The Peace Corps and our military forces are engaging in "civic action" projects designed to improve the health conditions in rural areas of foreign countries. Periodically, citizens or government committees belatedly ask: "What about America's poor? Are their health needs being met?"

---

[7] Vincent A. Siragusa, "The Psychological Effects of Poverty on the Community" (unpublished paper, Norman, Oklahoma, April 22, 1970), 1–3.

The limited availability of medical personnel and hospital beds in rural counties compared to urban counties is well documented in the *Health Manpower Source Book* published by the U.S. Department of Health, Education, and Welfare in 1965.[8] There are three times the number of physicians per one hundred thousand population in urban as in rural areas. Urban residents on the average spend more for total medical care than rural residents. Related to these statistics is the fact that urban residents make more visits to physicians and dentists than their rural counterparts. Medicare has helped somewhat but it alone is not enough. It is significant to note that average family costs for medical services are nearly the same for both groups. Physicians, dentists, and hospitals do not as a rule adjust their rates to reflect the significant regional differences in family income. Most rural communities are without any medical services.

Health facilities and services

Many studies have documented the ill-health of low-income urban and rural children. Suffering from malnutrition, physical defects, and social neglect, they are over-represented in the ranks of low school achievers. And when they grow up, they are likely to replace or join their parents as unemployed or underemployed adults. The inability of central city and rural residents to secure adequate physical and psychological health care relegates to them the role of breeders of the poor.

At a time when the nation is considering ways to curb the population explosion, central cities and rural communities offer the greatest challenge. They not only have a disproportionate share of poor families but also a disproportionate share of large families. White rural farm families with low incomes have a birth rate nearly 50 per cent higher than for the nation as a whole; while the average for nonwhite rural farm families with low incomes is over 150 per cent greater. Similar rates are found in low-income central city families. Few low-income families have access to information and medical advice related to family planning.

The law of the land states that every child is entitled to twelve years of free education. To the uninformed bystander this type of quantitative equality implies an equality of educational opportunity. In reality, of course, this is far from being the truth. All children do not attend schools with adequate facilities, qualified teachers, and optimum class size. It is also true that the quality of education available

Educational facilities and services

8 Maryland Y. Pennell and Kathryn I. Baker, "Location of Manpower in Eight Health Occupations," in *Manpower Source Book* (Washington, D.C., U.S. Department of Health, Education, and Welfare, Public Health Service, 1965).

to the child varies greatly between urban, rural, and suburban schools.

Only about 3 per cent of the total schools in America are the one-room type characterizing the nation's first public schools. On the other hand, half the total high schools in America have enrollments of less than three hundred students and educate less than 15 per cent of all high school students. Lacking the minimum number of school-age children (one thousand) to support adequately a four-year school with three hundred students, many rural communities—especially in the Plains, Southwest, Rocky Mountain, and Far West regions—are consolidating school districts in order to provide a better quality of instruction. (At a time when urban communities are balking at busing school children a few blocks to achieve racial desegregation, rural school districts have a long history of busing children many miles to attend consolidated schools.)

An examination of the financial support of the public schools reveals an inverse ratio between funds and funding sources. The sources with the least amount of funds bear the highest share of education expenses. In 1968–69, 52 per cent of total revenue for public elementary and secondary schools came from local school districts, 41 per cent from the states, and 7 per cent from the federal government. Thus it becomes evident that school districts located in areas with limited resources are handicapped in terms of their ability to secure funds through real estate and personal property taxes.

Central cities are losing their tax base as industrial plants and commercial establishments are following the white middle-class exodus out of the city to the suburbs. Commuters from suburban communities also add to the financial plight of central cities. Their presence in the city requires additional police, fire, maintenance, sewage and garbage collection. Yet they often contribute nothing to meet these extra costs. It is no great surprise that many urban school districts are faced with deteriorating physical plants, inadequate budgets, and a declining quality of instruction.

Most rural schools are in the same financial condition as central city schools. Limited resources and an inadequate tax base have always plagued most rural schools. Even though relieved of some of these pressures by the exodus of unemployed residents to urban areas and the consolidation of one-room schools into large districts, most rural schools still have an inadequate tax base.

Efforts of local school districts to secure additional revenue through bond elections are being met with great resistance. The elderly population remaining in central cities and rural communities can see little reason to vote themselves additional taxes to support schools in which they no longer have children. Young homeowners use bond elections as a means of saying no to increased living costs and forced school desegregation.

The high expenditures per pupil for some rural districts also reflect the high costs encountered when children are scattered over wide areas. The major problem encountered by low-income rural areas is to provide a top quality of education without spending an excessively large proportion of their income. Unfortunately, low-income districts—urban and rural—do not have adequate funds to meet their greater-than-average needs for new facilities, more flexible and relevant curricula, and in-service training programs.

As stated earlier, other problems confronting urban and rural schools include high teacher turnover and pupil drop-out rates, and racial desegregation. But the foremost school problem is to improve the low self-images of alienated students wherever they reside. Urban and rural children are alike in their capacity to learn and in their fear of being rejected. The problems of blacks, Mexican-Americans, American Indians, Puerto Ricans, and poor whites are basically problems of inadequate opportunities. In short, educational disadvantages are debilitating in any community. It is the lack of equal opportunities that causes children to differ. The challenge to teachers is clear: find a way to maximize the education of each child. Some teachers are more successful than others. This, contrary to popular views, is not a function of class size or school location. People —teachers, administrators, counselors, and others—make the difference.

Youth subcultures

There is a consensus among social scientists that an adolescent subculture does exist and that there is sufficient evidence to support this proposition. James Coleman stated that the youth culture is a self-contained adolescent society with only a few threads of connection with the outside adult society.[9] Most upper- and middle-class youths outgrow the manifestations of their adolescent subculture and become integral parts of the adult community. In time, they stop rebelling and join their parents as gatekeepers of the status quo.

There is, however, another group of youth for whom the future is not so certain. They are the young people who are described as "impoverished," "culturally deprived," "lower class," "working class," and "socially or culturally disadvantaged." Whatever name

9 James S. Coleman, *Adolescents and the Schools* (New York, Free Press, 1961).

we choose, it is clear that this group is in need of special assistance. As many studies point out, not all disadvantaged youth are found in urban communities. Rural schools are also beset with problems centering on disadvantaged pupils.

While middle-class youth are more likely to perceive older siblings, parents, peers, and teachers as being able to help them attain their educational goals, lower-class youth find few acceptable referents in their quest for a good education. They become discouraged with school and drop out or are easily pushed out by insensitive teachers. But not all school problems are confined to low-income students. Affluent students form the bulk of the drug cases, suicides, and campus radicals. Both urban and rural schools are showing the signs of individual and group disorganization which grows out of urbanization.

The solutions to problems of rural people do not come automatically with migration to the city. Instead, their problems usually are pushed and pulled into even greater agonies upon initial arrival in the city. This is seen in the following brief discussion of mountaineers who migrate to urban areas.

Mountaineers in the city Because of clashing cultural patterns, the personal problems of mountaineers who migrate to the city often multiply.[10] Unlike city residents who tend to be *object oriented*, the mountaineer is *person oriented*. City dwellers are collectors of things but seldom people, while the mountaineer is constantly seeking out "home folks" to visit. Thus the mountaineer finds city dwellers to be cold, unconcerned neighbors. Nor can he easily get caught up in their preoccupation with getting consumer goods, amassing large sums of money, and being bound by demands for punctuality. On the contrary, his is a world of scarcity, low income, and carefree visiting—none of these traits fits well into urban demands for getting ahead.

The mountaineer is also *tradition oriented*. Survival in the mountains is based upon perpetuating old, familiar ways of life—especially housekeeping practices, speech patterns, and health codes. There is a strong resistance to change. Along with this commitment to the status quo comes passive resignation to unequal opportunities. Poverty, as an illustration, is not likely to be defined as being bad but, instead, the way things have been and probably will continue to be.

10 See Rebecca Caudill, *My Appalachia* (New York, Holt, Rinehart & Winston, 1966); and Jack E. Weller, *Yesterday's People* (Lexington, Ky., University of Kentucky Press, 1965).

Poverty becomes a vicious circle from which the mountaineer seldom seeks to extricate himself. In short, the mountaineer prefers to live today in the same manner as he lived yesterday.

Finally, the mountaineer is *religion oriented*. He is likely to believe that whatever happens to him is God's will. Such a fatalistic view of life does not spark the mountaineer to become an organization man or scholar. Relatedly, too much book learning, money, or sex may, according to some views, imply that an individual is in league with the devil. For these and other reasons, the mountaineer finds urban patterns of adjustment too demanding and unpredictable. Equally important, he is confused and tormented when forced to change in order to survive. In a real sense, he is a social dinosaur in a twentieth-century environment.

The lack of cultural press toward formal education makes the successful urban adjustment of mountain people even more improbable. "A little readin' and writin' " seems sufficient for most southern immigrants. Because of this condition, only a few schools—rural or urban—have been able to involve southern white parents in order to raise the educational aspirations of their children. Most of these parents do not seem to be against educational systems but, equally debilitating, they are *indifferent* to them. Thus their children enter school with a readiness to drop out and a susceptibility to being pushed out.

The physical size, heterogeneity of students, and sterile decorum of the school quickly crush what little emotional security the mountain child may have had when he first entered school. The net effect of these conditions is to accentuate shyness and reticence. School, too often, is something that is happening to the children and not for them. They see little relationship between school and the world of work as reflected in their parents' jobs.

The educational problems of the low-income rural migrants to urban schools begin *before* they enter the urban school. First, their subculture usually does not inculcate the middle-class press for educational success. Second, their basic problems centering on physical survival usually overshadow the less concrete educational problems, causing students to become impatient with a process that will not immediately meet their physical needs. Third, the high mobility rate of low-income families thwarts school efforts to provide continuous and progressive learning experiences.

By now it should be evident that while this illustration is based on mountain families who migrate to urban areas, we could have substituted blacks, Mexican-Americans, or American Indians for the mountaineers. The problems created by urbanization are accentuated in the youth subcultures that we observe in the schools.

Attitudes
affect
behavior As we have noted, the concept "rural"—like the concept "urban"—is merely a state of mind. It exists only in the imagination of its classifiers. Therefore, we should not be surprised to learn that rural schools are as different as the people describing them.

To some people, the rural community is an *alien port*, harboring alien people—the culturally deprived, culturally disadvantaged, and culturally different. These aliens must remain there until they can secure an adequate income to serve as passage to urban communities. Unfortunately, most rural people secure just enough money to migrate to urban communities that frequently are worse than their rural communities.

To many people, the rural community is a *plantation* and the owners live elsewhere. Schools on these plantations are administered and taught by paternalistic—and sometimes sadistic—overseers. Discipline is the foremost activity of the overseers who are on constant alert for student (slave) rebellions. Rebels are beaten, failed, and pushed out of school.

To other people, the rural community is a *battlefield* and school personnel have declared war on low-achieving students. The search and destroy tactics of these teacher-administrator-warriors are quite clear: they use laws to force children into elaborate booby-trapped classrooms; once in the classroom, children meet their educational deaths through a variety of excruciating tortures—meaningless assignments, failing grades, and ridicule.

To still others, the rural community is a *foreign country* where administrators and teachers with missionary zeal try to teach uncivilized, lower-class heathens. Risking disease, boredom, and low social status, these self-styled martyrs use any means, including withholding love and acceptance, to force their students to unlearn lower-class patterns of behavior. School successes are measured in terms of converts to middle-classness. Of course, students who do not adopt middle-class behavior are defined by these teachers as individuals doomed to social hell as poor white trash, poor blacks, poor Indians, and poor Spanish-speaking people.

To a few observers, the rural community is a place of great challenge and enormous rewards. Those who help rural children to succeed in school are likely to be helping them out of poverty and despair. The small core of effective rural school administrators and teachers are beautiful people. They are beautiful because they *care* about all children. They are beautiful because they *dare* be creative in their efforts to improve the quality of education in rural schools. There are too few effective teachers in either rural or urban schools.

The U.S. Department of Agriculture farm income studies show that farmers have been moving up on the income scale. In 1969, the *gross income* of farmers was $54.6 billion, up $3.6 billion from 1968. However, higher farm production expenses kept 1969 from being a record *net income* year. Even so, the 1969 *net income* of $16.2 billion was the third highest on record, exceeded only by 1947 ($17.1 billion) and 1966 ($16.3 billion).

Current trends

On a *net income per farm* basis, the $5,437 figure in 1969 was a record, surpassing 1968 by $500 and 1967 by $1,000. This was largely due to the fact that there were fewer farms to split the income in 1969 than in previous years. Farms selling $10,000 and less have been declining in number during the past ten years (down from 1,848,000 to 1,223,000), while farms in the $40,000-and-over sales category have increased in number from 113,000 in 1960 to 211,000 in 1969. Farms with less than $2,500 sales accounted for 41.2 per cent of all farms, but their cash receipts made up only 2.7 per cent of the total. On the other hand, farms with sales of $40,000 and over made up only 7.1 per cent of all farms, but accounted for 51.3 per cent of all cash receipts.

In 1969, farms in the $2,500 and less sales category had an average *total income per farm* of $8,093 with an average *net income* of $1,082. At the same time, farms in the $40,000 and over category had an average *total income per farm* of $32,967 with an average *net income* of $27,503. It is also worth noting that the low-income farms had more nonfarm income than the high-income farms.

As a percentage of the total national income, farm income has been shrinking noticeably since the late 1940s. It has dropped from 9.4 per cent of total national income in 1948 to 2.9 per cent in 1969. Furthermore, there has been a significant shift in the relative importance of crops and livestock as farm income producers. Once the great income producer, crops now are a distant second to livestock. In 1969, livestock receipts were $28 billion compared with $18 billion from crops.

The rural counties are far from becoming extinct. Many industries are relocating in the towns and small cities of the rural countryside. During the 1960s, nonfarm job opportunities grew faster in rural and semirural counties than in metropolitan areas. This happened even though three predominantly rural states—North Dakota, South Dakota, and West Virginia—have lost population since 1960. Nearly half of the new manufacturing jobs in the past decade were in rural communities. In fact, rural counties in the South account for three-fifths of the nation's annual gain in manufacturing jobs. By 1975, it seems likely that the states extending across the southern tier of the country will account for almost half of the nation's industrial output, compared with 34 per cent in 1953.

Largely because of industry relocation and the attraction of non-urban living, the peak migration from rural areas appears to be over. Though persons living on farms dropped 64 per cent to 10.5 million between 1950 and 1968, rural areas as a whole lost most of their population (10 million) between 1950 and 1960. Many individuals who do not want to live in rural communities find the suburban communities to be more attractive than urban neighborhoods. The 1970 census reveals that for the first time in our history the suburbs have more population than the central cities.

The exodus out of the central cities includes a growing number of Negroes. Each year since 1964, an average of 85,000 blacks have moved to the suburbs. During the 1960s, more than 800,000 blacks migrated from the central cities. This is small compared with the 14 million whites who moved to the suburbs in the same period, but it indicates that the racial composition of near-rural and rural communities in most states will include a substantial number of non-whites. Joining the blacks in the exodus from the central cities are Mexican-Americans, Indians, and Puerto Ricans.

Plan of the book   In order to provide the reader with an updated view of the many forces bringing about the urbanization of rural schools, this book is divided into six parts. Each part contains articles selected for their insight and relevance to our over-all theme of change through urbanization. Rather than merely presenting a collection of readings, each of the following six parts includes introductory comments that contain materials not covered in the articles. Thus each introduction is also a complete article. I have selected materials which provide both "objective" and "subjective" views of rural school problems, related problems, the background of these problems, and, in many instances, their solutions.

Part One presents a glimpse of rural poverty throughout the United States. It points up conditions that are especially severe in the non-urban areas, conditions which better educational programs could in many cases alleviate. The ten studies in Part Two make up a general picture of rural American schools today. The road to improvement of the situation is shown in parts Three and Four to be a combination of people—teachers, administrators, and interested community members—and innovative ideas and equipment.

Part Five deals with the special problem of desegregation in public schools. The articles do not all deal primarily with rural or small schools, but the human problems involved—narrow-mindedness, resistance to change, and lack of concern for each student as an individual of importance—are problems which are at least as relevant to rural schools in general as to the urban communities studied here. Many rural schools in the nation are just now facing the question of integration and can perhaps avoid many of the problems encountered in earlier desegregation attempts if they are made aware in advance through readings like the present book.

The last section, "If We Fail," is a look at some of the fatal consequences that await us when we ignore rural schools and fail to desegregate them and to provide all their students with a top quality of instruction. Urban schools do not have a monopoly on educational problems or solutions. Urban and rural schools together represent a large share of our nation's most pressing unfinished business.

Part One. **The Rural Poor**

Introduction to Part One

FREQUENTLY, social commentators define the widening gap between black and white Americans as our most pressing domestic problem. There is yet another problem that may be even more serious than conflicts involving race per se: the extreme income gap between affluent and poor families. While it is true that there is a great disparity between black and white median family incomes, there are also significant intragroup differences. Recent civil rights activities such as the "Poor People's March on Washington" in 1969 have pointed up the severity of poverty in America.

Urban poverty is much more visible than rural poverty. Dilapidated buildings, garbage-strewn alleys, and rats are all too often the dominant characteristics of urban slums. These conditions tend to blur the memory of clean, well-kept buildings which also characterize many urban poor neighborhoods. While it is difficult to change the negative image of the urban slum, it is almost impossible to erase the idyllic picture of rural poverty.

Tourists driving through the countryside are likely to define the blight they see as being "quaint," "picturesque," or "Americana." Nearly 40 per cent of rural Americans are poverty-stricken. In Appalachia, for example, welfare has become a way of life. Small children grow up aspiring not to finish high school but to get their own welfare case number. Elsewhere we can see the haunting images of over three hundred thousand migrant harvesters whose average annual family income is less than nine hundred dollars per year.

Who Are the Poor?

It is impossible for those who have not experienced poverty to fully understand what it is like to be poor. Jo Goodwin Parker's article, "What is Poverty?" describes some of the physically, psychologically, and socially debilitating conditions that accrue to the rural poor. To many readers, this article will seem like an amateurish bit of fiction

23

writing. Unfortunately, it is not fiction but Mrs. Parker's life that is so vividly described. It is a portrait that brings into sharper focus life in the other America, characterized by conditions of *not enough.*

Generally, when affluent people go without soap, hot water, lights, heat, food, and medicine, it is because they elect to do so. When poverty-stricken people go without these items, it is usually because they have no choice. Therein lies a major difference between the poor and the affluent. The former is controlled by the economic system and the latter controls the economic system.

Poverty has a smell—a smell of rotting garbage and sour foods. It is the smell of children's urine and unwashed bodies. Above all else, it is the smell of people denied an equal opportunity to live like their affluent peers. What keeps the poor going? How can they come back again and again for more heartache and physical pain? Could it be because they, like other people, cling tenaciously to life, no matter how painful? Yes, even the Mrs. Parkers want to live. Like a thin thread spun by a master weaver, Mrs. Parker's tale is hung together by pleas for a chance to live in a better environment. Interestingly, her primary concern is not for herself but her children, who are already damaged by the time they get to school.

Within the stark reality of this situation, a more challenging question emerges: How can we rebuild poverty-stricken spirits? The first steps in helping the poor are understanding their plight and caring enough to assist them in altering their condition. Too few people seem either to understand or to care. But understanding and caring are not enough. Action is needed at all community levels.

The War on Poverty

Bill Kovach and Nat Caldwell's article, "The Plight of the Rural Poor," points out the inadequacies of state and federal programs set up to abate rural poverty. Hardly optimistic, these writers conclude that the rural poor have been ignored in the past and are likely to be ignored in the future. Currently, most of the poor who live in rural areas are not being helped by governmental antipoverty programs. Lacking strong community organizations and political power, the rural poor do not have the collective voices they need in order to be heard. Their muted cries are, like the words of a popular song, blowing in the wind.

In many ways, the evaluation reports of programs designed to help the rural poor read like ill-conceived Broadway plays doomed to failure. Few government programs are designed to attack rural poverty. Urban-trained and urban-based administrators are attempting to adjust their programs and guidelines to rural communities. And when these programs fail, the brunt of the criticism falls on the rural residents. Perhaps, the critics conclude, the rural poor *are* shiftless and lazy. There are few successful projects such as the one in Tazewell and New Tazewell, Tennessee, described by Kovach and Caldwell. Most rural antipoverty programs are plagued with problems such as those described by James McElrath in his article, "Obstacles To Planning."

Minority Groups

Almost all articles about the poor focus on blacks and whites. Missing is a description of the problems faced by two other large groups: Mexican-Americans and American Indians. There are more than five million Mexican-Americans and 650,000 American Indians, concentrated mainly in the Southwest and the Far West. Both groups are marginal, being neither black nor white. And both frequently are victims of more discrimination than either blacks or whites. Their marginality reflects individual searches for identity and the unsuccessful attempts of whites to "assimilate" them.

Second- and third-generation descendants of early Spanish settlers are usually affluent, but second- and third-generation descendants *Mexican-Americans* of agricultural workers tend to be poverty-stricken. There is still a third group: First-generation children of *braceros*—migrant farm workers from Mexico. The first two groups usually are quite Americanized; they have little knowledge of their Spanish heritage and speak little or no Spanish. Conversely, children of migrant workers speak fluent Spanish and cling tightly to Mexican customs and traditions. All Spanish groups are discriminated against by the *Anglos*— the white majority.

Ozzie Simmons ("The Mutual Images and Expectations of Anglo-Americans and Mexican-Americans") does an outstanding job of describing the differences in expectations and attitudes of Anglo-Americans and Mexican-Americans. Both groups reflect their social position in the larger community, and that factor alone places the Mexican-American in a disadvantaged position. To state simply that Mexican-Americans desire the best of both cultures is to slide over even more penetrating questions: Is obtaining the best of both cultures possible? Will Anglos assimilate with a large number of Mexicans whom they believe to be socially inferior? If the answer to the latter question is yes, then there are more questions: What will it cost the Mexican-Americans? Their language? Their cultural heritage? Their identity? Assimilation American-style tends to result in minority groups losing their identities. Perhaps most Mexican-Americans will decide that the social price for assimilation into the Anglo culture is too high. Then the cries for Brown Power will, like Negroes demanding Black Power, enhance the growth of the minority culture.

American
Indians

American Indians are at the bottom of the economic ladder. As a whole, they have the highest rates of unemployment and school dropouts, live in the poorest housing, and are often accorded the lowest social status in their communities. Most government programs have failed to assist Indians in their efforts to maintain individual dignity and cultural identity. As ludicrous as it may sound, white Americans are still trying to Americanize the Indians. Conflicts between white and Indian cultures are found on reservations, in small communities, and in big cities.

Joseph S. Roucek's article, "The Most Oppressed Race in the United States: The Indian," gives a historical overview of conscious efforts by the federal government to deprive the Indian of his land, culture, and dignity. Unable or unwilling to realize that we do not have an Indian problem but a white problem of oppression, the federal government has established government-controlled Indian bureaus, and reservation and assistance programs. Each of these poorly conceived plans has contributed to the continued second-class citizenship of Indians. In school, Indian children are set apart as being "different" because of their dress, speech, and patterns of cultural adjustment. The war on poverty in Indian communities is not likely to be solved until someone declares a truce in the white middle-class social game of snobbery.

Approximately 450,000 of the total 650,000 Indian population live on 56 million acres of reservations in twenty-six states. Part of their frustration comes from the following statistics: Indians have 90 million *fewer* acres of land today than in 1887; their average life expectancy is forty-four years; over 40 per cent of the Indian school children—almost double the national average—drop out before completing high school; nearly 60 per cent of the adult Indian population has less than an eighth-grade education; infant mortality—twenty-six deaths per thousand—is more than ten points above the national average; 50 per cent of the Indian families have annual incomes below two thousand dollars, 75 per cent have annual incomes below three thousand dollars; unemployment is nearly 40 per cent—almost 10 times the national average.

During 1970, Indians expressed a growing mood of militancy

when they staged mass protests in Denver and Cleveland, seized Alcatraz Island, stormed Fort Lawton outside Seattle, and tried to take over Ellis Island. Navaho Indians acted out their frustrations with the "white man's way" by starting their own schools in Ramdah, New Mexico; while the Salt River and Zuñi tribes won approval for control of their federal programs.

Feeling trapped and powerless in a world controlled by non-Indians, a large number of rural and urban Indians have not become militant but, instead, have withdrawn. Overgeneralizing from this group, representatives of the white Establishment pass on stereotypes about shiftless and drunken Indians. There is a saying in some towns, "If you hire an Indian, never pay him the first day if you want him to come back the second day. He'll take the money and drink it up." But it is not only what is said about Indians that is detrimental but also what is not said. Seldom are they recognized as a minority group. Until the 1970 United States census, Indians were not even listed as an identifiable ethnic group. Little wonder, then, that some automobiles owned by Indians display bumper stickers that say "Custer had it coming."

Black Americans

No group has been subjected to as much suffering at the hands of white Americans as black Americans. Martin Luther King, Jr., once referred to black Americans as victims of "creative brutality." Certainly, all of the plight of poor blacks cannot be attributed to white hostility. Much of it, as noted by Foster Davis in "Darkness on the Delta," has grown out of inhumane technology and shortsighted government regulations.

Many of the so-called antipoverty programs are designed to help poor blacks even if by doing so the unemployment rolls will increase. These "cures" that kill the initiative and self-determination of people have caused some government officials to echo the lines of Pogo, a comic strip character: "We met the enemy and they are us."

Migrant workers

The 300,000 migrant workers in America are a composite of all poverty-stricken Americans. They are people of many colors—white, brown, black, red, and yellow. More important than their diverse colors are their common conditions of poverty. The children of migrant workers, for example, move with their parents through the citrus groves of Florida or California, stoop over the beans and tomatoes in Texas, pick cherries and blueberries in Michigan, hoe sugar beets in western Kansas, and crawl through the potato fields of Idaho and Maine. Life for the migrants is seasonal: a day here, a week there. They sleep in dilapidated structures that almost always lack adequate heat, refrigeration, and sanitary facilities. In addition, they walk and play on garbage-strewn grounds infested with internal parasites and drink polluted water.

A 1970 study funded by the Field Foundation of New York clearly illustrated the physical plight of the migrants. The study conducted in the Texas counties of Starr and Hidalgo described children who were dying because of neglect or growing up without hope because malnutrition and disease had left them unequipped physically or mentally to cope with life in an urbanized society. Most of the children examined by the teams of fifteen physicians were infected with intestinal parasites; most had chronic skin infections; all had dental problems; and a large number had chronically infected ears that resulted in partial deafness. In 1969, the federal government spent $564,677 for migrant health services in Hidalgo and Starr counties and $5,502,000 on the eradication of diseases in animals. The Field Foundation study noted that the current hospital procedure requiring a cash deposit before granting hospital admission places an impossible burden on those least able to afford being sick. Furthermore, communities in which migrants work tend to lack even minimally adequate medical care and health services.

But the plight of the migrants is not limited to poor health. In 1969, the migrants averaged seventy-eight days of work for pay of $891. They had an accident rate of over 300 per cent of the national average. The migrant's life expectancy is forty-nine; infant and maternal mortality is 125 per cent of the national average. Migrants and other farm workers are excluded from coverage by the National Labor Relations Act, which protects the rights of other workers to organize in an effort to improve their working conditions. The minimum wage law affects only the largest farms and the minimum for these workers is set considerably below that of other workers. However, within the past few years, there have been a few hopeful signs.

On July 29, 1970, twenty-six grape growers signed contracts with Cesar Chavez's United Farm Workers Organizing Committee. The agreement with 65 per cent of the growers ended decades of struggle to upgrade the working conditions of the migratory workers. The contract called for a wage of $1.80 an hour, plus 20 cents for each box of grapes picked. In addition, growers agreed to contribute 10 cents an hour to the union's health plan and 2 cents for each box to an economic development plan. The contract also included stringent safety requirements on the use of pesticides. Other unions have accelerated their efforts to organize agriculture workers.

Also in 1970, the Coca-Cola Company pledged to improve what it termed the "deplorable working conditions" in its Florida citrus groves. The company's long-range plan would effectuate higher wages, better housing, and social services for migrant workers. By the end of 1971, the plan calls for three hundred of the one thousand migrants who work part-time for Coca-Cola to be given steady work and fringe benefits. In addition, several one-stop child-centered social services centers and sixty to seventy new homes are to be constructed during the first phase. Obviously, the Coca-Cola program will not solve the problems of very many migratory workers, but if other growers mount a similar effort, the Field Foundation study will cease to be an adequate description of the living conditions of migrant workers.

Religious Orientation

"Nobody knows the trouble I've seen," begins a Negro spiritual. Perhaps the general faith in God and the particular faith in a religion offers a ray of hope to the poor. Or perhaps it does not. Berton Kaplan's article, "The Structure of Adaptive Sentiments in a Lower-Class Religious Group in Appalachia," suggests that religion—especially Christian religions—does not offer a way out of poverty but a rationalization for being poor. Although his study was of the Free Will Baptist Church in Appalachia, Kaplan described many other Christian denominations.

The premises of the Free Will Baptist Church—we are poor people, but we have a mansion in heaven; thou shalt not be angry; give your love to Jesus; we belong to the fellowship of sufferers—can be construed by church members as doctrines for being poor. Indeed, a deep pride in suffering can be instilled in the faithful. This is not to imply that there is a religious scheme to keep people impoverished. Rather, it implies that the religious sentiments are functional for those seeking to cope with social disintegration. When all else seems lost, it just seems to make things right by getting on one's knees and saying "amen!"

The Roman Catholic church is not unlike the Protestant churches. It acts as a bulwark of conservatism and presents obstacles in the path of progress and emancipation from poverty. The Roman church teaches obedience to its doctrines, to authority, to one's parents, to the supervisor at the place of employment. Acceptance of poverty is taught as a virtue that, like patience, will be rewarded in Heaven. Besides, it is seen as God's will.

2. What Is Poverty?

Jo Goodwin Parker

YOU ask me what is poverty? Listen to me. Here I am, dirty, smelly, and with no "proper" underwear on and with the stench of my rotting teeth near you. I will tell you. Listen to me. Listen without pity. I cannot use your pity. Listen with understanding. Put yourself in my dirty, worn out, ill-fitting shoes, and hear me.

Poverty is getting up every morning from a dirt- and illness-stained mattress. The sheets have long since been used for diapers. Poverty is living in a smell that never leaves. This is a smell of urine, sour milk, and spoiling food sometimes joined with the strong smell of long-cooked onions. Onions are cheap. If you have smelled this smell, you did not know how it came. It is the smell of the outdoor privy. It is the smell of young children who cannot walk the long dark way in the night. It is the smell of the mattresses where years of "accidents" have happened. It is the smell of the milk which has gone sour because the refrigerator long has not worked, and it costs money to get it fixed. It is the smell of rotting garbage. I could bury it, but where is the shovel? Shovels cost money.

Poverty is being tired. I have always been tired. They told me at the hospital when the last baby came that I had chronic anemia caused from poor diet, a bad case of worms, and that I needed a corrective operation. I listened politely—the poor are always polite. The poor always listen. They don't say that there is no money for iron pills, or better food, or worm medicine. The idea of an operation is frightening and costs so much that, if I had dared, I would have laughed. Who takes care of my children? Recovery from an operation takes a long time. I have three children. When I left them with "Granny" the last time I had a job, I came home to find the baby covered with fly specks, and a diaper that had not been changed since I left. When the dried diaper came off, bits of my baby's flesh

From an unpublished speech (Deland, Florida, December 27, 1965). Printed by permission.

came with it. My other child was playing with a sharp bit of broken glass, and my oldest was playing alone at the edge of a lake. I made twenty-two dollars a week, and a good nursery school costs twenty dollars a week for three children. I quit my job.

Poverty is dirt. You say in your clean clothes coming from your clean house, "Anybody can be clean." Let me explain about housekeeping with no money. For breakfast I give my children grits with no oleo or cornbread without eggs and oleo. This does not use up many dishes. What dishes there are, I wash in cold water and with no soap. Even the cheapest soap has to be saved for the baby's diapers. Look at my hands, so cracked and red. Once I saved for two months to buy a jar of Vaseline for my hands and the baby's diaper rash. When I had saved enough, I went to buy it and the price had gone up two cents. The baby and I suffered on. I have to decide every day if I can bear to put my cracked, sore hands into the cold water and strong soap. But you ask, why not hot water? Fuel costs money. If you have a wood fire it costs money. If you burn electricity, it costs money. Hot water is a luxury. I do not have luxuries. I know you will be surprised when I tell you how young I am. I look so much older. My back has been bent over the wash tubs every day for so long, I cannot remember when I ever did anything else. Every night I wash every stitch my school age child has on and just hope her clothes will be dry by morning.

Poverty is staying up all night on cold nights to watch the fire, knowing one spark on the newspaper covering the walls means your sleeping children die in flames. In summer poverty is watching gnats and flies devour your baby's tears when he cries. The screens are torn and you pay so little rent you know they will never be fixed. Poverty means insects in your food, in your nose, in your eyes, and crawling over you when you sleep. Poverty is hoping it never rains because diapers won't dry when it rains and soon you are using newspapers. Poverty is seeing your children forever with runny noses. Paper handkerchiefs cost money and all your rags you need for other things. Even more costly are antihistamines. Poverty is cooking without food and cleaning without soap.

Poverty is asking for help. Have you ever had to ask for help, knowing your children will suffer unless you get it? Think about asking for a loan from a relative, if this is the only way you can imagine asking for help. I will tell you how it feels. You find out where the office is that you are supposed to visit. You circle that block four or five times. Thinking of your children, you go in. Everyone is very busy. Finally, someone comes out and you tell her that you need help. That never is the person you need to see. You go see another person, and after spilling the whole shame of your poverty all over the desk between you, you find that this isn't the right office after all—you must repeat the whole process, and it never is any easier at the next place.

You have asked for help, and after all it has a cost. You are again told to wait. You are told why, but you don't really hear because of the red cloud of shame and the rising black cloud of despair.

Poverty is remembering. It is remembering quitting school in junior high because "nice" children had been so cruel about my clothes and my smell. The attendance officer came. My mother told him I was pregnant. I wasn't, but she thought that I could get a job and help out. I had jobs off and on, but never long enough to learn anything. Mostly I remember being married. I was so young then. I am still young. For a time, we had all the things you have. There was a little house in another town, with hot water and everything. Then my husband lost his job. There was unemployment insurance for a while and what few jobs I could get. Soon, all our nice things were repossessed and we moved back here. I was pregnant then. This house didn't look so bad when we first moved in. Every week it gets worse. Nothing is ever fixed. We now had no money. There were a few odd jobs for my husband, but everything went for food then, as it does now. I don't know how we lived through three years and three babies, but we did. I'll tell you something, after the last baby I destroyed my marriage. It had been a good one, but could you keep on bringing children in this dirt? Did you ever think how much it costs for any kind of birth control? I knew my husband was leaving the day he left, but there were no good-bys between us. I hope he has been able to climb out of this mess somewhere. He never could hope with us to drag him down.

That's when I asked for help. When I got it, you know how much it was? It was, and is, seventy-eight dollars a month for the four of us; that is all I ever can get. Now you know why there is no soap, no needles and thread, no hot water, no aspirin, no worm medicine, no hand cream, no shampoo. None of these things forever and ever and ever. So that you can see clearly, I pay twenty dollars a month rent, and most of the rest goes for food. For grits and cornmeal, and rice and milk and beans. I try my best to use only the minimum electricity. If I use more, there is that much less for food.

Poverty is looking into a black future. Your children won't play with my boys. They will turn to other boys who steal to get what they want. I can already see them behind the bars of their prison instead of behind the bars of my poverty. Or they will turn to the freedom of alcohol or drugs, and find themselves enslaved. And my daughter? At best, there is for her a life like mine.

But you say to me, there are schools. Yes, there are schools. My children have no extra books, no magazines, no extra pencils, or crayons, or paper and the most important of all, they do not have health. They have worms, they have infections, they have pink-eye all summer. They do not sleep well on the floor, or with me in my one bed. They do not suffer from hunger, my seventy-eight dollars keeps us alive, but they do suffer from malnutrition. Oh yes, I do remember what I was taught about health in school. It doesn't do much good. In some places there is a surplus commodities program. Not here. The county said it cost too much. There is a school lunch program. But I have two children who will already be damaged by the time they get to school.

But, you say to me, there are health clinics. Yes, there are health clinics and they are in the towns. I live out here eight miles from town. I can walk that far (even if it is sixteen miles both ways), but can my little children? My neighbor will take me when he goes; but he expects to get paid, *one way or another*. I bet you know my neighbor. He is that large man who spends his time at the gas station, the barbershop, and the corner store complaining about the government spending money on the immoral mothers of illegitimate children.

Poverty is an acid that drips on pride until all pride is worn away. Poverty is a chisel that chips on honor until honor is worn away. Some of you say that you would do *something* in my situation, and maybe you would, for the first week or the first month, but for year after year after year?

Even the poor can dream. A dream of a time when there is money. Money for the right kinds of food, for worm medicine, for iron pills, for toothbrushes, for hand cream, for a hammer and nails and a bit of screening, for a shovel, for a bit of paint, for some sheeting, for needles and thread. Money to pay *in money* for a trip to town. And, oh, money for hot water and money for soap. A dream of when asking for help does not eat away the last bit of pride. When the office you visit is as nice as the offices of other governmental agencies, when there are enough workers to help you quickly, when workers do not quit in defeat and despair. When you have to tell your story to only one person, and that person can send you for other help and you don't have to prove your poverty over and over and over again.

I have come out of my despair to tell you this. Remember I did not come from another place or another time. Others like me are all around you. Look at us with an angry heart, anger that will help you help me. Anger that will let you tell of me. The poor are always silent. Can you be silent too?

3. The Plight of the Rural Poor

Bill Kovach and Nat Caldwell

A fourth of all farms and a fifth of all other rural homes lack running water. Children receive, on the average, two years less education than in the city and its quality is apt to be inferior. Unemployment and underemployment runs at a rate of 15 per cent, more than twice as great as the national average. Moreover, the tools for rebuilding rural areas are not available—rural residents have less access to credit for housing, for business expansion, and for public utilities. As Secretary of Agriculture Orville L. Freeman has said, "Rural America is a place from which the poor, the uneducated, the unskilled, the hopeless, migrate to the cities when they cannot find jobs in their home communities." And, he might have added, these poor are usually not needed or even usable when they get there.

Rural poverty is largely regional. Of the thirty poorest congressional districts, twenty-nine are in the rural South. The backbone of rural poverty is that broad strip running from southern New York to central Alabama along the Appalachian Mountains. There are wide pockets in Mississippi, Arkansas, Louisiana, and Texas. The problem is also serious in Florida, Minnesota, Wisconsin, Oklahoma, and California, with its great numbers of migrant farm workers.

During the last year it has become clear that a large part of the sixteen million poor who live in rural areas—nearly half of the total in the entire nation—are not being reached by the federal agencies created and charged with eliminating poverty. Slowly and painfully, rural leaders and federal officials have become aware of the special character of rural poverty that has confounded every agency and program created to deal with the problem. An almost complete lack of basic facilities has repeatedly frustrated agencies concentrating on the development of physical resources. Industry, jobs, and business cannot be stimulated in areas lacking water systems or educa-

From *The Reporter*, April 21, 1966, pp. 27ff. Reprinted by permission. Copyright 1966 by The Reporter Magazine Company.

tional, recreational, and sewage facilities. The Office of Economic Opportunity, which concentrates on human development, cannot function adequately in areas robbed of local leadership by years of migration and whose population is so widely scattered that community action is almost impossible. In the rural South, the application of all the programs has run into an inherent resistance to integration and drastic economic change, especially in areas of substandard development dominated by a single industry such as mining or cotton.

One big reason why the rural poor have been neglected as compared to those in cities is that they produce no political leverage. In describing the plight of migrant workers, an Office of Economic Opportunity official summed up the helplessness of rural poor everywhere: "They seldom vote, so they have no political power, and what they have is so widely dispersed it is ineffective. They have little money to spend, so they have no power in the commercial world. They just don't reach the power structure of our society."

In the Appalachians, rural poverty is the result of years of state neglect. "The states," according to Harry Caudill of Kentucky, "never cared about their Appalachian counties." Caudill, a lawyer whose book *Night Comes to the Cumberlands* established him as an authority on the region, points out that the rotting, inadequate schools are state schools, that the crumbling roads are state roads. But outside Appalachia the picture is generally the same. Long-standing state neglect of the problems of a locally exhausted resource like coal, or the plight of subsistence farmers, migrant workers, and sharecroppers, has made the new federal efforts to solve them even more difficult.

Finding a balance   Federal action on the nation's poor was slow in coming, and when it arrived, the rural areas got short shrift. By February, 1965, it was clear to President Johnson that federal programs were failing to meet the needs of the rural poor. In a message to Congress, he demanded that any department or agency administering programs that could benefit rural people "assure that its benefits are distributed equitably between urban and rural areas."

The president ordered the formation of an office in the Department of Agriculture as the co-ordinating arm in promoting development programs in rural areas. But this office, the Rural Community Development Service (RCDS), has barely started to function. At the moment, its main activity is to help rural residents qualify for Social Security and Medicare, and to work with rural leaders in he direction of local projects. Eventually, a major function of the RCDS will be to act as a liaison between Department of Agriculture field workers on the county level and all federal agencies administering rural programs. Nine offices in eleven states are now open, and it is hoped that twenty-three will be in operation by June. But the RCDS has been slow appointing state directors, partly because of red tape, partly because of the difficulty of the job. Each state office consists of only one man—the state director.

The new service has also received little help and even less co-operation from other federal agencies. Agriculture officials complain that OEO co-operation is especially lacking. "They're all city oriented over there," one Agriculture aide said, "and they look on us as an old stodgy bureaucracy that can't handle problems as well as they. What they overlook is the fact that we have field workers in almost every county in the nation who could serve as representatives to develop rural programs—but it's going to take co-operation."

By September, President Johnson's plea for equitable distribution of benefits had resulted in so little action that sixteen senators joined Gaylord Nelson (D., Wisconsin) in calling for a new effort to get federal help into rural areas. Two months later, in November, the vice president noted the persistence of the problem at a national OEO press seminar and called for "a better working relationship . . . between OEO and the Department of Agriculture." Other OEO officials promptly agreed. Joseph A. Kershaw, in charge of evaluating programs for OEO, admitted that the urban-rural investment ratio was far out of balance, probably "because the urban problems are easier to get at." He promised that "Next year at least 45 per cent of the (OEO) budget will be in rural programs."

When queried last month, however, Kershaw was less optimistic: "I don't think we'll make the 45 per cent figure."

Officials in OEO have been reluctant to discuss the extent of the gap between urban and rural programs. A meaningful breakdown of rural-urban expenditures is hard to come by. But OEO's total expenditures for the past year give some indication: for the period from November 24, 1964, through November 1, 1965, OEO figures show an investment of $741,784,368 in urban programs as contrasted with $222,378,423 in rural ones.

Richard Wenner, the OEO representative on a task force considering rural problems, has given another and more specific indication of the gap. Recently he told rural leaders at a Chattanooga, Tennessee, meeting that OEO expenditures in rural Community Action programs amounted to only 15 per cent of the $637 million allocated for fiscal 1966. But if funds for Head Start projects (preschool educational programs) are excluded, only 7 to 8 per cent of OEO's Community Action budget remained for rural programs. Since many other programs (rural loans, migrant-worker aid, Job Corps camps, and others) have rural impact, OEO officials argue, and with some justification, that such figures are misleading.

While efforts such as the Labor Department's vocational training program or rural loans have been helpful, they hardly strike at the roots of rural poverty. The rural loan program is an example of the narrow objectives of such remedies. A farmhand in Mississippi, for instance, receives $1,850 (with up to fifteen years to repay at 4.125 per cent interest) to set up a small garage and purchase tools. The expectation is that his $2,500 annual income will rise by about $1,000 so that he can better care for his ten dependents. In other cases, even such limited objectives are not met. A sharecropper who has coveted a tractor obtains one through the rural loan program only to learn that his problem goes much deeper than the lack of a tractor.

OEO guidelines make urban treatment easier. A recent experience in West Virginia is a case in point. The key to an effective attack on rural poverty is a Community Action Program designed to bring the full force of co-ordinated federal help to bear on a given community. Mineral and Hardy counties in West Virginia set up their Community Action Program in November, 1964—the first such rural project financed in the nation. Later, through OEO's request that an effort be made to reach as many people as would an equivalent program in an urban area, the project was expanded to include four other counties. But then urban-developed OEO guidelines got in the way. As R. E. Fisher, publisher of the Moorefield *Examiner*, tells it, OEO "said we had to have more representation from the poor—the poor being defined as having less than $3,000 a year income. They never seemed to realize that the six-county area consisted of three thousand square miles and that people just don't come to meetings at the drop of a hat, especially in the daytime." Fisher reports that the entire program is bogged down in the "ever-changing guidelines."

High and dry As with OEO, the Appalachian Regional Commission (ARC) has placed little money into rural pockets. A greater share of the commission's funds—some $840 million of the initial $1.1 billion appropriation—is being invested in a highway system that currently benefits contractors from large cities who merely shift machinery and men from massive interstate projects to these rural jobs. The conclusion drawn by Sar A. Levitan in a study of "Programs in Aid of the Poor," financed by the Upjohn Institute, was that the unskilled, rural or urban, "might qualify for no more than a fifth of the total man-hours generated directly by construction projects" financed by the commission.

Similarly, the application of the Economic Development Administration's program, which now includes the old Area Redevelopment Administration and the Accelerated Public Works projects, does not immediately reach the rural poor. As the Upjohn Institute study pointed out, by "directing its aid to employers and not to the unemployed, the program is based on the belief that federal efforts should concentrate on the business community which, in turn, will create new jobs to help the unemployed." Both the EDA and the ARC programs are based on the hope that they will eventually aid the rural poor as an indirect result of their investments in going enterprises. But a look at how these federal programs are working in rural areas indicates that the programs themselves tend to keep the rural poor from receiving any significant benefits.

Just as the shortage of human resources in rural areas militates against present OEO solutions, the shortage of economic resources interferes with aid from the Appalachian Regional Commission. Two basic actions by the ARC have provided grounds for criticism. The first applies to the highway program, which has so far consumed the bulk of ARC money. Not only do the road-construction projects supply few jobs for the region's poor but when the roads are completed, according to the Upjohn study, the kind of jobs created in the "growth centers" served by them "will be seasonal and low paying, and may still not allow the workers to escape the threshold of poverty."

Many observers, including some ARC officials, consider the decision to have the highway system run mainly north and south the biggest mistake of the program. Appalachia's depression has developed to a large extent because of an isolation due to a lack of access through the mountains. State governments have traditionally built their highways along the north-south axis, ignoring east-west routes wherever possible because of the high cost of building roads in the mountains. Thus, traffic has flowed around Appalachia as river waters flow around an island. Only in flood times such as a wartime boom does the surrounding prosperity spill over.

The second basic action of the commission that has been widely questioned was the adoption of the "economic growth center" concept. Little money has been invested in resource development in sparsely populated rural areas. According to John L. Sweeney, the federal co-chairman on the commission, the ARC is not going to "sprinkle an area of 182,000 square miles with just temporary construction jobs." The commission, he says, is building a base for permanent jobs, higher incomes, and better conditions for investing in areas demonstrating a growth potential. To qualify as a growth center, a community must meet standards of population density, existing wealth, educational facilities, and other advantages that write off the neediest rural areas and concentrate federal aid in cities or towns. The concept has been described as a new application of the old "trickle down" theory of economics—invest the money at the top and it will eventually trickle down to those who need it. Critics point out, though, that the region has always supported islands of prosperity. Birmingham, Knoxville, and Pittsburgh are all in Appalachia, but their presence has not prevented hunger in the surrounding countryside. The sense of hopelessness that this city orientation engenders in rural areas is obvious. There is a general feeling that only continued migration or welfare offers a long-range solution for deprived rural areas, and the Community Action Program created for McDowell County, West Virginia, for example, frankly aims at preparing residents of this area to adapt themselves in out-of-state cities.

The explosive migrant — If nothing else, the fact of an increasing migration to the cities has focused Washington's attention on the rural dilemma. Following a White House meeting last August, a study on agriculture and rural life was ordered under the direction of Secretary Freeman. The study was to be conducted by a task force of representatives from the departments of Health, Education and Welfare, Agriculture, and Labor, the Office of Economic Opportunity, the Housing and Home Finance Agency, and the Bureau of the Budget. Among the key targets of this task force was the proposal of programs to "stem farm migration to the cities and encourage a return to rural communities."

Robert G. Lewis, head of the Rural Community Development Service, crystallized this thinking in the preface to the program the task force hoped would be submitted to the present session of Congress: "The tragedy that occurred in the slums of Los Angeles . . . began as depression on the farm. Fundamentally, it was not a 'race riot'—but rather an explosion growing out of the poverty and despair of rural people lost in an urban slum existence that had eroded away whatever social capability and discipline they had at the start."

Although a detailed program suggested as a result of the study has been temporarily shelved because of budget conflicts—some observers feel the squeeze of current Great Society programs and Vietnam left no room for major legislation of its kind—it has stimulated further study and some further investment in rural problems. This increased interest in new ideas for rural solutions was evidenced in President Johnson's request in January for five million dollars for pilot projects to combat rural poverty. The president envisions a common planning effort aimed at community development and the pooling of resources in rural areas.

"Our purpose," his message said, "is to demonstrate how a common effort can provide the needed district vocational school in one county, the hospital in another, the police training in a third, industry or an adequate library in a fourth—and how it can avoid the waste of duplication or, worse still, the total lack of any such facilities or services in a wide area because of a failure to pool common resources. Our purpose is not to supplant present efforts of local, state, or federal governments—but to supplement them; not to forsake the small community, but to help it avoid underrepresentation in decisions that affect its life."

An example of the effect that such a co-ordinated attack could have in a depressed rural community may be seen in the neighboring towns of Tazewell and New Tazewell, Tennessee, which have a population of some two thousand. There, in 1962, the Area Redevelopment Administration gambled a million dollars on a public-works project to develop water and sewage facilities. Three years later, that initial federal investment has been matched by $9.5 million of other public and private investment and has brought the Tazewells to the point where they will qualify as a potential growth center under the Appalachian Commission formula. As a result of the ARA's million-dollar gamble, they have attracted plants manufacturing trailers, plastics, textiles, and furniture, creating seven hundred new jobs. Public and private building has been stimulated; credit has opened up for local development; twenty-two members of the 1954 graduating class at the local high school who left the Tazewells for the higher pay of the cities have returned home.

The central idea of the task-force program that was dropped was the proposal for Opportunity Homesteads. Loans on liberal terms were planned to help a family to develop land on which it lived or to purchase and develop a homestead on land in areas where economic development appeared feasible. A probationary period was to be required in which the homesteader would improve the property and develop a subsistence farming operation; the participation of all adult members of the family in vocational, home-management, and general education programs would be required. The end result would be the transfer of equity in the homestead to the family; because of the required training programs, it would be better prepared to develop economic independence.

Since the homestead farm was conceived only for subsistence purposes, off-farm employment would be provided in the first years by federal investment in rural work projects. Planners point out that there is a backlog of needed work requiring low levels of skills, including soil, water, and wildlife conservation, forestry, and beautification. While such investments would be expensive, they would, unlike present relief expenditures, have a lasting value in developing natural resources, human skills, and a strong rural economic base.

A chance to grow   Supporters of rural programs know that in President Johnson and Vice President Humphrey they have two men attuned to rural problems. As a lobbyist for the National Farmers Union said recently: "These guys know us, they know our problems. For the first time in a long time I don't feel as if I'm speaking a foreign language in Washington when I talk about rural affairs." The optimism of people like this, however, has suffered a setback with the increasing concern over Vietnam. Not only are the chances dim for new programs and increased poverty-program spending; as city job opportunities open up with increased military spending, another massive migration of the rural poor comparable to that of the second world war and the Korean War is apt to occur. Moreover, migrants have higher hopes and deeper hostilities than those of the 1940s or 1950s. The gap between what they possess and what they desire is infinitely wider.

Watts and Harlem and South Chicago and the other ports of entry into America's cities are not equipped to absorb many more of the rural dispossessed. Unless a solution is found for rural poverty where it exists, the human and physical resources of the countryside will be forfeited, and their forfeiture will serve as a continuing drain on the vitality of urban America.

Already the frustration and disappointment of small-town and rural leaders is being voiced. Recently the Appalachian Regional Commission decided that a highway could not be economically justified in Hancock County, Tennessee. When he heard of it, Mayor Charles Turner of Sneedville, the county seat, remarked, "I'm sorry to jump on you fellows about your programs. They're all real fine programs. It's just that I've put my whole life into this town and this county, and only now they're telling me it doesn't have a chance to grow anyhow."

4. **Obstacles to Planning**

James McElrath

ONE of the first obstacles which stands in the way of long-range progressive planning on the part of the CAA[1] is the difference in ideas between what the local community and what the federal legislators and regional staff interpret as priorities for the War on Poverty. This difference of opinion was the reason many people gave for the failure of CAAs to launch meaningful action. One director felt that community involvement and participation on the part of the poor had failed because ". . . in the past when the CAA tried to get the community or neighborhood involved, the people responded at first. Then they decided on a program they wanted; it was packaged up, and applied for, and it would come back refused. It was hard to keep people interested when this happened time after time." He said, "If Community Action is really to be what it is supposed to be, the government will have to allow more freedom to the individual communities to decide which programs they want to have." This was a representative feeling and also applied to attempts of local CAAs to agree upon program priorities.

Many people also felt that the federal-local polarity was bad because ". . . those people up in Washington (or down in Austin) just don't know what it's like here in Adair, or Cherokee, or Delaware, or Sequoyah County [Oklahoma]." The feeling of most persons interviewed, was that "the feds" were trying to take decision-making away from the local community. Most used the consolidation required of the four counties as an example of this federal "power grab."

Another obstacle to long-range planning for action on the part of the whole community is the lack of understanding on the part of the board members as to what the real purposes of the War on Poverty are. Many do not understand the basic philosophy of the Community

From "A Multi-County Community Action Program Planning for Action," Southern Regional Education Board, August, 1968, pp. 5–9. Reprinted by permission.

[1] Community Action Agency.

43

Action Program and some do not know the goals of some of the programs offered by their CAAs. A woman was interviewed who had been on the board for about eight months and still knew little about CAP. This board member did not even know by what process she had been elected. In another county I attended a board meeting at which important questions were raised and votes taken. One new member, very recently elected to the board, said again and again, "I don't even know what's going on." He had received no training. He was not aware of CAP goals and guidelines. This lack of training and knowledge was true of many board members interviewed.

Another obstacle to participation in planning by the whole community is the resistance to change which is characteristic of many of the people in the area. Many of these people do not want conditions to change for the poor, especially when it will affect them economically or politically. Associated with this resistance to change is the political power structure of these four and many other rural counties. The people who control the county politically, economically, and socially are the ones who often are most resistant to change. They want to "help the poor," but they don't want to give up any of their economic or political control. This is a real obstacle to any attempts at providing real Community Action. What makes it an even greater obstacle is that these people mean well and often feel that they really are doing the right things to help "those poor people." They are paternalistic because they feel that the paternal attitude is appropriate. Unfortunately, these influential people often control the CAP boards. (I use the word "unfortunately" because CAP boards are often run in the same way as county politics. Personalities and personal favoritism come strongly into play; and the few poor who *are* on the board are often carried along somewhat bewilderingly). Although it is necessary that such influential people be on CAP boards in order to represent a cross-section of the community, it is regrettable that such a basically good concept of equal representation is often misused or exploited in such a way as to leave the poor without much influence. The CAP was created to give the poor a predominant voice in solving their difficulties, and a CAP board should be the last place where petty county politics and power plays are not only noticeable but sometimes prominent. (I realize that asking for such a CAP is a little unrealistic; however, striving for greater representation on the part of the poor themselves should be a top-priority item.)

One example of the misuse of the representation of the poor which was encountered was the use of "representatives of the poor," rather than the poor themselves, to the CAP board. Although this is allowed by CAP guidelines, it is often done to the extent that the poor are really left unrepresented (by their own voice) on the CAP board.

A curious combination of the two CAP board figures described above (the influential county "politicians," and the "representatives of the poor") was the school superintendent or principal. Very often these men would be quite powerful on the board, and they were already usually fairly powerful, or at least well known, throughout the county. More than one person whom I interviewed described the school superintendents, who are often powerful politically, as "little rulers in their own kingdom." They are often elected to CAP boards as "representatives of the poor." For many years they have been the only ones to whom the poor could turn for help. As a person in one of the communities put it, "The school is the only real stable structure in many rural communities, literally and figuratively. Whenever a new family moves in, the superintendent finds out in one way or another and goes and talks to the people. He finds out whether they have a job, how many children they have, whether they need to get on welfare rolls, etc. He may offer to take them to the welfare office or to town when they need to go. In the course of events, people become dependent, in one way or another, on the superintendent, and become, or feel, personally indebted to him. This tends to draw the support of the people to him. This is probably why superintendents are often the representative of the poor on the CAP board." In most cases, I doubt if the superintendents in these situations have any "designs" on the people; they are probably trying to help. However, even if they have good ideas about what the community needs and about what the poor really need, they are usually so closely aligned with the power structure and its ideas and have known the people who are powerful for so long that they feel somewhat indebted to the established point of view and fail to "buck the system" when it most needs it. Moreover, the representation of the poor by the people in power is a *very weak* substitute for the voice of the poor themselves.

Some people to whom I talked were aware of the workings of the local CAP. They felt that "those politicians should be removed." However, many times they tended to substitute what they saw as "regular, concerned people" for the politicians. Usually they still had the paternalistic attitude that "we need to help those poor people," and they usually did not understand the need of the poor to learn to speak for themselves and to eventually develop real power, political and otherwise. Very few CAP board members who were interviewed seemed to see the problems of the poor as the poor themselves see these problems. This situation could be greatly alleviated by having more poor people on the board. (One study of CAAs suggests that any representation of the poor on CAP boards in an amount less than 51 per cent "is a patent fraud.")

This misunderstanding of the plight of the poor is further complicated by the fact that so many of the poor in northeastern Oklahoma are Indians. The Indians, unfamiliar to white customs, had and still have difficulty fitting into the dominant society. In the past they have been repressed; they are still discriminated against; and many still see the white man as evil. Indeed, many of the hardships they now experience were often caused by the white man. Often, they were not as easily able to recover from the loss of land as the white man. Their bottomland was flooded out, and they were moved back up on the rock mountains. The Great White Fathers gave them welfare, helping them to eke out their subsistence, and at the same time salving the consciences of the whites. The dominant, profit-motivated society rapidly left them behind. It was easy to forget the Indians living out in the hills and hollows, easy to dam their streams and flood their gardens. Easy to ask, "What's wrong with those lazy Indians (or black men)? Why can't they be like white men? All they want to do is sit out there and collect welfare."

The Indians, however, share many conditions with the rest of the poor. Both groups are often bereft of hope. They are both often on welfare or pitifully underemployed in the town's leading canning or plucking factory. Very few of the poor, white, Negro or Indian, *want* to be on welfare. However, many people still have such feelings as: "Those poor people are just sorry people—they haven't got any incentive. Why, I have five hired hands, and I pay them good money; only one of them that isn't leaning on his hoe half the time. I pay them good money, too—$1.15 an hour. I guarantee him at least nine months out of the year—when it's not snowing, or raining, or something. If those poor people want to work, I'll let them work. They just don't want to work." These are representative comments which I heard in Oklahoma County when I visited.

The following is a fictional monologue based on real people and actual conditions. It presents an attitude which stands in the way of any real Community Action or any action on the part of the community over a long period of time. "If those poor people don't want to hoe soybeans, they can always pick strawberries or something. They just don't want to work. They just want to draw welfare checks. Who, me! No, I wouldn't pick strawberries. I got an education. Picking strawberries only lasts about three weeks. A man needs a full-time job if he's going to support his family. Besides, those Indians like living out in the hills (or blacks in ghettoes). They got a feeling for those places. No, I wouldn't like it; I've known a better life. No, I would not like to be on welfare; I've got *pride*. That's what's wrong with the poor people—they don't have any pride. . . . How should I know why they don't have any; I've tried to give them some. I am on the CAP board, and I talk to them when they come into my store. I loan them money at my bank; I rent them my houses. I give them all they need. What else can I give them? I've got everything they need. All they need to do is ask for it."

Planning to get programs to give more of what we've got to the poor is not planning for a War on Poverty. It is planning for job-creating and community conscience-salving.

5. The Mutual Images and Expectations of Anglo-Americans and Mexican-Americans

Ozzie G. Simmons

A number of psychological and sociological studies have treated ethnic and racial stereotypes as they appear publicly in the mass media and also as held privately by individuals.[1] The present paper is based on data collected for a study of a number of aspects of the relations between Anglo-Americans and Mexican-Americans in a South Texas community, and is concerned with the principal assumptions and expectations that Anglo- and Mexican-Americans hold of one another; how they see each other; the extent to which these pictures are realistic; and the implications of their intergroup relations and cultural differences for the fulfillment of mutual expectations.[2]

The community   The community studied (here called "Border City") is in South Texas, about 250 miles south of San Antonio. Driving south from San Antonio, one passes over vast expanses of brushland and grazing country, then suddenly comes upon acres of citrus groves, farmlands rich with vegetables and cotton, and long rows of palm trees. This is the "Magic Valley," an oasis in the semidesert region of South Texas. The Missouri Pacific Railroad (paralleled by Highway 83, locally called "the longest street in the world") bisects twelve major towns and cities of the Lower Río Grande Valley between Browns-

From *Daedalus*, Journal of American Academy of Arts and Sciences, Spring, 1961, pp. 286–99. Reprinted by permission.

[1] See John Harding, Bernard Kutner, Harold Proshansky, and Isidor Chein, "Prejudice and Ethnic Relations," in Gardner Lindzey (ed.), *Handbook of Social Psychology* (Cambridge, Addison-Wesley Publishing Company, 1954), Vol. 2, pp. 1021–61; and Otto Klineberg, *Tensions Affecting International Understanding* (New York, Social Science Research Council, 1950), Bulletin 62.

[2] The term "Anglo-American," as is common in the Southwest, refers to all residents of Border City who do not identify themselves as Spanish-speaking and of Mexican descent. The Anglo-Americans of Border City have immigrated there from all parts of the United States and represent a wide variety of regional and ethnic backgrounds. The terms "Mexican-American" and "Mexican," as used here, refer to all residents of Border City who are Spanish-speaking and of Mexican descent. The term "Spanish-speaking" is perhaps less objectionable to many people, but for present purposes is even less specific than Mexican or Mexican-American, since it also refers to ethnic groups that would have no sense of identification with the group under consideration here.

ville, near the Gulf of Mexico, and Río Grande City, 103 miles to the west.

Border City is neither the largest nor the smallest of these cities, and is physically and culturally much like the rest. Its *first* building was constructed in 1905. By 1920 it had 5,331 inhabitants, and at the time of our study these had increased to an estimated 17,500. The completion of the St. Louis, Brownsville, and Mexico Railroad in 1904 considerably facilitated Anglo-American immigration to the Valley. Before this the Valley had been inhabited largely by Mexican ranchers, who maintained large haciendas in the traditional Mexican style based on peonage. Most of these haciendas are now divided into large or small tracts that are owned by Anglo-Americans, who obtained them through purchase or less legitimate means. The position of the old Mexican-American landowning families has steadily deteriorated, and today these families, with a few exceptions, are completely overshadowed by the Anglo-Americans, who have taken over their social and economic position in the community.

The Anglo-American immigration into the Valley was paralleled by that of the Mexicans from across the border, who were attracted by the seemingly greater opportunities for farm labor created by the introduction of irrigation and the subsequent agricultural expansion. Actually, there had been a small but steady flow of Mexican immigration into South Texas that long antedated the Anglo-American immigration.[3] At present, Mexican-Americans probably constitute about two-fifths of the total population of the Valley.

In Border City, Mexican-Americans comprise about 56 per cent of the population. The southwestern part of the city, adjoining and sometimes infiltrating the business and industrial areas, is variously referred to as "Mexiquita," "Mexican-town," and "Little Mexico" by the city's Anglo-Americans, and as the *colonia* by the Mexican-Americans. With few exceptions, the *colonia* is inhabited only by Mexican-Americans, most of whom live in close proximity to one another in indifferently constructed houses on tiny lots. The north side of the city, which lies across the railroad tracks, is inhabited almost completely by Anglo-Americans. Its appearance is in sharp contrast to that of the *colonia* in that it is strictly residential and displays much better housing.

In the occupational hierarchy of Border City, the top level (the

3 For the historical background of the Valley, see Frank C. Pierce, *A Brief History of the Lower Rio Grande Valley* (Menasha, George Banta Publishing Company, 1917); Paul S. Taylor, *An American-Mexican Frontier* (Chapel Hill, University of North Carolina Press, 1934); and Florence J. Scott, *Historical Heritage of the Lower Rio Grande*, (San Antonio, the Naylor Company, 1937).

growers, packers, canners, businessmen, and professionals) is over-whelmingly Anglo-American. In the middle group (the white-collar occupations) Mexicans are prominent only where their bilingualism makes them useful, for example, as clerks and salesmen. The bottom level (farm laborers, shed and cannery workers, and domestic serv-ants) is overwhelmingly Mexican-American.

These conditions result from a number of factors, some quite distinct from the reception accorded Mexican-Americans by Anglo-Americans. Many Mexican-Americans are still recent immigrants and are thus relatively unfamiliar with Anglo-American culture and urban living, or else persist in their tendency to live apart and main-tain their own institutions whenever possible. Among their disadvan-tages, however, the negative attitudes and discriminatory practices of the Anglo-American group must be counted. It is only fair to say, with the late Ruth Tuck, that much of what Mexican-Americans have suffered at Anglo-American hands has not been perpetrated delib-erately but through indifference, that it has been done not with the fist but with the elbow.[4] The average social and economic status of the Mexican-American group has been improving, and many are moving upward. This is partly owing to increasing acceptance by the Anglo-American group, but chiefly to the efforts of the Mexican-Americans themselves.

Anglo-American assumptions and expectations
Robert Lynd writes of the dualism in the principal assumptions that guide Americans in conducting their everyday life and identifies the attempt to "live by contrasting rules of the game" as a characteristic aspect of our culture.[5] This pattern of moral compromise, sympto-matic of what is likely to be only vaguely a conscious moral conflict, is evident in Anglo-American assumptions and expectations with regard to Mexican-Americans, which appear both in the moral principles that define what intergroup relations ought to be, and in the popular notions held by Anglo-Americans as to what Mexican-Americans are "really" like. In the first case there is a response to the "American creed," which embodies ideals of the essential dignity of the individual and of certain inalienable rights to freedom, justice, and equal opportunity. Accordingly, Anglo-Americans believe that Mexican-Americans must be accorded full acceptance and equal status in the larger society. When their orientation to these ideals is uppermost, Anglo-Americans believe that the assimilation of Mexi-

---

[4] Ruth D. Tuck, *Not with the Fist* (New York, Harcourt Brace and Company, 1946).
[5] Robert S. Lynd, *Knowledge for What?* (Princeton, Princeton University Press, 1948).

can-Americans is only a matter of time, contingent solely on the full incorporation of Anglo-American values and ways of life.

These expectations regarding the assimilation of the Mexican are most clearly expressed in the notion of the "high type" of Mexican. It is based on three criteria: occupational achievement and wealth (the Anglo-American's own principal criteria of status) and command of Anglo-American ways. Mexican-Americans who can so qualify are acceptable for membership in the service clubs and a few other Anglo-American organizations and for limited social intercourse. They may even intermarry without being penalized or ostracized. Both in their achievements in business and agriculture and in wealth, they compare favorably with middle-class Anglo-Americans, and they manifest a high command of the latter's ways. This view of the "high type" of Mexican reflects the Anglo-American assumption that Mexicans are assimilable; it does not necessarily insure a full acceptance of even the "high type" of Mexican or that his acceptance will be consistent.

The assumption that Mexican-Americans will be ultimately assimilated was not uniformly shared by all the Anglo-Americans who were our informants in Border City. Regardless of whether they expressed adherence to this ideal, however, most Anglo-Americans expressed the contrasting assumption that Mexican-Americans are essentially inferior. Thus the same people may hold assumptions and expectations that are contradictory, although expressed at different times and in different situations. As in the case of their adherence to the ideal of assimilability, not all Anglo-Americans hold the same assumptions and expectations with respect to the inferiority of Mexican-Americans; and even those who agree vary in the intensity of their beliefs. Some do not believe in the Mexican's inferiority at all; some are relatively moderate or skeptical, while others express extreme views with considerable emotional intensity.

Despite this variation, the Anglo-Americans' principal assumptions and expectations emphasize the Mexicans' presumed inferiority. In its most characteristic pattern, such inferiority is held to be self-evident. As one Anglo-American woman put it, "Mexicans are inferior because they are so typically and naturally Mexican." Since they are so obviously inferior, their present subordinate status is appropriate and is really their own fault. There is a ready identification between Mexicans and menial labor, buttressed by an image of the Mexican worker as improvident, undependable, irresponsible, childlike, and indolent. If Mexicans are fit for only the humblest labor, there is nothing abnormal about the fact that most Mexican workers are at the bottom of the occupational pyramid, and the fact that most Mexicans are unskilled workers is sufficient proof that they belong in that category.

Associated with the assumption of Mexican inferiority is that of the homogeneity of this group—that is, all Mexicans are alike. Anglo-Americans may classify Mexicans as being of "high type" and "low type" and at the same time maintain that "a Mexican is a Mexican." Both notions serve a purpose, depending on the situation. The assumption that all Mexicans are alike buttresses the assumption of inferiority by making it convenient to ignore the fact of the existence of a substantial number of Mexican-Americans who represent all levels of business and professional achievement. Such people are considered exceptions to the rule.

Anglo-American images of Mexican-Americans To employ Gordon Allport's definition, a stereotype is an exaggerated belief associated with a category, and its function is to justify conduct in relation to that category.[6] Some of the Anglo-American images of the Mexican have no ascertainable basis in fact, while others have at least a kernel of truth. Although some components of these images derive from behavior patterns that are characteristic of some Mexican-Americans in some situations, few if any of the popular generalizations about them are valid as stated, and none is demonstrably true at all. Some of the images of Mexican-Americans are specific to a particular area of intergroup relations, such as the image of the Mexican-American's attributes as a worker. Another is specific to politics and describes Mexicans as ready to give their votes to whoever will pay for them or provide free barbecues and beer.[7] Let us consider a few of the stereotypical beliefs that are widely used on general principles to justify Anglo-American practices of exclusion and subordination.

One such general belief accuses Mexican-Americans of being unclean. The examples given of this supposed characteristic most frequently refer to a lack of personal cleanliness and environmental hygiene and to a high incidence of skin ailments ascribed to a lack of hygiene practices. Indeed, there are few immigrant groups, regardless of their ethnic background, to whom this defect has not been attributed by the host society, as well as others prominent in stereotypes of

---

6 Gordon W. Allport, *The Nature of Prejudice* (Cambridge, Addison-Wesley Publishing Company, 1954).

7 For an analysis of Mexican-American value orientations and behavior in the occupational and political spheres, see Ozzie G. Simmons, "Anglo-Americans and Mexican-Americans in South Texas: A Study in Dominant-Subordinate Group Relations" (unpublished doctoral dissertation, Harvard University, 1952).

the Mexican. It has often been observed that for middle-class Americans cleanliness is not simply a matter of keeping clean but is also an index to the morals and virtues of the individual. It is largely true that Mexicans tend to be much more casual in hygienic practices than Anglo-Americans. Moreover, their labor in the field, the packing sheds, and the towns is rarely clean work, and it is possible that many Anglo-Americans base their conclusions on what they observe in such situations. There is no evidence of a higher incidence of skin ailments among Mexicans than among Anglo-Americans. The belief that Mexicans are unclean is useful for rationalizing the Anglo-American practice of excluding Mexicans from any situation that involves close or allegedly close contact with Anglo-Americans, as in residence, and the common use of swimming pools and other recreational facilities.

Drunkenness and criminality are a pair of traits that have appeared regularly in the stereotypes applied to immigrant groups. They have a prominent place in Anglo-American images of Mexicans. If Mexicans are inveterate drunkards and have criminal tendencies, a justification is provided for excluding them from full participation in the life of the community. It is true that drinking is a popular activity among Mexican-Americans and that total abstinence is rare, except among some Protestant Mexican-Americans. Drinking varies, however, from the occasional consumption of a bottle of beer to the heavy drinking of more potent beverages, so that the frequency of drinking and drunkenness is far from being evenly distributed among Mexican-Americans. Actually, this pattern is equally applicable to the Anglo-American group. The ample patronage of bars in the Anglo-American part of Border City, and the drinking behavior exhibited by Anglo-Americans when they cross the river to Mexico indicate that Mexicans have no monopoly on drinking or drunkenness. It is true that the number of arrests for drunkenness in Border City is greater among Mexicans, but this is probably because Mexicans are more vulnerable to arrest. The court records in Border City show little difference in the contributions made to delinquency and crime by Anglo- and Mexican-Americans.

Another cluster of images in the Anglo-American stereotype portrays Mexican-Americans as deceitful and of a "low" morality, as mysterious, unpredictable, and hostile to Anglo-Americans. It is quite possible that Mexicans resort to a number of devices in their relations with Anglo-Americans, particularly in relations with employers, to compensate for their disadvantages, which may be construed by Anglo-Americans as evidence of deceitfulness. The whole nature of the dominant-subordinate relationship does not make for frankness on the part of Mexicans or encourage them to face up directly to Anglo-Americans in most intergroup contacts. As to the charge of immorality, one need only recognize the strong sense of loyalty and obligation that Mexicans feel in their familial and inter-personal relations to know that the charge is baseless. The claim that Mexicans are mysterious and deceitful may in part reflect Anglo-American reactions to actual differences in culture and personality, but like the other beliefs considered here, is highly exaggerated. The imputation of hostility to Mexicans, which is manifested in a reluc-tance to enter the *colonia*, particularly at night, may have its kernel of truth, but appears to be largely a projection of the Anglo-Ameri-can's own feelings.

All three of these images can serve to justify exclusion and dis-crimination: if Mexicans are deceitful and immoral, they do not have to be accorded equal status and justice; if they are mysterious and unpredictable, there is no point in treating them as one would a fellow Anglo-American; and if they are hostile and dangerous, it is best that they live apart in colonies of their own.

Not all Anglo-American images of the Mexican are unfavorable. Among those usually meant to be complimentary are the beliefs that all Mexicans are musical and always ready for a fiesta, that they are very "romantic" rather than "realistic" (which may have unfavorable overtones as well), and that they love flowers and can grow them under the most adverse conditions. Although each of these beliefs may have a modicum of truth, it may be noted that they tend to rein-force Anglo-American images of Mexicans as childlike and irrespon-sible, and thus they support the notion that Mexicans are capable only of subordinate status.

Mexican-American assumptions, expectations, and images

Mexican-Americans are as likely to hold contradictory assumptions and distorted images as are Anglo-Americans. Their principal as-sumptions, however, must reflect those of Anglo-Americans—that is, Mexicans must take into account the Anglo-Americans' conflict as to their potential equality and present inferiority, since they are the object of such imputations. Similarly, their images of Anglo-Ameri-cans are not derived wholly independently, but to some extent must reflect their own subordinate status. Consequently, their stereotypes of Anglo-Americans are much less elaborate, in part because Mexi-cans feel no need of justifying the present intergroup relation, in part because the very nature of their dependent position forces them to view the relation more realistically than Anglo-Americans do. For the same reasons, they need not hold to their beliefs about Anglo-Americans with the rigidity and intensity so often characteristic of the latter.

Any discussion of these assumptions and expectations requires some mention of the class distinctions within the Mexican-American group.[8] Its middle class, though small as compared with the lower class, is powerful within the group and performs the critical role of intermediary in negotiations with the Anglo-American group. Middle-class status is based on education and occupation, family background, readiness to serve the interests of the group, on wealth, and the degree of acculturation, or command of Anglo-American ways. Anglo-Americans recognize Mexican class distinctions (although not very accurately) in their notions of the "high type" and "low type" of Mexicans.

In general, lower-class Mexicans do not regard the disabilities of their status as being nearly as severe as do middle-class Mexican-Americans. This is primarily a reflection of the insulation between the Anglo-American world and that of the Mexican lower class. Most Mexicans, regardless of class, are keenly aware of Anglo-American attitudes and practices with regard to their group, but lower-class Mexicans do not conceive of participation in the larger society as necessary nor do they regard Anglo-American practices of exclusion as affecting them directly. Their principal reaction has been to maintain their isolation, and thus they have not been particularly concerned with improving their status by acquiring Anglo-American ways, a course more characteristic of the middle-class Mexican.

Mexican-American assumptions and expectations regarding Anglo-Americans must be qualified, then, as being more characteristic of middle- than of lower-class Mexican-Americans. Mexicans, like Anglo-Americans, are subject to conflicts in their ideals, not only because of irrational thinking on their part but also because of Anglo-American inconsistencies between ideal and practice. As for ideals expressing democratic values, Mexican expectations are for obvious reasons the counterpart of the Anglo-Americans'—that Mexican-Americans should be accorded full acceptance and equal opportunity. They feel a considerable ambivalence, however, as to the Anglo-American expectation that the only way to achieve this goal is by a full incorporation of Anglo-American values and ways of life, for this implies the ultimate loss of their cultural identity as Mexicans. On the one hand, they favor the acquisition of Anglo-American

[8] See *ibid.*, for a discussion of the Anglo-American and Mexican class structures.

culture and the eventual remaking of the Mexican in the Anglo-American image; but on the other hand, they are not so sure that Anglo-American acceptance is worth such a price. When they are concerned with this dilemma, Mexicans advocate a fusion with Anglo-American culture in which the "best" of the Mexican ways, as they view it, would be retained along with the incorporation of the "best" of the Anglo-American ways, rather than a one-sided exchange in which all that is distinctively Mexican would be lost.

A few examples will illustrate the point of view expressed in the phrase, "the best of both ways." A premium is placed on speaking good, unaccented English, but the retention of good Spanish is valued just as highly as "a mark of culture that should not be abandoned." Similarly, there is an emphasis on the incorporation of behavior patterns that are considered characteristically Anglo-American and that will promote "getting ahead," but not to the point at which the drive for power and wealth would become completely dominant, as is believed to be the case with Anglo-Americans.

Mexican ambivalence about becoming Anglo-American or achieving a fusion of the "best" of both cultures is compounded by their ambivalence about another issue, that of equality versus inferiority. That Anglo-Americans are dominant in the society and seem to monopolize its accomplishments and rewards leads Mexicans at times to draw the same conclusion that Anglo-Americans do, namely, that Mexicans are inferior. This questioning of their own sense of worth exists in all classes of the Mexican-American group, although with varying intensity, and plays a substantial part in every adjustment to intergroup relations. There is a pronounced tendency to concede the superiority of Anglo-American ways and consequently to define Mexican ways as undesirable, inferior, and disreputable. The tendency to believe in his own inferiority is counterbalanced, however, by the Mexican's fierce racial pride, which sets the tone of Mexican demands and strivings for equal status, even though these may slip into feelings of inferiority.

The images Mexicans have of Anglo-Americans may not be so elaborate or so emotionally charged as the images that Anglo-Americans have of Mexicans, but they are nevertheless stereotypes, overgeneralized and exaggerated, although used primarily for defensive rather than justificatory purposes. Mexican images of Anglo-Americans are sometimes favorable, particularly when they identify such traits as initiative, ambition, and industriousness as being peculiarly Anglo-American. Unfavorable images are prominent, however, and, although they may be hostile, they never impute inferiority to Anglo-Americans. Most of the Mexican stereotypes evaluate Anglo-Americans on the basis of their attitudes toward Mexican-Americans. For example, one such classification provides a two-fold typology. The first type, the "majority," includes those who are cold, unkind, mercenary, and exploitative. The second type, the "minority," consists of those who are friendly, warm, just, and unprejudiced. For the most part, Mexican images of Anglo-Americans reflect the latter's patterns of exclusion and assumptions of superiority, as experienced by Mexican-Americans. Thus Anglo-Americans are pictured as stolid, phlegmatic, cold hearted, and distant. They are also said to be braggarts, conceited, inconstant, and insincere.

A number of students of intergroup relations assert that research in this area has yet to demonstrate any relation between stereotypical beliefs and intergroup behavior; indeed, some insist that under certain conditions ethnic attitudes and discrimination can vary independently.[9] Arnold M. Rose, for example, concludes that "from a heuristic standpoint it may be desirable to assume that patterns of intergroup relations, on the one hand, and attitudes of prejudice and stereotyping, on the other hand, are fairly unrelated phenomena although they have reciprocal influences on each other. . . ."[10] In the present study, no systematic attempt was made to investigate the relations between the stereotypical beliefs of particular individuals and their actual intergroup behavior; but the study did yield evidence that both images which justify group separatism and separateness itself are characteristic aspects of intergroup relations in Border City. One of the principal findings is that in those situations in which contact between Anglo-Americans and Mexicans is voluntary (such as residence, education, recreation, religious worship, and social intercourse) the characteristic pattern is separateness rather than common participation. Wherever intergroup contact is necessary, as in occupational activities and the performance of commercial and professional services, it is held to the minimum sufficient to accomplish the purpose of the contact.[11] The extent of this is not constant for all members of the two groups, since it tends to be less severe between

Intergroup relations, mutual expectations, and cultural differences

9 Robert K. Merton, "Discrimination and the American Creed," in R. M. MacIver (ed.), *Discrimination and National Welfare* (New York, Harper and Brothers, 1949), 99–128; John Harding, Bernard Kutner, Harold Proshansky, and Isidor Chein, *op. cit.*; Arnold M. Rose, "Intergroup Relations vs. Prejudice: Pertinent Theory for the Study of Social Change," *Social Problems*, Vol. IV (1956), 173–76; Robin M. Williams, Jr., "Racial and Cultural Relations," in Joseph B. Gittler (ed.), *Review of Sociology: Analysis of a Decade* (New York, John Wiley and Sons, 1957), 423–64.

10 Rose, *op. cit.*   11 Simmons, *op. cit.*

Anglo-Americans and those Mexicans they define as "high type." Nevertheless, the evidence reveals a high degree of compatibility between beliefs and practices in Border City's intergroup relations, although the data have nothing to offer for the identification of direct relationships.

In any case, the separateness that characterizes intergroup relations cannot be attributed solely to the exclusion practices of the Anglo-American group. Mexicans have tended to remain separate by choice as well as by necessity. Like many other ethnic groups, they have often found this the easier course, since they need not strain to learn another language or to change their ways and manners. The isolation practices of the Mexican group are as relevant to an understanding of intergroup relations as are the exclusion practices of the Anglo-Americans.

This should not, however, obscure the fact that to a wide extent the majority of Mexican-Americans share the patterns of living of Anglo-American society; many of their ways are already identical. Regardless of the degree of their insulation from the larger society, the demands of life in the United States have required basic modifications of the Mexicans' cultural tradition. In material culture, Mexicans are hardly to be distinguished from Anglo-Americans, and there have been basic changes in medical beliefs and practices and in the customs regarding godparenthood. Mexicans have acquired English in varying degrees, and their Spanish has become noticeably Anglicized. Although the original organization of the family has persisted, major changes have occurred in patterns of traditional authority, as well as in child training and courtship practices. Still, it is the exceedingly rare Mexican-American, no matter how acculturated he may be to the dominant society, who does not in some degree retain the more subtle characteristics of his Mexican heritage, particularly in his conception of time and in other fundamental value orientations, as well as in his modes of participation in interpersonal relations.[12] Many of the most acculturated Mexican-Americans have attempted to exemplify what they regard as "the best of both ways." They have become largely Anglo-American in their way of living, but they still retain fluent Spanish and a knowledge of their traditional culture, and they maintain an identification with their own heritage while

---

[12] For cultural differences and similarities between Anglo-Americans and Mexicans, see Simmons, *op. cit.*; Tuck, *op. cit.*; Lyle Saunders, *Cultural Differences and Medical Care* (New York, Russell Sage Foundation, 1954); Munro S. Edmonson, *Los Manitos: A Study of Institutional Values* (New Orleans, Middle American Research Institute, Tulane University, 1957), Publication 25, pp. 1–72; and Margaret Clark, *Health in the Mexican-American Culture* (Berkeley, University of California Press, 1959).

participating in Anglo-American culture. Nevertheless, this sort of achievement still seems a long way off for many Mexican-Americans who regard it as desirable.

A predominant Anglo-American expectation is that the Mexicans will be eventually assimilated into the larger society; but this is contingent upon Mexicans' becoming just like Anglo-Americans. The Mexican counterpart to this expectation is only partially complementary. Mexicans want to be full members of the larger society, but they do not want to give up their cultural heritage. There is even less complementarity of expectation with regard to the present conduct of intergroup relations. Anglo-Americans believe they are justified in withholding equal access to the rewards of full acceptance as long as Mexicans remain "different," particularly since they interpret the differences (both those which have some basis in reality and those which have none) as evidence of inferiority. Mexicans, on the other hand, while not always certain that they are not inferior, clearly want equal opportunity and full acceptance now, not in some dim future, and they do not believe that their differences (either presumed or real) from Anglo-Americans offer any justification for the denial of opportunity and acceptance. Moreover, they do not find that acculturation is rewarded in any clear and regular way by progressive acceptance.

It is probable that both Anglo-Americans and Mexicans will have to modify their beliefs and practices if they are to realize more nearly their expectations of each other. Mutual stereotyping, as well as the exclusion practices of Anglo-Americans and the isolation practices of Mexicans, maintains the separateness of the two groups, and separateness is a massive barrier to the realization of their expectations. The process of acculturation is presently going on among Mexican-Americans and will continue, regardless of whether changes in Anglo-Mexican relations occur. Unless Mexican-Americans can validate their increasing command of Anglo-American ways by a free participation in the larger society, however, such acculturation is not likely to accelerate its present leisurely pace, nor will it lead to eventual assimilation. The *colonia* is a relatively safe place in which new cultural acquisitions may be tried out, and thus it has its positive functions; but by the same token it is only in intergroup contacts with Anglo-Americans that acculturation is validated, that the Mexican's level of acculturation is tested, and that the distance he must yet travel to assimilation is measured.[13]

13 See Leonard Broom and John I. Kitsuse, "The Validation of Acculturation: A Condition to Ethnic Assimilation," *American Anthropologist*, Vol. LVII (1955), 44–48.

Conclusions   There are major inconsistencies in the assumptions that Anglo-Americans and Mexican-Americans hold about one another. Anglo-Americans assume that Mexican-Americans are their potential, if not actual, peers, but at the same time assume they are their inferiors. The beliefs that presumably demonstrate the Mexican-Americans' inferiority tend to place them outside the accepted moral order and framework of Anglo-American society by attributing to them undesirable characteristics that make it "reasonable" to treat them differently from their fellow Anglo-Americans, but are also a substantial support for maintaining the relation as it is. The assumptions of Mexican-Americans about Anglo-Americans are similarly inconsistent, and their images of Anglo-Americans are predominantly negative, although these are primarily defensive rather than justificatory. The mutual expectations of the two groups contrast sharply with the ideal of a complementarity of expectations, in that Anglo-Americans expect Mexicans to become just like themselves, if they are to be accorded equal status in the larger society, whereas Mexican-Americans want full acceptance, regardless of the extent to which they give up their own ways and acquire those of the dominant group.

Anglo-Americans and Mexicans may decide to stay apart because they are different, but cultural differences provide no moral justification for one group to deny to the other equal opportunity and the rewards of the larger society. If the full acceptance of Mexicans by Anglo-Americans is contingent upon the disappearance of cultural differences, it will not be accorded in the foreseeable future. In our American society, we have often seriously underestimated the strength and tenacity of early cultural conditioning. We have expected newcomers to change their customs and values to conform to American ways as quickly as possible, without an adequate appreciation of the strains imposed by this process. An understanding of the nature of culture and of its interrelations with personality can make us more realistic about the rate at which cultural change can proceed and about the gains and costs for the individual who is subject to the experiences of acculturation. In viewing cultural differences primarily as disabilities, we neglect their positive aspects. Mexican-American culture represents the most constructive and effective means Mexican-Americans have yet been able to develop for coping with their changed natural and social environment. They will further exchange old ways for new only if these appear to be more meaningful and rewarding than the old, and then only if they are given full opportunity to acquire the new ways and to use them.

6. The Most Oppressed Race in The United States: The Indian

Joseph S. Roucek

THE four hundred thousand American Indians living today on reservations constitute "the most oppressed minority group in the United States," according to the then Senator Hubert Humphrey, who pointed this out at the beginning of May, 1964, at a national conference in Washington on improvements in education, housing, and health for the underprivileged citizens. He stressed also that the average family income is low, and that their unemployment rate was "seven or eight times" the national average. "Poverty is the everyday life of the American Indian. No other group in American life is so victimized," he said.

Another example of the fate of the Indians is provided by the current treatment of the Seneca Indians. They are being driven from their homes by the rising waters of the Kinzua Dam in western Pennsylvania, although in 1794 the United States signed a treaty with the Seneca Indian Nation granting it a reservation along the banks of the Allegheny River in western New York which the Senecas were to enjoy undisturbed "forever" or, at least, "as long as the grass grew green."

Obviously, governments, like young suitors, should not be taken seriously when they use words like "forever," for the Indians are being dispossessed, because most of their land will be submerged under water when the Kinzua Dam flood control project twenty-seven miles downstream will have been completed.

The Indians may, in their wisdom, understand that the living cannot always be bound by the promises of the dead. In 1794, the America west of the Atlantic coast was a great wilderness that Thomas Jefferson thought would take a thousand years to settle, and no one could foresee that the United States population would multiply 45 times in 170 years. No man dreamed of the mechanization, the rapid

From *The Educational Forum*, May, 1965, pp. 477–85. Reprinted by permission. Copyright 1965 by Kappa Delta Pi, an honor society in education.

transportation, and all the other things that created a larger human gap between 1964 and 1794 than existed between the infant United States and the Roman Empire.

One thing, however, the Indians cannot understand is why it should take so long for them to be paid for their land. A twenty-billion-dollar reparations and rehabilitation bill, passed by the House (and cut down to $9.1 million by a Senate subcommittee), lay in limbo sidetracked by apparently more pressing business, although some 140 Indian families had to find new homes by October 1. They no longer referred to the president as "the Great White Father," and as far as they can tell, the white man still speaks with a forked tongue.

Johnson's war on poverty Yet, the problems of the Indian have not been entirely forgotten in Washington. With the accession of Lyndon B. Johnson to the Presidency, the administration's war on poverty has been focusing attention on the American Indian such as he has probably not enjoyed since the end of the Indian Wars in the late nineteenth century. The Indian has been singled out in talks by President Johnson, Secretary of the Interior Stewart L. Udall, and, of course, by United States Indian Commissioner Philleo Nash, as a special target of the antipoverty campaign. The emphasis on Indian poverty has been, in turn, focusing attention on the great confusion that sometimes results when people start trying to find practical means of fighting poverty. For, ironically, the Indian in the United States has been the subject of such concern by the federal government for a longer time than any other group in the nation. In fact, the special character of the Indian problem is attested by the foundation of the Indian service as a branch of the federal government with no counterpart in all the other American minority situations—although the problem of the American Red Man concerns directly less than one-half of one per cent of the total American population.

Mr. Udall says that he agrees with Senator Humphrey that the logical opening battle against poverty would be pilot projects on Indian reservations. Both men agree that a major problem involved in fighting Indian poverty—and no one denies it is some of the worst poverty in the nation—centers on the reservation. Should the aim be to end the reservation system and force the Indian abruptly to enter the "mainstream" of American life? Or should it be to strengthen the reservation, to cause the Indian to turn more toward his own culture and its ways of solving problems?

These two approaches represent the two extremes. The latter was the policy of the New Deal under which Indian Commissioner John

Collier sometimes set up schools to teach Indians their own language. The former was the policy of the Eisenhower administration which sought to "terminate" Indian tribes, to bring to an end the special relationships they had had with the federal government.[1]

Nevertheless, neither approach appears to have brought the Indian very far up from poverty. All evidence shows that the "terminated" or otherwise "landless" Indians have frequently ended up in Indian slums, such as can be found in Rapid City, South Dakota, or in Billings and Great Falls, Montana. The responsibility for the care of them has been simply shifted from the federal to local governments. On the other hand, the Indian living on a reservation has realized a strong sense of identification with it, often becoming completely dependent on a paternalistic federal government, refusing to be budged into any movement toward self-sufficiency.

Using as a guide a report prepared by a task force headed by Commissioner Nash, the John F. Kennedy and Johnson administrations tried to find a middle way and, at the same time, have stressed less a "way" than a pragmatic approach to each problem, an approach geared to the general belief that self-sufficiency is needed.

"There are many encouraging signs of success," claim some Indian leaders.[2] But these leaders also emphasize that these programs have been scratching only the surface, and that they must be greatly expanded before they make a significant and permanent dent in Indian problems.

Most of the Indian leaders agree that training or educating young Indians so that a large percentage can live away from the reservation is an important goal. They add, however, that many Indians will remain on the reservation, and that general welfare programs, housing, sanitation, and education there must be improved. *The role of education*

The whole history of the efforts of the federal government to "educate" the Indians is rather sordid, since the Federal Bureau of Indian Affairs has often failed to interest the Indians in education and self-improvement and has come to be looked upon as a "father figure" which would solve the Indians' problems. Thus, the Indians have declined in a "welfare culture" basically alien to them. In fact, this is one of the most pitiful stories of the misguided educational efforts in American educational history in regard to America's original "minority."

1 John Collier, "A New Deal for the Red Men" in W. E. Washburn, *The Indian and the White Man* (New York, Doubleday, Anchor Books, 1964), 392–96.
2 Dick Gilluly, "War on Poverty Fixed on Indians," *Christian Science Monitor*, June 8, 1964.

The historical background is quite interesting in this respect. The original colonies were little interested in Indian education, although several colleges, including Dartmouth and Harvard, made provisions for tuition-free admissions of the Red Man, and the Continental Congress employed, in 1775, a schoolmaster for the Delawares.[3] The Revolution stopped educational efforts on behalf of the Indian, and until 1819 Indian education was left entirely to a few missionary societies; from that year to 1873 ten thousand dollars was appropriated annually for the work, and most of it was turned over to the missions.[4]

In 1871, Congress decreed that no Indian tribe shall be acknowledged or recognized as an independent nation, tribe or power, with whom the United States may contract by treaty,[5] thus marking the beginning of a definitely new phase in Indian-white relations. The Indians became wards of the federal government, a unique status for any minority group in the United States. The policy of the Indian Office from that time on aimed at weakening the tribal organization of the Indians, destroying their culture, and forcing their assimilation as individuals into the normative American way of life.

One phase of forced assimilation concerned the educational program. Indian children of school age were taken out of their tribal homes and placed in boarding schools, where the use of Indian languages and the practice of Indian folkways and mores, such as dress and hair styles, were prohibited. The curricula there were largely those of the white schools, without any consideration as to the particular needs of the Indians. Whatever practical training the Indian children secured either for making a living or making better homes was gained from the labor they performed to help to support the schools; thus a mediocre school system tried to prepare Indian children to live as white people, when in fact most of them would return home to live as Indians.[6]

It is true that the appropriations by the federal government were increased regularly after 1873; but until 1929 Indian education had been a hodgepodge. Most Indians attended public schools—and this is still true—while large numbers went to mission schools. Many attended boarding schools, both on and off the reservations, estab-

---

[3] Alden Stevens, "White American Indian," *Survey Graphic*, Vol. XXIX (March, 1940), 168–74.

[4] For details, cf. Clifton E. Olmstead, *History of Religion in the United States* (Englewood Cliffs, N. J., Prentice-Hall, 1960), 179–82, 415–18.

[5] Ray A. Billington, *Westward Expansion* (New York, The Macmillan Co., 1949), 668; pp. 651–80 cover Indian-white relations from 1860 to 1887.

[6] Gordon Macgregor, *The Changing Indian Warriors Without Weapons* (Chicago, University of Chicago Press, 1944), 116–27.

lished late in the last century on the theory that Indian education needed the removal of the children from their parents and home life, so that they could be "civilized." Force was often used to take them from their homes, and the schools were characterized by a rigid discipline and a standardized, outmoded course of study. Half of the time was devoted to school work, the other half to doing routine institutional tasks such as laundering, cleaning, wood-chopping and food preparation. Since the work was hard, physically, and required many hours a day, this often affected the health of the pupils. Conditions were worsened by insufficient operating funds, resulting in dangerously low standards of living. Forbidden to speak their own language in school, out of touch with family and tribal life, denied the normal experience and education needed to prepare them for life as Indians, the children would return home from school dissatisfied misfits, unable to readapt themselves to reservation life and equally unable to find a place in a white community. They had learned to read and write, but they were unfamiliar with the customs and language of their own people, and found their schooling of little use in making a living. . . .[7]

The New Deal policy replaced this first phase of the Indian reservation policy in 1934. Yet, even the new ideology has hardly made any dent in the over-all problem of Indian education. Economically, the American Indian was pauperized, and the education of the younger Indians had made them marginal individuals *par excellence,* not ready to take their place in the white American world, and unsettled for Indian life. This policy of "acculturation" had failed simply because the forms of Indian culture patterns still were more divergent from the dominant WASP (White-Anglo-Saxon-Protestant) culture pattern than that of any other American minority. A complicating element was introduced by the record of low standards of personnel of the Indian service.[8]

It is true that World War II did much to have the American Indian accepted into the American stream of life, yet, in September, 1951, John R. Ride, Winnebago Indian killed in action in Korea, could not be buried in a cemetery in Sioux City, Iowa, because he was not of the "Caucasian race." It was only because of the direct intervention

The Indian program since World War II

---

7 Stevens, *op. cit.*
8 Clark Wissler, "American Indian Tribal Groups" in Frances J. Brown and Joseph S. Roucek, (eds.), *Our Racial and National Minorities* (New York, Prentice-Hall, 1937), 37–55. Also Robert F. Heizer, "The American Indian" in Brown and Roucek, (eds.), *One America* (New York, Prentice-Hall, 1952), 27–31, and R. A. Schermerhorn, *These Our People: Minorities in American Culture* (Boston, D. C. Heath, 1949), 57–82.

by President Truman that he was buried with military honors in the Arlington National Cemetery.[9]

Furthermore, in spite of the hopes to liquidate the government's responsibility to the Indians by the policy of "relocation" and "termination," the United States has been unable to convert the American original natives to the "American way of life."

In 1952 the Bureau of Indian Affairs scheduled the Voluntary Relocation Program under which reservation Indians, as individuals or as families, were granted financial and other help to move to industrial centers for permanent employment and settlement. The bureau put the proportion of relocated Indians who by 1955 had returned at about 24 per cent. This program hardly influenced the more basic problem of helping the reservation Indians to develop viable economies, to work out their own problems, and to decide how much of the traditional Indian heritage they might want to retain.

On August 1, 1953, Congress passed the "termination" program, aiming to have tribes request termination of their relations to the federal government. But this meant also in many cases dissolution of tribal organizations and the division of tribal assets among the members, with the resulting demoralization and pauperization of many tribes.

Perennial educational problems Noteworthy in the present situation are the difficulties faced by the Indians of school age.

The Indian youngster, even today, lives in a continuous state of conflict. This is especially true in regions where the color line is not sharply drawn, and where there are no absolute prescriptions marking off the role shared by all other citizens and the role of Americans shared only by those with colored skin. Under such circumstances, the Indian can never be certain of his status or sure of his welcome. While restricting caste-ways are undoubtedly detrimental under any conditions, they are bound to be more traumatic to the individual when they are not an integral, inevitable, and therefore impersonal part of the social structure. School segregation in former days also had a most unfavorable effect on the Indian pupils, seriously interfering, in extreme cases, with both their work and play. Confused by the failure of the authorities to offer a rational explanation for it, such children sometimes reached the conclusion that it must be a form of punishment for being "red." Many, therefore, on the basis of surface impressions, developed defenses against their anxiety by

9 Joseph S. Roucek, "The American Indian in Literature and Politics," *Il Politico*, Vol. XXVII, No. 3, (1962) 569–85.

repressions, substitutions, overcompensations, and antisocial behavior.

This, therefore, presents the perennial problem of American education when confronted by the existence of "minorities": how to relate the concepts of cultural pluralism to total assimilation. Should young Indians be integrated into American society as Indians, or should they be encouraged to acculturate as rapidly as possible to the typical "American way of life," although this might lead to complete estrangement of their families' background?

Obviously, the integration of Indian children into schools off their reservation has been a mixed blessing. The Indian child's clothes, language, and social customs set him apart psychologically, and the situation has been complicated by his inability to participate financially in most extracurricular and social activities on equal terms with his white classmates. This feeling of being different accounts in large measure for the 60 per cent drop-out rate among Indian high school children.[10]

Then there are the conflicts in the educational goals. While the typical American educational system favors individualism and competition, the Indians are group-minded. For the Navaho Indian, for instance, to take initiative in any obvious manner has the psychological effect of separating him from his own social group. By training and experience he works best as a "member of a familial group where authority is diffuse, informal, and shared, and where adequate performance is enforced by the subtle action of 'shaming.' "[11] In fact, most American Indians see no value in competition. To strive to excel in games or compete in school work is to them quite impolite, to say the least. For instance, some Hopi school children evidenced embarrassment and resisted the injunction to turn around from the blackboard just as soon as they had finished a problem. Distinction of this sort was not a part of their culture.[12]

The "deculturalization" of the Indian child has, in turn, produced quite an abyss between the world of their families and of the school, reaching the point where the federal government once withdrew rations on an Indian reservation to force Indian parents to send their children to school.[13]

Underlying all these factors has been the persistent race conscious-

10 "U.S. Indians," *New York Times*, May 31, 1964.

11 Dorothea Leighton and Clyde Kluckhohn, *Children of the People* (Cambridge, Harvard University Press, 1947), 107.

12 Franklin J. Shaw and Robert S. Ort, *Personal Adjustment in the American Culture* (New York, Harper & Row, 1953), 33.

13 E. E. Dale, *The Indians of the Southwest* (Norman, University of Oklahoma Press, 1949), 182.

ness of dominant-status Americans, often evaluating Indians as "colored" people and hence, as inferior.

The contemporary goal of governmental policy toward the American Indian is for him to attain economic self-sufficiency and develop skills in retaining his lands and natural resources. The assumption is that this will make Indians no more vulnerable than other Americans and enable them to compete with the rest of the world. The goal is also to have the Indian assume full responsibilities for citizenship, including payment of taxes on land now held in trust for him by the government. (In the opinion of most specialists this is not likely to be reached any earlier than the year 2000.) In fact, some critics stress that there is still no firm, definite program to reach such goals, and no rigorous timetable to achieve it. Nor, they claim, is there even a real trend of policy or a vigorous drive among officials to head for it. Indeed, the Bureau of Indian Affairs has been accused of arbitrary methods that inadvertently reverse the advance of the Indians toward "complete self-reliance and delay the end of their paternalistic supervision by the government."[14]

The views of the Indians So far, we have been viewing the problem of the American Indian from the "American" point of view. Little is actually known about the social attitudes of the Indians, especially of the youngsters. In this respect, two pieces of research on Indian attitudes—from a relatively small sample—by Spindler using the Rorschach technique lead to some interesting conclusions.

The Spindlers describe a rather remarkable group of Indians "who had attained occupational and social positions equivalent to those of high status in the nearby white towns," and had undergone a psychological transformation toward the middle-class American value system: in the other case, the Indians who have appeared acculturated gave evidence of a corroded psychological structure, in which such shifts as had taken place were "regressive and disintegrative."[15]

The conclusion of the Spindlers is that there are some older Indians still holding to the ancient values of their people with conviction, but that the great majority of adults stand between the old and the new in various degrees of confusion and society. But all are "insecure."[16]

14 Milton L. Barron, *American Minorities* (New York, Alfred Knopf, 1962), 154.

15 G. D. and L. S. Spindler, "The American Indian Personality Types and Their Socio-Cultural Roots," *The Annals of the American Academy of Political and Social Science,* Vol. CCCXI (May, 1957), 152. Also, A. T. Hallowell, *Culture and Experience* (Philadelphia: University of Pennsylvania Press, 1957), Chaps. 5, 19, 20.

About half of the American Indians are under the age of twenty, and we can only guess how much regression and disintegration found by the Spindlers among older Indians exists among them. We do know, however, that the young Indians tend to leave school earlier than white children. While the average number of years of schooling for adults over twenty-five in the general population is over ten years, for Indians on reservations it is between five and six.[17] The proportion of Indian children who graduate from high school is less than two-thirds of whites.[18]

An analysis of the hopes of the young Indians is offered by Hoyt, who studied 582 essays on "My Hopes for My Life in Leaving School" from Indian children fifteen to seventeen years of age in all types of schools (boarding and day, federal public integrated and public exclusively Indian, missionary, vocational and nonvocational institutions) in the Southwest. He then secured 207 essays from white children of the same ages for purposes of comparison.[19]

Hoyt's report is that reference to the old values of Indians "was entirely negative. This is the more striking since the essays were from the Southwest. There was incidental reference to values learned in school, values some children wanted to carry back to their people." But nearly one-third of all these children featured love or concern for their parents, family or tribe, "references to family being about twice as common as references to tribe, and especially common among the children of the least sophisticated of the schools. No white child of native parentage spoke of love for parents or family, but a few white children spoke of love for humanity or desire to serve it."[20]

Regarding the material aspects of the standard of living, one-third of the Indian children wanted to own something of their own, "car" being most frequently noted. But white children favored cars, too, although "less frequently, no doubt taking them for granted." Thus "in general the frequency of expression of interest in material things to be owned was similar among Indian children and white children."

Most interest was shown in a job by the Indian children: 91 per cent wanted a regular job, and most wanted it off the reservation. Nearly the same percentage of white children wanted a job, but mentioned nothing steady or regular about it "which was no doubt taken for granted."

16 Spindler, *op. cit.*, 154–67.

17 *Educational Cutdown* (Washington, D.C., Bureau of Indian Affairs, 1959), 9.

18 *Today's Dropouts, Tomorrow's Problems* (Washington, D.C., Bureau of Indian Affairs, 1960), 2.

19 Elizabeth E. Hoyt, "Young Indians: Some Problems and Issues of Mental Hygiene," *Mental Health*, vol. XLVI, No. 1 (January, 1962), 41–47.

20 *Ibid.*, 44.

"The concentration of interests in jobs and the remarks relating to achievement—and possible frustration"—were the most striking thing about these essays. The mention of "steady" and "regular" was particularly interesting in view of the fact that Indians have the reputation for being interested primarily in casual or seasonable labor, tasks which require a major but temporary concentration of effort.

But these children knew hardly anything about the jobs available to them or what was needed as preparation for them. The uncertainty of Indian children seemed primarily to be uncertainty as to what possible jobs there might be; the uncertainty of white children seemed to rise from knowledge of too many jobs, from which they could not choose.

In general, "Indian children in integrated schools knew somewhat more about jobs than the other Indians; these schools were in urban communities and the Indian children were rubbing shoulders with other children whose fathers had a variety of jobs." And the second "most striking thing about the essays was the psychological insecurity some children expressed. They had much more humility of ambition and much more lack of confidence than the white children." In fact they had "various fears that they might not 'make the grade,' even for low-level jobs. Many were concerned for their family and tribe should they have to leave them for jobs. While the older and embittered Indians ascribe Indian failures to the prejudices of whites, these children felt no bitterness about this."

It is obvious that formulating an approach to the war on poverty among Indians is immensely complex, and that much confusion exists. Undoubtedly this is true of the war on poverty in general, and Indian leaders and federal officials hope that the Indian experience will produce some useful knowledge which can be applied to similar situations.

7. **Darkness on the Delta**

Foster Davis

THE cotton in Mississippi's Delta has grown well this year. Plants as tall as a man march in rows across vast, flat fields where picking machines lurch along spewing the dirty-looking gray bolls into a hopper.

Picking cotton in the fall and chopping weeds from the plants during the growing season once was work for men and women who knew no other life. Then came the machines, and year by year thousands of Mississippi's Delta Negroes have found their already precarious existence threatened by technology and government regulation to the point of desperation.

Talk of acreage reduction and minimum-wage legislation is nearly meaningless to these workers. An estimated total of fifty-five thousand people are being uprooted from the plantations where they were born and where they expected to work out their lives. Perhaps twelve thousand more who live in towns and once earned a scanty living by day labor on the plantations are also without employment this year. Such local, state, and federal efforts as there have been to aid these people have not yet reached more than a small fraction of them.

The available statistics tell a portion of the story. In 1953 Mississippi planted over 2.5 million acres in cotton. By 1966 that figure, because of steady reductions in the federal cotton allotments, had dropped to 1.03 million. In 1960, according to the Delta Council, a trade organization devoted to the economic interests of the Delta, over thirty thousand seasonal workers were employed. By last year that figure had dropped to less than seventeen thousand.

Mississippi's Delta is an eighteen-county area of smooth, mellow soil formed by what once was the periodic flooding of the land by the river systems that bound it. On the west there is the Mississippi

Cures that kill

71

River. On the east there are the lesser systems of the Coldwater, Tallahatchie, and Yazoo rivers. The Delta measures precisely 196 miles from north to south and approximately fifty miles across at its widest point.

Since the region was settled in the early years of the nineteenth century, the Delta has depended on cotton. Men talk about cotton here the way the weather is discussed in other areas. And until recent years, picking that cotton crop would have been impossible without the ready labor supply provided by the Delta's large Negro population.

The gradual reduction of the amount of cotton a farmer could plant and still participate in the federal price-support programs has been a continuing concern in the Delta. The Delta Council has lobbied hard to try to keep cotton allotments high, without notable success. Two additional factors, however, have combined to make this an exceptionally difficult year for the Delta.

Those two factors are the 1965 farm bill, which made its presence felt last year, and the agricultural minimum-wage legislation. The former provides for direct cash payments from the federal government to farmers who agree to reduce their acreage by up to 35 per cent. Most have done it, with a corresponding decrease in their needs for labor. The minimum-wage legislation, which became effective last February 1 and provided a $1.00 per hour minimum for farm laborers, extended to farmers who used more than five hundred man-days of labor in any calendar quarter in 1966. In effect this means any farmer who raises cotton on more than a patch of land. Next February the minimum goes to $1.15. The year after that it goes to $1.30.

For farmers who had been accustomed to paying workers closer to thirty cents an hour, or from $3.00 to $3.50 a day, the requirement snuffed out the flickering demand for hand labor. Laborers who could drive the expensive machinery used in cotton farming were in demand. (There are perhaps twenty-five thousand such Negroes in the Delta.) But the props were kicked out from under the less fortunate Negroes without such skills. The immediate effect has been that people who had a small but reliable income now have almost nothing or literally nothing. Some of them are going hungry. And things will be worse when the weather turns cold.

Hardship has long been a fact of life for the Negro in the Mississippi Delta. Typical housing is an unpainted shack with one leaky stove and no inside water or other plumbing. The children often have bad teeth and swollen bellies. Such conditions are so commonplace that they tend to go unnoticed even among the Deltans who consider themselves concerned about the plight of the Negro farmhand.

The diet of Delta Negroes has never been good, but this year it is worse. In the past most of them could count on a regular supply of yellow meal and beans provided under the Federal Commodity Program. But now, in more and more counties, the program is being replaced by a food-stamp plan under which a family is given stamps redeemable for food in local markets in exchange for a certain cash contribution. The concept is sound enough: it substitutes self-help for the dole and makes for a more balanced diet. But the difficulty with the food-stamp program is that it requires what is for a poor Mississippi family—black or white—a major cash outlay at one time. Stamps may be purchased once or twice a month. The family's contribution varies with the income and the number of mouths to feed. A typical household of six persons with a monthly income of $50 must plunk down $22 to get stamps good for $74 worth of food. The result is that many families don't participate in the program. Civil-rights groups are hoping to persuade the Department of Agriculture to change the program so that poorer people can get the stamps free. They have had limited success: the department says it is "reviewing" the program and a change has been made affecting those with a monthly income of less than $50. A person with a monthly income of $49.99 or less now can get $12 worth of stamps for fifty cents. Unfortunately, however, many elderly Negroes get exactly $50 per month through the state's aid for the aged program, which prices them out of the reduced-cost phase of the program.

The issue of hunger in the Delta began as a skirmish in April when Senators Joseph Clark and Robert F. Kennedy visited Mississippi to gather ammunition for the annual battle over money for the anti-poverty program. Clark is chairman and Kennedy is a member of the Senate Subcommittee on Employment, Manpower, and Poverty. They returned to Washington with reports of severe malnutrition, prompting a team study by the Department of Agriculture that led to the liberalization in the stamp program.

Hunger, visible and invisible

The issue really flared up, however, after a six-man team of doctors, one of them a Negro from Yazoo City, toured six counties, two of them in the Delta, and then issued a report entitled "Hungry Children" through the Atlanta-based Southern Regional Council. The team's work was done at the request of Friends of the Children of Mississippi, a massive Head Start program trying to get the U.S. Office of Economic Opportunity to finance it in the counties the doctors visited. The doctors' twenty-seven-page report was a strong indictment of Mississippi.

What caught the headlines was a personal report added to the
team report by Dr. Raymond M. Wheeler of Charlotte, North Carolina. Dr. Wheeler, chairman of the SRC executive committee, wrote
that what he had seen led him to place more credence in the charges
that there was a tacit policy by "those who control the state to
eliminate the Negro Mississippian either by driving him out of the
state or starving him to death." White Mississippi, with its customary
genius for saying the wrong thing, made an almost predictable response. Much of the state press declared that Mississippi had been
libeled. Governor Paul Johnson said that he, for one, had never
seen any hungry Negroes. In fact, he added, the Negroes he saw "are
so fat they shine." The state's congressional delegation responded in
like tone, except for Senator John Stennis, who said that he did not
believe there were people in Mississippi going without food but if
there were they should be fed. In midsummer he introduced and got
quick Senate passage of a $75-million emergency food and medical-
service bill to alleviate conditions in poverty areas in the nation. That
action seemed to offer an effective rebuttal to those who were charging a deliberate policy of starvation, but it is not likely to have any
substantial effect upon the condition of Delta Negroes by the time it
trickles down through the state welfare department.

The plantation shacks in which most of these Americans were
born and raised still dot the flat, distant fields. Many of them are still
inhabited by Negroes who have been told they may remain on the
plantations although there is no longer any work for them. Many
more of these shacks, timeless billboards of poverty, are empty, their
windows gaping vacantly at fields where cotton once grew from the
dark earth. The Delta Council has even begun a program to raze the
shacks in order to improve the appearance of the landscape. And
where the cotton grew there now are soybeans, wheat, or, often,
nothing but pastureland. More and more, the men and women who
lived crowded into these faded little buildings are fleeing.

They move in impossibly broken-down old cars into the slum
sections of Greenville, a way station for the trip to Detroit, Chicago,
and the other embattled cities of the North. They are fleeing the
collapse of a way of life which, though it had never enabled them to
live well and in dignity, did provide them with a roof, food, sporadic
medical care, and a sense of community. Now, with the disintegration
of a one-crop economy, they are losing these.

The picture is not entirely bleak. Relief efforts are being made in
several directions. The Delta Council estimates that there are twenty-
one thousand more industrial jobs now than there were ten years ago,

a 361 per cent increase. Perhaps 25 per cent of these are filled by Negroes, usually in the lower-paying positions.

A number of federally financed job-training and antipoverty programs are at work in the Delta. There is a basic education program, several Head Start programs, Manpower Development and Training Act programs, and the Neighborhood Youth Corps. But these reach at best 15 to 20 per cent of those who need help. Washington County, for example, has an estimated total of five thousand children who could benefit by Head Start. Perhaps fifteen hundred are served by it.

The basic education and job-training program can handle several hundred students at a time, but thousands are in need. A greatly increased program of child-care education is needed. Sixty-two of every thousand Negro babies born in Washington County die in the first year of their lives. They rarely if ever die from malnutrition, but more often from the mother's ignorance or carelessness. A Public Health Service official commented: "Take an example. Here's a mother fifteen years old. She's barely literate, she has no concept of working in a modern environment at all; she has a baby. The first two or three babies are experiments. Those that are better educated and can learn, do learn; those that can't, don't."

On malnutrition, this same doctor said: "There is some malnutrition. There are some homes in which there is not enough food for the family to get adequate nutrition. But these homes are also the homes in which the most ignorant and the most unable to help themselves live. Short of just going down and raising them as children and not giving them food stamps but actually telling them what to buy and what to eat and setting up their menu for them, I don't know what you can do."

Much help is needed for these Negro Mississippians. The technique is not simply one of providing a trade and sending the former hoe hand into the job market. The experience of job-training programs has been that the cotton chopper cannot be sent routinely through a program and then routed to an employer. It is too much of a change. A job-training and basic education program run by the Catholic church in Mississippi, for example, took Negroes from the plantations and taught them to read, write, and do simple arithmetic. They were then hired by a local chicken-freezing plant with rather simple jobs. They did not do well; production-line pressure upset them.

Experiences of this sort are producing some changes in the approach of state and federal officials. The newest concept is "outreach."

This is governmentese for going out and finding those who need help, including whatever medical care they may need to give them health and vigor, placing them in a job, and then keeping track of them to see how they fare.

Black leadership in the Delta, unlike that of the Black Power advocates in the Northern cities, now has as its goals the almost quaint-sounding ones of employment, a decent place to live, the respect of other human beings, and perhaps some special help for the very old and the very young. The white community can ill afford to miss this opportunity for co-operation. It may not last for long.

8. The Structure of Adaptive Sentiments in a Lower-Class Religious Group in Appalachia

Berton H. Kaplan

SROLE et al. point out in the Midtown Study[1] that we know little about the adaptive significance of membership in different religious traditions. As they point out, the literature on the subject is very meager.[2] Consequently, we are concerned with the socially shared sentiments which appear to interfere with or facilitate the process of striving as reflected in the religious sentiments of a Free Will Baptist group.

Theoretical Approach

The above general problem can be asked more specifically: How do a religious group's sentiments reflect important strains, satisfactions, and mechanisms of control? This question has a theoretical history in the work of Durkheim and in the central hypothesis for *The Elementary Forms of the Religious Life*[3]:

> The general conclusion the reader has before him is that religion is something eminently social. Religious representations are collective representations which express collective reality; the rites are a manner of acting which take rise in the midst of the assembled group and which are destined to excite, maintain, or recreate certain mental states in these groups. So if the categories are of religious origin, they ought to participate in this nature common to all religious facts; they too should be social affairs and the product of collective thought. At least—for the actual condition of our knowledge of these matters, one should be careful to avoid all radical and exclusive statements— it is allowable to suppose that they are rich in social elements.

For Durkheim, the origins of religious sentiment lie in the social

From the *Journal of Social Issues*, January, 1965, pp. 126–41. Reprinted by permission. Copyright 1965 by the Society for the Psychological Study of Social Issues.

[1] Leo Srole et al., *Mental Health in the Metropolis: The Midtown Study* (New York, McGraw-Hill, 1963), 300.

[2] *Ibid.*

[3] Emile Durkheim, *The Elementary Forms of the Religious Life* (New York, Collier Book Edition, 1961), 22.

and psychic necessities of life, in the nature of the human condition. Society is assumed to be the reality behind religious sentiments and rituals.

Assuming that religious sentiments reflect social and psychic necessities, it seems "allowable" to examine how such sentiment reflects some of the basic definitions of life strain and the modes of adaptation. In so doing, we were initially guided by Harvey Smith's[4] formulation on social sources of stress, or stressors, as social "presses." It is also worth examining how religious sentiments reflect the major sources of goal seeking in a society.[5] In this way, it is also possible to examine religion as a channel of emotional adjustment to areas of strain.[6]

In order to implement this point of view, we will utilize Leighton's "theory of sentiments" which deals directly with how one studies the mental health implications of a way of life, in this case, in terms of the social definitions which interfere with or facilitate goal-directed behavior. Indeed, Leighton's two fundamental assumptions in his theory of sentiments are as follows:[7]

A given personality exists more or less continuously throughout life in the act of striving; and interference with that striving has consequences which in turn often lead to psychiatric disorder.

Although not intended as definitive, Leighton proposes ten essential striving sentiments:

1. Physical security.
2. Sexual satisfaction.
3. The expression of hostility.
4. The expression of love.
5. The securing of love.
6. Securing of recognition.

---

[4] Harvey L. Smith, *Society and Health in a Mountain Community Working Paper* (Chapel Hill, Institute for Research and Social Science, 1961), 1–4, 23–25.

[5] See Weston LaBarre, "Transference Cures in Religious Cults and Social Groups," *Journal of Psychoanalysis in Groups*, Vol. I (January, 1963), 68. LeBarre hypothesizes that religion is a "royal road to an understanding of the major tensions in a society."

[6] Talcott Parsons, *Social System* (Glencoe, The Free Press, 1951), 370–78.

[7] Leighton, Alexander, *My Name Is Legion*. (New York, Basic Books, 1959), 136. It seems appropriate to make a few comments on Leighton's conceptual scheme. It would appear that all of the categories of Leighton's theory of sentiments need to be expanded in order to enrich both description and analysis. For example, the needs and dimensions of group membership and hostility expression can encompass a larger theoretical framework than used. Also, if we are interested in the process of adaptation, the flow of events in the social system, it would appear that it might be useful to consider the convergence of Leighton's theory with social systems theory in the spirit, for example, of Smelser's work on conductiveness, types of strain, definitions and assessment of the problem, the mobilization of responses, and the operation of social control. It seems furthermore that there is a need to develop additional categories on coping and adaptive behavior, possibly in the light of a social system framework. In so doing Leighton's "tree of hypotheses" can be expanded.

7. Expression of spontaneity (called variously positive force, creativity, volition).
8. Orientation in terms of one's place in society and the place of others.
9. The securing and maintaining of membership in a definite human group.
10. A sense of belonging to a moral order and being right in what one does, being in and of a system of values.[8]

Although these goals or objects are not precisely defined, their implicit meaning is useful for exploratory purposes. As Leighton points out, other cautions are in order. All of these goals may not be equally relevant at the same time; this list is by no means exhaustive, but can be considered as a central governing complex.[9] All are assumed to be important to the maintenance of physical health. If these essential sentiments are reasonably well met, we have an integrated society, giving rise to a higher level of mental health. If not, we have criteria of disintegration of varying degrees with a predicted higher degree of mental disorder.[10]

Social definitions which help meet the ten postulated objects would be considered to facilitate the means-goal problem. Leighton points out furthermore that there are at least three types of interference with striving towards these ten goals; interferences due to defects in the objects; defects in the personality; and intervening social circumstances which block achievement or anticipation of the postulated goals.[11] We are concerned solely with the first type: conflicting and/or ill defined socially shared sentiments about the listed goals as objects.

It is necessary also to consider a bit further the definition of the concept of sentiments. Hughes, Tremblay, Rapoport, and Leighton[12] point out that sentiments can be regarded in terms of three modes: what is, what ought to be, and what is desired. What is refers to an orientational mode, that of charting the world in terms of what people expect, interpret, and act upon. What ought to be refers to those sentiments represented by values, those standards of behavior for oneself and others. What is desired refers to what an individual may want. In this case we are concerned with the sentiments which define the ten essential striving goals in terms of all three modes.

Other comments on sentiments are in order. These sentiments are considered as being individually and/or socially shared and may

8 *Ibid.*, 148.
9 *Ibid.*, 235.
10 *Ibid.*, 315–33.
11 *Ibid.*, 149–57.
12 Charles C. Hughes et al., *People of Cove and Woodlot* (New York, Basic Books, 1960), 137–38.

be loosely or tightly interconnected.[13] Next, the concept of sentiments is assumed to be a bridge between the analysis of social and cultural processes and personality processes, since sentiments function in terms of social, cultural, and personality integration. Furthermore, some of these sentiments may have higher valence than others. In addition, the concept of sentiments is considered to parallel closely the concept of themes and values in groups. Finally, the concept of sentiments focuses on mental health, not just on mental disorder.

The Setting of the Research

This study took place in a changing, but previously isolated, community in the remote mountains of western North Carolina.[14] Indeed, the community was isolated up until about World War II. After the war, new industries and electricity opened the community to the influences of the larger society. The religious life was especially changed and we wish to report on one of the new religious modes of confronting an altered environment.

It is especially important to point out that the organization of a Free Will Baptist group was relatively new to this still remote community. In fact, when this data was collected, they had been in formal existence about three years. It should also be emphasized that the members of this group were white and very poor. The men of all work ages were usually without regular work. Considered social outcasts in terms of the community prestige system, the Free Will were referred to by most other members of the community as the "sorry" class. And the "sorry's" saw themselves as being looked down upon and shut out. It should also be pointed out that about half the members of this group were what the local people called the "drifters" from out of the area. Many had come to Mountain Community to follow timbering or sawmilling, unstable and low paying occupations at best. The remainder of the group were said to be of local origin.

In addition to the aspects of social deprivation as described above, it is also important to indicate that this group represents a population largely left out by the urbanization that had occurred in the Mountain Community area in the last ten to fifteen years. Without an education, without skills fitted for the new industries, the men in this group were usually isolated from participating in the new opportunities brought about by the development of factory work in the local area. Thus, in another way, they were shut out from the possible rewards of the

---

[13] Leighton, *My Name Is Legion*, 226–75.
[14] Berton H. Kaplan, "Social Change, Adaptive Problems, and Health in a Mountain Community" (unpublished dissertation, Chapel Hill, University of North Carolina, 1962).

rapidly changing community about them, and they were keenly aware of this.

We have a group, then, who were in an apparently deprived social situation which appeared to provide considerable motivation to form the new church. We have, in effect, most of the conditions for examining the sentiments of a new religious group which apparently developed around particular strains in their life situation. The question then is what personal-social sentiments did this newly formed religious group find compatible as adaptive responses to social strains of considerable importance?

Method

Methodologically,[15] using participation observation methods over three summers, sentiments are observed in terms of what is, what ought to be, and what is desired. We followed the Stirling County format for inferring sentiments. Hughes et al.[16] suggest several criteria for assessing and inferring group sentiments: depth of affect, prevalence, position, and salience. Depth refers to the wide sharing of the sentiment. Position refers to the sharing of the sentiments by strategically located people in the group whose influence is usually felt. And salience refers to the sentiments which are important to the processes of the group.

The Essential Socio-cultural Striving
Sentiments in the Free Will Baptist Group[17]

Indeed, the members of the Free Will Baptist Church are the poorest in the community. Unstable jobs, small, unproductive farms on the poorest land, poor housing, a lack of education and occupational skills, inability to secure industrial employment—these factors contribute to making them the poorest in the community and the most concerned with the elementary securities of adequate food, clothing, and housing. Yet, the Free Will Baptist sentiments do not encourage economic activity; rather, they emphasize that one's rewards—the "real ones"—will be forthcoming in heaven. It is not surprising to find an economically dispossessed group projecting their aspirations into the "other" world. What is somewhat interesting is that the church of origin (Missionary Baptists), from which the hard core

Physical
Security

"We are
poor people,
but we have
a mansion
in heaven"

15 Hughes et al., *People of Cove and Woodlot*, 140–61.

16 See Robert Brown, *Explanations in Social Science* (Chicago, Aldine Press, 1963), 14–47, for a discussion of ways of reporting data. We followed the reporting model of Hughes et al., *People of Cove and Woodlot*, as an example.

17 See James S. Brown, "Social Class, Intermarriage, and Church Membership in a Kentucky Community," *American Journal of Sociology*, 57 (November, 1951), 232–42, for a rough comparison with considerable differences.

membership of the Free Will group derived, did encourage hard work and economic success and had a view of trying to overcome economic hardship. Thus, it would appear that in the Free Will group we find projective sentiments which may reduce some of their tensions about economic insecurity and some of their tensions about being unable to derive adequate income from the new economy.

The other problem is that they teach these sentiments to their children—discouraging the securing of an education, for example—which may set up future interferences, which will likewise isolate their children from new job opportunities of an urbanizing economy. In this sense, the system becomes self-contained and self-perpetuating. We would wonder if the offspring of this group might not be even more economically dispossessed than their parents since their subsistence basis is becoming more and more tenuous.

One other observation seems very important. It appears that the formation of the Free Will group and their sentiments about securing the important rewards later, in one's after life, may act as a tension reducing defense. But there appears to be a good deal of conflict, of dissonance, in that decision. The preacher, particularly at revivals, frequently made comments about the desirability of economic well-being, and would then hurl abuse at those around them who were well off, to which the congregation would fervently "amen." It appeared to this observer that a double-bind type set of sentiments existed: the first rejected this world for the rewards of heaven in the future; the second strongly desired economic well-being in this life and hated those who were so positioned.

Sex

"Sex is evil"

If positive and accepting sentiments about sexual feelings and experience facilitates mental health, then in the Free Will group we find religious sentiments which appear to interfere with rather than facilitate this goal. Viewing man's impulses as basically evil, sex was referred to in unequivocally evil terms. The basic sentiment was like a simple equation: Sex is evil. For example, the preachers constantly stated this sentiment in their sermons. Sex was frequently referred to as "nasty and bad." Sex was seen as the devil within man. Indeed, sexuality was said to be the cause of most marital discords. Even in marriage, if sexual feelings were felt to be especially welcome and strong, then such feelings were indicted as another source of evidence of the evils within man. For example, we observed at one revival, during the group confessional, a woman get up and confess to enjoying her relations with her husband. In her mind, and within her group, pleasure was worldly; sex was pleasurable; therefore, she was sinning.

At least, this appeared to be a frequently stated equation of sentiments in the group, especially for the women.

All of these related sentiments about the evils of sex were a constant preoccupation of the members and their preacher. The sermons frequently centered around the twin topics of sin and sex. Yet, it was interesting that in this group three preachers had compromised themselves within a three- or four-year period. One was caught with someone else's wife in the church at night; another had run off with the choir leader; and a third had run off with a member's wife. Sex was an evil to these preachers, as well as a strong preoccupation.

The dominant sentiment about expressing anger was their eleventh commandment—"Thou shalt not be angry." In this group, this sentiment was expressed in different ways. The emphasis was that God was angry at them for all of their sinful thoughts and experiences, but it was unpardonable for men to be angry. It was as though the sentiment's equations went something like this, "God is angry at us; God equals anger; and anger is an emotion reserved for God." It was as if man became too powerful if he allowed anger to be expressed and recognized, consciously at least. We often heard typical comments to this effect from members of the group: "It is safer to keep our angry feelings to ourselves."

Convincing evidence indicated that anger was said to make men sexually aggressive. For example, an informant said:

> If a man gets mad, he gets to feeling like the devil will take over. When that happens, it scares the woman. Then a man wants sex all the time.

Furthermore, they distrusted man's capacity for controlling feelings which had to do with sex and anger, often equating the two. The preachers, for example, frequently talked about the brutish and nasty devil within man and urged people to confess to these and other "hidden" thoughts publicly. These forces must be guarded against at all costs, so the members fervently stated. Indeed, a basic purpose and reward of their membership, so the preachers urged, was to control all these potentially unmanageable impulses—the devil in man—the mixed equation of sex and anger. For example, when, during a revival, the time came for people to come forward to recount religious dreams, this theme was commonly expressed: the devil was usually sex, anger, and pleasure; and this group would help them defeat the devil.

Hostility
"Thou shalt not be angry"

Giving Love

"Give your love to Jesus"

It appeared to us that the major direction of giving affective sentiments was to bestow affection on Jesus, as Savior. Interpersonally, "People don't really trust each other," as we heard it expressed in our participation or from informants. Indeed, a pattern of distrust of others was a common theme in the sermons and in our personal discussions. It was only Jesus whom you could love and hopefully trust. An informant stated it as follows:

> We feel that people can't be depended on. It's hard to love folks like that. Our salvation is from Jesus. He loves us.

The concept of love was defined as something you receive from Jesus, not something you give. The entire sermon and revival foci were more on receiving His love than on giving it. On the more interpersonal level, the emphasis was on a receiving rather than on a more symmetrical relationship.

Securing Love

"We belong to the fellowship of sufferers"

An informant stated their dominant and intense sentiment about love:

> They emphasize a life of suffering, pain and dreariness from which death will rescue them. They look for a mansion in the sky. They see no love in religion or life.

Indeed, rather than the religious group as a source of love, the preacher told them how unwanted and unloved they were by others and by God, although loved by Jesus. As an informant put it:

> Their preachers like to scold them. They will come again and again and listen to this. They love to be scolded by their preachers.

As a friend of mine in this group so aptly put it: "We are the fellowship of the damned. I know that is true." But in this sense of fellowship, considerable rewards were expected and derived.

In terms of their definition of God, we found other evidence for their sentiments of suffering and being unloved. They stated that God is an angry judge who is very aware of their sins. And they believe themselves to be basically sinners, basically bad. Indeed, God was not seen as a source of love.

Recognition

"It is hard to stay saved"

If recognition refers to rewards for adequate role performance, then we find considerable sentiments of interferences amongst Free Will Baptist members. The key religious role is to become saved. To be saved is the crucial and central religious role. To be saved means to accept Jesus Christ as Lord and Savior. To be saved is an act of faith. To be saved is an emotional act, in that one feels it deeply, and to be saved is publicly stated and ritually confirmed.

Indeed, to be saved is without a doubt the most important goal in the life of the Free Will Baptist in this community. To be saved means to bestow one's sin on Jesus who will act as sin bearing substitute. To be saved means life eternal, the afterlife with Jesus and God in heaven. Particularly, for Free Will Baptists, the saved role is practically the only role which is defined as being rewarding. To be saved means to achieve all those rewards which are defined as infinitely important to a member of the Free Will Baptist Church. For those few who can maintain this state, crucial rewards are gained.

Yet, those who become Free Will Baptists must deal with a serious problem. Let us indicate the problem by comparison. As Missionary Baptists, from which most of these members broke away, to be saved means to be saved for all time. You may sin, but you never fall from grace; forgiveness is easily acquired. In contrast, in the Free Will Church, once saved does not mean always saved at all. Indeed, if the smallest sin is committed one is again out of a state of grace and is consequently no longer saved. And even if one is saved, it is an uncertain status, because one may have sinned and may not be aware of it.

We repeatedly heard comments and great concern about "Am I Worthy?" This meant an expression of personal crisis over the lack of assurance of being saved and hence being a worthy person. We heard repeated concern about losing one's salvation. As a result, they hold frequent revivals which allow one to become saved and saved again. The problem is that the role is never defined as fixed. In effect, the role rests on the hot fires of their institutionalized uncertainty, with a literal promise of a furnace of hell as a result of their defined uncertainty.

For example, they have a term for people who cannot remain saved. They are referred to as the "Bible hardened." The "Bible hardened" are people who have been saved again and again, but feel they cannot remain "sin free," an almost impossible expectation in any system. Consequently, they give up. And, in terms of our observations, we would hypothesize that the common ways in which this group gives up are through apathetic withdrawal, alcoholism, and probably other mental illnesses.

Consequently, the most important sentiment and related role in the group, being saved, is one of the most uncertain roles in their life, and to be unsaved, we must emphasize, means to live with powerful and real fear of eternal damnation, and the conquest of one's feelings and action in this life by the "devil."

Spontaneity
"We have a lively church"

The free expression of feelings in rather uninhibited ways is a dominant sentiment in the group. Enter a revival and one will witness yelling, wailing, crying, and the talking in tongues. During the sermon the audience participates in frequent and emotional "amens." The sermons are long with emotional outpourings of frequent yelling and prancing about. The songs are sung with the fullest possible emotional commitment, often with tears. After singing, the preacher and the congregation often break into what is called "talking in tongues," which is an expression of whatever comes to mind in a seemingly disorderly way with unique words, which are seen as presumably the divine speaking through man.

As an informant put it:

> We really have a good time. We sing and if we feel like it, we yell. It's just about the only place I know where man can really let go. I like religion with feelings. It's the only way God can talk to us and we to Him. You see, I like the ole timey religion.

If members in this group were motivated by a search for group emotional catharsis, then it would appear reasonable to assume that they had found a sentiment which allows for some expression of deep feelings in a spontaneous way. We would hasten to add, in terms of our observations, that the emotionality was undirected and somewhat primitive, despairing more often than joyous, driven rather than free and spontaneous.

Orientation
"We are the fellowship of sufferers"

Religious membership does, indeed, bestow membership for them in a group. With unstable work situations, infrequent neighboring patterns, and a complete absence of any organized group life, we can describe a group in which membership in primary relationship groups is infrequent and tenuous. But in the church group, they do belong. However, they define their belonging in suffering terms. It appeared to be like a group of complainers getting together to share the misery. This is stated in the sentiment of, "We are the fellowship of sufferers,"—a constant theme in the sermons or interviews. Thus, the group does provide some memberships, belonging, and group support, but it is that of common misery.

If we look at religion as a defined set of religious sentiments about the meaning of human existence, then the Free Will Church appears to offer more sentiments which interfere than facilitate this process. For example, as already indicated, the basic goal and key value is that of "being saved." But this is really a most uncertain role due to the conflicting sentiments about it. Second, the values about life center around the sentiments concerning sin. And sin is usually defined as anything that gives pleasure. The definition of sin also includes the violations, of course, of the Decalogue, but the greater emphasis in this group is that whatever is pleasurable is sinful. Consequently, we have a group whose sentiment is that of "sin equals pleasure" and in which the key role of salvation is an uncertain one because man, as they define him, cannot really be sure of his salvation, as all men are inveterate sinners and unable to stay saved. It is thus reasonable to hypothesize that this group does not facilitate the essential goals of being in and of a system of values which give a sense of belonging and assurance of correctness and meaning about life and man's place in the scheme of things.

Belonging to a System of Values

"Saved or not saved?"

These then were the structure of sentiments among the Free Will Baptist religious community.[18] Although it may appear that selective focus has been on the interfering sentiments, we had no such intent. This is the way things were, however negative.

We must emphasize that if we were to describe these sentiments apart from the religious context, we would have essentially the same definitions of the situation.

Discussion

To achieve a rigorous understanding of the system of sentiments we have just described would require, in an ideal sense, a social, cultural, and psychiatric understanding of the dynamics of their way of life from child-rearing practices to their present social structure. Indeed, each sentiment or cluster of related sentiments would have to be examined developmentally, as well as situationally. But this large analytic task is far beyond the scope or intent of this short paper, although the protocol for such an undertaking is suggested by the work of Leighton. We will restrict our discussion to the examination of several devices to cope with the problems of disintegration.

In view of our hypothesis that religious systems not only reflect some of the strains and satisfactions in a way of life (as discussed), we also assume that they can provide compensating behavior mech-

18 Leighton, *My Name Is Legion*, 168–71.

anisms. In this regard, the work of Poblete and O'Dea[19] and Holt[20] would suggest that such sects represent attempts at social control through attempts of social reorganization. Indeed, if we follow Smelser's[21] recent examination of social movements as responses to strain, we do have an example of the development of a value-oriented religious movement as a collective attempt "to restore, protect, modify, or create values."[22] In this case, a pessimistic sect, typical of the disinherited, seeks through millenarianism both hope and an escape. Although faced with a costly social environment, they strongly anticipate future rewards. In terms of Festinger's concept of cognitive dissonance, the frustrated tend to then diminish the value of the unattainable, which then reduces the dissonance and the frustration.[23]

Although this group appears to provide a reactive safety valve in the projected value of salvation in the other life, this was not by any means the only coping mechanism in effect. It was apparent that at least two other self-correcting or disintegration-inhibiting mechanisms of a more social psychological type were of considerable importance: social masochism and ritually expressed tensions, as devices characteristic of adaptive retreats from successful coping.

We will examine these two mechanisms of adaptive retreat in terms of Menninger's theory of adaptation.[24] In the face of disorganizing threats, tensions are evoked. If normal coping devices are not effective, special devices are utilized to maintain an equilibrium, although of an increasingly lower level of adaptation. Menninger classifies five regressive stages[25] of adaptive retreat from adequate coping: first order dyscontrol: nervousness—slight but definite impairment of adaptive control; second order dyscontrol: neurotic syndromes—an increased disorganization leads to more expensive tension-reducing devices; third order dyscontrol—the escape of destructive impulses; fourth order dyscontrol—reality is abandoned completely or very largely; and fifth order dyscontrol—beyond the psychoses to the abandonment of a will to live.

The data on the Free Will group strongly suggest that some of

19 Renata Poblete, S. J., and Thomas F. O'Dea, "Anomie and the Quest for Community: The Formation of Sects Among the Puerto Ricans of New York," *American Catholic Sociological Review*, 21 (Spring, 1960), 18–36.

20 John Holt, "Holiness Religion: Cultural Shock and Social Reorganization," *American Sociological Review*, Vol. V (June, 1940), 17–24.

21 Nell Smelser, *Theory of Collective Behavior* (New York, Free Press, 1963), 313–81.

22 *Ibid.*, 314–19.

23 John W. Thibaut and Harold H. Kelly, *The Psychology of Groups* (New York: Wiley and Sons, 1959).

24 Thomas S. Langner and Stanley T. Michael, *Life Stress and Mental Health* (New York, Free Press, 1963), 422.

25 *Ibid.*, 162–63.

the sentiments are reactive attempts to cope with their social disintegration, as defined, in terms of several adaptive retreat devices, social masochism and ritualistic control of aggression, which fall within Menninger's characteristics of the second order state of retreat.

The second order of dyscontrol is characterized[26] by a detachment from the environment, by aggressive escapes, by a lowering of productivity and achievement, by a diminished reality testing, and by symptoms of anxiety and discomfort—all of which seem to fit our description of the Free Will group. Our following discussion of the behavioral mechanisms of social masochism and attempted control of aggression and tension through religious rituals, which were very prominent in the way of life of the group, illustrate aspects of a second order retreat, as defined by Menninger.[27]

It appeared to us that one of the most obvious adaptive retreat mechanisms in evidence was what Reik refers to as social[28] masochism or Menninger's self-punishment. Reik in this case emphasizes that social masochism does not involve a completely abject, subjected, and passive attitude. What appears to be abject subjection is only a mask for strong underlying resistant aggressive and hostile feelings. As such, social masochism is a mechanism for releasing aggression. Social masochism is acted out by demonstrations of helplessness, subjection, unworthiness, and the like, as well as aggressive fantasying. This behavior is intended to secure responses within themselves and within the group which reinforce their self-images of being bad. Grinker,[29] for example, points out that negative self-images can be a point around which people organize and integrate themselves with considerable vigor.

In the Free Will group, social masochism took the form of seeing themselves in what appeared to be painfully unpleasant ways with frequent comments, especially from the preacher, as well as among themselves, of being miserable, bad, unworthy, sinful, devils, social outcasts, helpless, and of being subjected to terrifying forces. Indeed the whole group could be characterized, as they do themselves, as the "fellowship of sufferers." It was our impression that they got some genuine group cohesiveness out of this feeling of brotherhood through

Self-punishment [marginal note]

26 *Ibid.*, 174–75.
27 Bateson, Gregory, *Naven* (Stanford, Stanford University Press, 1950), 289; I am indebted to John Gulick for this approach and related ideas in *Cherokees at the Crossroads* (Chapel Hill, Institute for Research in Social Science, Monographs, University of North Carolina, 1960), 166–69.
28 Theodore Reik, *Masochism in Modern Man* (New York, Grove Press, 1941).
29 Roy Grinker, "Self-Esteem and Adaptation," *Archives of General Psychiatry*, Vol. IX (October, 1963), 418.

suffering, indeed an identity, which provided them with social contacts and a group context for expressing self-aggression in this way, publicly whipping their "self," as a group of supportive "brothers" and "sisters."

Ritual In terms of ritually organized[30] ways of acting out wishes and anxieties, it appears that the role of the minister in this group and the congregation's reaction to him were quite revealing of an adaptive retreat device if examined as a rough parallel to the role of the shaman in "primitive" culture. In Geza Roheim's description, the shaman is described as the exorciser of demons, which is like the role of the minister among the Free Will Baptists, who especially during revivals urges that they all fight the devil together and publicly. Roheim goes on to indicate:

> In every primitive tribe, we find a shaman in the center of society. It is easy to show that he is either neurotic or psychotic, at least that his art is based on the same mechanism as a neurosis or a psychosis. The shaman makes both visible and public the systems of symbolic fantasy that are present in the psyche of every adult member of society. They are the leaders in an infantile game as the lightning conductors of common anxiety. They fight the demons so others can hunt the prey and the general flight from reality.[31]

During sermons, or especially during revivals, the preacher would encourage the people to express themselves in the most uninhibited ways. People would begin to talk incoherently, thrash around in orgiastic ways, and allow great permissiveness to their feelings and thoughts. For example, many would get up and cite dreams, or literally free associate or come to the front and free associate with ecstasy; and, if they could reach a babble of incoherence, they would reach a highly rewarded state within the group. In fact, such a condition was defined as "a person who had power," or someone who had received the message of God himself and who could consequently talk in tongues. The preacher, like the shaman, also addressed himself to, and tried to bring to the surface of expression and make very permissive, the "devils," and "evils," and "sins," within the members of the group, but when the meeting was over, such permissiveness was supposed to stop, as it is to stop after the analytic hour. Indeed, the permissiveness allowed during the sermons and especially in the revival closely parallels, in our view, the permissiveness allowed within the psychoanalytic context, and that in both cases the permissive-

---

[30] Parsons, *Social System*, 304–305.
[31] LaBarre, "Transference Cures in Religious Cults and Social Groups," 71.

ness allows for the uninhibited release of thoughts, especially primary process thoughts.[32]

The Free Will preacher thus encourages fears, fantasies, destructive wishes, primitive feelings, and anxieties to be placed on public display, as the demons to be exorcised, all with permitted religious legitimacy. Then, towards the end of the sermon, the preacher emphasizes and assures his congregation that the demon can be controlled, that Satan can and is being defeated within the group and within themselves. He thus gives them support and helps restrict their uninhibited expression to the religious context.[33]

These two mechanisms were most prominent, and reflected, in Menninger's scheme, major aspects of a second order retreat from adequate coping. Our position would be that these second order retreat mechanisms inhibit or control a more serious regression or disintegration in this poverty-stricken group.

Summary

In Durkheim's terms, it seems allowable to infer that the religious sentiments described are indeed rich in social elements reflective of their general life situation—their search for meaningful membership and identity, even if it be that of the fellowship of sufferers with the assurance of rewards hereafter. The problems of impulse control and expression (hostility and sexuality), alienation from changing opportunity structure, general economic deprivation, and chronic economic and life uncertainty—these are all key life problems and are projected within their religious sentiments.

We find then a group, characterized by social deprivation, forming a new church in the community. The sentiments of this group, as defined within Leighton's scheme, appear more interfering than facilitating of postulated essential goals. But the sentiments of the group are by no means all negative. This sect is characterized as a value-oriented movement with attempts to cope with these strains by projected rewards into the future afterlife. The group also offers its members several other adaptive retreat devices: public self-flagellation and the public exorcism of inner devils. This religious group thus represents aspects of a second order retreat in Menninger's scheme, adaptive retreats from successful coping, which may be quite functional in inhibiting even more severe social and psychological disintegration. Deprived and beaten back as this group has been,

---

32 Parsons, *Social System*, 300.
33 *Ibid.*

they in fact had few, if any, other institutional or value alternatives to correct or cope with their environment. This then raises a key problem for those whose life is characterized by poverty and disintegration: how are more successful coping devices built into such a way of life?

As Durkheim pointed out, the religion of a group does appear to reflect strategic social and psychic realities. In this Appalachian community, the poverty warriors would miss a very strategic part of the system if they neglected the many and pervasive functions of the religion of the poor. In my opinion, the religious sentiments of the Free Will help maintain their poverty. How is the cycle broken?

The larger "causal" chain which explains the culture of poverty, in Appalachia or elsewhere, should be one of our pressing intellectual requirements. In this respect, the institutional resources of coping successfully or unsuccessfully appear to be crucial,[34] and the religious systems of the poor may be invaluable foci for studying this problem.

[34] Langner, "Life Stress and Mental Health."

Part Two. **The Educational Challenge**

Introduction to Part Two

IN attempting to discuss the problems of schools, an important question is: "Who are the disadvantaged pupils?" The literature on this particular topic gives many definitions. However, most authors agree that children of low-income parents tend to be overrepresented in the ranks of those who do not receive a fair or an equal share of the educational opportunities. The National Educational Association's Educational Policies Commission gave the following definition of the typical disadvantaged child:

> First, the disadvantaged child is likely to be very poor. Persons whose cultures keep them apart from the mainstream of American life find the gravest difficulties in employment, partly because they tend to lack . . . the job skills which would enable them to acquire the increasingly difficult job skills of an intellect-based economy. But for a significant group among the disadvantaged, there is a still worse handicap: the persistence of racial prejudice in employment. There are occupations in America today which are virtually closed to Negroes.[1]

The definitions of a disadvantaged child have taken on many synonyms, such as the physically handicapped, the socio-economically handicapped, the culturally deprived, and the slower learner. Obviously, both white and nonwhite children are among the disadvantaged. Duncan and Gazda derived their definition from the characteristics of the child's family and community:

1. Insufficient income to accommodate a reasonable level of living.
2. Dependency on service agencies for basic needs.
3. Lack of competitive spirit.
4. Inability to become a part of the majority culture because of isolation and discrimination.
5. Emotional and psychological problems not serious enough to require constant attention or institutional confinement.

1 Educational Policies Commission, *American Education and the Search for Equal Opportunity* (Washington, D.C., National Education Association, 1965), 4.

6. Short range individual and family goals.
7. Poor educational background.
8. Poor health and nutrition.
9. Semi-skilled or unskilled family heads.
10. Lack of motivation for improving their lot in life.
11. Excessive unemployment.
12. Isolation from educational and employment opportunities.
13. Prevalent physical disabilities and mental retardation.
14. High proportion of disrupted and broken homes.
15. Little interaction among family members.
16. Substandard housing.
17. Feeling of pessimism, defeat, despair, hostility, and apathy.[2]

Considering the above descriptions of the disadvantaged child, it becomes evident that there are many types of disadvantages. Nonetheless, it seems that the disadvantaged child is, to a large degree, a by-product of poverty. Therefore this condition becomes the overriding force creating a circle from which few such children can escape. Rural schools are, like urban schools, faced with the Herculean task of overcoming environmental forces which they neither created nor control. In addition, the sheer spatial isolation of rural youth adds a physical dimension to their alienation.

Home situations The degree of powerlessness experienced by adults in rural areas detracts significantly from their parental concerns for their children's social development. To be unemployed or underemployed in rural communities likely is not to be a seasonal but a continuing condition. Few new jobs are added to replace the low-paying agricultural activities being phased out by advanced technology. Feeling trapped in an impersonal system of work, low-income adults in rural areas pass on their feelings of powerlessness to their children. Nonwhite adults give their children an additional legacy: resignation and defeat which reflect racial segregation and discrimination.

To the poverty-stricken child, as well as the affluent child, members of his family are important; they are the people with whom he communicates and from whom he receives a substantial portion of his socialization. The negative effects of the home on the disadvantaged child were noted by one educator as follows:

> The home is a crowded, busy, active, noisy place where no one child is focused upon. There are too many children for this, and the parents have too little time. Consequently, the children spend much more time in each other's company and with the relatives. Individualism

[2] Jack A. Duncan and George A. Gazda, "Significant Content of Group Counseling Sessions with Culturally Deprived Ninth Grade Students," *Personnel and Guidance Journal*, Vol. XLVI (September, 1967), 11–16.

and self-concern on the part of the children is much less likely to emerge and is, in fact, discouraged in this more family-centered home.[3]

Of course, many affluent homes fit the above description. The major difference between poverty-stricken and affluent homes often is not the degree of parental interaction with children but, instead, the number of *parent substitutes* made available to the children. Affluent parents "buy" baby-sitters, tutors, recreation leaders, and psychiatrists to care for their children. In many rural communities, such parent substitutes are few or nonexistent. Another issue that will not be discussed here is the number of low-income parents who themselves need rest and psychological relief. For a variety of reasons, affluent rural and urban families adequately prepare their children for school. Families which give their children adequate preparation for succeeding in school have been described as having the following:

A family conversation which: answers his questions and encourages him to ask questions; extends his vocabulary with verbs and with adjectives and adverbs; gives him a right and a need to stand up for and to explain his point of view on the world.

A family environment which: sets an example of reading; provides a variety of toys and play materials with colors, sizes, and objects that challenge his ingenuity with his hands and his mind.

Two parents who: read a good deal; read to him; show him that they believe in the value of education; reward him for good school achievement.[4]

More often than not, the parents of the disadvantaged child will view the school with pessimism. Generally, this is due to the fact that their own school experiences were unpleasant. Therefore, they have difficulty convincing their children that school is a good place. This does not mean that all of the parents are hostile toward the school; most of them hope that somehow their children will achieve success in school. Education is still perceived by most low-income parents as *the* way out of poverty for their children. Rather than being against education, most are hesitant to become involved with it. Of course, some low-income parents have been completely "turned off" from formal education by their own childhood failures.

When a child is born he initially receives the social class standing of his family. To say that all men are created equal then does not

3 Helen E. Rees, *Deprivation and Compensatory Education: A Consideration* (Boston, Houghton Mifflin, 1968), 46.
4 Robert J. Havighurst, "Who Are the Socially Disadvantaged?" *Journal of Negro Education*, Vol. XXIII (Summer, 1964), 212–13.

fit the realities of everyday life. Equality of opportunity and social position does not exist for all people. All children, for instance, are not born into affluence or even into the solid comfort of the middle class; many children are born into a poverty-stricken existence, sometimes referred to as "the wrong side of town." Scientific studies of social class in several regions of the United States illustrate that it is a major molder of individual decisions and social actions; every aspect of American life is directly or indirectly influenced by social class. Rural family life is not immune to the effects of social class.

In simple terms, socialization can be described as learning to play the "game" of life, which includes a knowledge of the rules as well as knowing who made the rules and what the expected payoff will be. In addition, the rules governing people depend on their social class. It is not an exaggeration to say that low-income children learn to be losers, while middle- and upper-income children learn to be winners.

Probably the greatest gap between the disadvantaged child and his advantaged counterpart is that of social training. Usually the family of the disadvantaged child does not stress social etiquette, vocabulary, and personal hygiene—the hallmarks of our middle-class school systems. The list of neglected areas in minority-group homes is quite extensive. Briggs and Hummel noted the following:

> Because of their social deprivation, many minority group boys and girls need special help in developing good habits and better understanding in regard to personal hygiene and grooming, social adjustment, vocabulary, speech, applying for jobs, filling out application blanks, interview behavior and pointers, diet, sleep, medical and dental care, study habits, and numerous other social skills which most boys and girls acquire unconsciously by virtue of their environment.[5]

Frank Riessman made similar comments on the needs of all disadvantaged children, including disadvantaged white children:

> A basic weakness of deprived youngsters which the school can deal with is the lack of know-how, including the academic know-how and the know-how of the middle class generally—knowing how to get a job, how to appear for an interview, how to fill out a form, how to take tests, how to answer questions, and how to listen. The last is particularly important.[6]

[5] William A. Briggs and Deal L. Hummel, *Counseling Minority Group Youth: Developing the Experience of Equality Through Education* (Columbus, Ohio, Ohio Civil Rights Commission, 1962), 21.

[6] Frank Riessman, "The Culturally Deprived Child: A New View," *School Life*, Vol. XL (April, 1963), 5–7.

For children in families that are forced to subsist on minimal or subminimal incomes, inadequate satisfaction of nutritional needs are further compounded by insufficient rest and sleep. These conditions heighten the probability of their being unable to perform competently in school. Breckenridge and Vincent documented how deficiencies in basic physiological needs impede learning. They found that even if the child does become accustomed to a lower level of living and to rarely knowing a sense of well-being, he may have such a low level of energy as to be easily fatigued and to have little endurance for the complex and demanding tasks of learning.[7] In a related study, Catherine Bruner concluded that families with severely limited income are preoccupied with obtaining the bare necessities of life. These parents are so caught up with meeting daily needs that they often have little concern or time to spend with their children or to help them derive full advantage from available experiences.[8]

In almost every phase of health care and behavior, deprived families behave differently from affluent families. Understandably, poverty-stricken families have a higher rate of physical and mental illnesses. They receive much less benefit from community health programs. Many children suffer irreparable dental and bodily damage because the family finances are more needed for food, shelter, and clothing and cannot be spared for other needs.

According to the World Health Organization, health is the complete physical, mental, and social well-being of the individual, and not merely the absence of disease or infirmity. If the concept of good health entails the complete physical, mental, and social well-being of the individual, then economically-deprived children are obviously in poor health insofar as their social well-being is concerned. This, in turn, shows up in their high course failure and school drop-out rates.

There is almost unanimous agreement that prior satisfaction of the basic needs is necessary before human beings can become concerned with and perform higher-level functions. In order for a child to realize his potential in school, he must be healthy. Therefore, adequate nutrition, sleep, living conditions, clothing, exercise, and medical care all contribute to increase the student's capability in school. Merely meeting physical needs will not necessarily lead to

7 Marion Breckenridge and E. L. Vincent, "Nutrition and Growth", in J. M. Seidman (ed.), *The Adolescent: A Book of Readings* (New York, Holt, Rinehart and Winston, 1962), 73.

8 Catherine Bruner, "Deprivation, Its Effects, Its Remedies," *Educational Leadership*, Vol. XXIII (November, 1965), 105.

optimum learning. What goes on inside the classroom is as important as what goes into the child's body.

Tests of
Intelligence
Recent research has demonstrated that for children growing up under deprived circumstances their IQ may be depressed by a significant amount and that intervention at certain points, especially in the period from ages three to nine, can raise the IQ by as much as ten to fifteen points.[9] Several studies have demonstrated that many children who test in the seventies can—with proper intervention—have their IQs raised to the norm (100) or higher. For the severely disadvantaged child, IQ scores are more a measure of his intellectual stimulation than of inborn potential. Schools in impoverished communities have a high concentration of children with low IQs, a clear result of the impoverishment of their total environment.

Most findings concerning the intelligence of disadvantaged children indicate that the environment of these children causes depression of intellectual functioning. However, with positive changes in their home or school environments they often show considerable increase in IQs. Even short-range training in perceptual skills, following directions, and other school-related tasks have experimentally produced marked increases in intelligence test performance. Thus, levels of intellectual functioning have been found to be quite changeable for the culturally deprived and greatly affected by environmental experiences. In most instances, it seems correct to assume that the measured intelligence of deprived children does not reflect a ceiling level of their learning ability; however, their full learning ability will be realized only under the proper environmental conditions in the home and the school. Many urban and rural schools are raising IQs by improving the students' cognitive skills.

A child's intuitive cognition takes place very early in life through the sensory modalities such as vision, hearing, touch, and even taste and smell. This *perceptual development* is stimulated by environments which are rich in experiences. Experiences which make use of games, toys, and other objects which may be manipulated are important in cognitive development. Equally important is the necessity for the opportunity for interaction between the child and adults at meals, playtimes, and other activities. When homes do not provide these experiences—and most low-income homes do not—schools should.

Closely correlated with inadequate perceptual development is *linguistic development*. Bernstein studied the language behavior of

9 Benjamin S. Bloom, Allison Davis, and Robert Hess, *Compensatory Education for Cultural Deprivation* (New York, Holt, Rinehart and Winston, 1965), 72.

families that relate to the intellectual development of their children and distinguished between two forms or types of language. One form of language is called "restricted" and the other form is called "elaborated." According to Bernstein, a family which employs restricted language gives a child a language environment characterized by the following:

1. Short, grammatically simple, often unfinished sentences with a poor syntactical form stressing the active voice.
2. Simple and repetitive use of conjunctions (so, then, because).
3. Little use of subordinate clauses to break down the initial categories of the dominant subject.
4. Inability to hold a formal subject through a speech sequence; thus a dislocated informational content is facilitated.
5. Rigid and limited use of adjectives and adverbs.
6. Constraint on the self-reference pronoun; frequent use of personal pronoun.
7. Frequent use of statements where the reason and conclusion are confounded to produce a categoric statement.
8. A large number of statements/phrases which signal a requirement for the previous speech sequence to be reinforced: "Wouldn't it? You see? You know?" etc. This process is termed "sympathetic circularity."
9. Individual selection from a group of idiomatic phrases or sequences will frequently occur.
10. The individual qualification is implicit in the sentence organization; it is a language of implicit meaning.[10]

On the other hand, a family which employs an "elaborated" language gives the child a language environment characterized by the following:

1. Accurate grammatical order and syntax regulate what is said.
2. Logical modifications and stress are mediated through a grammatically complex sentence construction, especially through the use of a range of conjunctions and subordinate clauses.
3. Frequent use of prepositions which indicate logical relationships as well as prepositions which indicate temporal and spatial contiguity.
4. Frequent use of the personal pronoun "I."
5. A discriminative selection from a range of adjectives and adverbs.
6. Individual qualification is verbally mediated through the structure and relationships within and between sentences.
7. Expressive symbolism discriminates between meanings within speech sequences rather than reinforcing dominant words or phrases, or accompanying the sequence in a diffuse, generalized manner.

[10] Basil Bernstein, "Language and Social Class," *British Journal of Sociology*, Vol. XI (1960), 271–76.

8. A language use which points to the possibilities inherent in a complex conceptual hierarchy for the organizing of experience.[11]

A child who has learned a "restricted" language at home is likely to have difficulty in school, where an elaborate language is used and taught by the teacher; and, unless he learns the "elaborate" language that is expected in the school, the difficulty of the child is likely to increase as he goes further in school.

Readings   The increasing demands placed on rural schools make it impossible for teachers to be the jack-of-all trades as Alphatique Thomas described in her memoirs, "A Teacher Reminisces." Reasons for the change grew out of rural systems described by Dennis Farney ("As a Tiny Rural School Nears End of the Line, Feelings Are Mixed") in which teachers were, as a whole, undertrained, underpaid, undersupervised, and underrated as to their importance. The complexity of the challenge to upgrade rural education was spelled out in 1944 by the White House Conference on Rural Education in "A Charter of Education for Rural Children."

In "Emeralds of Opportunity in Rural Education," Douglas MacRae underscored the importance of rural schools. Believing that population growth and unfavorable urban industrial conditions will cause millions of Americans to return to rural areas, MacRae suggests that we accelerate our efforts to improve rural schools. James Moore and Paul King note the academic differences between urban and rural children. Their article, "A Comparison of Rural and Urban Pupils on Achievement," offers this somber conclusion: "It is believed by the authors that the poorer background received by the rural students prevents them from catching up completely."

While it is true that many rural schools graduate outstanding scholars, we cannot ignore the inadequate curricula described by Richard Frost in "Education and the Other America." Like the central city, rural schools' curricula do indeed reflect the impact of white middle-class—often prejudiced—materials. In "The Schools of Appalachia," Peter Schrag documents the irrelevancy and conservatism of many rural schools.

Robert Coles ("What Migrant Farm Children Learn") and Maxine Greene ("The Teacher and the Negro Child: 'Invisibility' in the School") point out the negative effects of irrelevant school materials and activities. Finally, Walter Daniel's article, "Problems of Disadvantaged Youth, Urban and Rural," examines the similarities and differences between disadvantaged urban and rural youth.

[11] *Ibid.*

9. A Teacher Reminisces

Alphatique Thomas

IT was not an imposing structure—a small, three-room building badly in need of a new coat of white paint. The well, with its zinc water bucket, was located at one side of the square plot, and the two outhouses were located quite a distance behind the building at opposite sides.

Two dirt roads crossed here, and there was a cluster of mailboxes at the corner. No other buildings were in sight, except two rural homes and the small, unpainted house for the principal.

One of these rural houses was where I would live for seven and one-half months. The primary teacher would live in the other house with her aunt.

This was the first school my grandfather attended; and now, I was one of the three teachers!

As I walked the half-mile distance in a slow rain the day school opened, I had many questions rushing through my mind. What should I do first? How many pupils would I have? Would I be able to perform the duties expected of me? Just what did the parents expect me to do? Would I be able to put into practice all those wonderful theories I had been studying for the past three years? Would I be able to be the teacher that I knew my mother had been?

By this time, I was near the school, and I saw the other two teachers walking toward the school, too.

When I went to my room, I counted twenty-two children's desks, chased an enormous rat from the huge wood box behind the large stove, opened the windows, and began to take books from the book room which adjoined my room. I had the third, fourth, and fifth grades, but I did not know how many pupils I would have in each grade, nor how many I would have in my room.

Soon, my pupils and some of their parents began to arrive. Of course, the three trustees were on hand to assist in our opening

From *Texas Outlook*, May 1967, pp. 53ff. Reprinted by permission.

ceremonies. The partitions between the three rooms could be opened for such occasions. The chairman of the trustees introduced each of the teachers, and several of the parents gave short talks.

About the middle of the morning the rain stopped, and we let our pupils have a short recess, while we teachers assembled the books and some supplies we had purchased. When my twenty eager children returned, I looked over their report cards of the previous year and issued textbooks.

Since many of our pupils had to walk several miles to school, the end of the day came at 3:00 P.M. This gave us time to sweep our rooms and prepare materials for the next day.

We teachers had no expense account with which to buy supplies, no duplicating machines, and a most limited library. (We furnished most of the books from our own libraries.) So we resorted to the mail-order catalog for art materials, a hectograph, construction paper, and anything else which we thought we could use and afford, for our salaries were less than one hundred dollars a month.

I used my personal encyclopedia set, a set of four books concerning birds, flowers, trees, and animals, and several other individual books to aid me with science.

Can you imagine a teacher in such a locality inviting the district game warden to speak to the entire group of sixty pupils on animal and fowl conservation?

Well, I did! I thought that I had brought to the pupils some valuable information. But, after our guest had left, my pupils told me more about birds and their habits than the learned guest had told them.

That event was strike one so far as theory was concerned, but I was not one to admit defeat.

My next adventure was a field trip to see the effects of erosion. One farmer near the school had terraced his farm, so we visited it first. It was ideal for my project. The next farm we visited was an excellent example of what erosion could do to good farm land. Too, I found many breeding places for mosquitoes. (I couldn't let an opportunity to teach health go by.)

But that night I had a visit from one of my trustees telling me that I was not employed "to go traipsing around the country," that a teacher should remain in her room so that the children could "learn books."

Down went my theory of field trips as well as speakers, and my spirits of teaching as a career really "knocked the bottom out of the bucket."

My father came for me that weekend, and I poured out my troubles to him and Mother. Daddy and Mother were comforting and under-standing. I returned to school with great ambition and renewed vigor, but I did not have another speaker, nor did I take my pupils on a field trip.

We had good basketball, baseball, and volleyball teams for both boys and girls. Many of our Friday afternoons were spent competing with other schools in our area. Since none of the teachers had cars, one or more of our parents brought their wagons to take us to play. During the winter, we had covers over the wagons and used kerosene lanterns to keep us warm. Many of the parents rode horseback to see their children play.

Yes, we had such good times! When we returned, we generally went home with one of the children for a party. This would mean making candy, popping corn, playing games, or singing to the accompaniment of a guitar and fiddle or an old-fashioned organ.

We entered the County Interscholastic League Meet in several fields. We did not win first place in any event, but one of my pupils won third place in subjunior division spelling. I believe that I was happier than the pupil.

The nearest large town was about twenty-eight miles away, and the only way to go shopping was with my parents or the parents of the other lady teacher. I could, therefore, save most of my salary. I was so very proud as I saw my assets growing.

So, I decided to return to school the next year to receive my degree. With one year of experience and a degree I could apply for work in larger systems. Experience and a degree were so very important during depression years, but experience overshadowed the degree in most cases.

Looking back on that initiation into teaching, I feel that my traveling along the road of helping mold young minds in so many facets has been most rewarding. It is not the years that count—but the mileage.

10. As a Tiny Rural School Nears End Of the Line, Feelings Are Mixed

Dennis Farney

RED Cloud, Neb.—North and west of here, where the land tilts up toward higher, rougher country, the weathered white frame building sits amid the native prairie grass. It is the Pleasant Prairie grade school —seven children in six grades, one teacher and ninety-five years of rural history that, quite possibly, will end tomorrow afternoon.

That's when the people of District 41 will gather at the three-room schoolhouse for the potluck dinner that traditionally marks the close of school. There will be fried chicken and baked beans, and maybe softball if the weather is right. There will be report cards and gifts from the teacher. Then in the late spring afternoon everyone will go home and someone will lock the schoolhouse door.

The door may never open for classes again. For the Pleasant Prairie, like thousands of rural districts before it, is confronted with a battery of pressures: new state legislation designed to encourage school consolidation, a long-term population outflow and, finally, the question of whether its children can best be served in its isolation and solitude. "I hate to say it, but I think the time is here when we ought to go to town (the Red Cloud school)," says James Richardson, a District 41 school board member. "The kids are missing too much."

All this arouses mixed feelings here in Webster County, the childhood home of Nebraska novelist Willa Cather and the setting for some of her best-known works. Webster County is a tradition-conscious place. And Pleasant Prairie has been a part of local history since the district was formed in 1875, a time when the settlers were still subduing the waving prairie grass and, as Miss Cather once wrote, "There was nothing but the land: Not a country at all, but the material out of which countries are made."

Setting for a story
The district began with a sod schoolhouse. But in the early 1880s,

From *The Wall Street Journal*, May 8, 1970. Reprinted by permission.

John Copley, two of whose great-granddaughters are enrolled at Pleasant Prairie today, donated two acres of prairie for the school and a third for a country cemetery that still stands nearby. Once a church as well as schoolhouse, the frame building erected on Mr. Copley's land apparently was the setting for one of Miss Cather's short stories. She called it "The Best Years," and it was about a country schoolteacher whose school was next to a cemetery—"very few graves, very much sun and waving yellow grass, open to the singing from the schoolroom and the shouts of the boys playing ball at noon."

The native grass is gone from much of Webster County now, destroyed by the plow. But it still flourishes among the tombstones and across the broad school yard. And a visit to the school finds other echoes of an earlier time as well.

The day is cold and wet, and inside the main classroom an electric fan whirs to spread the heat of a propane stove. Pleasant Prairie's pupils sit working before Mrs. Ardis Yost, a vivacious teacher whose home is Red Cloud. The children represent only three farm families: the Lovejoys (Roger, six; Jerry, nine; David, ten; and Earlene, twelve); the Dorns (Melanie, five; and Iantha, nine); and the Richardsons (Greg, eight).

It is early morning, time for kindergarten reading. Melanie, a little girl with shoulder-length brown hair, joins Mrs. Yost at a large table in the center of the classroom and haltingly begins a familiar story. ("No, no Tip. The ball is not to play with. . . .")

Fifteen minutes later, Mrs. Yost sends Melanie back to her desk and calls up Greg and Roger, two crew-cut youngsters. They're soon racing to identify the flash cards she holds up, shouting out the words almost in unison. Mrs. Yost declares Roger a narrow winner, and then, after admonishing him about a particularly vivid bit of grammar ("I don't got a dog of my own") sends him and Greg back and calls up David.

A lesson in grammar

While one class is reciting at Pleasant Prairie, the other children are supposed to be studying, an arrangement that generally works well. But the plan inevitably results in distractions, and some crop up during David's class

Mrs. Yost must keep a watchful eye on Melanie, whose attention span is about average for a five-year-old. And David must read against the background noise of Greg and Roger, busily stapling papers together in a project accompanied by much shuffling of feet and whispered consultations. (Later on, a sudden clatter would interrupt another class as Roger, for reasons never explained, nearly fell out of his chair. "You falling apart, Roger?" Mrs. Yost asked mildly, and the class went on.)

Midmorning means recess time—time, if the weather were fair, for tag or softball, a game apparently as appealing to the girls as the boys. ("I'm a good catcher," volunteers the irrepressible Iantha. "Well, if Roger doesn't pitch, I can catch them.") But on this dreary day, the children dash into the big north room, put a record on the phonograph and square dance.

Mrs. Yost, however, has work to do. She dons a soiled pair of gloves and throws another chunk of coal into an iron potbellied stove that supplements the propane heater. Among her other miscellaneous chores are keeping the school clean and, each morning, collecting a container of water from the outside well and bringing it inside to heat on the stove. The children use it to wash their hands before dipping into their metal lunch boxes at noon.

A 1926
yearbook Rural schools have some obvious educational deficiencies: The teaching aids are often scanty and the quality of teaching can vary widely from school to school. The small library here at Pleasant Prairie does include a modern set of encyclopedias and some recent textbooks, but many of the books, like the 1926 Yearbook of Agriculture, are plainly outdated.

"If a country school gets a poor teacher, the year is just wasted," says Miss Edyth Beezley, Webster County's school superintendent. "One of the biggest deficiencies of rural schools is that the children have no competition. The teacher has to teach so many grades that she doesn't have time to devote to the extra things. And many times, teachers aren't well enough trained to spread themselves that thin."

But that isn't the case here at Pleasant Prairie. Mrs. Yost, who signed on last fall for five thousand dollars a year, has seven years of teaching experience and works hard to make school interesting and the lessons relevant. Knowing that the limited curriculum and limited competition can leave children ill prepared, intellectually and emotionally, for the faster pace of high school, she tries to cover a variety of subject areas. "If I can at least hit the top of a subject," she says, "they won't be awed by it when they come to it again."

The children's art work covers the classroom walls and in the north room is "Maplewood Store," where Greg and Roger learn arithmetic while playing. To stimulate interest in science lessons recently, Mrs. Yost divided the children into the Mammals vs. the Reptiles and staged a quiz contest. (The Mammals won.)

She also uses the kind of audio-visual aids that would have been undreamed of at schools like this a decade ago. The north room boasts a tape recorder and a movie projector, and the children see two educational films a week, drawn from hundreds available through an area-wide educational program.

Mrs. Yost believes that if Pleasant Prairie's children were exposed to the advantages of a modern city school, they would "never want to come back" to their rural classroom. "They're happy here," she explains. "But they like it because they have never been exposed to anything different." *Private tutoring*

Nevertheless, she believes, Pleasant Prairie does offer some definite advantages over urban schools. "How many teachers could take two first-graders and give them this much time each day?" she asks. "With Melanie, I'm practically a private tutor." An even bigger advantage, she feels, is an unspoken bond that binds this rural community together—and binds the school to the community.

"People care," she says. "(As a pupil) you feel that you're responsible, not only to your parents, but to the entire community."

This bond was evident last December 23, when more than eighty friends and neighbors crowded into the north room for the annual Christmas program. The children sang the old carols and their rhythm band (Jerry and Earlene on the cymbals, David on the drum, Iantha on the tambourine and the rest on rhythm band sticks) gave a rousing rendition of "When the Rhythm Band Starts to Play." There were plays and readings and refreshments afterward. David recalls the night as the most fun he has ever had in school: "*Everybody* was there," he says.

On this afternoon in the spring, the children are still talking about that night—about how nervous they were and how they all put coins in their shoes for luck. They relive it as they decorate plaster figures in art class, the last of the day. Then, at 3:15, they don their jackets, pick up their lunch boxes and head for the school yard, where their parents wait in cars to take them home to the family farms.

11. A Charter of Education for Rural Children

THE first White House conference on rural education presents the following as the educational rights of every rural child and pledges itself to work for their achievement.

I. *Every rural child has the right to a satisfactory, modern elementary education.* This education should be such as to guarantee the child an opportunity to develop and maintain a healthy body and a balanced personality, to acquire the skills needed as tools of learning, to get a good start in understanding and appreciating the natural and social world, to participate happily and helpfully in home and community life, to work and play with others, and to enjoy and use music, art, literature, and handicrafts.

II. *Every rural child has the right to a satisfactory, modern secondary education.* This education should assure the youth continued progress in his general physical, social, civic, and cultural development begun in the elementary school, and provide initial training for farming or other occupations and an open door to college and the professions.

III. *Every rural child has the right to an educational program that bridges the gap between home and school, and between school and adult life.* This program requires, on the one hand, co-operation with parents for the home education of children too young for school and for the joint educational guidance by home and school of all other children; and, on the other hand, the co-operative development of cultural and vocational adult education suited to the needs and desires of the people of the community.

IV. *Every rural child has the right thru his school to health services, educational and vocational guidance, library facilities, rec-*

From *The White House Conference on Rural Education* (National Education Association, 1944), 14–15. Reprinted by permission.

reational activities, and, where needed, school lunches and pupil transportation facilities at public expense. Such special services, because they require the employment of specially qualified personnel, can be supplied most easily thru enlarged units of school administration and the co-operation of several small schools.

V. *Every rural child has the right to teachers, supervisors, and administrators who know rural life and who are educated to deal effectively with the problems peculiar to rural schools.* Persons so educated should hold state certificates that set forth their special qualifications, should be paid adequate salaries, and should be given by law and fair practices security in their positions as a reward for good and faithful services. The accomplishment of these objectives is the responsibility of local leadership, state departments of education, the teacher education institutions, and national leaders in rural education.

VI. *Every rural child has the right to educational service and guidance during the entire year and full-time attendance in a school that is open for not less than nine months in each year for at least twelve years.* The educational development of children during vacation time is also a responsibility of the community school. In many communities the period of schooling has already become fourteen years and should become such in all communities as rapidly as possible.

VII. *Every rural child has the right to attend school in a satisfactory, modern building.* The building should be attractive, clean, sanitary, safe, conducive to good health, equipped with materials and apparatus essential to the best teaching, planned as a community center, and surrounded by ample space for playgrounds, gardens, landscaping, and beautification.

VIII. *Every rural child has the right thru the school to participate in community life and culture.* For effective service the school plant must be planned and recognized as a center of community activity, the closest possible interrelationships should be maintained between the school and other community agencies; and children and youth should be recognized as active participants in community affairs.

IX. *Every rural child has the right to a local school system sufficiently strong to provide all the services required for a modern education.* Obtaining such a school system depends upon organizing amply large units of school administration. Such units do not necessarily result in large schools. Large schools can provide broad educational opportunities more economically, but with special efforts small schools can well serve rural children and communities.

X. *Every rural child has the right to have the tax resources of his community, state, and nation used to guarantee him an American standard of educational opportunity.* This right must include equality of opportunity for minority and low economic groups. Since many rural youth become urban producers and consumers, it is necessary for the development of the democratic way of life that the wealth and productivity of the entire nation should aid in the support of the right of every child to a good education.

These are the rights of the rural child because they are the rights of every child regardless of race, or color, or situation, wherever he may live under the flag of the United States of America.

12. Emeralds of Opportunity in Rural Education

Douglas G. MacRae

. . . I want to talk to you on the subject of "Emeralds of Opportunity in Rural Education," for I know you who are committed to it look upon its opportunity as emeralds.

A corroding irony in the attitude of this nation, including that of many high councils of government and of education itself, is the minimal thought directed toward problems of rural education. For it seems the greater the problem is, the less attention our leaders feel it deserves. They view the problem quantitatively—seldom qualitatively.

Surely, we agree that the most dramatic problems are in the bursting, bulging cities. It has required no gift of prophecy, no straining of the ear at a demographic Delphi, no eagle eye or owlish wisdom to see and to know the dusty legions of the damned, trudging the hopeless road from the place where they cannot make a living to the place where they cannot make a living.

The ugliest leprous spots on the sociological and educational scene in this land are in the big cities where teachers in dim corridors are stabbed in the back by hoodlums; where, out of the fester and ooze of poverty, dope-sickness, violence, cruelty, and racism a bewildered and half-crazed youth seeking a security they don't understand, could one day in this land form a goose-stepping Gestapo like that which thirty years ago pranced in iron pride down the Wilhelm Strasse in a choreography of terror.

Since writing these very lines, I have picked up two publications: The *Christian Science Monitor*, of January 31, and *Education U.S.A.*, of February 3. The lead story in page 1 of the *Monitor* is about an American city where "Many fear to walk at night; where the assistant principal of a high school was shot fatally last week as he chased three youths who had grabbed $350 from the school bank." The front page of *Education U.S.A.* carried a story reading, "For two

From *Rural Education News*, March, 1969, pp. 1–4. Reprinted by permission.

113

years two schools in a large American city have played their annual football game in absolute secrecy. Even the players are not told the game site in advance. They board a bus and are taken to a neutral field."

In Charles Silberman's book *Crisis in Black and White*, he speaks of one element, among many others, which he says has a devastating psychological impact upon the bright and awful quicksilver of developing young minds—the element of noise—the continuously, crashing decibels of noise: garbage trucks, galvanized cans, the smelly roar of bus exhausts, and strident voices. Silberman says the child soon tunes everything else out but the noise, the noise, the noise!

Is it any wonder that many of the most athletic and creative minds in American education—leaders of the educational enterprise in the great cities of this favored land—have either crumbled under the strain, become disgusted with the frustration and have quit the scene, leaving American educational leadership much the poorer.

These are some of the reasons we are pouring massive manpower and massive millions upon the problems of urban America and the problems of education in urban America; and perhaps we should. Yet, somehow, there persists in my mind a small, but persistently nagging, thought that we may be treating the problem on the surface; that we have developed a set of oversimplified phrases and conclusions about the urban-rural picture in America.

One thing is for sure: the problem is not localized. The rain of educational troubles, while it may come in scattered showers, is just as torrential in country field and town as on steel and stone and manswarm on a hundred pavements.

The chemistry and the physics of such rain is the same. We used to talk about the problems of the rural poor; now, it seems we are devoting our whole attention to the problems of the urban poor.

But, this is wrong, for, in many respects, the problems of rural education escalate in direct ratio to the increased size of the urban education establishment. Therefore, these problems call for more attention, not less.

—In 1960, 3,700,000 adults in rural America were functional illiterates.
—The percentage of uncertified rural teachers is twice that of urban teachers.
—The drop-out rate is highest among rural children.
—Only half the proportion of rural youth goes to college as that of urban youth.
—With all the talk of the ugliness of urban poverty, one out of every

four persons lives in poverty in rural America, while one out of eight lives in poverty in urban areas.

There is little value in suggesting culpability for either economic or educational poverty except that in the critique we may identify some of the causative factors behind both.

But I suggest that, in a real sense, we are all responsible for the poverty in the country, for the futile flight to the city, and for the disillusionment and abandoned hope of millions who have moved to the city; finding there pollution and disease in place of clean air and conservation, homelessness instead of home, bleak unemployment instead of an energizing job.

Yes, I say that to an extent greater than we would like to admit, we are all responsible for this. We have not provided equal educational opportunity for the boy on the Dakota plains or the little girl in the lean-to shack at the foot of a West Virginia hill. Few of us have fought more than a milk-toast fight for federal dollars, unrestricted and on a per capita basis, for the only ultimate defense other than God Almighty, the defense which lies in the heart, spirit, and mind of man. Not only have we failed to fight; we have damned those who have. Few of us have done much to make possible a fair and equitable local effort in terms of either dollars or equal education by combining counties, districts, employing the device of the intermediate unit, using shared services, or the like.

Would to the Lord we had done more of these things! If we had, we could, I think, have built throughout the broad rural areas of this republic, an education and an economy of solid rock on which millions of our people might have stood firm and planned and built and prospered, and not moved away leaving behind them ghost towns of swirling dust and trash, and a lonely wind banging the shutters in empty, wooden lament of what might have been.

I believe the future of rural life and rural education is fully as bright as any emerald!

First of all, it is bright because it has the richest tradition of leadership.

The leadership in rural education has been, can be, and must continue to be, a precious, flawless emerald.

Secondly, rural education can be bright because it must be flexible. In many respects, through sheer necessity, it has already been more flexible than most divisions of American education. I have heard so much about individualized instruction in recent years that the term actually sickens me into green nausea. Without fanfare of trumpet, rural teachers have been doing individualized instruction for years.

Furthermore, rural educators have been innovating for years. For example: In a little ranch and oil town in northwestern Colorado called Meeker, there is modular scheduling, team teaching, and a co-op work program.

In a little elementary school in West Pecos, New Mexico, all the children every day study the Spanish language by the oral-aural method with a Chilean-born teacher in order to develop a functional bilingualism most appropriate for their section of the country.

In the tiny town of Hawksville, Utah—population 111—the school, with the co-operation of the Western States Small Schools Projects and a very modest grant from the Ford Foundation, has an amplified telephone system over which the governor of their state and the vice-president of the United States, among others, have talked with them.

In short, rural schools can be creative if their leadership wills it.

But gone with the wind is the exclusive emphasis in rural education on the musty vocational agriculture courses possibly appropriate for the days of Rutherford B. Hayes. The new vocational courses should address themselves to not only farm, but nonfarm vocation, as well as basic academic and cultural experiences.

Education for rural youth can prepare them for life wherever they may be—farm or city—if, instead of concentrating altogether on farming, it includes such things as park and estate forestry, soil conservation, pollution control, veterinary service, landscaping, horticulture, and food processing.

Five per cent of the United States' work force remains on the land today. Again I say, all the more reason for rational planning of their education. For within the framework of this 5 per cent figure, a full half-million high school students are in rural schools and only three out of eight are taking anything but the old traditional vocational agriculture courses. This is irrational; this is tragic; this is destructive of the potential of young life. Education must give youth the equipment to stay on the farm, go to the small or big city, or to the university. Ten million workers are needed, just to process farm products in the towns and cities.

One thing is lucidly clear in all this: If we provide the competent specialized instruction and the breadth of educational opportunity I have been referring to, we must use co-operative services; we must develop administrative units large enough to support, corporately, the services which tiny individual units cannot possibly do. We must employ new structures for education.

Finally, the future of rural education is bright because the problem of it is at once the promise of it. Implicit in the smallness of its population density is the greatness of its potential service to the people of America.

There are many glimpses we have in this life into the unspeakable joy of heaven. For me, one of them is sitting by the side of the sea, high above it on the bulkhead, leisurely smoking a Robert Burns panatela, and watching the mighty, cresting, swelling high tide smash with spume-spattered fury against the sea wall beneath me. The wall is an unfailing bulwark, and the angry waters recoil from it and swirl and wash back out into the deep.

This, I believe, symbolizes what is happening as the tides of people roll upon the great cities. Much of the tide is going to be driven back because it can't get in. This is exactly what an article in the *New York Times* meant when it stated, in effect, that rural education is not all it should be "primarily because our prosperity has not yet washed into a great many farm areas."

Herein is Orville Freeman's insistent thesis, the starkly incredible fact that seventy per cent of our people live on one per cent of our land. The Frankenstein of bigness is horribly strangling much of the health, the morality, the stability, and the density of this nation, and its education as well.

One hundred million additional people will be in this country by 1999. Where will they go? Obviously, the only place for them to go and the only Lebensraum for our congested cities is the 99 per cent of the land of this America where people are not living.

But captives of urban congestion are not going to cross over into a barren Canaan. Mere annexation of areas contiguous to tremendous cities is not the basic answer, for the extension of the boundary lines of the city of itself will not move ten people from slum, ghetto, unemployment, and poverty.

The Canaan which will beckon people from the captivity in which we have placed them must be lush and fertile in jobs, in housing, in education, in recreation and culture. Hundreds of small towns and small cities flung like a handful of emeralds over the map of this country in what are now farm areas is far better than piling bigness upon bigness.

Basic in the development of these little Canaans is industry and business—their willingness to go there. For when they go they create jobs and markets and employment. They lay the foundation for services which people desire and require; and we are making progress here. In the annual report of the secretary of agriculture to the president last month, he reports that almost half of the million dollar plants opened in 1966 were outside the metropolitan areas and that the increase in private nonfarm employment between 1962 and 1967 was between eight and tenfold annually.

Business needs incentive if it is to revitalize the farm and nonfarm areas—loans, grants, government subsidy (for all this is in the interest of the country)—special loan rates for the housing of its workers, etc.

But more basic than all this, industry needs the floor of education under it, and the right kind of education; not only to give its workers the functional skills they need, but also to attract talented leadership and talented population to these communities of tomorrow.

Remember the words of Thomas Jefferson, spoken, to be sure, in a different age but which have the same meaning for our country today: "Preach, my dear sir, a crusade against ignorance; improve the law for educating the common people. Let our countrymen know that the people alone can protect us."

I suggest that the 99 per cent of our land where only 30 per cent of our people now live has the breath of opportunity, not only for this 30 per cent, but for a substantive population increase and redistribution in which this nation may find protection.

Says John Fischer in *Harpers*: "I have a feeling that I have been given a glimpse of the exciting time just ahead. It may be a time when we find a new national purpose: to resettle the deserted hinterland; to discover ways of moving people and jobs away from megalopolis before it becomes both uninhabitable and ungovernable."

Mr. Fischer's words are emeralds of opportunity for rural educators.

13. A Comparison of Rural and Urban Pupils On Achievement

James C. Moore and Paul T. King

THE common practice of classifying children's intelligence on the basis of a single standardized individual or group intelligence test is inadequate.

The question of urban and rural differences too often is answered by the administration of a single test or a test battery. These tests seem to give advantage to the urban child because of the general make-up of the tests.

It has been shown that high school class rank is one of the better predictors of college success. With this in mind, class rank was taken to be a good measure of school achievement.

For the purpose of this study, the criterion of achievement will be defined as a student's rank with respect to his classmates.

Although achievement was the main item of investigation, the question of differences in intelligence seemed important enough to be taken into consideration.

Many investigations have been made on this subject with conflicting results. Duchapt (1952) found that children from rural areas are (1) of more rugged physique; (2) equally endowed mentally; (3) a bit more sluggish in intellectual tasks. Shepard (1942) indicated urban superiority was not justified.

Others (Lehman, 1959, and Hinds, 1922) found the urban child to be superior intellectually. These differences, when found, are usually done on an IQ comparison basis. This seems inadequate and is very well demonstrated by Sullivan (1957). His investigation found rural children to be inferior on the Wechsler-Bellevue, Form I, which stresses verbal and numerical abilities.

When the same children were given the Progressive Matrices Test, Sullivan found that there was no difference between the two groups.

This cultural bias of many of today's intelligence tests seems to contribute to the differences between urban and rural children.

From *School and Community*, November, 1964, pp. 28–30. Reprinted by permission.

119

In view of this contradictory information, it was decided to investigate the achievement of urban and rural children by two methods. First, two groups of urban and rural children were matched with respect to IQ (California Test of Mental Maturity).

Secondly, independent samples were used to answer the same questions asked of the matched groups.

The following hypotheses were investigated:

1. There is a significantly greater proportion of urban students in the two upper fifths of class rank in the ninth grade.

2. There is a significantly greater proportion of rural students in the two lower fifths of class rank in the ninth grade.

It is reasoned that after attending a rural school for the first eight grades, a rural student may well be behind his urban classmates.

These factors could cause the rural student to achieve less when, at the beginning of the ninth grade, he is put on a bus and shuttled into the city schools. Thus, at the end of the ninth grade, the average rural child would rank lower than the average urban child.

It is also considered reasonable that after spending five days a week with his urban peers for a period of four years, this difference might no longer be present. The third hypothesis is stated as follows:

3. There will be no difference between urban and rural children in class rank at the end of the senior year.

The 1962 graduating class at Hickman High School in Columbia was used in the testing. Each student met the following criteria:

1. A rural student must have attended a rural school for grades one through eight and completed his schooling in the Columbia city schools.

2. An urban student must have attended the Columbia city schools for grades one through twelve.

3. It was also necessary that each student had graduated and had taken the California Test of Mental Maturity.

Of the 311 graduating seniors, 151 urban and 46 rural students were found to meet these standards. The 114 students not used came under several classifications. Some had transferred into Columbia, others did not have CTMM IQ scores. The matched and independent groups were then investigated against the three hypotheses.

Before checking the hypotheses, a test of significance of the difference between independent means was run on the IQs of the urban and rural groups.

A grade point average was computed for each student on the basis of his grades in courses carrying a full credit. The grade point averages were then ordered and each student was assigned a ranking from 1 to 197.

The mean ranking was computed for urban and rural students in both matched and independent groups at the ninth and twelfth grade levels, and a t-test of significance of difference between means was run. Before computing the t-tests, the variances were checked for equality.

Differences between urban and rural students for the hypotheses in the matched group were small. The urban children had a larger proportion of students in the upper middle fifth of class rank in the ninth grade.

There was also a greater proportion of rural students in the lower fifth of the ninth grade class rank. Both of these differences were significant at the .05 level. However, as was hypothesized, there was no difference between urban and rural achievement at the end of the 12th grade.

When the study was extended to independent samples, nearly all of the hypotheses were confirmed. There was a significantly greater proportion of urban students in the two upper fifths of class rank (hypothesis 1), and a significantly greater proportion of rural students in the two lower fifths of class rank (hypothesis 2) in the ninth grade.

Hypothesis 3 was not entirely borne out in that a significantly greater proportion of 12th grade urban students were found to be in the upper fifth of class rank. However, there were no differences found in the other four fifths of class rank. All of the differences were at the .05 level of significance.

There were no significant differences in IQ means between urban and rural children for independent and matched groups. It should be noted that when grade point averages are considered, there are significant differences between urban and rural students at both the ninth and twelfth grades.

Also there is no difference between the rural students' rank in the ninth and twelfth grades, and also no difference in the urban students' rank in these same grades.

The findings favoring the students of urban schools in the present study have several implications for educational practices. The movement of students from rural schools to larger city schools has been in progress for many years. The present study, as well as others, shows that education received by students in rural schools is not as effective as education received by urban students.

One implication of these findings is that upgrading of rural schools seems to be needed.

Reorganization of small rural schools into larger city administrative units seems to be a second implication. It is not uncommon practice for some rural schools to close and send their students to the city schools on a tuition basis.

Reorganization of these schools would not only equate the tax burden between the urban and rural people, but also would enable the district to better educate their children.

With fast, economical transportation, it is no burden to transport students many miles to and from the city schools. But some may ask, "What about the effect of riding buses on our children's achievement?"

To begin with, most of the rural students have to ride buses to the rural schools anyway.

A study by Dunlap, Harper, and Hunka shows that second grade rural children vanned to city schools showed higher scores on the Stanford Achievement Test than urban students. They also found no difference in scores on the SAT in grades four and six, indicating that the bus ride to and from school has no adverse effect on the rural children.

It was noted that there was a significant difference between mean grade point rankings of the two groups at both the ninth and twelfth grades. This may seem to be contradictory to hypothesis 3.

However, hypothesis 3 was made on the proportion of students in each fifth of class rank. Even then there was a significant difference favoring the urban students in the upper fifth of class rank in the twelfth grade.

Does this really indicate an improvement by the rural student while attending city schools? It is the authors' belief that it does.

At the end of the ninth grade, it was plainly shown that the urban students were well ahead of their rural friends in achievement. This was true two ways: the differences in proportion in the upper two-fifths of class rank, and also in mean rank.

By the end of the twelfth grade, this difference in proportion was almost completely eliminated. Even though there was still a difference in mean rankings, the results still show that the rural students did gain on the urban students, but did not quite catch up with them.

It is believed by the authors that the poorer background received by the rural students prevents them from catching up completely.

It is also believed that this lack of proper background could be eliminated by reorganization and consolidation of the small rural schools.

14. Education and the Other America

Richard T. Frost

BEFORE coming to Washington, I had a tasty confrontation with several school officials over the issue of busing children to reduce racial imbalance in five grade schools. One put his position in a nutshell. Said he, "You are social engineers. We are educators." That remark is sickening—not only because it is so silly, but because it summarizes the whole history of twentieth-century education and the astonishing blinders it has pasted onto its face.

Education is now and always has been the grandest form of "social engineering" known to man. How could any of us ever have forgotten that? But we did, and now we reap the sour harvest of a long and ugly century of disgrace.

We in the education industry have much to answer for. We have permitted ourselves to reflect unchallenged values instead of taking our part in creating important national values. We have failed to involve education with life as it is lived and now education has its own crisis in relevancy.

I should like to speak to that crisis in relevancy; to the anatomy of the crisis, and to some hopeful signs that something is being done about it. But first, may I suggest one of the prime causes of it.

On my first visit to Berkeley, several years back, I was walking along the campus with Martin Meyerson, then dean of the School of Environmental Design, later acting chancellor and now president of the state university at Buffalo. I remember a huge building, of the 1910 "monument era." Across its front, deeply etched into what I took to be a limestone, was the following phrase: "DEDICATED TO THE PRESERVATION OF RURAL VALUES IN AMERICA."

An unfriendly wisecrack by me brought Meyerson's retort, "I never knew they were in jeopardy."

That was 1963 or so and Meyerson was right—then. I now feel

From *Teachers College Journal*, January, 1967, pp. 188–91. Reprinted by permission.

that, for the first time, *really*, there are signs that the overbalance of rural influence on American institutions is actually challenged. Nevertheless let's remember how tenacious and abiding is the anticity theme in this country.

There have been almost no friendly pieces of urban literature in America for its 180 years. Even the city's apparent hymn-writers—Mumford and so on, really don't like cities. His last book suggested their imminent death and how necessary and even desirable this is.

The city has no anthem, no theme, no catechisms, and no rituals. It has no flag, no central symbol, no citadel, if you will. Its preoccupation with mere public service generated the only two songs it could ever sing—"efficiency" and "economy," while its newer high priests, the city managers, croak out these hymns as though they mean something to center-city citizens.

The city suffers badly from a seriously unfavorable balance of payments. It must import both commuters and new immigrants, the former paying little for the privilege of crossing its borders five days a week; the latter are an important drain on meager resources.

The hymns sung in the city's churches have an almost exclusively rural imagery. People, faced with the tensions and complexities of big cities still sing "Bringing in the Sheaves"—whatever they are—and "We Plow the Fields and Scatter"—whatever that means—and there are always complaints when a pastor lists that one about "Britain's dark, Satanic mills."

The school books my youngsters bring home are replete with rural settings, or small, seacoast towns, or little white cottages in suburbia with green rugs in front of them. "Up, Spot," "Hello, Dick," "Goodbye, Jane," and all that. My six-year-old still brings that silly little book home. And, just the other night, I examined my twelve-year-old son's English grammar book, although it wasn't called that. Sprinkled throughout are all those lovely, idyllic scenes of the countryside, the mountains, fishing along the great Colorado River—and *canoes*. There must be a hundred canoes sliding gently through the pages.

Now, I believe that fantasy is an indispensable and delicious element in a child's life. But a book almost wholly fantastic seems a bit too much, particularly one that doesn't intend to be.

Television has its "Lassie," always a small-town story with a simple, small-town message, and television also has its seemingly endless series of crime shows that put the city in its apparently "proper light."

The tyranny of the "white suburban and rural culture" reigns on.

The music teacher deals with Beethoven or Bartok, or Gershwin or you name it, but jazz is for "after class" or not at all, because, hadn't you heard, "white is right." Negro girls spend enormous amounts of time straightening their hair while white girls do the reverse and, as Pete Seeger says, somewhere along the line, things got "all mixed up."

Alas for the American city—home for crime, for drifters, for noise, for dirt, for dope, for shysters, for illicit sex, for God knows what else, while in suburbia, or out there in the countryside, there is purity and fresh air, straight-forwardness and honesty; no politics and certainly no corruption.

The noncity scene is blessed with a real ritual of its own. Bolstered by decades of American literature, by thousands of speeches and millions of sermons extolling the rural life, the anticity is symbolized by "no sidewalks" (what a great and noble goal!). The songs of suburbia are the songs of the children, the single most important product issuing from this sector. And while there may be occasional and intense disagreement about noncity objectives, to one all-embracing principle do the patriots readily repair—the city must be repelled, for it is BAD.

But let me remind anyone in this room who is forgetful; that murmur you hear in suburbia is not the symphony of life. Let us convert the dangerously irrelevant school systems attended by center-city children to ones which provide significant preparation, not only for surviving, but even for flourishing in an urban environment. Let us teach in school what some store-front lenders really charge to rent their money. Have you heard the Joan Baez song about Pretty Boy Floyd in the 1930s in Oklahoma:

> *Well, it's through this world I've rambled,*
> *I've seen lots of funny men.*
> *Some rob you with a six-gun,*
> *Some, with a fountain pen.*

Let us teach in school what consumer habits might get a buyer a little more for his buck. Let us explain clearly what the pattern of local social services is, and how one takes solid advantage of those services. Let us explain what due process of law means and how to behave in confrontation with the police.

Let us stop classifying kids as "slow learners" (if not "retarded") when they come to school suspicious of authority figures, unwilling to say much and befuddled by educational settings and imagery which have little or no relevancy to them.

Let us educate youngsters for an urban future in a multi-racial world. And let such education be offered not only in urban settings —for the children of rural areas need to understand cities and the problems of cities because they will probably live much of their own later lives in metropolitan settings. . . .

What we need are educational systems that will produce citizens whose background, motivation, and education, in combination, will equip them not only to look out for themselves, and later for their families, but also to help our society to cope more effectively with the problems of urban life. . . .

Thousands and thousands of foreign students have been accepted for admission. We have been highly pleased by their presence on our campuses—cosmopolitanism and all that. In judging them, we have been aware of their language difficulties, social adjustment problems, and inadequate preparation; thus we have been especially impressed with their great progress and we have tended to grade them on that progress.

There is another kind of "foreign student" now knocking on the door. From the ghettoes of Camden or Cleveland or Roxbury or Watts, or the backwoods hollows of Eastern Kentucky or West Virginia, they too have "language difficulties" and "social adjustment problems" and "inadequate preparation." . . .

Whether from rural America, or, as will be the majority, from the central city, these students, like all students, will show their backgrounds. They may be just a little less reticent about expressing a point of view. They may use language a little more pungent than we're accustomed to, or different from what we've always heard. They may scoff at a national rhetoric that says white is always right, or that men have equal protection of the laws, or at the tribal incantations of a Greek-letter group on a campus. They just might even question the automatic right of a professor to label his interpretation of some facts as "true" or "right." And, they might create a little turmoil in the social system of higher education by ignoring it as merely "silly," and this might be the unkindest cut of all; or they might just "clam up" in response to a different and somewhat threatening environment to which they are not accustomed.

In short, they may not be adept at the great middle-class rituals which nicely lubricate the higher education scene. And how will we respond to this? . . .

Many of these youngsters are the children of poverty and yet of promise. When you judge them, consider all they had to go through to get where they now stand; the handicaps they faced in developing themselves enough to knock on your door. Perhaps their test scores are not impressive; but were you assessing the horsepower of two engines rather than two students, you would not have one haul a load uphill and the other one haul a load downhill, and then compare the size of the loads they moved.

We must remember that the children of poverty have been going uphill all the time and we must weight their test scores accordingly. Theirs has not been an easy life. They have developed some intellectual and visceral strength which has allowed them to survive and which, if you give them a chance, will allow them to grow, gain strength, and flourish in their personal lives and in their contribution to society.

Some of the youngsters will have lower scores than others whom you might otherwise admit; yours is a difficult choice. But, as always, diversity is one of the strengths of America. We should inject this diversity of background into the higher education setting where a now dangerously homogeneous studentry lives.

This exhortation extends also to those of you who in your high schools are specialists in fostering admission of youngsters to appropriate post-secondary institutions. To you I extend a special appeal. You know better than I that often you are pressured by parents to facilitate college admission for reasons of social status even when the students show limited potential to profit from the experience. And since the wheel that squeaks the loudest gets the grease, it is only natural that you try to give appropriate help to these youngsters.

In the stress of this process, remember the bright children who may not be seeking admission to college—who may have to be sought out and encouraged and assured that the American dream can really come true for them, too. Seek them out and encourage them as early as you can, and encourage their parents who may be hesitant to urge their children to higher attainments lest they strive for too much and suffer the bitterness of disappointed hopes.

I would urge also, and this is particularly important, I think, that you look for these boys and girls even earlier than has been your customary practice. I'm told that when youngsters go from grammar school into high school, they and their parents are often advised if they plan on college attendance, they should take a program of studies appropriate for preparation for college. To those of us in this room, this is perfectly natural, but for many of the children of poverty and their families, often college is never mentioned or considered as a realistic possibility. So I say to you, do not wait until those youngsters who might be truly "upward bound" are assigned, at the beginning of high school, to terminal programs.

Locate them; encourage them; get them on the college track; give them a chance to grow and learn so that, with increasing maturity, they may take real choices instead of having the doors closed on them before they really know where those doors are and what's on the other side of them. A student can always transfer from a college preparatory program to a vocational or general course, but students committed to the latter often find the initial decision almost irreversible. . . .

We hope with this effort to lead the way in fostering a fundamental shift in the important dynamics of career sorting, so that a youngster's potentiality and a youngster's potentiality alone, rather than the social circumstances of his birth, will be the more determining factor in how far he will go in the educational system and hence, what level he will achieve in the occupational structure of American society. . . .

In order to do that, we all will have to alter our basic assumptions somewhat. We will have to depend less on our goals of social efficiency and more on a goal of social justice. We will have to diminish our dependence on Newtonian physics as a basis for deciding educational questions and increase our use of the heart, itself. We will, in short, have to respond to the "other America" which now says, "Us, too"; "We want, in, too"; "Give us the chance, too."

This does not suggest a simple and silly process of judging youngsters by intuition alone. No rational world could be built on that basis. But, it does demand an enlargement of the criteria we have used in the past and a greater variety of tools by which we *include* and *exclude* people.

15. The Schools of Appalachia

Peter Schrag

GOLDIE Bell is an experienced American elementary school teacher who has never been asked about phonics, the new math, or the college potential of her pupils. The Scuddy School, where she works, can be reached only by crossing a muddy creek from an unpaved road which winds its way into one of the many blind valleys of eastern Kentucky. Down the road from the school live the coal miners—many of them now unemployed—who would be eligible for the Scuddy School PTA, if the school had one.

Mrs. Bell teaches five grades—fourth, fifth, sixth, seventh, and eighth—in her half of the wooden building that comprises the school. In the adjacent room a younger woman teaches grades one, two, and three. The walls are painted gray and brown, bare bulbs provide light, and a potbellied, coal-burning stove affords an uneven heat in the winter. There is a constant murmur in the room; most of Mrs. Bell's thirty-eight children must work on their own, the older ones helping the younger, the faster giving aid to the slow. One child has no shoes, many have no socks, and several look prematurely old. They are the children of some of the poorest people in America. A few are reading a story:

> Jane and Spot were going up the street as fast as they could. So were Jack and Jim. (Jane is blond and wears a blue dress; two boys follow on roller skates.)
> "Get out of the way," called the boys. But just then Jane stopped. The boys stopped, too.
> "Look boys," said Jane. "See what I have in my pocket."
> "Pennies!" said Jack.
> "What are you going to buy with them? Is it a toy for Spot?" (Later in the story they go for a spin in the family's green and white cabin cruiser.)

From the *Saturday Review*, May 15, 1965. Reprinted by permission. Copyright 1965 by the Saturday Review, Inc.

As they read, Mrs. Bell is asking another group about a different story.

> "Who is it that's driving the big tractor?" she asks.
> "Jack," says one of the pupils.
> "What's the girl doing?"
> "Washing dishes."
> "What would she like to do?"
> "Be out with the boy."
> "They had one of those dishwashers," Mrs. Bell says, "Not many of us are lucky enough to have one of those."

The Scuddy School is one of twenty-odd one- or two-room schools in Perry County, and one of several thousand in Appalachia; many have been closed in recent years, but hundreds will remain because transportation over the "hollows" is difficult and because—strangely enough—local pride and suspicion of the world outside demand that they be kept open. Many are built of wooden slats though some have been replaced since World War II with cinder block structures —usually because "the old school burned down." The potbellied stove and the outdoor privy are the only standard pieces of equipment. A miscellany of old desks, benches, tables, and chairs comprise the furniture; decorations come from old magazines and calendars.

The one-room schools of eastern Kentucky are staffed by a mixture of people—some, like Mrs. Bell, are dedicated veterans, others are women who have not met certification requirements, and still others are persons who once taught in the better consolidated schools but who were "sent up a hollow" for an academic or, more commonly, a political offense. Teachers are rarely fired, but if they identify themselves with the wrong faction in a local election, they will be sentenced to an inferior school, sometimes as much as fifty miles from home.

The presence of the one-room schools, and the fate of some of the teachers, are symptoms of the problems that plague education in Appalachia. In eastern Kentucky, which has never had a tradition of public education beyond the three Rs, schools mean jobs as bus drivers, teachers, and lunchroom employees; they mean contracts for local businessmen, and they represent power for county politicians. In Breathitt County, for example, Mrs. Marie Turner has been superintendent of schools since 1931; her husband held the office for six years before, and several in-laws controlled it before that. The Turners own the building in which the Board of Education is located, and they take rent from the board. According to the

Lexington Leader, which ran a series of articles on school politics in Kentucky—with little apparent effect—the Turners have profited from the schools' purchase of coal, gasoline, and school buses, and from the deposit of school funds in local banks. Elsewhere in Kentucky school boards purchase real estate from the sons and daughters of board members, and hire each other's children and wives as teachers. In Perry County, where Goldie Bell teaches, and where the board followed common practice by naming a new school for the superintendent, Dennis G. Wooton ("We don't wait till they die," someone said), Mr. Wooton's son-in-law, Curtiss Spicer, is principal of the Wooton School, and his daughter, Mrs. Spicer, is one of its teachers.

This kind of nepotism is almost inevitable in an area as ingrown as eastern Kentucky: of the nineteen pages in the Hazard telephone book, the Perry County seat, two are filled with listings for people named Combs, four persons named Combs teach at the Dilce Combs High School, and recently a high school science teacher named Combs was exiled to a one-room school for supporting a school board candidate named Combs against an incumbent named Combs. Virtually all the teachers in the Perry County schools grew up in the county, or within a few miles of its borders, and many are teaching in the classrooms where they sat as students not many years before. Even if an outsider wanted a job in eastern Kentucky—and few do since the average salary is just over $3,000—he would have difficulty obtaining one. "Outsiders just wouldn't be happy here," said one of the county superintendents.

The consequence of the inbreeding is that few new ideas have reached the schools of the area. Even the consolidated high schools operate largely with antiquated equipment, irrelevant textbooks, and obsolete material. Although many teachers sincerely strive to teach children in the best possible way, the years of previous miseducation make the task difficult. Sharon Barnett, a young, attractive English teacher at M. C. Napier High School near Hazard (Napier was superintendent when the school was built) spends the first semester in her senior course diagramming sentences; in the second semester she hopes to have her students read Macbeth. She knows that such an undertaking is difficult, but she desperately wants to bring something of the culture of the outside world to her community. She has come back to teach in Perry County because "my life is here," because "I love these people." And she knows what she's up against. "We could do so much more for these kids if their background were not so poor," she said. "They've had poor teaching in the country schools; some of the teachers are disliked so much that the kids are determined not to learn in order to hurt the teacher."

Yet despite all efforts—and there are other teachers like Sharon Barnett—the schools remain irrelevant for most of the students. Of those who started first grade in Perry County in 1948, about twelve per cent graduated in 1960. Many boys drop out, as a teacher said, "to get a job, a car and show off," and the girls quit to get married. A substantial number leave school and do nothing other than stand on the street corners of the towns. In Perry County, where the unemployment rate is about 17 per cent, the children fall into two groups: those who are ambitious and want to go north, especially into Ohio and Indiana, and those who see no value in any education, and have given up. When a grade school teacher recently asked her pupils what they wanted to do when they grew up, several answered, "to get on the welfare."

The content of the school curriculum provides little incentive for academic effort. Students are rarely challenged to work on their own, laboratory equipment is scarce and rarely used, and the courses in social studies are largely devoted to the clichés of American history and American life. The required civics book in Perry County proclaims, characteristically:

> Our economic system is founded on these basic principles: free private enterprise, competition, the profit motive, and private property. Businessmen and others must compete against one another in order to earn profits. These profits become their private property. This system is known as *capitalism*. By means of our capitalistic system we have built the most productive economy, bringing Americans the highest standard of living that the world has ever known.

Since the county does not furnish free books in the high schools, students who use the civics text are not only required to read it but to pay for it. When relevant issues come up they fall outside the formal curriculum. In a discussion of civic responsibility and community planning, a high school teacher told his class: "In case something goes wrong in city government, the citizens should protest, they should write letters, and keep the officials on their toes."

"My uncle says he'll lose his job if the Democrats don't get in," a student exclaimed. Another student interrupted to say "In Hazard they don't care . . . if they cared they'd fix it up."

"It's not that bad," a third student said. "You just don't appreciate what we have."

"That's because there's nothing to appreciate. . . ."

"All the money goes to the hifalutin' big shots. You know the clothes they sent in after the flood, it didn't go to the people that needed it. They got a little bit so they could take pictures for the newspapers."

Discussions like this are rarely encouraged or channeled. Some teachers are nervous because others have been exiled to one-room schools, and because the community tolerates few heresies. The textbooks are safe and therefore irrelevant—the best teachers will admit privately that "we're not giving the kids what they should have."

Many teachers and principals are now making serious efforts to keep children in school. Sharon Barnett challenges her students to visualize themselves in ten years. "I ask them about what kind of job and home they think they'll have, and I tell them that the drunks on the street once had dreams like theirs. They've been protected by their parents and by the mountains. They don't know what the world is like. The mountains are terribly high." These efforts sometimes mean that a principal must find shoes for a boy who has none, or a loan for this year's books, repayable at twenty-five cents a week, or a special trip to a cabin in a ravine to convince a family that staying in school is important.

Many of the mountaineers value education even though most never went beyond the eighth grade themselves. They want lives for their children that are better than they have had, but they do not know, and cannot know, what a good education is, or the kind of effort it requires. Although eastern Kentucky, with substantial amounts of state aid, has made great progress in education in the past five years, eliminating one-room schools, raising teacher salaries, and increasing the proportion of teachers who are certified with a degree from a college, the education its schools provide is still far behind most of the nation. Perry County has some new elementary schools that are bright and well equipped, and the Hazard Vocational School, which children from the county high schools can attend, provides training in a number of useful trades. But even the most recent advances have failed to bring education in Appalachia to an effective level. In an age of technical sophistication, most high schools in eastern Kentucky have little laboratory equipment, and sometimes no laboratories at all. A biology student in one school said that his experimental work in biology consisted of "looking through a microscope once." There are few school libraries and few schools with gymnasiums, language laboratories, films, tapes, or records. For many, the most elaborate equipment is the coke machine, and in an area as carbonated as Kentucky, there are many of those. Meanwhile, school authorities confront incredible problems of transportation. Schools open in mid-

August because snow in the winter often makes the roads impassable, forcing the schools to close sometimes for several weeks. Perry County, with about 7,800 public school children, spends $144,000 a year busing them.

Despite these difficulties, the respectable citizens of the county towns—some of which have separate school systems—remain smug and provincial; many of them deny that there is any poverty in Appalachia, and they resent outside help. Hazard, which is surely one of the ugliest small towns in America, is ringed with signs, sponsored by a local bank, proclaiming "We Like Hazard" and "We Like Perry County." While thousands of tons of coal flow almost untaxed from mechanized mines, and the region's topsoil flows down the muddy rivers, and the ambitious kids move to the north, no one takes much local interest in the problems of education in the county. School officials shrug with a kind of hopelessness about their overcrowded, inadequate buildings, saying they are "bonded to the hilt," but rarely mentioning the incredibly low county tax structure; the town burghers say the schools are fine, that "they're doing a good job," and the women's church groups resent the idea that some of the clothing they gave for the poor was actually returned to the same counties in which it was donated.

Local pride rests in high school football and basketball teams, but few take any active interest in the minds of the kids. In those schools where Parent-Teacher Associations are active, the parents help raise funds for library books and team athletic equipment, without much protest about the fact that the Board of Education provides neither books nor a program in physical education. With the exception of the Hazard *Herald,* which has criticized some of the more flagrant manifestations of school politics, there is not one organization in all Perry County that is critical of the schools. Ever since the coal companies began to exploit eastern Kentucky and its people, outsiders have been suspect, and no one wants their advice now. Thus even those with the best intentions must work carefully and cooperate with the local politicians. To do otherwise is to be ineffective.

Although large amounts of state and federal money are going into public education and welfare programs in eastern Kentucky—90 per cent of the Perry County school budget comes from the state— attempts to achieve educational reform on the state level have been frustrated. Harry Caudill, the Whitesburg attorney who is author of *Night Comes to the Cumberlands,* was a member of a special legislative committee that proposed, among other things, a strong educational Hatch Act to prohibit teachers from engaging in school politics and the election of school board members on a countywide basis, rather than from intra-county districts. "A great howl went up," Mr. Caudill said. "We were called agents of the Pope and a whole lot of other things." Since other political issues diverted the attention of those who might have supported them, the committee's proposals were never enacted.

Despite its poverty, Appalachia remains perhaps the most typically American region; its people have not entirely shaken their frontier attitudes about the conservation of resources, about the value of education, and about relations with the outside world. Rivers are polluted with trash and garbage, refuse dumps foul scenic valleys, and the hulks of abandoned cars line many highways. While most of the nation has become more European, more cosmopolitan, Appalachia has changed but little, remaining behind its protective mountains. Thus there remains a suspicion of change, and of anything but the most conservative education.

Nevertheless a few voices have been raised recently to challenge the old isolation, the brightest of them being Harry Caudill's. And even conservatives like Mrs. W. P. Nolan, the editor of the *Herald*, are expressing a new consciousness. Like some of her fellow citizens, she is worried about Communist infiltration and outside interference in Kentucky. But she also concedes that something is drastically wrong with the schools. "Someone should talk about short-changing the kids," she said. "If we'd had good education in this state fifty years ago, we wouldn't be so embarrassed now before the nation and the world. A lot of this welfare money goes down the drain. We really need help on just three things: flood control, highway construction, and education. If we got that, we could take care of ourselves." Indications are that federal support will be forthcoming for the first two items. If it is, then perhaps there is also a chance for the schools.

16. What Migrant Farm Children Learn

Robert Coles

RUTH is an eight-year-old girl who has traveled widely and knows quite a bit about life and what sustains it. She was born in the hill country of Arkansas and lived there a solid two years. For the past six years, however, she has never lived anywhere more than six months, and at times she will spend more days of a month moving about with her family than settling into some kind of home life.

There are hundreds of thousands of children like Ruth, migrant children, sons and daughters of wandering, seasonal farm hands. They are boys and girls whose lives bear so little resemblance to those of other children that to comprehend them requires knowing a good deal more than the statistics of poverty.

Ruth, for example, looks at first glance to be a pretty, blonde girl with light blue eyes and a fetching smile that would seem to caution any social reformer against too grim a view of her life. True enough, she commonly takes her meals by hand rather than with fork or spoon, and on the floor (or whatever nearby field is her temporary backyard) rather than on a table, but she eats lustily and with no evidence of dismay at her family's living conditions. I am sure many middle-class children would envy her the sticky mess she can regularly make of a meal, pushing her fingers at will through pork fat, potatoes, gravy, and wet, spongy bread, staining her faded denim dress with them all. That dress was made for an older girl; it reaches halfway from her knees to her ankles and looks as if it had fallen upon her, hanging out of balance, her left shoulder bare, her right one covered halfway up the neck. I suppose many children already burdened by the daily lessons that have to precede any future respectability might wish such a dress, too.

When I saw Ruth's smile I saw her poor teeth. When she walked I noticed the toughened but still bruised and infected soles of her

From the *Saturday Review*, May 15, 1965. Reprinted by permission. Copyright 1965 by the Saturday Review, Inc.

feet. Her unkempt hair was dry and stringy; she had sores on her body; her eyes hurt in the sunlight; her skin was coarse, some of it blistered, some of it decisively marked with lines of dirt or old scars. My son might wish that he, like Ruth, never would see a dentist or doctor, though I doubt he would want to pay the price she has.

Ruth's school habits are another source of possible envy to children like mine and yours: she goes to school only occasionally, sometimes missing classes altogether for several weeks, at other times going to them days and even weeks in a row. When she *wants* to go to school, and when there is a school available, she will go. On the other hand, when she feels vaguely hesitant about leaving home, or is interested in staying home with her brothers and sisters to work in the fields with their mother at gathering a particularly lush harvest, there is no question about her sovereign right to make her own choice.

Families like Ruth's live in persisting if incredible contrast to the way most of us do in this country. Since we are now beginning to take notice of poverty, their kind of existence will, one hopes, concern us more than ever before. It will be terribly difficult, however, to achieve an effective means of truly reaching such families and interrupting their style of living where it counts: in the education and training of the large number of children they produce.

Until now, sharecropper families could choose either to leave their cabins, forsaking the only kind of work they knew, for the ghettos of Southern or Northern cities, or give up any hope of a stable home in the interests of at least securing their jobs as farm hands. Thus migrant farmers, like sharecroppers, are essentially the rural poor who have shunned becoming the urban unemployed. They are people who know a great deal about how to survive on little money—many of them see less than $1,000 a year. They know how to buy stale bread at low cost, or soda pop instead of milk for their children. They know that candy takes you a long way on its calories, and that for a pittance, fat, which subdues hunger, can be obtained. They know not to worry about changing clothes, or looking at them too fondly; pants or dresses are simply to cover you when you leave home to work or travel, or walk the road to a store. They know to sleep together when it is cold, or outside when it is warm. Finally, they know that children are born and children die, even as they themselves are lucky to have lived to the working age of ten or twelve, the marrying age of fourteen or fifteen. Owning little else, they cherish their infants and want more of them, in the fearful expectation that not all those conceived, born, or even reared through infancy will live long enough to start their own families.

Such knowledge in migrants helps keep them moving, and because of their work we manage to eat well; a large share of our fruit and vegetables is picked by migrant farmers, and by their wives and children. Unfortunately, migrants have no reason to want to know very much about reading and writing. In my experience most of them are illiterate, and they suffer not at all for it. Their lives go on without newspapers, books, even letters. They have no mailing address anyway. And they are ineligible to vote or even own library cards.

Not only our political life is grounded in the laws of the local community. Our educational system consists of thousands of separate systems, and what co-ordination they have is supplied (and limited) by the individual states. Ruth's family travels from state to state, and Ruth as a child comes under the jurisdiction of many schools. Though legally few of them would deny her a desk—in truth, they would assert her obligation to come seek one—in point of fact, thousands upon thousands of children like Ruth slip through our countryside, attending school in the most desultory fashion, if indeed at all.

If we are concerned about such a state of affairs, then I would imagine we would have to ask how we might come to meet and educate the rural poor. However, in order to be of help to people who often are not actively seeking it (and are suspicious when it does come) those in a position to be of service must try hard to learn the assumptions which they as middle-class citizens do and do not share with the poor and the needy. Untold millions of dollars can be earnestly spent to try to help people who see the offering only as a devilish plot.

The experience of many ministers, doctors, social workers, and nurses indicates that it is not always easy to obtain the gratitude and co-operation of those people, even when such attitudes would seem to their evident advantage. Well-intentioned efforts to treat sick people, or change their diet for the better, have been seen by migrants as senseless intrusions at best; often they are feared and rejected outright as harmful. When people daily learn that they have little in common with the lives and habits of "others," they yield to outsiders slowly and reluctantly. To a migrant, for example, the presence of a doctor may indicate the increased likelihood of death. Similarly, the desirability of sending his children to school is by no means apparent. Nor do migrant children escape the doubts, fears, and suspicions held so fixedly by their parents.

For the past two years I have been interested in the family life of migrant farm and sharecropper children, the work life that occupies their parents, and often them, too, and the relationship between such social and environmental influences and the quality of thinking and feeling in the children. I have been particularly anxious to learn how such relatively impoverished and isolated farm children—there are still millions of them in America today—manage at school. Again and again, from growers as well as those concerned with the living conditions of the people who harvest their crops, one hears that vague word "education" summoned in rare unanimity as an "ultimate" answer to a vexing problem: What, in fact, do migrant children learn when, and if, they go to school? Moreover, what relationship does such learning have to those other lessons that inevitably come upon them?

Ruth's sister, for instance, is not illiterate. At ten she can print her name and she knows about half the letters of the alphabet. A word or two come readily to her as she tries to read, but it is generally tough going. Like her parents, who also had a sporadic kind of education, geared to accomplishing a signature and a rather limited recognition of words, she now knows more than she will know in the future; for older migrants soon slip back when it comes to reading and writing. In the words of Ruth's mother: "I learned the writing and reading in school, but I left off when I was old enough to work steady and not be bothering my folks. Now, to tell the truth, I've forgotten all I learned. . . . We don't have no use for writing and reading."

Ruth's drawings, or those of her sisters and brothers, show quite clearly what she expects of life. I repeatedly asked her to draw a school. She responded with silence and a few aimless gestures of the crayon in her hand. She could draw woods and fields, birds and a nearby lake, but not a school building. Nor could she easily draw her home; she told me quite directly that there were many, and asked me casually which one I had in mind. Eventually she was able to draw one, a composite of many nondescript cabins she knew. Nearby, indeed touching the home, was a car. She clearly intended to let me know that the car, too, was her home. I was struck at how naturally she could draw the terrain on which the house stood; the house itself was sketched quickly and very poorly, then ignored—as if she had obliged me at the price of her own annoyance. "I'd rather sleep outside than in the car," she told me as she pushed the drawing in my direction. I was being pointedly told that the family car really meant more to her than the succession of temporary shacks I might call her various "homes"; and, in any case, she was more tied to the outside world than *any* quarters.

The school building Ruth finally managed to draw was distinctly small, dwarfed by a giant pine tree and on to one side of the paper. Ruth drew it hastily as she had the house. She used a black crayon, and supplied no windows or doors. In fact it was an isolated box, essentially irrelevant to the carefully drawn landscape.

What can one make of such productions, after all, but the work of one child? In the first place, Ruth's view of both home and school is shared by other migrant children I have studied. Moreover, the drawings of these young boys and girls contrast markedly with those I have accumulated over the years from children I have treated from middle-class suburbs, or Negro and white children I studied as they attended newly desegregated schools in the South. Comparing the sheaves of drawings collected from migrant farm children with hundreds of others reveals how specifically children learn to define the make-up of their world. Those from comfortable, suburban neighborhoods lavish attention on the homes they draw, fill their pictures of schools with windows and doors, plants and flags, people and books; for that matter, they sometimes sketch pictures within pictures, so that the corridors of the buildings will faithfully resemble those real ones they daily walk. Even the very poor Negro and white children I have come to know so closely these recent years in cities like New Orleans or Atlanta see their homes and schools as central to their lives, worthy of concern and care in representation.

Migrant farm children, on the other hand, live in a number of makeshift homes and see schools as ultimately irrelevant to their future. As a matter of fact, so do many of the earnest, hard-working teachers who watch them come and go. Those windowless, doorless schools in Ruth's pictures tell the observer that for such a child there is little connection between anything that happens in school and the events of the world. Windows and doors, after all, connect a building with its environment.

Migrant children, like their sharecropper cousins, have little connection with "our" environment. That is what Ruth meant to say with her crayons, and that is the truth of life for millions of our citizens. I have talked with growers and plantation owners, those who employ Ruth's parents—sometimes even her. Some of them are bedeviled, caught between their rude needs for quick, seasonal, cheap labor and their recognition as sensitive human beings that there is something terrible indeed about the kind of life their farm hands have. While one grower may fall back upon angry dismissal of all his workers as born fools or incompetents, lucky to survive on the pittance they earn, his neighbor, no less anxious to employ hundreds of seasonal workers, will speak with genuine concern for a way to end the predicament. A very wealthy farmer told me. "I wish we could end this by developing machines to pick every crop cheaply, and educating the children of these people. . . . Only by educating them will they get out of the rut they're in now."

Fair enough; it is not unpopular these days to recommend more "education" for our children, especially those who are poor and likely to remain so without increased literacy and skills. Much harder is the specific task of figuring out what to do and how to do it. In the case of the migrants no beginning will ever be more than a futile stab in the dark unless it is characterized by a real concern for how the people themselves see their lives, and what they make of worlds other than their own. I am not so sure that a few more days at school, a few more lessons learned, make any difference at all to those rural poor who *do* send their children to school.

People who spend their lives growing and harvesting food, whether on plantations where they live or on farms scattered over the nation, have little use at present for what education they already have. The world for them is one of sunrise and sunset, seeds becoming plants, plants producing vegetables, or cotton to be picked by their hands. Children for them come into the world as it is, and are expected to live or die in that same world. Yes, there is hope; but it is a hope unattached to specific time, to a particular generation. "Low is de way to de upper bright world," I've heard sharecroppers say, but they do not have themselves or their children in mind. If we mean to bring that bright world to them, we had best think out what its nature will be, and what strengths and values in their present world are perhaps very much worth being preserved.

For many of these rural children are sick in body, uneducated in mind, yet quite strong and effective psychologically, so long as their strength and capacity to manage their lives are judged by the standards—the obligations and challenges—of their own world. One migrant put the issue quite directly to me: "I don't care about books for my kids. If it be different, they could need them, but not now." A Negro, he had fled the South to find his social and political freedom in Chicago. Eventually, faced with the alternatives of the ghetto and the relief rolls, he determined that seasonal farm work, mostly in the South, offered a better life: "It's hard, I know; but we can do as we know to, and I believe it's better on you than being in the city, sitting yourself on the stairs all day." His feelings are shared by many white folk of Appalachia who also have come to Chicago and other cities these recent years, and eventually departed.

If we really wish to reach such people, we can do it. They are not clinging to what little they have out of vain contrariness or inherited foolishness. They are stubborn all right, as human beings often are when confronted with the grim alternatives of life and death, endurance or surrender. They may even be suspicious, defiant, and almost mischievously aloof in the face of our occasional generosity—those sudden, good-spirited moments when we send parcels, medicines, books, and our own high intentions. I do not decry those intentions; but I do wonder whether we all might not clarify those intentions as a prerequisite to their fulfillment.

I think hundreds of thousands of rural parents and children want a better life, *as they know life.* They want steady work, at higher wages; a chance to live in homes that are theirs, on land they know, near towns and people they know. Many of them picture their children going to school some day, learning those numbers and letters which—they vaguely know it—lead to an improved kind of existence. However, they picture the day in the *future,* and they have learned to be circumspect—even harshly doubtful—when that future comes knocking on their door. Too many valuable announcements have already come their way only to leave them still as they are: roads bringing the traffic of people and progress; electricity lighting their homes or social security deductions promising them a retirement with at least some income—few migrants live to collect it. It would be a further irony if more schools were built in rural areas, yet migrants and sharecroppers found their hand-to-mouth existence untouched.

What is to be done? Our cities need no more refugees, candidates for the wasted, heavy hours of the slums. Our farms will need less and less labor as machines gradually replace hands in harvesting. Still, for some years to come sharecroppers and migrant families will continue to live on farms, or move about on them; and they will be needed. It is their children who are going to require the kind of education that will enable them to achieve that different, kinder world their parents never really dare imagine near at hand. I once heard a sharecropper tell his grandchild, "Some day the sun will shine on us all day; but that's off from now." Maybe not.

"I want my child to go plumb through school, but if he does, then what will he do?" That is the problem facing us. Only when that mother and her child find a sensible connection between what happens in school and in their lives will they be interested in classrooms.

Until now only a few impressive and lonely ministers, teachers, or public health workers (doctors, nurses, social workers, dieticians) have cared much for the welfare of these people and earned their respect. There is no reason why more of us cannot join their company. Mobile teaching units—I once worked on a mobile medical unit— can go to people quite afraid to ask for help, quite unaware that such help might be forthcoming. Schools can be established on the basis of the needs and lives of these people, rather than the habits and interests of the rest of us.

It scarcely makes sense, for example, to expect people chronically on the move to respect the primacy of the town school. On the contrary, regional networks of schools are badly needed, many of them mobile, all staffed by teachers specifically concerned with the customs and beliefs of the rural poor, white and Negro. Also needed will be some real interest in these people on the part of business, labor, and government—interest enough to supply small, diversified industry to employ them. For if they are not to swell the ranks of the bitter, urban unemployed, or the shiftless, rural unemployed, they will, rather obviously, need jobs. Moreover, they will need education and training for those jobs. (Such remarks are clichés, worn and blunted; the reason that is the case is their continuing relevance. There is no original, beautiful way to dress up the tired but urgent facts of human distress.)

Our needs—for work, for knowledge—fall back upon one another; they cannot be considered separately. Migrant children want their own books, require their own lessons. Their special language, their ways of dressing and eating and getting along with one another, must be understood and made part of the life of the school—even as our own ideas and habits inform the spirit of our middle-class neighborhood schools.

I do not wish to overwhelm the reader with the dismaying facts that together make for a sad spectacle in our national life. It is not alone a matter of people exploited until their backs are broken, their spirit destroyed, their minds numbed. Many incredibly poor farm families are made up of tenacious and willful people. Theirs is the tragedy of inner strength—consolidated and tested by a hard life— in search of its own fulfillment. As a nation founded essentially by farmers and built to its present greatness by wanderers, can we continue to deny many farm children their reasonable future without losing, at the very least, a good deal of our own self-respect?

17. The Teacher and the Negro Child: "Invisibility" in the School

Maxine Greene

IN a fundamental sense, the civil rights struggle is a struggle for dignity, for what Martin Luther King calls "somebodiness." The goal may not be so defined by the rank and file of activists; nor may the mass of Negro people articulate it in such terms. But this is the note sounded most often in literature by and about the Negro since the Civil War. It is one of the aspects of the Negro revolt with which teachers must be concerned.

The acknowledged purpose of the public school today is to teach all children to think as intelligently as they can, to conceptualize, to form their worlds. No classroom teacher, however, can ignore the difficulties due to the "degenerating sense of 'nobodiness'" which, we are told by Dr. King,[1] afflicts every Negro, adult as well as child. To feel, in James Baldwin's language, "faceless" is often to feel indifferent to the demands made by the world. In the classroom, this may result in failure to master elementary skills; it may affect an individual's attitude towards any sort of work and make him "play it cool" when asked to feel responsible for what he does or does not do. If this happens, the effects of early impoverishment are confirmed. The disabilities most obvious to employers—unreliability, poor work habits, lack of skills[2]—are built into character and style. And the vicious circle that supports so much discrimination is tightened once again.

This is not, of course, to say that the predicament of the Negro is the "fault" of those who have taught him in the school. It is to suggest that one of the contributing factors may be dealt with in the school

From *The Education Forum*, March, 1965, pp. 275–80. Reprinted by permission. Copyright 1965 by Kappa Delta Pi, an honor society in education.

[1] "Letter from a Birmingham Jail," in *Why We Can't Wait* (New York: Harper and Row), 84.
[2] Abraham L. Harris, "Education and the Economic Status of the Negro," in Robert A. Goldwin (ed.), *100 Years of Emancipation* (Chicago, Rand McNally & Co., 1964), 152–53.

if teachers can be brought to see the meaning and somehow feel the pain of "facelessness." As the widow of Willy Loman says in *Death of a Salesman,* "Attention must be paid."

One way to see and to feel is through imaginative engagement in presentations like Ralph Ellison's exemplary novel entitled—all too relevantly—*Invisible Man.* The nameless hero of that work suffers from what he calls "invisibility," a condition not of his own making but due to a "peculiar disposition in the eyes"[3] of others. Those others are white people; and it makes little difference if they are benevolent or malign. The disposition in their eyes enables them not to see the Negro as a living human being, a creature of "substance, of flesh and bone, fibre and liquids,"—of mind. They see him, rather, as an object, an abstraction: "Negro," "member of a subculture," "culturally deprived."

Ironically, it is the humanitarian concern for the poor and underprivileged that has led to teaching teachers terms and categories like these. They are obviously useful if linked to understanding of special circumstances influencing learning in the school. But they are also potentially dangerous. They may lead some teachers to regard their pupils as "cases," even "causes,"—to forget that they are individuals, to impose on them (with the best of intentions) a new invisibility.

This is important because of the duality of the work the classroom teacher is asked to perform. The teaching act is on the one hand a behavioral affair, rationally conducted, and guided (hopefully) by theory. On the other hand, it is an affair of face-to-face encounters, dependent for their validity on the teacher's own authenticity, on his ability to identify imaginatively.

If he has been recently educated in the art of teaching, he is likely to be familiar with the structure of his subject matter. He is probably equipped to organize the materials of his teaching in accord with the logic of the subject and, at once, with the conceptual level of the learners concerned. There is no question but that he knows more and communicates more effectively than some of those who were taught to teach "not the subject, but the child."

If the teacher is a fairly recent graduate, he is also likely to be committed to a subject matter specialty which he finds exciting, complex, "real." He may be exposed, therefore, to a frustration unknown to some of his older colleagues; and this may make it even harder for him to engage in encounters with youngsters innocent of the joys of learning, pupils who "couldn't care less."

3 Ellison, *Invisible Man* (Signet Edition), 7.

When we link such frustration and estrangement to the increasing professionalism and precision of instruction in the schools, we can easily envisage the consequences for the nurture of identity. Yet neutrality and, perhaps, impersonality may be a function of the cognitive orientation becoming characteristic of the schools.

This orientation has been accounted for by Sputnik I and the subsequent panic over "mediocrity." More significant, however, is the general acknowledgment that it is the only appropriate educational response to a society growing more organized, automated, and intricate each day. The person adequately prepared for the jobs to be done requires more than rudimentary literacy. The citizen equipped to make a choice in an election or in a local controversy must be able to conceptualize, to form the world about him in a variety of cognitive ways. We have only to recall some of the recent battles over school desegregation or housing exclusion laws, or the issues raised in the presidential campaign. Far more than factual information is needed in each case. The individual asked to take a stand must know how to reason, how to visualize alternatives, how to evaluate—how to think. The recent innovations in the fields of curriculum construction and subject matter organization have been responses to these necessities.

Further research, further experience in programming teaching machines, for instance, may increase our understanding of the slow learner and his requirements; but the special problem of the Negro child in the slum school may still remain. This is in part because of the ineradicable effects of deprivation in early life. It is also because of the larger problem of the Negro in America, and the uncertainty regarding his identity. Although—theoretically—every child can be taught any subject, the actuality of the Negro child's expectations is not yet fully understood.

There is a growing consensus that severe impoverishment in early childhood makes "normal" concept development impossible.[4] If a child is deprived of a range of sensory stimulations, of linguistic experiences, individualized care, security, and continuities, he is likely to be doomed to perpetual "underachievement" when measured against the cultural norms.

The only hope is said to be compensatory prekindergarten education, as in the experimental programs developed by Martin Deutsch and his associates at the Institute for Development Studies in New York. The focus there is on pre-school enrichment, "to reduce the

4 See, for example, Bruno Bettelheim's review of Benjamin Bloom, *Stability and Change in Human Characteristics* in *The New York Review of Books*, September 10, 1964.

attenuating influence of the socially marginal environment."[5] Because the pupils are three- and four-year-olds, the teachers can devote themselves to cultivating the sense of individual personhood, enriching sensory experiences, cultivating curiosity, teaching the children to know their names. The work done already gives evidence of releasing some children from the limitations of impoverishment, of enabling them to learn to learn.

But there are thousands of equally impoverished youngsters moving through the grades and into high schools. If not helped before the age of six, we are told, the influence of the early environment cannot be reduced. In any case, the Deutsch program—qua program—can scarcely be adapted to grades where skills and subject matter must be taught. It holds clues, nonetheless. Something must be done to nurture child identity, even if it is too late for him to be "saved."

The teacher, then, confronts ambiguities and perplexities of all sorts when he takes the responsibility for a Negro child. He realizes that he will be hard put to motivate and teach if there is little feeling of self-regard or worth. He may realize, too, that there is little hope of the child's becoming cognitively excellent if he has not been helped when very young. To complicate his task, he may find that his own view of worth—because of his commitment to subject matter and to learning in general—is linked to his prime regard for capacity to learn.

The very terminology of his trade, "cultural deprivation" and the rest, may intensify this difficulty. A majority or middle-class bias is implied; and, although it may be pragmatically warranted, it is potentially hurtful as far as certain patterns of individuality are concerned. The bias may be reinforced by the teacher's own middle-class values, which often interact with commitment to his discipline to form a kind of screen in front of him. And the screen, once again, obscures his vision of the Negro child as creature "of substance, of flesh and bone. . . ."

He no longer is made to feel guilty about being middle class, as he might have been ten or fifteen years ago. With the exception of those public school people who romanticize the working class and the values they ascribe to it (lack of hypocrisy, delinquent "chivalry"), most teachers tend now to acknowledge at least the expediency of middle-class restraints, aspirations, codes.

Even if he has no feeling of guilt or shame at being middle class and intellectual too, the teacher must still break through the barrier

5 Martin Deutsch, "The Disadvantaged Child and the Learning Process," in A. Harry Passow (ed.), *Education in Depressed Areas* (New York, Teachers College, 1962), 163–79.

his loyalties tend to raise. If he does not, he will not succeed in "fascinating" children, as Frank Riessman puts it,[6] with what there is to be known. If he cannot reach his pupils, he will be unable to discern the variety of "learning styles" that may be used. If he is unable to individualize the members of his class, he will be unable to adapt the strategies at hand, the techniques that might involve them, as individuals, in the struggle to learn. Clearly, he must do all he can to promote the cause of rationality—using flexible time schemes, allowing for alternative ways of framing material and responding to it, being permissive with some children and structured with others. But as he attempts to promote the cause in diverse ways, he must also try to enlarge his own conception of worth. He cannot exclude the life styles which seem to him to be nonrational, frivolous, shallow, "low"; because, if he does, he excludes individuals from his category of the worthy—and, perhaps, from his category of the human. And he cannot teach those he excludes.

If he succeeds in diversifying, in enlarging his conception of worth, if he succeeds in distinguishing among individual youngsters—his task has only begun. He cannot be "color-blind" when he considers his pupils; since this is often to become unintentionally discriminatory. He cannot treat his Negro pupils and his middle-class white pupils equally; since that would lead to thrusting the children of the poor into fixed positions of inequality. He needs to make distinctions and to be nondiscriminatory as well. He needs to find a way of permitting every child to express his own uniqueness visibly, to "become" in his own authentic way.

What is authenticity for a Negro child? And how is the white teacher to know? If he cannot know, if he cannot empathize, it will be difficult to move a child to trust—to trust in a way that builds what Erik Erikson calls "fidelity," one of the building stones of personal identity. How can the white teacher find out how it is with his Negro pupils, what it is like to yearn (as a Single One who is deprived and Negro) to become someone—to be?

He is told by some articulate Negroes that he can never know, not if he is the Man, "Mister Charlie," white. LeRoi Jones, in his play called *Dutchman*, suggests that no white man can conceivably know, that no white man can even comprehend Negro jazz or Negro blues. When Robert Kennedy met with Dr. Kenneth Clark and James Baldwin, the estrangement between Negro and well-meaning white was dramatized in the public eye. Kennedy, taken unaware, was told that he could not possibly understand. John Oliver Killens, the novel-

6 *The Culturally Deprived Child* (New York, Harper and Row, 1962), 94.

ist, explains this with talk of a difference in "psyche"[7] and in emotional chemistries. Yet all stress the importance of respect and regard; all speak of integration; all give voice to the need for a recognition of identity.

The teacher, with his unique responsibility, cannot expect clear directives from the side of his profession or from the Negro people themselves. Day after day—unless he chooses to remain "scientific" and impersonal—he will find himself asked to make particular choices, urgent choices; and no one, in or outside his school, will be able to tell him with certainty that his choices are right or wrong. If he is fortunate, he will have contact with the parents or with other people from his students' neighborhood. It may be that some of them will be equipped to mediate, somehow, between his professional function and the particularities of life on the streets and in tenement rooms. It may be that he will come in touch with the fabric of puzzlements on which his Negro pupils are trying to work with their few cognitive skills. Or he may become acquainted with the jobs that are open—and the jobs that are not. He may learn to help them develop a conception of work for work's own sake, for the sake of meanings in their lives.

It is important for him to try. It is important for his professional effectiveness to consider the significance of encounters, of what Martin Buber (and Martin Luther King) call the "I-Thou." His own humanity may deepen if he reaches out and tries to see, since he could not even begin to reach without becoming open to himself.

Again, literature may play a part. There is not only the possibility of vicarious participation when he reads; there is also engagement on his own terms, engagement in the fundamental human quest for meaning, identity, "somebodiness." He will find no final answers, certainly not to questions about the crippled and the illiterate and the poor; but he will, among all the ambiguities in what he reads, experience the power of possibility.

In *Invisible Man*, there is the question: "Yes, but what is the next phase?" There is the perception of diversity and oneness in America; there is the fruitful decision "to put it down," to refuse to "file and forget." And there is, just before the end:

> I denounce because though implicated and partially responsible, I have been hurt to the point of abysmal pain, hurt to the point of invisibility. And I defend because in spite of all I find that I love. In order to get some of it down I have to love. I sell you no phony for-

7 Killens, "Explanation of the 'Black Psyche'," *New York Times Magazine*, June 7, 1964.

giveness, I'm a desperate man—but too much of your life will be lost, its meaning lost, unless you approach it as much through love as through hate.

Through encounter, through the search for meaning—the forms can be imposed and the children can be taught to make sense of it too, to try to learn in their own terms, "to put it down."

The teacher can do no more than explore and pay heed and try to see. He can act as if understanding were possible, as if youngsters will become visible once he chooses to open his eyes. And he is likely, after a time, to discover that nothing is lost where mastery is concerned—that he has it in him to be a teacher when he becomes a man.

18. Problems of Disadvantaged Youth, Urban and Rural

Walter G. Daniel

THE socially disadvantaged children and youth suffer from disabilities which result from their birth and nurture in environments which impose handicaps rather than provide the opportunities for their development into competent citizens. They are growing up in an increasingly complex urban, industrial, and democratically oriented society. An expanding American economy needs their manpower—intellect and skills. As the metropolitan areas spread, they dominate both urban and rural life. And they also attract culturally or socially dissimilar people whose differences are more easily recognized than their similarities. There results a clash which disrupts communities, fragments them into segments, brings pressures upon the social agencies, and interferes with progress. The schools, especially, feel the impact and are challenged to become more realistic and effective in fulfilling their functions.

Migration or increased geographic mobility and the expanding mass media have brought urban and rural people under the same socializing influences and general values. Subcultures or segments of the population, however, quickly develop and the areas or communities become sectors or neighborhoods that are labeled according to their geographic location or identifiable inhabitants. We tend to think of urban communities and rural ones. Or there are the sectors that begin with "inner city" and radiate into "edge-of-the-city" and "suburbia." The rural areas are farm and nonfarm, while there are types of farms which are characterized as commercial, subsistence, commuting, etc. The central city becomes the slums and the rural area is labeled "played out." Given enough problems, any area may be labeled as "depressed."

General comparisons of urban and rural youth As previously stated, the opportunities for acquiring the advantages

From *The Journal of Negro Education*, Summer, 1964, pp. 218–24. Reprinted by permission.

152

of the urban society are not enjoyed by all, even all of those who inhabit the cities. Various studies report data that indicate the nature of difference or social disadvantage. The following summary states the major differences in the over-all background of youth in these areas:

1. The education of parents, which will be lower in the rural areas, for few have finished high school.
2. The income of the family, for most of the rural parents work in the lower-paid occupations or live in areas where wages are lower.
3. The isolation of the rural area which leads to a lack of cultural stimulation and a lack of regulation and order.
4. The decline in population in the rural area which reduces the flow of "new blood" into the population or limits new ideas or dental, medical and other necessary welfare services. Less favorable social and economic influences result in limited educational opportunities. Buildings, teaching staffs, curricula, on the whole, are not as good as those which are available in the cities. (However, we should add quickly that the students who live within the central portions of the city do not generally have the advantages of good buildings, good teachers and curricula, etc., when compared with those who live beyond the central areas.)
5. The earlier average age of marriage. This fact is related to the other factors just mentioned, especially education and income, and contributes to the failure of developing a culturally stimulating environment and reinforces the need to move to the city for employment.

The immediate environment offers the model for youth behavior. The first reference group is the family, and there are great differences in the degree of identification of children and youth with their families. As they grow into adulthood, young people seek independence from their families. Research indicates that rural youth may retain family influences and close relationships longer than city youth.

Youth behavior and social reference groups

Some sociologists regard youth as rebellious and conclude that they tend to form a rebellious subculture. Others say that this behavior is not an indication of rebellion and the rejection of adult values but is the expression of independence and the desire to be accepted into adult society. The manner of this expression differs and varies according to geographic location, ethnic origin, socio-economic class, or a combination of these factors. In their backgrounds, however, there are the common elements of low family income, limited parental education, histories of intellectual and educational retardation, low aspirations for parents and children, and circumscribed participation in the social, economic, and political life in the areas in which they reside.

Disadvantaged
Inner city
youth

The usual adolescent drives for independence are multiplied many times in the inner city. The symbols of affluence are seen daily and the apparent success of fraud, of disregard for law and of exploitation of others induces lawlessness, delinquency, and resentment of authority. The youth of the central city often display a strong ingroup feeling, a lack of shame, much rudeness, little restraint, and few inhibitions. They are likely to have little regard for the property of others but may be quick to share with others regardless of origin. There is often a keen sensitivity to insult, status, and emotional tension. They are quick to feel social or psychological alienation. And those whose families move often within the city do not acquire close affiliations in school or in the neighborhood.

Disadvantaged
rural
dropout

Research on rural youth is most inadequate. Several studies regarding selected areas do throw some light on the problems involved. Among them is one on dropouts in Louisiana which concluded that conflicts between school and home concerning norms for behavior contributed to feelings of insecurity and alienation from school and led to voluntary withdrawal from school as a way of resolving the conflicts. An additional finding was the less favorable position of the nonwhite segment of the population.

An investigation in Iowa identified six major types of predisposing factors that were associated with dropping out of school. These were (1) school too difficult, (2) lack of acceptance, (3) disruptive home situations, (4) financial needs, (5) school program inadequate, and (6) engagement or marriage.

Some reports on the problems of rural youth have indicated that those who must travel on buses for long distances have difficulties maintaining regular attendance, and that others of this group experience alienation or lack of acceptance because of school cliques. High school student bodies have been known to be divided between the "bus kids" and the others, with resulting damaging effects upon school spirit, human relations, and educational programs. Other schools have been disrupted by racial, religious, and social class antagonisms inimical to the unifying functions of American education. Both family and social group support are essential to good performance and success in school. Their absence means the loss of the kind of reinforcement which rural youth need.

Employment
disadvantages
of farm and
nonfarm youth

Employment opportunities for urban youth are generally considerably more favorable than those for their rural counterparts. But just as there are differences among the urban group, there are also differences among the rural. According to the latest statistics there are 7.5 million rural youth between the ages of fifteen and twenty-four. Of these, 5.7 million are classified as nonfarm and 1.8 million as farm. The youth reared on farms receive some kind of training for farm life, and many will remain and others will go to the city. The nonfarm rural youth, however, have a more difficult adjustment because of the tremendous changes in the pattern of demand for the employment opportunities which are associated with recent technological changes. These changes have reduced the demand for unskilled and semiskilled workers and thereby have eliminated a large number of jobs which have most frequently been the entering positions for new workers and for those changing from farm to nonfarm work. The over-all rate of economic growth in the past five years has been sharply below the growth rate of the previous ten years. Employmentwise this fact has meant that the rate of employment growth has slowed down significantly in the nonfarm sectors. The number of persons on nonfarm payrolls has been expanding at half the rate of the post-war decade, while the goods-producing industries such as construction, manufacturing, and mining have experienced an actual decline to give way to the service-producing industries which are increasing. These trends suggest that there will be a redistribution of rural nonfarm employment that must be accompanied by a high degree of geographical and social mobility.

Another segment of the population that experiences extreme problems comprises the families of agricultural workers who travel to work locations on a seasonal basis, often traveling through several states and returning to a home base after the crop season is over. The average size of the migrant families ranges from two in Florida to six and seven in Texas. In 1960 migrant farm workers earned average wages of nineteen dollars a week, while the nonmigrant farm worker earned twenty-two dollars and the factory worker ninety dollars per week. Here are represented tremendous differences in family background, school availability and economic and social opportunity. *Migrant children and youth*

Forced by economic necessity to travel, the migrant child must move from school to school and tends to fall behind in his studies. In one study, 87 per cent of the migratory children were found to be below normal grade level at age fifteen. Associated with extreme mobility and low income are poor health, poor nutrition, poor housing, irregular school attendance, and community rejection. The educational effects are poor work and study habits, low achievement, and defeat.

Since youth are members of families who depend upon seasonal farm employment, their fates are tied to parental employment patterns. Solutions to their problems must be found in the context of answering the two major questions of (1) how to give the farm worker steady work and (2) how to give the farmer a dependable supply of labor when and where he needs it. The effective approach to untangling some of the difficulties must begin at the local level, must be focused upon upgrading the skills and living conditions of migrant families, must utilize supportive services as a step toward self-development, and must include the co-operation of all agricultural, governmental, and educational agencies with the local comunity.

Disadvantages of race Whether they are in an urban or a rural area, Negro youth suffer additional disabilities because of their race. In 1962, about one out of every four nonwhite teenagers in the labor force was unemployed, as compared with one out of every eight white teenagers. Those who live in the city are nearer a wider range of employment opportunities than those who live in either the farm or nonfarm areas.

Most of the teenagers now growing up in rural-farm areas will not find farm jobs when they enter the labor market. The majority of rural youths face a choice of underemployment on farms or in rural areas and small towns or movement to urban areas for employment. Many young persons on the farms are fully employed only during the relatively short peak seasons of work. For the rest of the year, they work on a part-time basis and do not fully utilize their potential.

Most youth who come to the cities will remain, but race affects mobility. Initially they will live in the central part of the city. Large numbers will crowd into the deteriorated portions where they will live until they make enough money to move into the sections that radiate into the suburbs. If they are white the movement is faster. If they are Negro, they will find it more difficult to make the money to move, more difficult to achieve a high living standard. White or Negro, however, the majority of those who migrated to the city from the country will remain in or near the inner city, trying to rear families without much knowledge of urban life and without much participation in the economic and social structure.

While both whites and Negroes will be shifted and shunted around as expressway construction and urban renewal proceed, the Negroes will bear the greater amount of deprivation and discomfort. They will be forced into the deteriorating neighborhoods and will bear the marks of oppression and restriction. The seeds of discontent are flowering into resentment and mistrust to such an extent that in many parts of the country, both urban and rural, there is an uneasiness that must be recognized if problems are to be dealt with effectively and if the nation is to advance toward the goals of equality for which it stands.

Urbanization, industrialization and democratization will continue. Educational planning, therefore, must take into account the economic, social, and political influences which govern the needs and make the provisions for meeting them. For the disadvantaged learners, who have been discussed in this chapter, the principal educational problems involve the lack of readiness, the poor quality of experiences, and the restricted opportunities derived from their background and environment. Improvement lies in changing the community framework and in providing the needed school staff, physical facilities, and supplementary services.

Overcoming disadvantage

Our study of selected disadvantaged youth population groups shows three outstanding problems, namely communication, employment, and social relationships. Youth from the backgrounds described have experienced an "oral-aural" tradition. While they are generally effective in "face-to-face" situations or can communicate with their peers, they will avoid situations which require them to read or write. The growing emphasis upon taking qualifying written examinations or filling out application forms, or following directions will require that specific preparation or direct teaching be planned.

There needs to be direct teaching for outcomes that will aid these youth in getting and holding jobs. Their experiences have helped them to develop initiative, realistic outlooks, some self-reliance or independence. At the same time they are often impulsive in attitude, irregular in attendance, or may resent supervision and criticism and may become discouraged. They are often preoccupied with immediate needs for money to obtain food, clothing, and housing and will accept short-range goals. There are frequent tendencies to passivity, discouragement, and feelings of futility.

When they realize that they occupy the lowest positions in the socio-economic scale, they may conclude that knowing someone or "having pull" is more important than having skills. Oftentimes these youth have experienced so much failure in school and elsewhere that they have acquired no faith or confidence in their own ability to succeed. For many, life is "shuffle" rather than progress. Life experiences have done little to develop security, stability, orderliness, and sequence or continuity. Most of them have moved about, have little self-discipline. Because society has treated many of them as children or as naïve if not primitive people, they have failed to develop maturity through the intellectual and emotional experiences.

Community responsibility

The ultimate responsibility for improving the educational and employment opportunities of youth must be assumed by the adult community. Adults must change their attitudes toward assimilation. When culturally different people meet on a continuing basis, community progress and integration require some type of assimilation. Usually the group that is numerically superior will try to assimilate the group that is different. Hence the disadvantaged crystallize their resistance, or run the risk of oppression, or learn to accommodate. A fundamental issue is raised: How can dissimilar elements of the population work together for the development of society and themselves? Inasmuch as some groups are used to control other groups, another question needs to be raised: How do persons who are urban and middle class and who administer the schools, the social agencies, and all other organizations of the community relate effectively to the people who differ from them?

The greatest change must take place in the hearts and minds of the leaders who control community policies and organizations. These leaders must see that urban renewal and modern transportation do not add to the disabilities and inconveniences of the disadvantaged. Hence the problem of the community must be attacked simultaneously with the planning for the education and preparation of the youth. The leadership must not overgeneralize from sociological observations. For example, the broken home with matriarchal domination has been represented as damaging to youth identification; yet the inspirational effect of mother has been praised annually and the stability achieved in some matriarchal homes has been amazing. Similarly, the failure to appreciate education upon the part of parents has been misrepresented since studies have shown interest in education despite dissatisfaction with schools.

A high degree of parental and community support is essential for dealing with youth problems which arise out of their background; but such support must be intelligent, prepared, and constructive. The Norfolk Division of the Virginia State College has been engaged in a program which has sought to identify and retrain former workers who offer potential talent.

The one hundred men chosen for the initial pilot group of persons to be retrained represented the lowest in the socio-economic scale. They were distrustful, often unenthusiastic or resentful or frequently unreliable. The staff had to use unusual methods to locate them, establish rapport, maintain their interest and follow through. It would have been easier to work with people of greater promise and responsiveness. Yet, improvement efforts must be directed at working with the adults and youth in the lowest levels of the community.

The American economy needs all the manpower available for its **Conclusion** wholesome expansion. Urban and rural youth constitute the sources of supply but many of them are disadvantaged because of conditions of birth and environment. Urban and rural communities are interdependent and must learn ways of co-operation and co-ordination in the national interest. Schools must meet the challenge by implementing specific programs which take into account the characteristics and problems of their pupils. But the responsibility for solutions must be shared with community agencies. Indeed the citizens of the adult community must take the lead. Real progress depends upon the constructive and imaginative leadership of both professional and lay people. There must be genuine community support for improving human relations, for recognizing cultural pluralism in the social structure, for paying the cost essential to operate effective programs, for achieving economic, social, and political participation of all elements in the population, and for attaining a significantly greater measure of equality in opportunity now. Our nation has the human and material resources. We must use them to accomplish our announced goals.

Part Three. **Quality Education Is People**

Introduction to Part Three

THE change in the proportion of rural population and the widening gap between education in urban and rural schools became so noticeable by the latter part of the nineteenth century that some educators demanded drastic curriculum changes. In 1897, the National Education Association (NEA) appointed a committee on rural education— the Committee of Twelve. The committee's report significantly influenced rural school improvement for the following twenty-five years. It made recommendations concerning curriculum and method, internal organization and management, secondary education, problems of vocational education, school buildings and equipment, teacher preparation, and finance. Out of this study came a boost to the idea of consolidation of small schools and transportation of pupils at public expense. Later, the Country Life Commission appointed by Theodore Roosevelt in 1909 dealt with social and economic problems of rural life. This commission's report contained a comprehensive section on rural education. It recommended developing programs in agriculture and home economics, teaching the advantages of rural life, and the development of community centers.

The First White House Conference on Rural Education (1944) was **New goals** a turning point for the modern development of rural schools. At this conference rural educators finally agreed that rural education need not be second-best. As noted in Part Two, they concluded that a top quality education is the right of all rural children because it is the right of every child regardless of race, color, or situation, wherever he may live in America. Ten years later, the 1954 National Conference on Rural Education suggested three areas for intensive study.

1. Review the decade of progress since the 1944 White House Conference on Rural Education.
2. Study persistent and emerging problems now affecting rural living.

163

3. Explore broad questions of policy for the future.[1]

Every major committee convened to study rural education has shown that while rural schools have many problems similar to urban schools, they also have many problems unlike those of urban schools. Rural schools, most committee reports conclude, ought to be institutions whose programs reflect the needs and experiences of pupils and communities oriented toward small town concerns. These needs and experiences require special attention. As they undergo the process of increased urbanization, rural schools are faced with even greater curriculum problems. In final analysis, teachers and administrators, not their concepts and materials, provide the most important quality of instruction found in a school.

Rural education includes all the problems of education in general and of rural communities in particular. Although it is true that rural schools differ somewhat from urban schools, it is also true that they differ from each other. For instance, rural schools in the cotton belt differ from rural schools in dairy communities.

Problems of change   Indispensable to the realization of a better quality of rural school education as encouraged in this book are better-trained and better-paid school personnel. At both the elementary and the secondary school levels most rural school personnel face unusually difficult assignments. For example, it is not uncommon for rural teachers to instruct children in three to six different grades. Rural teachers in general receive far less supportive services than their city colleagues in administering programs designed to meet the needs of disadvantaged pupils. In addition to most textbooks and state courses of study being prepared from the viewpoint of urban conditions and needs, qualified administrators and supervisors are ordinarily not available to help with the task of adapting courses and devising supplementary material. Rural teachers seldom have the benefit of well-equipped classrooms and adequate instructional materials.

In every community, but especially in rural communities, the teacher's job has been made considerably more difficult by the school's attempt to serve the emotional and physical, as well as the intellectual, needs of its pupils and to relate itself more intimately to the community it serves. In urban schools, experts are often available to relieve teachers of many responsibilities in connection with special types of work, such as guidance. In the typical rural school the teacher must be prepared to guide his pupils in almost every area. Similarly,

[1] National Education Association, *Rural Education: A Forward Look* (New York, Department of Rural Education, NEA, 1955), xv.

the demands of school-community relations tend to be heavier in the country than in the city. The rural teachers must be able to understand —and if possible exercise leadership—in the adult affairs of the community he serves.

To fulfill such responsibilities the modern rural teacher must have outstanding personal qualities and adequate preparation for his work. He must possess commitment, initiative, and self-reliance. And, of course, he must understand children and adults, know how to deal with them, and—if his daily schedule is not to overwhelm him— enjoy dealing with them. He should have training in rural sociology and have an intimate knowledge of the particular community he serves. Because he must teach many subjects and advise pupils on a wide variety of problems, he should have a broad educational background and a sound understanding of the contemporary world.

Far from being adequately prepared for his work, the typical rural teacher, from the point of view of personal qualifications, education, and experience, is at the bottom of his profession. He has had less general and professional education than his city colleague, is less experienced, and has spent a shorter time on his current job. Unfortunately, teachers in rural schools, who face particularly exacting assignments, as a group have the greatest deficiencies of all.

The student, the most important person of any educational system, is hurt by an inferior educational system. This is not to imply that all, or most, rural schools are inferior. Some of our best schools are in rural areas, but unfortunately many of the worst ones also are found there. In general, however, innovation and new techniques are likely to be developed in urban areas. A major question to be asked is: How adequately are rural children being educated? First, it must be conceded that few children from any part of the country are being adequately prepared to become integral parts of our post-modern world. Adding to the special problems of rural schools is their weaker financial and social attractions for outstanding teachers and administrators.

The rural school is an anomaly in our society geared for rapid communication and instant change. (But so too is the urban school.) Rural schools are among the slowest changing organizations in America. Their snail-like rate of change continues despite education being one of the more powerful means used outside school to reshape other organizations. It seems that educators seldom practice what they teach.

When changes occur, they usually come largely as a response to external prompting and pressures rather than as a response to definitions of problems initiated within school systems. For example, the changes in mathematics followed Sputnik I, racial desegregation of public schools began in 1954 with the *Brown* decision of the United States Supreme Court, and programs of cultural enrichment were added in large numbers after private foundations and the federal government provided "seed" money for implementation.

Aside from a few changes, rural schools are still a main bulwark of institutionalized inequality; they reflect and perpetuate the conservative elements in our social class and racial stratification systems. Adding to this process are many rural administrators who themselves are committed to maintaining the status quo.

Administrators School administration did not become an applied science in America until the twentieth century. The early superintendents of schools were little more than clerks, while principals had even less power and prestige. Local communities were reluctant to turn their schools over to professional educators. Many rural communities still maintain great control over their schools and school personnel. Changes in operation of schools cannot be attributed to a single cause. Certainly, foremost causes of the emergence of administration as a discipline include the extension of compulsory school attendance laws and the hiring of additional personnel to deal with truancy problems.

In the early 1900s, school officials known as county superintendents began to acquire professional status. By 1930, some states required that county superintendents meet certain educational qualifications. In most rural communities, however, the major criterion for being a county superintendent was community acceptance. A 1934 study of 850 county superintendents noted that the average superintendent

> was a native American of long-established American ancestry and tradition. He was middle aged, a married man with at least two children. He had been reared in a large family on a farm by parents with a common school education who were church members and regular attendants. As for intellectual background, his reading opportunities were narrow and his travel in boyhood limited, his work largely confined to the farm, and his avocations healthy but poor in the intellectual and aesthetic ranges. In his community situations, he was a joiner and an active participant in all respectable organizations. A member, active worker, and regular attendant at church, he also served as a member of the board of such groups as the Rotary Club, the Chamber of Commerce, the Masons, and the Young Men's Christian Association. Probably much more than other professional men, he is drawn into all sorts of ex officio relations. . . . The spread of

his social and professional affiliations is from one to twenty, and the average eight.[2]

A similar study conducted in 1964 by the American Association of School Administrators noted little change in the characteristics of county superintendents. Rural school principals tend to have backgrounds similar to their superintendents.

School administrators can make the teachers' job a joy or a curse. Rural school teachers who can work with their administrators rather than having to work around them are indeed fortunate. Although most administrators are concerned with developing team spirit within their staff, few know how to do it. Consequently teacher morale becomes a school deficit, and staff attitudes in turn influence and affect the pupils.[3] Administrators in the better-run rural schools see to it that an orientation program for new teachers clearly defines the school's policies.

In carrying out policies, the principal must assume leadership in helping his staff to understand administrative policy. It is commonly agreed that the members of a teaching staff will more willingly accept and more effectively carry out policies which they understand. The principal can develop this understanding by presenting the reasons which led to each policy. The reasons behind policies may be related to state legislation, local pressures, or research. . . . Teachers have a need to be informed about current legislation, the trend of public opinion, the impact of educational research, and other pressures. Some teachers do not have the opportunity to grow in understanding unless they receive help.[4]

The interaction between administrators and teachers is much like the employer-employee relationship found in large businesses. The higher status of administrators sets the outer limits within which teachers can officially function. Unfortunately, most rural administrators have little training in supervisory techniques. This, however, is gradually changing as more rural school administrators are getting certificates and degrees in school administration. Most administrators realize the importance of such training.

The rural school principal frequently is in the awkward position of having to mediate between the ideal of allowing teachers and students academic freedom, and placating his generally conservative

2 Willis Rudy, *Schools in An Age of Mass Culture* (Englewood Cliffs, New Jersey, Prentice-Hall, 1965), 79.
3 Roy J. Haring, *The Role of the Superintendent in the Interrelationship of School and Community* (New York, Columbia University Press, 1953), 25.
4 Hilda Stocker and Dorothy Witted (eds.), *The Roles of Superintendents, Supervisors, and Principals in the Improvement of Instruction, with Respect to Current Forces Affecting Education* (Columbus, Ohio, Ohio State University, 1956), 30–32.

community. The intimate face-to-face interaction in small towns places more pressure on rural administrators than their urban counterparts. Those who conform to community norms are labeled "good old boys" who think the "right" way. Because urban school administrators are not as close to their communities as rural administrators, in many ways, it is easier to innovate in urban schools.

Effective administration of any school is difficult. Effective administration of inadequately financed and staffed rural schools is almost impossible; too many tasks simply cannot be completed. Some rural administrators double as teachers or clerical help in order to guide their schools through an academic year. Yet, there are isolated cases of rural administrators who manage to encourage and initiate innovative projects within their schools despite budget limitations.

In most rural schools, the principal provides such guidance services as are available. One major disadvantage of this practice is that he is responsible for the enforcement of school regulations as well as becoming a confidant of the pupils. Hence it is difficult for him to establish the comfortable, almost permissive kind of relationship with pupils that is basic to good counseling. Certainly, there are exceptions to this.

In some larger rural schools an assistant principal is responsible for guidance and counseling, while infractions of school regulations come under the jurisdiction of the principal. In other schools, the principal just happens to be the kind of person who can convey the warmth, empathy, and genuine interest that young people need and thus is able to dispel some of the fear and anxiety that most pupils associate with a visit to the principal's office. Most counseling and guidance, however, is unofficially given by the teachers.

Teachers　The percentage of well-qualified rural teachers is constantly increasing and many studies point to an even greater improvement in the future. Both educators and laymen alike have become aware of the importance of rural teachers being better prepared for their responsibilities. In all states certification requirements for rural teachers have been raised, and there is a pronounced upward trend in the amount of training rural teachers receive. The increase of small, consolidated schools and the growing tendency of teachers to shy away from big city assignments highlight the importance of nonurban schools. More well-prepared and able young teachers than ever before are entering rural schools. Furthermore, increased attention is being given to the kind of preparation prospective rural teachers should receive. More relevant programs for those preparing for rural teaching assignments are emerging in many teacher-education institutions.

The role of today's rural teachers can be thought of in terms of how they perceive of their own role or in terms of how others perceive it. Traditionally, teachers have thought of themselves in roles such as imparters of knowledge, disciplinarians, test givers, paper checkers. There is considerable research which tells us how nonteachers categoize teachers' roles. One author categorized the duties of teachers into six areas which in varying degrees could be thought of as the determinants of the teacher role: (1) a director of learning, (2) a counseling and guidance person, (3) a mediator of the culture, (4) a member of the school community, (5) a mediator between school and community, and (6) a member of the teaching profession.[5]

The more effective teachers quickly realize that in order to be successful they cannot overlook the backgrounds, needs, and problems of their students. The problems that the students bring to school affect their ability to profit from the school experiences, and the teacher's awareness of these problems and his behavior in relation to them influence each student's attitudes toward the teacher and toward school. An effective teacher must be able to assist the students in understanding and handling their problems and in making intelligent choices. Rural teachers who are unaware of these factors are likely to be ineffective in their classrooms. Every teacher is involved in guidance, whether he wishes it or not. His influence will not be neutral and it may be negative. He can weaken a child's self-confidence, increase his frustrations, and otherwise make his school adjustment difficult.[6]

There must be good rapport between teachers and pupils. A teacher should be able to give guidance and encouragement. Effective teachers stimulate pupils to express their own ideas and think for themselves. Not enough teachers help their students to be creative persons rather than sponges that soak up facts and drip them back when squeezed by examinations.

Although most rural school teachers have to do their own guidance, some small schools are fortunate enough to have guidance personnel whose function is the co-ordination of the guidance activities of the entire school. Teachers and guidance counselors who really care about their students are rare in any school system. Too many teachers

[5] Clarence E. Fishburn, "Learning the Role of the Teacher," *Journal of Teacher Education*, Vol. XVII (Fall, 1966), 329–31.

[6] Edgar G. Johnston, Mildred Peters, and William Evraiff, *The Role of the Teacher in Guidance* (Englewood Cliffs, New Jersey, Prentice-Hall, 1959), 7.

consider interaction with children as an obstacle standing between them and an annual salary. If they could get the salary without the interaction, they would do so. (But so would most other school personnel.) Few urban or rural teachers seem to like the children whom they must teach.

A student can be viewed as intelligent, an asset to the class, most likely to succeed; or he can be defined as being stupid, a trouble-maker, a born loser. At some point in the semester, most students are able to determine how their teachers define them, and they learn to play such roles. Teachers' attitudes are that powerful. Some teachers also engage in character assassination of certain children, especially low-achievers. In these instances, the student does not have a chance: he is branded for the duration of his life in the system. Little wonder these students drop out of school.

Where do teachers fail? Each one must ask himself, or perhaps a more significant answer would come from asking their failures— the dropouts. The thoughts of a dropout recorded by Marian Franklin is something each teacher should hear and ponder deeply.

> Teachers come in many sizes and shapes—large, small, young, old, tired, fresh, black, white, rich, poor.
> Some are kind, and some are not.
> Those who are mean are stinky.
> Some teachers know how to make you feel good;
> Others make you feel bad all over, deep down.
> Some help you not be afraid;
> Others keep you scared all the time.
> Some show you what you might try;
> Others tell you that you can't do it.
> They are No-No teachers. They're stinky.
> Lots of teachers go to college after they finish teaching you to see if they can learn some more.
> Some learn; some don't. Some it helps; some it don't.
> Those who don't try to learn and understand are stinky.
> Some teachers make you want to come to school every day; some teachers make you want to skip out as often as you can.
> I've had two who made me wish I had school on Saturday.
> I've been lucky. Some kids never find teachers like that.
> Some bring you lots of things to work with;
> Others make you stay in your seat and fill in blanks and memorize stuff.
> Those teachers are stinky.
> They say stinky words, give you stinky looks, and grade you on stinky report cards.
> Some teachers are great. Like I said, I had two like that.
> They put bandages on my hurts—on my heart, on my mind, on my spirit.

> Those teachers cared about me and let me know it.
> They gave me wings.[7]

The relationship between teachers, parents, administrators, and other teachers is important; but the interaction between the teacher and his students is the most important. In a few words: The climate of the class is set by the behavior of the teacher. The behavior of the teacher spreads through the class and is present even when the teacher is out of the room. The initial climate that a teacher develops is usually continued throughout the year. The opinion the teacher has of a child and the opinion a child has of himself affects his learning. Children who are expected to succeed will usually do so and children who feel good about themselves will usually succeed. Also, the converse is true.

It takes a special kind of commitment to be an effective teacher in a small school that can offer neither salaries nor instructional materials comparable to larger schools.

There is a tremendous staffing problem in rural school districts. **Problems of** Rural schools have a disproportionate share of teachers with provi- **recruitment** sional or substandard certificates. Except for those who have an altruistic desire to teach in "difficult" schools, rural schools offer little attraction to outstanding teachers. In many communities there is even a lack of adequate housing for teachers. Furthermore, community apathy is apparent regarding the quality of the teachers townspeople seek, their biggest desire merely to have a "warm body" to do a little teaching. Teachers aware of this latter condition are in danger of doing as little as possible, therein becoming victims of professional stagnation. Parents often add to this condition by their own low level of expectation of their children's abilities. Finally, many urban-oriented teachers do not easily adjust to the life-styles and norms of rural communities.

Securing better teachers for rural schools involves more than the improvement and lengthening of the teacher preparatory programs. It is equally important to secure better teacher candidates by making rural teaching more attractive and by developing procedures for selecting the best-qualified individuals from among the available candidates. In many communities, as a consequence of unsatisfactory experiences with "well-educated" teachers, rural people have lost faith in the value of extensive formal education for prospective teachers. In most instances lack of success in teaching was due not

[7] Marian Franklin, "Some Thoughts About Teaching and Teachers," *Today's Education* (February, 1970), 15.

to the amount or quality of preparation but to individual personality traits and an inability to adjust to the requirements of rural communities.

A very large problem in the area of staffing is the fact that rural schools are used by student teachers or teachers without certificates as a place to gain a year or more of experience. Once they earn their degree or certification, they go on to larger systems. Even worse, teaching in a rural school system is often used by college professors as a threat to low-achieving student teachers, or by placement agencies as a dumping ground for teachers who are believed to be too incompetent to teach elsewhere. When a particularly good teacher is found in the rural system, he is wooed by big city personnel officers who offer promises of a brighter future in their schools. It is very difficult for men teaching in rural schools to pass up the higher salaries offered by urban schools.

Rural schools have not been able to attract or hold enough able teachers primarily because salary, tenure, and living conditions in rural areas are inferior in comparison with conditions prevailing in cities. Rural school patrons and the nation must face the necessity of offering salaries that will attract capable young people to careers as rural teachers and compensate them for preparation beyond the bachelor's degree. Slowly, rural communities are beginning to realize that salaries paid rural teachers must be higher or at least more nearly in line with those paid by urban schools. Several states have helped their rural school districts to meet these requirements by establishing state-wide minimum salaries and providing financial assistance for paying them. Unless the compensation for rural teaching is increased, the imposition of higher standards of preparation may actually result in a lowering of the quality of future personnel. Many outstanding students are likely to give up the idea of teaching in rural schools because of the disparity between the exacting requirements for the work and its rewards.

In addition to increasing the salary scales in their schools, many rural communities are also trying to improve the conditions under which teachers live and work. Retirement and tenure laws are being improved, and, what is perhaps even more important, the coercive and constrictive claims many rural communities made on their teachers' private lives in the past are being relaxed. Most intelligent, sensitive, committed young teachers—and they are precisely the type many rural communities want to attract—shun a school district in which they do not have a reasonable amount of social and intellectual freedom.

A major problem of staffing rural schools relates to community awareness. In order to be accepted in the community, the teacher must either be from a rural district or else be deeply aware of the rural community conditions. The rural teacher must feel equal to the people; he must not act superior or condescending. This type of restrained, educated person is hard to find in any community. It seems as though most colleges do not teach humility. Furthermore, most rural people who become teachers accept jobs in larger school districts. Few return home to teach. College education tends to make people less tolerant of their low-income home towns.

The lack of adequate funds in most rural schools is seen in their inadequate equipment, texts, library and laboratory facilities, etc. In some poverty-stricken communities, the school is set up in a dilapidated shack. The amazing thing is that rural school personnel are able to overcome these obstacles and graduate as many students as they do.

August Hollingshead's article, "The School System," describes rural **Readings** schools in the 1940s. Much of the provincialism found in Elmtown nearly thirty years ago still characterizes many rural communities. For this reason, the article offers an excellent overview into problems encountered by rural school administrators and teachers who try to update the curricula.

Harold Sebold and George Redfern's article, "Roadblocks to Recruitment," spells out many of the reasons rural schools have difficulty attracting competent teachers, while Frank Mayer ("The Teacher from Appalachia") and George Rhodes ("Why Consider Teaching in a Small School?") offer reasons why many competent teachers are attracted to and remain in small schools. Perhaps the most encouraging articles in this section are Susan Rucker's, "Room Seven," and Lawana Trout's "We Ain't Unteachable . . . Just Unteached." Miss Rucker's notes about her students, anxieties, and aspirations illustrate the type of commitment and skills effective teachers must possess. Mrs. Trout demonstrates that teachers can break down prejudices within the classroom.

In terms of leadership, small school systems need the same top quality of leadership as the big city schools. Stephen Knezevich's article, "Small Communities Need Big Men," suggests the type of leadership needed. Reasons for needing more competent administrators are vividly sketched out by Stephen Romine in "Current Influences Changing the Principal's Role." In fact, as Kenneth Sand and Dale Hayes ("Why Small District Hired Two Superintendents") illustrate, the task of administering small school districts may require more administrators instead of fewer.

Finally, unless the community is involved as suggested in the article, "Home-School-Community Relations," most of the new techniques and innovations discussed in this section will die because of inadequate support. School, at best, is an extension of the home, not a competitor.

19. The School System

August B. Hollingshead

THE school is the only tax-supported institution devoted exclusively to the training of young Elmtowners in knowledge, skills, and values cherished by the culture. Practically all children between six and thirteen years of age spend from six to seven hours a day, five days a week, from early September until the following June in and around a public elementary school located within walking distance of their homes. After age fourteen most children are connected with the high school for at least a brief period, but as they grow older an increasing percentage leaves school for the work world, so that approximately only one-third graduate from high school.

The Elmtown schools are operated by a combination of local laymen and professionally trained educators under the authority of state law. State law decrees that a school district must provide a common school education[1] at public expense; however, the school is essentially a local responsibility, particularly with respect to policy. State educational officials have little control over the Elmtown system beyond their power to withdraw state aid funds in extreme cases for violations of law or administrative rulings.

The territory encompassed by the Elmtown communal area is organized into thirty-three school districts. Thirty-two are rural districts that support one-room schools where grades one through eight are taught. Each of these schools is administered by three trustees elected by the citizens of the district. They are supported largely by real estate taxes levied by the school board on its taxing district, which coincides with the area of the school district, supplemented by some state aid funds. These rural schools have no connection with the schools in Elmtown.

From *Elmtown's Youth* (New York, John Wiley & Sons, 1949), 121–47. Reprinted and abridged by permission. Elmtown is a fictitious midwestern town.

1 The courts of Home State have ruled that a common school education includes four years of high school.

The Elmtown schools are organized into one district which includes the town and a few sections in Elm Township adjacent to one side of the incorporated area. There are three two-room ward schools, a central elementary school, and a high school in the system. Grades one through four are taught in the ward schools, one through eight in Central School, and nine through twelve in the high school. Since we are concerned primarily with high-school-aged young people, and since the high school is a center of conflict, our discussion will be confined largely to Elmtown High School.

Even though school districts are not required to maintain a high school—and none of the thirty-two rural districts within the communal area has done so—the state law, however, has made it obligatory upon the elementary school district to pay the tuition on a per capita basis of its pupils who wish to attend an available high school.[2] A statute passed in 1917 provides that, for the purpose of levying a tax to pay the tuition of eighth-grade graduates in high schools established in other districts or towns, the territory in each county not included in a high school district is a non–high school district. In accordance with this statute, all land in Home County not in a high school district is organized into a non–high school district and a tax levied to pay for the tuition of pupils who attend high schools in other districts. Inasmuch as the only high school in the community is located in Elmtown, pupils from the non–high school district covered by the rural portion of the communal area come to Elmtown High School. Thus, the rural territory is covered by two districts, the common school district and the non–high school district. This means the levying of two taxes, one to support the local elementary school and the other to pay high school tuition on a per capita basis for students from the non–high school area who attend high school. The tax rate levied to support the elementary school varies from one district to another, whereas the rate is uniform on all non–high school land in the county. Real estate within the Elmtown school system, however, is taxed only once, since this is a single administrative unit that includes all the schools under one board of education. The significance of this point will become clear when the relationship between the policies of the Elmtown Board of Education and land ownership is discussed.

The board of education Responsibility for the operation of the Elmtown school system rests

2 The courts have ruled that it is impracticable to maintain a high school in every district, but it is not impossible to give every child the benefit of a high school education by sending him to a convenient district where a high school is maintained.

in the hands of a seven-man board of education. The president of the board is elected annually at the school election held in April. Two members are elected also at the annual election for three-year terms. Theoretically, any adult citizen in the district may be a candidate for the school board, and, if he receives enough votes, elected. In practice, the members of the board of education come mainly from the two upper classes[3] and have to qualify under informal ground rules. Even to be considered for the board a person has to be male, Protestant, Republican, a property owner, preferably a Rotarian, or at least approved by the Rotarians. (Rotarians are proud of the way they have controlled the selection of the board for more than twenty-five years.)

When a vacancy is to occur, the selection of a man for the board of education is left to the president of the board. He discusses possible candidates with his friends on the board and in the Rotary Club. Generally he invites a fellow Rotarian with whom he believes he can work to become a candidate. The president then files this man's name with the election clerk; nothing is said publicly about the im-

3 Henry Dotson, a lifetime Elmtown resident prominent in business circles, described the top social class as follows: "The top class is what we call the four hundred or society class. . . . First, I'd say money is the most important. In fact, nobody's in this class if he doesn't have money; but it just isn't money alone. You've got to have the right family connections, and you've got to behave yourself, or you get popped out. And if you lose your money, you're dropped. . . . There's no use talking about people being in a certain class or a certain portion of a class unless they are accepted by the people in that group as equals" (p. 70).

Social Classes—Elmtown

CLASS I: The top social class in which wealth and lineage were combined through the economic, legal, and family systems in such a manner that membership in this class was fairly stable from one generation to another. Members of this class tended to have their position ascribed through inheritance.

CLASS II: Almost one-half of the families in Class II achieved their positions through their own efforts; the remainder inherited them, but a further rise was precluded, since their origins were too well known and enough time had not elapsed between the start of their ascent and their present position to allow them to be accepted in the exclusive circles of Class I. Class II is sometimes called the "new rich."

CLASS III: The pivotal position of Class III was demonstrated by the attitudes its members held. Members of Class III defined people in Class I and Class II as being superior to themselves. On the other hand, they believed themselves to be above "the masses" and "the common man." Class III families had sufficient income for the conveniences and comforts of life, but they had little surplus to invest in wealth-producing enterprises.

CLASS IV: Individuals in Class IV, on the whole, were aware of the inferior prestige position they occupied in comparison with the higher classes; furthermore they resented the attitudes most persons in the higher classes exhibited toward them. However, they took pride in the fact that they were not so badly off as the people in Class V. Persons in Class IV were wage earners who barely earned enough to live from week to week.

CLASS V: The lowest-ranking social class, looked upon as the scum of the city by the higher classes. When they worked, the men were unskilled and semi-skilled laborers or machine operators.

pending vacancy or the forthcoming election until after the last date for filing has passed. Then the *Bugle* runs a news item stating that the date for filing names for the school election has passed, that such-and-such men have filed as candidates for the board of education, and that Mr. X has filed again for president of the board. Little additional publicity is given to the election until the *Bugle* carries the necessary legal notices of the polling places and names of candidates. On election day, only a handful of voters go to the polls to elect the hand-picked candidates. . . .

The president was the key officer on the board. As its head and chief executive, he made day-to-day decisions in collaboration with the superintendent on all questions which involved the school's relation to the community. Since the president was closer to the administration of the system than the other members of the board, he played a more influential role than the others in the formation of policy. The board as a whole was responsible for salary schedules, maintenance of the school plant, appointment of personnel, and general policy.

Evidence derived from personal interviews showed that the members of the board of education for more than a generation have been concerned primarily with two phases: operating the schools as economically as possible, and seeing that teachers conform, in the classroom and in their personal lives, to the most conservative economic, political, religious, and moral doctrines prevailing in the local culture. Past and current board members believed that the school should reflect in its administration and teaching all that is traditionally good and wholesome in the Middle Western American small-town life— if it did not cost too much.

From interviews and attendance at board meetings it became clear that the question of cost was uppermost in their thoughts whenever any innovation was suggested. The problem of cost versus educational values was particularly acute whenever the high school was involved, for high school education was far more expensive than elementary training. The members of the board were of the opinion that not everyone had the ability to justify a high school education. They believed that many boys and girls who were in high school would have been better off on the farm or at the mill. They were interested, however, in seeing that everyone who could profit by high school education was provided with the necessary facilities, but they were not clear in their conception of who could profit by such an education. In general, they meant sons and daughters of the three higher classes, and of class IV, if they behaved properly Adolescents in class V were not considered to have enough ability to profit from a high school education. No board member was found who at any time believed that it was the responsibility of the community to provide educational facilities for *all* high-school-aged adolescents. When it was suggested that the traditional type of high school education might not be the type needed for the lower classes, the suggestion was countered usually with the argument that vocational education cost too much per student to be put into effect on a broad scale; besides, the boy or girl could learn the same type of skill "from life." . . .

Salaried personnel hired by the board executed its policies and made the school system function. Forty-one of the forty-five persons employed by the board were professionally trained. Forty were teachers licensed by the state. The school nurse, the clerk of the board, and the custodians were Elmtowners. The board followed two policies in the employment of teachers and administrators: local girls were hired whenever possible in the elementary schools; outsiders were appointed to administrative positions and in the high school. **Personnel**

These policies combined with the administrative organizations of the system and its shortage of funds produced a series of intraschool conflicts which kept practically every employee on edge. The clerk of the board functioned as the superintendent's secretary. She was hired by the president of the board and reported directly to him. Her family had been politically active in Elmtown for three generations. The superintendent did not trust her, and she did not approve his educational policies. The chief custodian was a strict Lutheran who reported "things going on at the high school" to the Lutheran minister and the Lutheran member of the board. His first assistant was a Norwegian and a Lutheran. Neither one approved of the high school dances, parties, and carnivals held in the school. The custodians were hired by the board and administratively directly under it, but for practical purposes they took their orders from the superintendent and principals. As local people, they believed in the rightness of the values prevailing in the board and the community in so far as they pertained to the training of boys and girls in the public schools.

Elementary teachers were split into two distinct groups, outsiders and local girls. Three-fourths of these teachers had been born, reared, and educated in Elmtown. After they had completed Elmtown High School, they had gone away to teachers' colleges or state universities for their professional training; then they had received appointments in the local system. These women generally came from class III families, with a few from class II. Local girls hired into the system followed one of two paths. They either taught for a few years, then married and raised a family, or stayed on year after year as "maiden ladies." Those who married had to leave the system immediately, as local sentiment would not tolerate a married teacher between 1930 and 1941, when so many persons were out of work. The "pedagogical veterans" who made teaching their career were often highly respected by families in the three higher classes. As a class I woman phrased it, "They are such fine teachers. They know the background of each child and teach accordingly." Class IV parents with some frequency accused them of "giving" good grades to the children of board members and the aristocrats. The local teachers usually lived at home with their parents, or in the family home if the parents were dead; so their living expenses were generally lower than those of the outside teachers, and they were better able to get along on the salaries they received than the outsiders.

All outside teachers were dissatisfied, for one reason or another, with either the school or the town. Their frustration was veiled carefully from the local teachers and the townspeople for fear of being considered "disloyal" or "unprofessional." Even among themselves they "guarded their tongues" for fear that their remarks would be carried to the town's gossips, the superintendent, or the board. As a group, they were frustrated by the controls imposed on them by the community and the low salaries they received. Their private lives were circumscribed by taboos, customs, expectancies, and obligations that ranged all the way from where they had to live to where they could buy necessities and to how they might utilize their leisure time without creating a chain of gossip that would reflect adversely upon the teacher, the system, and the profession.

Teachers were required to live in town, and it was suggested that they locate within the three better residential areas, but not in the four hundred area. Unmarried teachers were restricted to a relatively few homes and apartments. One man said that when he came to town he was told that since the houses and apartments owned by the members of the board and "a former County Superintendent of Roads" were all rented, he could rent from whomsoever he desired, but not near the canal, north of the railroad, or more than three blocks east of Freedom Street. "We were told that, if we got over on the east side close to the mill and down by the canal, we would be talked about and looked down upon." Yet this teacher severely criticized the elementary school principal when he bought a house outside the approved area. The president of the bank believed that the elementary school principal was presumptuous in buying a house. His comments were, "He doesn't need to think that because he bought a house the board is under any obligation to keep him. I don't think a person with a school teacher's salary shows very good judgment when he buys a house and puts a four thousand dollar mortgage on it."

Strong hints were made by businessmen, especially through the superintendent, to the effect that teachers should purchase their coal, clothes, groceries, cosmetics, and other accessories from locally owned stores. One teacher was criticized for buying her cosmetics from a drug store owned by a small chain with headquarters in another community. In this case, the wife of a local druggist called the superintendent's wife's attention to what the teacher had done, and he in turn enlightened the teacher. Teachers were forced to contribute to community enterprises, such as Girl Scouts and Boy Scouts, tuberculosis and cancer drives, and the milk fund for underprivileged children.

The community's interest in their religious life was not neglected. They were obliged to attend church, teach Sunday School classes, sing in the choir, act as youth leaders, and make annual pledges.

The outside teachers were largely isolated from the community's social life. The superintendent and the high school principal belonged to Rotary; the elementary school principal was in the Lions Club; but the other men did not belong to any civic or fraternal groups. The women teachers were invited into the Women's Club but, as one teacher said, "As complimentary members only—we don't actually belong." The superintendent related his feeling of isolation in these words:

> We have been here for two years now and I am convinced we are completely and absolutely outsiders. Actually, we have no friends. We don't have a single family in this town that we could call up and tell we were coming over to spend the evening. This is the worst town I have ever seen in that way. The people will be fine to you on the street or in church and treat you nice on public occasions. Everybody will shake hands and make pleasant remarks, but it doesn't go farther than that.

Teachers were not expected to hold parties or dinners and thereby attempt to further their interests by inviting townspeople to them. If they did, the local people criticized them for putting on airs. The superintendent warned his teachers on orders from the board not to smoke in public or to be seen in a tavern or at a public dance. The difference between what a teacher could do and what a board member could do is illustrated by this wishful statement of one teacher:

I would really like to see what they have in the Five Stars. I have been told they have good meals in there and a fine bar, a roulette wheel, a crap table, and other games. I have on occasion passed there and seen members of the board get out of their cars and go in there for an evening. I know some parents patronize it, but, if a teacher were seen in there, the board would ask for his resignation right now.

Demands on outside teachers and the low salaries produced a very high rate of turnover in the high school, where all the professional personnel were outsiders. All outsiders from the superintendent to the least experienced girl believed that they were inadequately paid. . . .

In the two years he had been in the system, the superintendent had lived through hectic experiences. Eight out of fifteen high school teachers were new in the fall of 1941; five had been hired the week school started to replace teachers who had resigned at the last minute to accept positions elsewhere. Three had been in the school a year or less, and four from two to three years; only one had been there four years, but he was desperately anxious to leave. He did resign at the end of the year under pressure from the board and the superintendent. Three of the four high school teachers who had taught in Elmtown more than two years were married men with families. They desired to leave, but their family obligations made them hesitate even though they received salaries that were lower than the average semi-skilled mill worker.

20. Roadblocks to Recruitment

Harold Sebold and George B. Redfern

RECRUITMENT of a teaching staff is a complex and difficult problem for any school system, but it is especially so for schools in rural areas and in urban centers where large numbers of pupils come from below-average backgrounds. A companion problem is retaining competent personnel once they have been hired.

Probably nothing is more basic to this whole area of concern than the increasing difficulty of convincing boards of education and the general public that a real and dangerous shortage of qualified teachers exists and has existed for many years. Too often school administrators, particularly those in rural areas, in conjunction with certifying officials have followed a policy of keeping classrooms open at all costs. The results are sometimes questionable.

In some instances lack of respect for appropriate qualifications has been apparent. Quality has been sacrificed for expediency and the public has learned to live too well with it. This is dangerous, for it may be a long road back to a high level of certification requirements.

Along with the need for quality in rural schools, another disturbing factor is the transient nature of personnel. In many cases, rural areas are simply intern training centers from which teachers move when opportunities become available in larger, often urban, systems. With district reorganization and improved working conditions, plus better salaries, this mobility has been lessened.

The whole physical environment which surrounds rural teaching makes it difficult to retain qualified teachers in rural areas. Consolidations frequently mean buildings far from suitable living quarters. Even buildings in small communities are frequently not accompanied by desirable living environments.

All too often the teacher is expected to do all the adjusting to a new environment, when some adjustment of the environment to the teacher would be more appropriate. School officials and community

From *Ohio Schools*, November, 1964, pp. 18–19. Reprinted by permission.

leaders have been slow to recognize their responsibilities in satisfying the personal comforts of the new teacher.

Recruitment of teachers for the nonurban school is at best a heartbreaking assignment. Early recruitment is almost impossible, since most qualified teachers are "looking over the field" and reserving their choices of position for the best offers—usually better-paying positions in urban or suburban areas. Unfortunately many rural administrators are becoming resigned to the acceptance of whatever staff is available.

The truth is that the rural scene need no longer exist as something inferior in its inducement for the new teacher. Recruitment for rural teaching could be vastly helped by a concerted effort on the part of rural school administrators to portray the real merits and advantages of nonurban teaching. Obviously, this effort needs to be sufficiently supported by such factors as adequate salary and an attractive living and teaching environment on par with other school districts.

The development of more adequate personnel staffs, whose prime responsibility would be the recruitment and management of teachers would be helpful. While small districts cannot presently afford this kind of administrative service, it may be hoped that development of large service centers for rural schools will provide this assistance.

An outmoded insistence on making a local school administrator be everything to everybody will never provide the solution to the particular and persistent problems of adequate staff personnel. Two staff members of a centrally located education center who are trained in recruitment practices and procedures could work toward filling one hundred vacancies as easily and efficiently as ten.

But all the personnel problems are not in the country. What about the slum and impoverished areas of cities? How may more teachers be prepared, employed, and retained here? One obvious answer is to increase the number who are specifically trained to work in schools serving culturally disadvantaged pupils.

It is essential for teachers in the larger urban school systems to understand the social changes that have been taking place in large cities and the implications these have for education. Urban renewal, changing community and housing patterns, pupil mobility, poverty, family disorganization as well as minority group upheaval are having terrific impacts upon schools. Changes in the inner cores of cities and the flight to suburbia by middle-class white families have created complex and persistent problems for teachers and school administrators.

The place to begin is in teacher preparation. Colleges and universities must do more "market research" and consider the possibility of specifically training a substantial number of teachers to work in schools having large lower socio-economic enrollments.

These teachers need to understand the complexities of urban life and the significance of the divergencies in the cultural characteristics of pupils who attend school in cities. This involves new emphases in knowledge as well as teaching techniques.

The demand for teachers in large cities is so great that specialized training programs are not likely to fulfill the need. It is essential, therefore, that school systems develop in-service programs which may give teachers already on the job some of the information, insight, and skill which will enable them to work more effectively with culturally disadvantaged pupils.

Such training must be in three areas: (a) a greater emphasis on the implications of cultural differences among pupils, with particular stress on understanding how pupils from lower socio-economic backgrounds behave and are motivated; (b) a fuller utilization of all the resources of the school system in promoting optimum learning situations, with emphasis on compensatory activities; and (c) a much greater familiarization with the community where the school is located. This means better acquaintance with community agencies, parents, church leaders and others who are a part of the environment of the pupils.

A large school system usually has a variety of positions to fill, which puts a premium on matching the individual with the position for which he is best qualified. Pressure should not be put on the applicant to accept an assignment for which he is not well suited. When he appears to have the potential for an assignment in a school serving culturally deprived pupils, however, there should be no reluctance to encourage him to accept the challenge. Once the individual accepts the assignment, he should be given every possible help to insure his success.

Turnover is costly—especially in schools serving underprivileged pupils—yet it continues to remain high in these schools. How may it be reduced?

Experience indicates that if teachers are specifically prepared to teach in schools in underprivileged neighborhoods, they are more successful and more likely to remain.

Care should be taken that teachers in these schools should not feel they are working in isolation. They should be helped to realize that they are an important part of a well-designed and challenging program; thus they are more likely to experience a sense of belonging to a vital educational venture.

Recognition of the teacher's success is also important. Above all, however, teachers of children with lower socio-economic backgrounds should be made to feel that they hold positions equal in prestige to any other in the school system.

21. The Teacher from Appalachia

Frank C. Mayer

EACH year, there is a flow of teachers from Appalachia to the better-paying Eastern and Midwestern school districts. This region, because of its low teachers' salaries, is a fertile recruiting area for many fast-growing districts which are in need of great numbers of teachers. Each year, more administrators from farther distances are visiting the area in search of teachers. Because Appalachian leaders are finding that the best teachers of the region are being lured out of state, teachers' salaries have been increased in an attempt to stop this attrition.

As an administrator in a district bordering Appalachia, I had the experience of recruiting, interviewing, engaging, and supervising many teachers from this area. Many of the district's finest teachers were reared and attended public schools and colleges there. Since drive and determination are needed to break family and provincial ties, these two qualities were possessed by the candidates.

In some districts, 50–70 per cent of the teaching staffs originate in Appalachia. This is especially true in fast-growing regions where large numbers of teachers have to be acquired quickly.

Where do Appalachian teachers relocate? How do they adjust in new districts? How are they accepted by outside staffs and communities?

Typically, these teachers locate geographically so that weekend trips home can be made as conveniently and quickly as possible. Because the teachers usually maintain strong family ties, home visits are made frequently. Some return each weekend. Several teachers had their wives and children stay in Appalachia, rented a room in the new district, and commuted home for weekends and holidays. Many maintain ties in the home towns by keeping the family homes or farms and renting them to local citizens. Presumably, it is a comfort to know that, if anything were to go wrong, the old homestead

From *School and Society*, October, 1966, pp. 324–25. Reprinted by permission.

would be available. Some continue to purchase home-state automobile licenses even though employed for several years in another state. These examples indicate a reluctance on the part of some of the teachers to cut the cords of the "old life."

The Appalachian teachers tend to feel more secure in school districts which employ teachers from or near their home areas. The social life of the teachers, for example, is largely restricted to activities among members of the group. Moving to the new area does involve adjustment problems, however. There is normally a higher standard of living which exists in the new community, and the way of life is considerably different. The new arrivals must adjust to a new value system, the mores are different, and the ways of rearing children, keeping house, food selection and preparation are different.

The members of the group as a whole seem to adjust remarkably well, but there are exceptions where the new candidates simply cannot adjust to the new environment. Two brothers decided to teach in Northern Ohio at salaries several thousand dollars per year more than they earned in their low-paying home area. After several weeks, one of the brothers failed to adjust to the new school and community and simply walked off the job. The other brother, experiencing similar difficulties, resigned prior to the completion of the first semester. Both brothers, having failed to adjust, returned to Appalachia.

In some cases, large segments of the family locate in the same district. After the first member of the family finds employment, news of the better teaching and living conditions soon reaches siblings, cousins, and friends. A chain reaction of moves sometimes follows to the new district, culminating with the parents, often teachers themselves, moving into the new area.

Often the new arrivals bring with them speech characteristics of their geographic areas. If the teacher has a heavy accent, communication problems may result. Students and parents experience difficulty in understanding some of the teachers. In one system, a supervisor administered achievement tests in order to provide uniform testing conditions. A principal complained that the tester had a heavy accent, the students had difficulty understanding him, and, as a result, the test scores were not accurate.

Another teacher who was conscious of her accent, used a tape recorder to judge her speech. She confided that she was concerned over her accent and asked for suggestions for improvements. She continued to work diligently toward improvement with the aid of the tape recorder.

Many of the newly located teachers were impressed with the school buildings and educational programs they found in their new location. As a part of an employment interview, I conducted a teacher through the building in which a vacancy existed. She was amazed at the beauty and caliber of the building. "You mean this beautiful room (a multipurpose room) is used for a cafeteria?" was a comment. The structure was one of the older buildings, built with P.W.A. funds, and in need of remodeling.

The teacher turnover rate among the relocated Appalachian teachers is low. After the initial move, a second move to a better school system would require, as a rule, moving farther away from home and family ties. It also would involve the risk of moving into a new area, meeting a new group of people, and perhaps adjustment to still another new set of values.

Are Appalachian teachers ahead, financially, when they move to better economic areas? Salary schedules are often one to four thousand dollars higher and retirement systems and sick leave provisions are better. Although living in the new areas involves higher costs, teachers are able to enjoy higher standards of living. Since people in the new community dress better, the Appalachian teacher, too, improves his manner of dress. They frequent new forms of entertainment which are available. The newcomers complain that they are not much ahead financially; that they could "bank" as much money or more back home. However, they enjoy the new higher standards of living and the improved working conditions. Seldom does one return to Appalachia on a permanent basis.

22. Why Consider Teaching in a Small School?

George S. Rhodes

TODAY the typical progressive business teacher often feels that he or she must seek employment in the large metropolitan school systems, which, of course, generally have large teaching units. The advantages viewed as accruing from such a position are higher compensation, more specialized teaching assignments, better facilities for teaching and a broader choice of cultural opportunities.

Although these advantages often do accrue to the teachers employed in typical urban school systems, I feel that the advantages offered to business teachers by smaller school systems are, in many instances, more attractive. In presenting the case for the teaching of business in the small high school I shall draw on three years of business teaching experience in a high school of approximately two hundred students.

As far as compensation is concerned, it is generally true that teachers' salaries in larger school systems are higher than the level prevalent in smaller systems. Quite often, however, because of the value accorded to the business education program by the smaller schools, local supplements are added to the basic teacher pay scale as an extra benefit for business teachers. Such supplements make the business teacher's salary comparable to, if not higher than, the average teaching salaries of urban public school systems. Why the business program is so regarded in the small community will be dealt with a bit later.

A second advantage claimed for the large business program is that it requires a large number of business teachers and allows each to specialize in a particular small area of instruction. Considering that business education itself is a specialized area, I feel that teacher specialization has reached a point of questionable returns. In one school that I am familiar with, the administration takes pride in the fact that each teacher instructs in only a narrow subject area, with

From *Business Education World*, April, 1965, pp. 17ff. Reprinted by permission.

one business teacher even being limited to teaching Typing I, another Typing II. This degree of specialization is defended on the grounds that it allows more competent and proficient teaching while at the same time requiring less teacher preparation. I feel that this develops a routine that leads to individual dullness and threatens to stifle professional growth. Another cost of such teacher specialization is that it also forces "specialization" in knowledge of students. All good instructors are truly interested in the total attainment of their students. The edge of this objective is blunted by specialization of instruction. Unlike the teacher in a small school, who has all business students for multiple classes over a period of years and comes to know them as individuals with their own aspirations and hopes, the specialized teacher is likely to be associated with his students in a very limited sense; he is often likely to refer to them by seat number rather than by name. Such a situation is likely to result from teaching a single subject to five different sections for perhaps a single semester. All teachers take pride in their professional accomplishments, which are reflected in their students' achievements. Who is likely to feel greater pride at the successful graduation and employment of a business student—the teacher who has taught him only a single course or the teacher who has conducted the entire business program?

The argument that better teaching facilities are provided by the larger schools is often true. Since, however, business education is so often regarded in a more favorable manner in the smaller schools, this difference in attitude is often translated into funds for providing facilities comparable to those of more able systems. Also, I feel that too much emphasis has been placed on teaching *equipment*, when such emphasis should properly be placed on teaching *abilities*. For that matter, as state influence becomes more and more evident in education, variations in school facilities occur less and less in proportion to the financial abilities of the local systems.

It is generally assumed that there is a close correlation between cultural and recreational opportunities and population concentration, and it might appear that this advantage cannot be offset by pleasant rural settings. Consideration must, however, be given to the vast improvements in communication in recent years, as evidenced by the greater prevalence of highway systems and automobiles. Today, no one really is isolated from cultural opportunities. Population concentration must also, in all fairness, be viewed from its negative side—traffic congestion, high crime rates, high cost of living, and so forth. The rise of suburbia provides evidence of the negative effects of urban life.

I have been defending the small school against larger school systems in general terms. I shall now point out some advantages of teaching *business subjects* in the small school that exist only to a very limited degree in large school systems. In typical rural school systems, the number of graduates going on to college work is relatively small in comparison with the number of college-bound graduates from the large urban schools. Consequently, the small school system has a great interest for employment by means of a terminal vocational program. The continuing expansion of office occupations and the number of young people entering them causes a high premium to be placed on the business program in these schools (as I have already pointed out in discussing salaries). Quite often, business education is the only vocational training program offered by the small schools.

The implications of these facts are obvious. In the urban schools, with as high as 90 per cent of the students—including the most able students—following college preparatory programs, the business program is often de-emphasized and is frequently filled with students of generally low ability. Thus, the business program of the small school usually occupies an enviable status, whereas its counterpart in the large schools often is valued at the opposite end of the totem pole, as college-prep curriculums, loaded with the so-called academic disciplines, crowd out the offerings of the business program. With the latter held in high regard in the smaller schools, the prestige of the business instructor in the community is, of course, on a similar level.

As a matter of fact, I feel that the teaching profession in general is held in higher esteem in nonurban communities. The population of these communities is generally drawn from the socio-economic middle class, the population stream that has developed and now maintains the predominant values held by our society. It is from this group that the vast majority of teachers come, and with whom they share common attitudes and values. Logically, teachers are comfortable in this occupational setting.

For the business teacher who desires variety with a minimum of routine in his work, the small school affords an outlet. This situation, I feel, permits the teacher to be better rounded, both as an instructor and as an individual. The close student-teacher relationship that exists in the smaller school enables the teacher to recognize his students' abilities and weaknesses. With all due respect for most schools' counseling programs, I believe that this knowledge makes the business teacher better qualified than any one else to render vocational counsel to students. But perhaps even more important is that the close student-teacher relationship develops friendships of association that go a long way toward making teaching a rewarding occupation. Teaching *individuals* is preferable to teaching seat numbers.

Although, as I have pointed out, greater flexibility is allowed the business teacher in the small school, it must be recognized that this, in turn, places greater responsibilities on the teacher. Certainly the business teacher going into the small school must be well grounded in the various sectors of business education—and, equally important, must enjoy teaching. Of course, it is apparent that more work is required to conduct a full business program than to teach a mere segment; but the rewards of the extra work are many. (I hasten to add that these remarks apply to many schools that, although small, employ more than one business teacher.)

It is not the purpose of this article to discourage teachers in urban school systems, but to persuade young teachers to investigate the opportunities of teaching in the nonurban schools, keeping in mind the advantages I have presented. Also, from a purely personal point of view, I desired to explain, for the benefit of those who have so often inquired, why I do not teach in one of the larger systems.

23. Room Seven

Susan Rucker

I began teaching special education intermediate the second week of school. Because I walked into a situation that had already been established, it was very difficult for me and for the children. On my side I had absolutely no teaching materials with me. I had never seen the children; I had never seen the books they were using. I had never seen their files. I had no idea of any of the rules of the county, the principal's rules, how to take your children to the lunch room, where the toilet was. It took me two days to find the teacher's toilet. I simply walked in at eight o'clock Monday morning and waited for my pupils to arrive. And they did!

On their side I was the fourth teacher in two weeks. The first question they asked me was: "How long are you going to be here, lady?" My pupils came in something like a tidal wave, and we struggled a great deal. We are still struggling, and I expect to be struggling for a long time. I don't know if I am so stupid I don't know what I am doing, or so stubborn I won't quit what I am doing. But we are going to manage, my class and I. We are going to manage.

Here I came, a new teacher, knowing nothing. And you know what? I had playground duty. That meant for one week I was not even able to look at my files. For the first week, I went over to Peg's room, the primary special teacher, and I cried. I went home and I cried some more. The second week was a little better because I didn't have the playground duty, and I had time over the weekend to work up some lesson plans. For the first six weeks I spent every night, three, four, five hours a night, doing work for my room.

The teachers who had been there before me didn't do very much. The room did not have crayons, scissors, or rulers. There were no construction or drawing papers. There was no soap at the sink or chalk at the blackboard. There were no staples; the stapler was bro-

From an unpublished speech, Bowie, Maryland, November 1, 1969. Printed by permission.

ken. There were no pencils; there was no paper to write on. There were few books. Some of the pupils didn't have books; some of them did have books. Some of them had picked up books that they thought they would like to read because they were sixth grade books and told me those were the books they were reading in. I just had to start from scratch.

The Students

The music and physical education teachers had scheduled the special education rooms with only one (thirty minute) session per week and one (thirty minute) physical education session per week. My pupils are almost all hyperactives. Their attention span is much less than the "normal" child of their own age. They are all so keyed up and so tense. Why, I've seen Carlette so tense that she literally devoured a brand-new pencil. I don't think she swallowed it, but she chomped it up in her mouth. It just disappeared from her hand, passed through her lips, and went into her mouth—even the metal piece! That's just a slight indication of how tense, how tied up in knots, these children are.

They needed more physical education and they needed more music. Music is a socially acceptable (I hate these words) way of releasing such tension. One thirty minute session a week, my God! With the co-operation of the physical education and music teachers, we now have at least one of the two things happening every day. My pupils are getting to the point now where they remember pretty much what comes when. This gives me a break, and I'll admit I need a break. They also need to get away from me.

Now I would like to tell you a little bit about each of my children. I walked in and I found ten little darlings, one of which the entire school is terrorized by. I have three girls and seven boys. I think I am more of a girl's teacher than a guy's teacher, but I'll learn. Of my ten, I have six blacks and four whites. All of the children are low income; several are welfare; four are free lunch, free breakfast.

Their home conditions initially appalled me. Given their disadvan- Carlette taged backgrounds, I was surprised that they knew as much as they did! When there aren't clocks on the walls, when there are eleven people standing because there is no place to sit, with coats on because there is no heat, in a three-room shack, linoleum hammered over holes in the floor, babies wetting pants and making presents of newspapers to me, it's amazing that they know as much as they do know and that they give and are as much as they really give and are.

No wonder Carlette shows you something she has from the other side of the room because with eleven people standing around you at home, you want space very badly, and you fight for space, and you fight for what you've got and what you hope to get because if you don't fight you don't get it. Carlette chops wood for the home in the afternoon after school because they don't have gas or electric heat. When she finishes chopping the wood, she gets buckets and carries water because they don't have inside plumbing. Somebody in the great somewhere gave Carlette a test and because she couldn't recognize items such as washing machines and irons, they decided she was slow. And they labeled her "special education retarded." But she can work like the very devil—chopping wood and carrying water, and math and reading. When she comes up to me and says, "I want to read this book now to you," and lays those big, wood-chopping hands on my arm, I listen. I listen not only because I know she can do me damage (which doesn't bother me one bit) but because she wants to read. There is not a child in my class who doesn't want to learn, and there is not a child in my class who cant learn. They do have problems learning, and their biggest problem is *social relations*.

Carlette is known all over the school as a fighter. She'll fight anybody, and you better not tangle with her. It's difficult to instill feminine virtues into such a creature. She has huge hands (I guess from chopping wood) and huge feet (I guess from stomping on heads). In addition, she has a chip on her shoulder you wouldn't imagine, and I guess there's a right for it to be there.

Her mother is a cripple. She sits in a chair in a corner, huddled up, shriveled, deformed. Her eyes don't focus, they sort of wander around. But the grandmother considers herself lucky to have that much of a daughter. Carlette's mother doesn't do much more than produce children, and she's had nine. Then there are Carlette's older sisters, who have a few illegitimate children. None of the children are legitimate in this family. They do claim the father. I think they even claim his name, but they don't claim anything else. Carlette's father doesn't give child support. He just comes in and lays Momma every once in a while and goes. So Carlette is super-sensitive about her father, who they say is called "Bo Diddily." And they call her that to tease her every once in a while. The reason she's so sensitive about Bo Diddily is because he's in jail. Who wouldn't be sensitive about that?

My little Carlette loves to read. This past month I've been weeding the readers out and lowering their standards a little bit. They've been overshooting their marks, and they can't handle it. It makes

reading a chore for them and for me. I've brought some of them down
the reading ladder as many as two steps, which means that I have
six or seven groups, and some of them are so enthusiastic that they
have finally found a book they can read. They bring me two or three
and want to read from each one at each sitting. Sometimes I read
in fifteen different books during the day for our reading block. Carlette decided that she wanted to read a second level book. She picked
up the workbook that was sitting by the readers, and that's what
she's working in.

At first, she would pout, stick her lower lip out, and thump people
on the head and beat them in the ears, and I mean beat them. She
tells me stories about beating an older sister with a copper pipe.
Carlette's no slouch when it comes to a good beating. But lately, in
the last two weeks, if I walk by, she doesn't turn her head, and she
doesn't shrug her shoulders, or whip around and not look at me.
She'll even come up to me and let me touch her. She lets me put my
arms around her, and she stands very close so that I will. I think I've
made some progress with Carlette. I'm not sure what it is, but she
seems to be a little more settled. And that's good because, as nasty as it
may seem, I singled her out, and I said, "That little black bitch right
there, she's going to be mine if I have her head on a platter. She's
going to be mine, and I'm going to do whatever it takes to win her.
At times, I'll lose her, I'll slide, but, God, I love that girl!"

I have one little guy whose name is Robert. He's terribly persecuted.   Robert
He's white. Robert is the best reader in the room, a nice boy. Last
year he was so passive that his body was not able to hold him up.
He would sit in a chair and slither out of it, under his desk, onto the
floor because that's how passive he was. He's doing much better
now. He's persecuted. He gets beaten up. But that's because he's a
nice guy. Because he wants to be liked, he does all the things that
would help a guy be liked. He gives, and then they take advantage
of him.

Robert is somewhat effeminate. He enjoys playing with girls much
more than with boys because who the hell likes to get beaten up on?
He's as eager to learn as any of the rest. He's been bugging me for a
long time to teach him his times tables. I'm not sure he's ready for it,
but Friday is his birthday, and I'm going to his birthday party and
give him a game that will teach multiplication. I'll help him with it
but first I want to see what he can do on his own. Robert's not quite
the lowest IQ I've got; he's next to the lowest. He's around an 80,
but he does much better than that. He doesn't have a pleasant home

situation, but he does have a mother and a father and a nice warm house, and he does get fed. That's more than I can say for some of the others.

Jerry   Jerry is spunky as all get out! I just adore him. Yet, as spunky and as harsh and as wild as he is, he's a marshmallow inside. He is very sensitive and frequently gets his feelings hurt. He's a hard worker, too. Oh, God, they all are! *They all want to learn.* I don't ever want to hear anybody tell me these kids can't learn because they can. There's a way to teach them what they want to know. My old Jerry, he's a wiry, spunky little kid and beautiful, oh beautiful! His name is Thomas; he's one of the Thomas clan. There's a whole group of Thomases, and I have two of them. They're cousins; I think it's an uncle that relates them.

Leroy   Leroy can be absolutely the funniest guy. He's another beautiful guy! A little, skinny, scrawny kid, a smart little kid, and I swear, he ought to be a drummer. Somebody has got to buy him drums because if he doesn't stop beating on the desk I'm going to beat on his head, and it will probably be hollow and sound lovely. But, he's a quick kid. He's a quick reader; he's brisk. He wants to get things done now, now, let's move. He's all right. He has a father and a mother. He was absent yesterday, the first day in the whole year he's been absent. When he came back, the note said that he had missed the bus. Well, that wasn't true. A younger brother squealed on him. They were both out. Both of them missed school for the first time in the whole year because a step-father of one of their step-sisters who happened to live next door was found dead the morning before. He died of a rat's bite, so they had been kept home for the funeral. Leroy's all right. He's all boy.

Donna   Donna is one of the white girls. I understand she was quite a fearful little lass, but the other special teacher managed to get that out of her. And now, she's got more spunk. She wants to help so badly. She'll do all the dirty work around the room. She'll pick up the floor and wash out the paint brushes and all that kind of stuff. She wants to help; she wants to learn; she wants to do more. They all complain that the work I give them is too easy and that I'm insulting them for giving them such easy work. Sometimes in my weak moments I give them more, but I know it's too hard for them, and they fail. And yet, I can't say, "See, I told you that you couldn't do the work; I told you that the work I was giving you was for you, special for you so that you could do it, and you could get up to the work I just gave you." They don't hear it. All they hear is the hurt in their heart that says once again they failed in school. Teacher gave them work that they couldn't do, and they failed. And then I'm always ashamed that I let their complaints get to me, and I let them bother me enough.

They are afraid to be wrong, so terribly afraid to be wrong. The work I have been giving them for the past many weeks has been very easy for them. For some, it's been easy; for others, it's stretching a little bit. But they need the ego boost more than anything in this world. Donna is one of those. If she makes a mistake she erases and fixes it; she can't stand to have anything but a perfect paper. But she's a spunky little kid. Her mother doesn't have anything nice to say about her, and I don't have much nice to say about her mother.

Rick is one of my white boys. He's hyperactive and becoming deaf which makes it difficult because you can't simply say something to Rick and know that he hears you. You have to question him; you have to say it five or six times to be sure that he does hear you. Often you would have to touch him to get his attention because he simply does not hear. And he's hyperactive; he can't sit in his seat. He's wandering around. He isn't necessarily causing trouble, but he wanders around the room picking up things, playing with whatever is there if it's a nail or a chair. He's crawling around on the floor and up and around the ceiling playing. If he did work at the very first of the semester it was because I was standing there watching him do it and helping him do it. Lately, for some unknown reason, when in September and October I had to force him to write five words on a paper, he's turning in papers to me complete.

I went to his home, too. I went to all their homes except two. As I mentioned earlier, he is deaf, getting deafer and his folks are not going to help him. His dad said: "Hmph, when you've got six kids, they've got to wait in line." Well, Rick's been waiting in line for a long time, and I think his problem is more serious than some of the others. Especially when I know that the operation, the hospital bed was reserved for my Ricky but Mom and Dad didn't take him. They couldn't afford time from the business, you know. So Ricky remains unable to hear.

William, God, he's a neat guy. I really like William; he is really wild. He is round, roly-poly, laughing, got stories to tell that go on forever and ever. I went to his home, too. He's the oldest of six children. He's eleven; his mother is twenty-six. She advised me very strongly not to have children. "They take up too much of your time. They cost too much, too much worry. Just don't have children," she told me. She's just four years older than I am, and she has six children, and the oldest is eleven, which is half my age. William's all right. He's as soft as putty. People make fun of his father, too. He's got a father and a step-father. His father's name is "Chick" and his name happens to be "Hawkins." So he gets all kinds of "Chicken," "Chicken Hawk," "Chicken Soup," "Hawkeyed," "Hawk-this," "Hawk—" he gets a lot of it. He puts up with a good deal of it, and he dishes it out too.

He's one of my guys who was reading in a 3.1 level book, when he couldn't manage a 2.1, when he could manage a 1.2 maybe. I managed to get him down into a lower book without losing face. I told him straight. I said, "Look, William, I don't know how you got into this 3 level book. I don't know how you did it, but that's the book you had when I came in, and it's too hard for you, William. It is. It's too hard. Now, let's back up; let's just take it easy, slow down, work up to that book. You can get there, but you should go step by step over the river. You should step on every rock. You can't just hop over; you can't fly over. It doesn't happen by magic. It's hard work. So, let's drop back, read in this book." And he's thrilled. In fact, he's finding three and four books at a time to read to me. I don't have time to listen to all my kids read. We'd miss lunch; I'd miss my breaks, and that groovy lunch room! My William, quite a guy!

Jonathon   Jonathon: what can you say about Jonathon? He's not the oldest in the room, but he's biggest, and he has a brother one year older than he is who has gone on to a special education class at a junior high. The two boys are very close, and Jonathon is very much under Thomas' thumb, or he was when Thomas was in this room with him. But now that Thomas is gone, Jonathon is really feeling his oats, and not only that—he's feeling that he is a man. He's approaching adolescence. So I have a big sex problem in my room. I've got my little girls being molested in the back, and nasty words being spoken, and all that kind of trash. Sex is raring its ugly, ugly head right here in front of me (it gives me weak knees).

Jonathon is contrary. It doesn't matter how much he wants to do something, by golly, if I suggest it, he's not going to do it. He'll stand there running a commentary: "I'm not going to do that; you can't make me do it. I'm not going to do anything like that. Boy, you won't find me doing anything like that, you dirty, white cracker. I'm not going to do it." Sometimes, depending on my mood, it's hysterically funny, that Jonathon is standing like a goose, squawking and nobody is really listening. Other times it gets on my nerves, and all I want him to do is shut up! And that's when we run into trouble. The minute I want something, he will not do it. But he's getting better. He does treat me though, as if I had leprosy. If I walk by, he runs the other way. God help me if I should touch him. He threatens to kill me, he threatens a lot of things though. He threatens to throw rocks at my windshield, but it doesn't bother me. I told him that I would collect insurance on it.

According to the counselor, Jonathon just might have a preadolescent crush on me. Heaven help me if I ever find any more preadolescents who want to have a crush on me. This guy could go a lot of places, he could be the leader of the room because they have the ultimate respect for Jonathon. It's just that he and I have to get together on something—I don't know what. He's going to the counselor regularly now and on the way down to her office, every step of the way, he says: "I'm not going to go; you can't make me go. . . ." I open the door and he walks in saying, "I'm not going to go; you can't make me go." When he comes back, he gives me the appointment slip for the next time, "Here's the appointment slip for next week, but I'm not going." And I usually answer, "Well, maybe you'll feel different about it next week, there's no need to decide right now." "Why, I'm not going to go," he ritualistically responds. And the next day it is: "I'm not going to go. You can't make me go to Miss Campbell." Every once in a while, he remembers to remind me, "Oh yes, I'm not going to Miss Campbell, don't forget that I'm not going."

And then there's dear Anna, a beautiful little blonde with beautiful Anna blue eyes, and never a sicklier child have I seen. She'll tell me that her kidneys of all things hurt. Her Mommy's this way. Her Mommy is a pusher and a gogetter, but Mommy's always sick. Mommy is our homeroom mother, and I should be nice about Mommy, because she is very nice. Anna is slow, very slow. I don't know why. I think she's slower than she should be. I think it's probably an emotional problem here with the room. She's very disturbed by these other guys. She would like very much that they all disappear. She is the primary object of their molestations, because she is a sweet passive little girl. But she tries. She gets discouraged and she tries again, then she gets even more discouraged. I need to give Anna more of my time because she is so easily discouraged, she needs constant care and feeding and medication, and a lot of love, too. She isn't very loving of me, though. But she doesn't run from me. It's all right, in time, I may win her or maybe she won't ever care for me, I don't know.

Leon   Leon is undoubtedly one of the lousiest kids I've ever known. I think I just simply do not like Leon. There are times when he is wonderful, but 99 per cent of the time he is unbearable. He lies, and that's something I cannot tolerate. I can't stand liars, and cheaters are the same thing to me. Cheating is a form of lying. Leon lies, and he looks at me straight in the eyes because he's afraid not to. He lies, and lies build on lies, and he doesn't get anywhere. He can't get out of it, and he can't save face. It's just very sad with Leon. He and Jonathon make such a pair as to be the terror of this room, and it's all that I can do sometimes to keep them under control. But we work at it. Leon wants to be biggest; he wants to be best, and if he falls short of biggest and best, he's nothing—in his estimation. He can do very well at this level and not that, but he wants the stars. Don't we all?

The Agony of Caring

I care. Teachers often care so much, and they want to give so much, but these children aren't accustomed to being given to. They're accustomed to being put down, "knocked upside the head," rejected. They're used to being put away, put aside, shoved around; and they're not used to people who care about them. They're not used to caring about their teachers. And it makes it doubly hard because you do care so much, and they don't understand. I've talked to the other new teachers in the building, and frequently I hear them say, "I want to take them home. I want to show them what an escalator is. I want to show them what it's like to do this and that." They want to give so much, and then they find that the hand that's feeding is being bitten. They don't understand why. Well, I'd like to take my kids home too. In fact, this weekend we are, about five of us, going to come back to my apartment, and bake some cookies. Nothing fantastic. Just bake some cookies and be together and have a nice time, I hope. *But you can't take away from children what they've already got, no matter how bad it is.* So they have a lousy home life. We must try not to make it seem any worse by throwing up the better world every chance we get. I've learned not to say, "Take this home to your mother and father," when I can just as easily say "your folks," because "your folks" for some children is an older sister, because they don't have a mother and a father. Or it's an uncle, or it's a grandmother, or it's the friend of the step-father.

I have a large race situation in my room. The problem comes from the blacks, especially Jonathon who's reaching the adolescent stage. The problem is whether or not the blacks are going to have to put up with these "white crackers." So, I'm finding that I have to teach tolerance to the blacks more than I thought I'd ever have to teach it to the whites. They're terribly rejecting of the whites. They're extremely sensitive to racial problems outside the classroom. You could look at my tests and see how liberal the stupid things say I am. What makes a difference, and what's important, is what my class thinks. And my class often thinks that I am horribly unjust, unkind, unfair. I hear comments a thousand times a day, "See that, she never picks on white guys." The law of averages dictates that when I have six out of ten that are black, I'm going to have to pick a black one once in a while. In the eyes of the blacks I'm being white; I'm being another "whitey," another "honky." It's awfully hard sometimes when I pour my gut out on the floor only to have them walk on it. The physical education teacher says, "Don't give up on them. Everyone else has; don't you give up on them."

I go back another day because there's something good about every single one of them. I hope I've said something good about every one of them because I really believe that there is something good about every single one of my children. I have a poster in the room on the wall at the back. It's a big flashy one with lots of colors, and it says, "Everyone has something to sing about." And it's true. Even these children. There's something good about them, and something good about their lives. For every single one, like Carlette. She doesn't have a moment alone. She has eleven people living in three rooms. I don't know where they sleep. They don't have any place to sit, but she's not alone. There are some people who are alone. She goes home to friends and family and people who love her. Some people don't have that. There's something for each one of them to hold on to, to be proud of, and to work from. I'm trying very hard to find that. Just today I had to teach them, "You don't teach an eagle how to run. You wouldn't teach a rabbit how to swim. You teach everybody what he can learn, and that's what I'm here to do. Somebody decided you needed special help, and somebody decided that I was the one to do it. I'm getting paid for it. You got put in this room. Let's get down to business. Accept it and go from there."

My class is a tremendous challenge. As good as the Cooperative Urban Teacher Education program (CUTE) was, it wasn't enough. It didn't prepare me well enough. I frequently feel grossly inadequate. I still don't know how to deal with a lot of problems. The mother-father name-calling problem. It's sort of like a game of verbal chicken. You start talking about somebody's mother, and you make a lewd comment, and then he makes another lewd, crude comment about your mother. The first one to get angry is the loser of that game. I think there's a name for it, but I can't remember it. Well, my kids do that, and it hurts their feelings. They do it to hurt each other's feelings, and it does. I took a couple of pupils to the principal very early in the year and explained what they were doing, and she said, "Now that's the silliest thing I ever heard, Miss Rucker. You know as well as I do that words aren't going to hurt anybody." I couldn't believe what she said. *Words do hurt.* Words hurt like nothing else can, and you can't ignore it. You can't ignore that kind of pain any more than you can ignore a broken leg. That's what she was asking me to do, and that's what she was asking them to do. And they can't do it, and I can't do it. They don't have the sense of security of their own worth and their parents' worth to fall back on. They can call my father whatever they want to, and it won't bother me because I know my father isn't that. I know my father's grand. They don't know that of their fathers.

I don't have any answers. I've got a million problems and no answers. I wish I had more backing than I do, not only from my cohorts at school but simply the people I live with. They have been brought up as not quite racists, but they edge that way. They would let me bring my kids over here, but perhaps one or two of their fathers better not find out. And there's the guy that I go with. It hurt me very badly, to the point of tears, when he said that what he would like to do with my class would be like what he would like to do with all niggers—ship them to Russia and exterminate them. I don't think very well in great huge terms, great generalities. I think of Carlette who's learning to be a little bit of a lady, and I think of Jonathon who's trying very hard to be a man, and of William who's quite a character. And I don't want them exterminated. I don't want to hand them everything on a silver platter the way they expect me to. You prove it in my room. You can read that book? Fine. Prove it to me first, then you get a harder one. I don't know. I don't have answers. I've got more problems than answers, and probably more stubbornness than problems. But for the same reason I put up with Bill for hating my kids, I put up with them. He doesn't know them, but he hates them. They're black. There's something good in them and in him. And somehow, maybe I can get a little bit of it to show, and if you can make a little bit show, a little more will follow. And eventually they can do it on their own.

My basic and major objectives for my class— I don't care if they never learn another word in my class—are (1) to accept themselves; (2) to have respect for themselves and respect for others, their time, their property, their life-space, their life-styles; and (3) to relax. They're extremely keyed up. They've got chips on their shoulders, and they're daring anybody and everybody to knock them off. I've seen them stand for ten minutes shoving each other, hoping to get somebody to fight them. If I can just make school something of a haven for these children who hate to go home. They dread weekends because they have to go home. They're wild on Fridays because they know that they're going to be spending two days there. They're wild on Mondays because of the things that have happened to them over the weekend. If I can make school a nice place to come, if I can make Room Seven a nice place to come, a refuge, a haven, some place where you can be yourself, some place where you can do what you want to do, where you can learn what you want to learn, and be with people who accept you for what you are, not what you could be, not measuring you against somebody else's yardstick but your own yardstick. If I can do that I will have had the most wonderful year that anybody could ever have.

If I could just leave them in the room alone and know that they wouldn't hate so much, and hate wouldn't ooze from every pore to the point that they have to hit and crush somebody's face. If I can teach them to respect each other. It's just a little thing like that. I wish I knew how. I want very badly to do that for them and to do that for me. It's been hard getting where I've gotten, and I've gotten very far since September. I still have far to go. I had to do it in what I think was a pretty rough way. Not as bad as some. My room is not by the garbage cans. I don't have leftover books and leftover supplies, but the *attitude* is leftover, and often the attitude is by the garbage cans. I want my pupils to feel good about themselves. I feel good about them. I get as mad as hell at them. I've been so mad that I've had to leave the room. But I get over it; I forgive them. And they forgive me an awful lot. I'm getting to be very fond of them, which is a curse in itself for both of us.

24. We Ain't Unteachable . . . Just Unteached

Lawana Trout

"WOP. Nigger. Cracker. Chink!"

"Like man, I'm tellin' you, there ain't no land of the free and home of the brave, and we gotta move."

I was teaching a unit on prejudice and propaganda to disadvantaged high school juniors in an institute for teachers of the disadvantaged held at Princeton University. Since that first class, I have taught the unit in several cities to classes that were all Negro, all white, and Negro-white, and to multiracial classes that included Puerto Ricans, Mexicans, Indians, and others.

President Kennedy said, "Those who make peaceful revolution impossible will make violent revolution inevitable." I wanted to evoke a peaceful revolution in my classroom—a revolution in thinking, a revolution in feeling, and a revolution in teaching. I ignored IQ scores and observed student performance. I forgot reading grade levels and searched for selections that spoke to the students. I was unconcerned about haircuts and dress styles, but I did care about what students thought and how they felt. At times I became a student, and each student became a teacher. I lost books, but I did not lose students.

During our study, I stopped periodically to discuss how different kinds of material should be covered. Should it be taught to everyone? to some? to which ones? I asked the students, "What problems do you think we will have to overcome as this class studies race problems?" The first day one boy asked, "Hey, you gonna let us talk about *Whitey* the same as us?"

Students were encouraged to disagree with anyone's ideas, including the teacher's. The one rule was, "You may say anything you like, but you must listen to everything anyone else says."

This English unit reveals how a speaker or writer achieves his goals through careful manipulation of words. It shows students the relation-

From *NEA Journal*, April, 1967, pp. 24–26. Reprinted by permission.

ship between words and emotions. I selected *prejudice, propaganda,* and *protest* because they are live topics for the students and they offered illustrations of the language situations I needed. The response of many students to the unit can be stated in the reaction of one: "I wasn't board a time." Some were bored, but the materials were more effective than most traditional ones.

We started by finding out how words are used to evoke feelings. Since the students were familiar with advertising, I used ads to make them aware of the "feeling" of words. I asked them to choose from a collection of pictures (Hondas, cigarettes, cars, record albums) something that they would like to sell, and then to write several types of ads about it.

The ads they wrote were serious, satirical, and humorous—for radio, television, magazines, or newspapers. Students "sold" their products to the class through reading and role playing. They slanted one ad in several different ways to appeal to different groups—teenagers, poor people, middle-aged women, young men.

The class compared different ways of expressing one idea—finest quality filet mignon: first class piece of dead cow. They played with personal slanting: "*I* daydream. *You* run away from the real world. *He* ought to see a headshrinker."

After we had written slanted descriptions of people and places, one student commented, "You can *make* people and things be anything you want them to be with the words you use."

Since the material was sometimes inflammatory and since I was a stranger to the students, tension was present until the class accepted me and my materials. Humor was my most vital ally. For example, one day I showed a cover of a popular magazine which pictured a boy carrying a small table and chair during the riot in Watts. "You are working for a magazine and you use this picture. Write one caption that will slant it positively and one that will slant it negatively."

After the class had provided several positive captions like "Innocent victim rescues furniture," I asked for some negative ones.

> Student: "Boy makes off with loot."
> Teacher: "Make it more negative."
> Student: (all Negro class) "*Negro* boy makes off with loot."
> Teacher: "More negative." (Hoping to get a word like *hoodlum, thief*) "What is the *worst* thing you could call this boy?"
> Student: (With a playful glint in her eye) "WHITE boy makes off with loot."
> Teacher: "I'm glad to see we've lost our prejudices in here."

From advertising we moved to the study of propaganda, which is, as one girl pointed out, another kind of selling. She noted, "Advertisers sell products, and propagandists sell ideas." We examined local newspapers for propaganda, and formulated a list of propaganda techniques.

Students examined simple editorial cartoons. Each student explained his cartoon to the class and we listed observations about what makes a cartoon. The class decided that symbolism is often used and that whether or not captions and situations have meaning often depends on the reader's familiarity with past events. Some questions were: If you were going to show hate in a cartoon, what would you use? How would you show love, peace, anger, or fear?

Our study of propaganda was not limited to newspapers; we looked at it in films like *The Twisted Cross*, which shows Hitler's rise to power, and in paintings like Picasso's "Guernica." The class was asked to give a one-word reaction to this painting. They listed *confusion, frustration, fear, struggle*. When one shy girl said, "Loneliness," the class roared with laughter. They stopped laughing when she argued, "These people are in trouble and afraid; fear makes people lonely."

We opened the study of prejudice with the book *Two Blocks Apart*, which reports the contrasting views of two New York boys from families of very different backgrounds—one, a poor Puerto Rican family; the other, a stable Irish Catholic family—on their neighborhoods, homes, schools, political views, and future plans. The book provoked many questions: Where do people get their views of others? Why do they accept them?

Students were asked to list various racial groups and to write, anonymously, positive and negative comments about each. We duplicated the combined comments and the class discussed the prejudice profile. One student observed, "People don't think about bein' prejudice. They just *be* it."

A boy reading *Black Like Me* played the role of Griffin and talked to the class about his trials in trying to understand and cope with prejudice. Hemingway's short story, "Ten Indians," and "A Question of Blood" by Ernest Haycox showed the Indian as a victim of prejudice. Several students read and liked *Letters from Mississippi*, accounts written by white students who went to Mississippi for the Student Nonviolent Co-ordinating Committee.

In an attempt to understand intolerance, we examined words that are weapons of prejudice. I asked for names referring to groups of people. Students supplied: Krauts, Kikes, Gooks, Frogs, Spiks,

Crackers, Wops, and others. After discussing their answers, I introduced Dick Gregory's autobiography, *nigger*. Since several copies had disappeared from the display table, I assumed that some were interested in his treatment of prejudice.

We listened to a record of Gregory's jokes about civil rights issues. I cut up his joke books, *What's Happening?* and *From the Back of the Bus*, and gave each student a joke to tell to the class. Then we talked about Gregory. Why did he entitle the book *nigger*? Who will buy this book? Why did he say, "Dear Momma . . . . if ever you hear the word 'nigger' again, remember they are advertising my book"?

Students prepared roles from *nigger* and read them for the class. One part dealt with prejudice in the classroom, and I asked how a teacher shows prejudice.

One boy responded immediately: "I once had a teacher who was always screamin' and yellin' at us. 'You dirty little colored kids are ruining our schools,' " he mimicked.

Others joined in. Some defended teachers, but others countered with comments like, "Yeah, but some teachers don't have to say anything to show they don't like you. They just give you that certain look."

Later in the lesson, I role-played several types of teachers, and the class reacted. Armed with a strong stare and a belligerent voice, I threatened, "I know all about you. I've heard about how tough you are. I want you to understand I can be just as mean as you can."

"I hate you!" exploded one boy.

After seeing the film *A Raisin in the Sun*, students discussed how the lines reveal the self-image of the characters. How did this image affect the characters' actions? What are some Negro self-images today? What are some white ones? How do these self-images affect individuals' actions regarding civil rights? What problems do they create? What is your image of the Indians? Of other races? Where did you get that image? How does one remain true to his own race and at the same time learn to live with other races?

By reading "The Odyssey of a Wop," the class got the picture of an Italian boy who denied his people until he reached manhood. Books relating to the search for identity included *When Legends Die* (Indian), *A Walker in the City* (Jew), *Autobiography of Malcolm X*, and others.

An examination of protest climaxed the unit. I searched for techniques that would help the students release their feelings. After we had looked at books of paintings and discussed expression through color and form, the students expressed some of their feelings about the civil rights struggle through finger painting.

A girl scratched her nails down the page—fingers tense, face tight. "This is hate," she said.

"This is King and his sissies being smothered by black power," said a boy as he distorted the quiet routine he had traced.

With a soft rhythm, a girl's finger traced human outlines. The rhythm flared as dark patterns of terror cut over the bodies. She titled her picture "Birmingham Sunday."

When the students had finished painting, they wrote brief interpretations of what they had sought to express and put them on the paintings.

As we evaluated possible solutions to the civil rights problems, we investigated the basic principles of several groups—Ku Klux Klan, Black Muslims, believers in black power, the defenders of the non-violence movement, and others.

They read the constitution of the Klan, and they examined copies of the Black Muslims' newspaper. They explored multiple definitions of black power, and they reacted to the newspaper put out by the National States' Rights Party, *Thunderbolt: The White Man's Viewpoint*. They took notes as they listened to recorded speeches by Malcolm X, Martin Luther King, and others. From these notes, they refuted the main arguments. Students also conducted interviews, television shows, and trials. One day when I praised them for good work, a boy flicked a half grin at me with, "We ain't unteachable . . . just unteached!"

The study concluded with a debate that opened by having a representative from each group present his basic ideas. Students were allowed to join any group or to remain independent. The different factions had filled the room with propaganda, signs, slogans, pictures, and projects. As members of the class played Martin Luther King, Malcolm X, the Imperial Wizard of the Klan, Stokely Carmichael, and others, students exploded like firecrackers all over the room.

"You mean to tell me you're gonna try to move the Negroes from the South to the North? They don't want us there, either."

"Man, Malcolm and his cats just yell and scream. We cool it" (a nonviolence speaker).

We also read from *Our Faces, Our Words: The Negro Protest*; *To Kill a Mockingbird*; *Huckleberry Finn*; *Crisis in Black and White*; and other books. Students read "Jewtown" from *How the Other Half Lives*, by Jacob Riis, and the article, "A Spanish Harlem Fortress"

(*New York Times Magazine*, January 19, 1964). They acted scenes from *In White America* and read several poems.

This unit allows every student to be an observer, a hero, a martyr, a crusader, an avenger. He is Jew *and* Gentile as the class reads Alfred Kazin's struggle to "be a Jew" and "become an American" in *A Walker in the City*. He is Indian *and* white as a student gives Tecumseh's speech against the white man's stealing Indian land. He is black *and* white as he discovers the meaning of Kenneth Clark's words: "The poetic irony of American race relations is that the rejected Negro must somehow also find the strength to free the privileged white."

In the classroom, students may bare their frustrations and fears, their loves and hates, their disillusionments in the past and their hopes for the future.

"Our English class was more instring then during the regeler time. I feel that if we had novolins we could all work together in one union."

"You're wasting your time. Whitey ain't chang and we are gonna get him."

"I don't think I'll ever be afraid of the word *nigger* again."

25. Small Communities Need Big Men

Stephen J. Knezevich

ADMINISTRATION is no job for "small boys" naïvely unaware of their responsibilities. This is true of administration in general—be it concerned with small or large situations. There are some who carry the mistaken notion that the small school systems can get along with "small" leaders, but the big systems must have the "big" leaders. Leadership responsibilities are the same in a small school system as in the larger one; the same in rural communities as in metropolitan areas. Human beings can cluster into small associations loosely referred to as small cities or small communities. They can also be part of many small neighborhood groups loosely federated into a large settlement or city. The need for leadership is not related directly nor inversely to the size of human associations in communal living. The need for an outstanding public school system is felt by people living in small communities as well as those living in larger settlements. It follows that, if administration can help contribute to the excellence of a school system, then good administration is as necessary in the small as in the large communities.

Medical attention, dental care, and legal counsel are as vital to people residing in small centers as those in the larger heterogeneous urban areas. Professional people such as doctors, dentists, and lawyers come to small communities to render their important and vital services. These professional men recognize that they serve people rather than a fictitious entity called a village, a town, a small city, or a metropolitan giant. They come happy to dedicate a lifetime career to satisfy needs for their particular professional services. It is not unusual to hear of a dentist, doctor, or lawyer who has spent his entire lifetime, and enjoyed doing it, in one small community. These professional people know that success in a chosen profession is not

From *Administration in a Small Community* (National Education Association, 1957), 6–13. Reprinted by permission.

necessarily related to the size of the community in which they practice their art.

School administrators in small communities should take note of other professional people contributing vital services in small communities. The professional challenges of educators in small communities are as great as the professional challenges of doctors, dentists, and lawyers. There is an all too prevalent notion that to gain prestige, fame, and fortune one must aspire to become a professional administrator in the very largest of urban settlements. This is a fallacy and a worship of false gods. It is fallacious because it confuses quantity with quality. The false god at the top of the ladder is pursued in the place of personal satisfactions derived from a job well done, regardless of the size of the school system. Prestige, fame, and fortune should be accorded to professional administrators in school systems which exhibit the finest quality of education rather than the greatest quantity of students. Good things can come in small packages in education as well as in Christmas gifts.

But small and large are relative terms. Schools in small communities should not be confused with the poorly organized school systems. To some people, small means the same thing as "too small" means to others. There are some communities which lack adequate financial resources, a sufficient number of resident pupils, and/or the human desire to provide necessary educational opportunities at a reasonable cost. Where the density of population, topography, roads, and other limiting conditions allow, reorganization into more efficient units should be accomplished. The growing and welcome trend toward the reorganization of inefficient school districts into satisfactory local administrative units has made it possible to achieve a quality program of education in small communities of America. It is not the purpose of the yearbook to plead for the perpetuation of school districts too small to meet the needs of present-day American children. Little can come from the worship of smallness for its own sake. Nor are big things always bad. The formation of satisfactory local units of school administration is a *must* if there are to be comprehensive educational programs in small communities. On the other hand, there will always remain some very small school systems because natural conditions make them necessary.

There was a time when it was almost impossible for the small community to hold on to the professional services of an outstanding professional school administrator. This need not be the case in small communities with satisfactory district organization containing adequate financial resources and resident pupil enrollments. *A high turnover among teachers or administrators is not conducive to the development of a quality educational program.* Continuity of administrative services is as necessary for effective educational programs in small communities as in larger ones.

The
"left-sittin'"
complex

The point of all this is that the school superintendent or principal serving the small but adequately organized district is confronted with an important job. He need not develop what can be called a "left-sittin' " complex, if he has failed to receive a call to come to a larger community. Even more disturbing is the case of the man who has done well as a small school administrator and would enjoy remaining. But he feels compelled to move when he has an opportunity to go to a larger system, lest his friends wonder if there is "something wrong" with him. If he stayed in a small community, his close associates might suspect him of losing ambition. It is hoped that professional school administrators will follow the lead of other professional people in small communities and consider remaining to enjoy a lifetime of service through the development of a high degree of excellence in the educational programs of the communities they serve. The alternative to this is continual adjustments necessary as one tries to scramble up a ladder that may lead to nowhere. Not everyone has the personal qualities needed to be a successful administrator in small communities. Many do, and these people should be encouraged to stay.

It follows that school board members must recognize the value of a long tenure of service for school superintendents and other professional administrators. In years past in certain small communities, discharging the school superintendent and other personnel was almost a spring sport. Such perverted pleasure or vulgar display of power is a detriment to the school and the community as a whole. The small community must prepare to reward its professional school administrators and teachers so that they may enjoy the standard of living and prestige that their counterparts in larger school systems enjoy.

This we
believe

Some administrators are tall and some are short; some are stout and some are lean. The physical characteristics of a person are poor clues to his effectiveness in education. They say that clothes can make the man. They can also help hide his incompetencies. Administrators come not only in various sizes, shapes, and dress, but also each holds various beliefs on important subjects. His fundamental beliefs have considerable influence on his effectiveness as an administrator. And it's what a man does about his beliefs that counts the most.

The precise role he feels the administrative leader should play in the school system is one of the more important beliefs. The professional and the social relationships between the administrator and teachers is another. Sometimes exterior trappings coupled with fanfare may hide real feelings. But truth will come out, and the hidden will be made obvious. It's what a man practices rather than what he preaches that tips his hand. The school administrator who openly declares that he is czar of all his domain is hard to find these days. To be called a dictator, benevolent despot, or "big boss" is not a compliment. The temper of the times makes democratic school administration the flattering remark. But can a man be democratic when he holds the reins of power? There is no question as to who has the authority to make teachers and students do his bidding. The power of the administrator is derived from the board of education. They give him authority to get a job done. Authority is a necessary accompaniment of responsibility. The question revolves around the use of delegated authority or authority inherent in a position. The very position of the superintendent or principal in the school organization makes him a leader in the sense that others are obliged to follow his demands. Being a leader by virtue of holding title to an office of responsibility and authority does not automatically make one a democratic school administrator. One's beliefs rather than one's legal or derived authority makes for democratic school administration. Power to force conformity to the will of the person in authority should be used only when the unusual situation demands it.

Faith in people is fundamental. Our schools are an integral part of our democratic cultural matrix. Without faith in the professional competence and personal sincerity of teachers there can be no democratic school administration. This is bedrock. You can't practice democracy if you envision the world as being populated with scheming incompetents who look after their own hide and will get yours if you don't watch out. The superstructure of democratic school administration rests on the belief that your professional colleagues in the classrooms are people who know enough to do the right thing at the right time. You must accept the idea that teachers desire to help build better schools. All the exterior trappings and fanfare aimed at proving to the public and yourself that your school is truly an expression of democracy in action will come to naught if there exists doubt in your mind of the ability of teachers to deliberate on vital school issues. The better professional preparation of teachers has made democratic leadership more of a practical possibility. No more can teachers be regarded as half-educated workers with barely enough skills to perform their classroom function with any degree of adequacy. Today's teachers are better educated than ever before; they are more alert and better informed on school problems.

There is also another side to this coin. Teachers must believe that professional school administrators are working with them rather than against them. The stereotyped bumbling and fumbling ogre in the school office must go the way of all superstitions. There have been attempts to depict educators as divided into fundamentally two warring camps, namely, teachers versus administrators. But the things that bind teachers and administrators together are far more important and numerous than those that tend to divide. Mutual distrust can reach the point of wreaking havoc. Mutual respect and understanding make for progress in education. Teachers must comprehend that superintendents and principals are better prepared professionally than ever before. Professional administrators are more sensitive to human relations than ever before.

One of the keystones of democratic leadership is that *the formulation of policy should involve those who are to be influenced by policies*. This means that teachers and administrators deliberate together and from such actions educational policies develop. There is little question that in recent decades great strides have been made in teacher-faculty participation in many aspects of the administrative process. One study pointed out that many teachers today feel that they have a right to participate in the determination of policies related to the curriculum and instruction, the salaries and working conditions, and to many other aspects of educational planning.[1] This same study underscored the idea that teachers who report opportunity to participate regularly and actively in making policies are much more likely to be enthusiastic about their school system than those who report limited opportunity to participate. It can be said that democratic leadership can promote a higher degree of faculty morale. Democracy in administration is not just something stylish to have around during these times; it is vitally necessary for continued progress in education. We cannot afford to neglect the creative talents of many teachers.

But all is not a bed of roses while operating democratically in school administration. At times faculty groups involved in policy formulation will tend to legislate rather than deliberate on needed educational policies. There is a tendency to solve dilemmas by "making a new rule." Intelligence does not result from compounding ignorance. Individuals with limited information in a particular area do not become mysteriously endowed with an expert's knowledge as

---

[1] University of Chicago, Midwest Administration Center, "The Teacher in Policy Making," *Administrator's Notebook* 1 (Chicago, The Center, May, 1952).

soon as they gather into a group. Decisions reached without adequate understanding of the problem are questionable, whether made by an uninformed group or delivered by an uninformed individual.

Furthermore, one does not become democratic by abdicating his responsibility for leadership to faculty members, even though they may be fully informed. There are some whose statements of democratic school administration imply that the superintendent's job should be limited to organizing faculty committees. When this is done, he sits back and waits until the committee makes up its mind on what he is to do next. This extreme leads to devitalization of the school executive's role in policy formulation and execution. The role of the leader in a democratically organized school system is not limited to counting the raised hands to determine who won or lost the decision on the policy to be adopted. A democratic leader is not the person who is pinned on the rack of indecision until all votes are counted. The specialized preparation and experiential background of the school superintendent must be fully utilized in policy formulation as well as policy execution. The truth of the business is that the superintendent has technical information which most faculty groups do not possess. The group process is not a replacement for the expert. The group process can be made more effective when it taps the resources of well-informed individuals. The extremes of autocratic control on the one hand and evisceration of executive powers on the other are to be avoided. It's no simple task to be a democratic leader.

To indicate that there are problems in democratic school administration is not to imply that it is a questionable practice. A person can gain strength if he is made aware of his weaknesses and does something about them. In any process, dangers must be recognized and appropriate action taken to correct them. Great strides have been made in understanding the dynamics of group work and the application of group effort to facilitate democratic school administration. But more needs to be done.

One area of concern is the function of the expert—the person who has the facts at his fingertips—in the group process. The great stress placed on arriving at decisions through the group process often results in unwillingness to yield anything on the basis of special knowledge and competence. Ignoring the opinion of the well informed or failing to give it proper weight is not favorable to progress. Theoretically, the consultant to the group should fulfill the expert's role. The current practice, which is particularly evident at educational conferences, to award almost anyone the title of consultant (to complete the group form of chairman, consultant, and recorder) belies the full appreciation of the importance of those who possess special knowledge and competence. The task is to wed the advantages of group action with the value of expert knowledge.

Still another problem remains unresolved in democratic school administration which places much emphasis on group effort in arriving at important decisions. We are not all endowed with superior intellects. There is evidence to support the contention that occasionally the brilliant mind is buried in the group process. At a time when great emphasis is being placed on the education of the gifted, it is folly to fail to fully utilize the contributions of the creative mind or the special talents of an individual with a background of rich experience to go along with it.

The small school administrator, with his many and intimate face-to-face contacts with his professional staff or laymen in the community, is in a fortunate position to promote democratic leadership. He is at the "grass roots" level. In larger school systems machinery must be set up to reach the "grass roots." Name tags at faculty get-togethers are not necessary in most small communities. First name greetings are generally the rule. The maze of special committees, steering committees, and executive committees so necessary in the large school systems are unnecessary here. The informal approach is well suited to schools in small communities. One might say that *the conditions in small school systems are ideal for the realization of the goal of democratic school administration.* There is no better laboratory for developing democratic administration than the small school system.

26. Current Influences Changing the Principal's Role

Stephen A. Romine

LIVING today has an explosive quality. People are continually subject to its impact. Noise, pressure, tension, impending change, and for some a sense of doom, exist in the midst of affluence heretofore unknown. We are gripped in a dynamism whose direction is unclear. Consequently, the role of all persons, including the school principal, is subject to many changing and conflicting conditions.

Time permits only brief mention of the more significant influences and their implications. Let us deal with them in three categories: (1) those within the educational establishment, (2) those outside the establishment in community, state, and nation, and (3) those on the international scene.

There are seven significant influences within the educational establishment that merit mention as follows:

Influences within the educational establishment

1. Growing centralism in education
2. Increasing innovation and specialization
3. A new breed of teachers and pupils
4. A power struggle in our semi-profession
5. Collegiate competition for teachers
6. Development of administrative theory
7. The size and complexity of schools

The movement toward centralism involves regionalism and nationalism, as well as statism. It tends to reduce local flexibility and to foster standardization and uniformity. In part this trend is a response to inability and unwillingness at local and state levels; in part it reflects the controversy over unequal educational opportunity; and in part it grows out of and supports the idea of the great society. Federal aid in large categorical or earmarked dosages has been a potent force in this movement.

From *The Education Digest*, February, 1968, pp. 35–37. The article first appeared in the *North Central Association Quarterly*. Reprinted by permission.

Automation, invention, and innovation wield much influence on education and administration. For example, the use of computers in scheduling is growing. The new biology programs developed by BSCS are widely used. Educational media of many types are being employed, hopefully to improve the process of teaching and learning. Only as educators can harness these movements and other products of scientific and co-operative development will they serve the schools well.

Teachers today are different from those we sent you twenty years or more ago. They are brighter and better educated. They are less tractable and more likely to speak out. They are not so conventional as teachers once were in their ethics, their ideals, or their motivation. Pupils, too, are today more rebellious and their backgrounds and expectations are less homogeneous. Alienation and estrangement characterize many members of both groups; more will be said on this point later.

In our semiprofession of education we have today the beginnings of a civil rebellion. If it continues, and this appears likely, we may postpone the time when ours becomes a real profession. Decision making is under scrutiny. Teachers are demanding a louder voice in virtually all matters, and administrators are increasingly suspect. Boards of education are caught up in this power struggle also, and the roles of all concerned are subject to modification. Much of this militant behavior is a result of the failure of administrators and trustees and citizens to meet legitimate needs of teachers. Now the pressure is on and it is mounting because it has been successful.

Collective bargaining and professional negotiation tend to restrict the leadership of principals and to legalize the means of its implementation. There seems to be little difference between bargaining and negotiation in their impact, and both reduce the status of administration. If this movement has not yet reached your community, you can expect it in the next several years, unless some unforeseen turn of events intervenes.

The democratization of higher education and the shortage of college teachers has initiated a widespread move to hire away from secondary schools their better-prepared teachers. Thus the problems of recruitment, induction, inservice education, and curricular improvement are being increased. The growing opportunity for collegiate teaching will also be involved as a lever in the power struggle mentioned earlier. Few principals can expect other than a growing personnel problem in the years just ahead.

Administrative theory is increasingly being developed and put to use in administrative practice. Bases of authority, decision making and implementation, power sharing, and other points of human relations and dynamics are undergoing change. The delegation of duties, the decentralization of authority, and related moves to broaden administrative participation are well known, although sometimes abused or disregarded. We know more about administration than we once did, we are more alert to errors, and we are permitted a smaller margin of error than ever before. Teachers are also more informed and/or opinionated about these matters, and they are impatient.

The size of our secondary schools, indeed of the total educational venture, has much influence on the principal. Complexity usually accompanies growth. I want to stress two developments that are particularly significant, namely those of communication and depersonalization. Administrators, teachers, and pupils feel these conditions that tend to reduce individual identity and promote a breakdown in the meaningful complex of group memberships. Communication failure and misunderstanding are increasingly likely as the size of a group grows, especially if this growth is accompanied by diversity of membership.

Outside the educational establishment and the school process, there are significant local, state, and national influences affecting the principal's role. Four that are crucial are as follows:

Influences on the local, state, and national levels

1. Population explosion, implosion, and mobility
2. Social and moral conflict, change, and improvement
3. Rising educational costs and taxation
4. Higher educational expectations

The interrelationship of these conditions is obvious.

Not only are we faced with more pupils to be educated, they are progressively concentrated in urban areas, and they are very mobile. About one-third of our families move each year. Problems of articulation, pressures for a more uniform curriculum, and the job of housing pupils and providing teachers combine to make school administration a great and sometimes frustrating challenge.

Add to these conditions such things as civil rights, deprivation, and segregation, and the task grows. Movements to improve economic, political, and social opportunity are rooted in education. No society can become great without first being well educated. If the schools are believed not to be effective, separate educational investments are then made, as we have observed. Thus schools feel compelled to respond quickly—whether ready or not—and the scope of educational responsibility grows much more rapidly than tax support.

In some ways the schools now serve as enforcement agencies of the courts and of governmental divisions handing out money. Cross purposes become involved and conflicting community attitudes cloud the educational environment. I am not judging these developments, but I do point out that social unrest and improvement enlarge upon the principal's responsibility and complicate his administration.

We live today with a great moral crisis. The restraints of long standing values have been loosened. The result is insecurity and for many a search for something around which to build new ideals. Youth is especially caught up in this period of questioning and questing. The young are idealists in many ways, but they are not blind to the denial of stated ethics in the behavior of people around them. And those of us who are older, too, feel some of the same fear and frustration.

The costs of all tax-supported agencies seem to be rising, including those of schools. The competition for dollars is often keen, and in many communities school tax increases have been denied repeatedly. Problems of housing, personnel, and program usually have some monetary basis. Many principals find that low-level fiscal support adds to their burden and underlies many of the divisive personnel developments in the schools.

The educational expectations of citizens are generally rising, and they are outspoken in criticism when needs are not met. Both quantitative and qualitative aspects of the schools are involved. Public relations assume growing significance, especially as conflict arises and various pressure groups seek to attain their own ends. Too often the ability of the principal to respond to challenges in this area is limited by conditions beyond his control, but he is expected to perform, nonetheless.

The International scene

It would seem that the influences already cited are enough to break the camel's back, but there are still more. On the international scene several major factors require attention:

1. World-wide social revolution and cold wars
2. The space race
3. Our ascending international role

Far removed from the principal's office though these influences may seem, they operate daily in the schools.

There is no doubt that various forms of capitalism, communism, fascism, nationalism, and socialism are in competition the world over. For many people the primary motive is a better life. The war in Vietnam is currently the hottest focal point of this conflict and this hope. Its impact on us as a people and on teaching and learning is apparent in most schools and dramatically so in some, especially at the college level. The draft creates opinions and pressures that are brought regularly to the attention of secondary school principals.

The race for outer space has stepped up school criticism and continues to advocate more and improved mathematics and science instruction. It is linked with the socio-political world revolution and to the growing international role our nation is called upon to play. All three of these closely related activities have tremendous tax implications.

The influences mentioned and others not touched upon constantly collide to create a great malady of this era—alienation. I use the term here in a broad sense to encompass a host of feelings that serve to destroy individual identity and weaken sustaining group membership. A few words about this condition in relation to educational challenge may be helpful. *Resultant national malady*

Upheavals and protests are noted across the world. Automation displaces people in some jobs and they are deeply and understandably concerned. On many college campuses the loud cry against impersonality is heard. Teachers strike or threaten to do so. Young people and old picket to protest a variety of conditions, real or imagined. Feelings run high and impatience and impertinence are prevalent. Never before has schooling in the traditional sense had so much competition for the time and effort of youth.

This widespread alienation, estrangement, and frustration touches all of us and affects our behavior. Each of us desperately needs personal identity, membership in groups, and a sense of integrity. Without these conditions we are at best unhappy and at worst a menace to self and society. And society loses its stability as the numbers of poorly identified and disintegrated individuals mount. We should, therefore, review our jobs carefully in the light of these influences and this malady.

A recitation of the many competing, supportive, and often contentious influences cited herein might overwhelm any but a strong or foolish man. But there is ample evidence that our principals are neither foolish nor weak. Most of them have tried hard to be responsive to the challenges at hand with the resources they have. Earlier discus- *Implications of these changing influences*

sion speaks directly to various limitations imposed by current influences and alludes to important administrative functions. A few closely related implications of these influences are now in order, and they are suggested solely with the intent of being helpful, not critical.

First, the principal should restudy carefully his role as a school administrator in the light of these influences, particularly as regards the growing dissension in educational ranks. There is no doubt that the job of the administrator is changing, and he of all people should have a hand in the process. He cannot wisely avoid the conflict or seek to shape his own destiny alone. It may be necessary, however, that he and other administrators organize to combat the power plays of others if dignity, fairness, reason, and professional integrity cannot otherwise be maintained. Whatever comes, tomorrow's administrator will be different from today's, and a willingness to participate in the direction of change is very essential.

Second, the principal should increasingly become a master of human relations and an expert in mediating and ameliorating conflict within individuals and within and among groups. Adeptness in making organizational and functional changes to involve others in decision making and implementation is very important. He should be able in delegation as well as in integration, which conditions call for more administrative help, likely from the ranks of teachers, than is typically provided today. It is not only the teachers who need lighter loads.

Deciding and doing are likely to encounter opposition from various quarters in the era ahead. Often no one of the possible alternatives will satisfy all concerned, indeed perhaps not even a majority. The principal in this endeavor will need to be unusually stable, possess considerable flexibility and great patience, and demonstrate talent in working with people. As one illustration, the problems of bargaining and negotiating are apt to be exceedingly trying in the next five to ten years.

Third, to bring greater wisdom and effectiveness to all his activity, the principal will need to find time to read and think more than ever before. How else can he keep abreast of influences and developments pertinent to his job? This will be more difficult to do later than at present, yet I see no other way to survive professionally. Hasty and poorly thought out administrative decisions have caused part of our current misery, and the future will be even less tolerant of error than the present. The principal will simply have to set definite and uninterrupted periods of time aside for this thoughtful approach to his job.

Fourth, and possibly most fundamental of all, the principal should lead a physically vigorous and culturally rich life apart from his job. The demands of this job are growing and only a person who is vigorous and varied in his nonvocational endeavor is likely to meet these demands. Resilience of body, mind, and spirit is quite essential in an administrative position, especially in working with people in an era of rapid change. This condition cannot be attained and maintained by one who is forever on the job, whether at home or in his office.

Redefinition of the role of the principal is in order, but this is not the occasion for this development. Such action is likely to require several years in view of the changing influences I have mentioned. This role is not static, indeed it will probably undergo much modification over the next decade. *A great, grave, and challenging time*

I am confident, however, that all is not lost and that good sense will see us through this trying period as in the past. No one of us escapes the destiny of his day; each is inevitably shaped and used by it. The wise and courageous man not only recognizes what is happening; but responds and attempts to shape and use that destiny for noble ends. School principals should do no less.

27. Why Small District Hired Two Superintendents

Kenneth W. Sand and Dale K. Hayes

EAGLE, Neb.—How does a small district find a superintendent who is qualified and will stay a while?

Faced with this problem, Alvo-Eagle public schools tried co-administrators, both on a half-time basis. The district, which was organized in 1961, serves a rural area of more than seventy-five square miles with a total population of approximately one thousand and two hundred. The certified faculty never exceeded twenty-one. Assessed valuation of the district was less than $4 million.

Teachers wouldn't stay   After three years, the district had been served by three superintendents at a one a year rate. Teachers left even faster. At the end of the second year only 26.3 per cent returned; after the third year 35 per cent returned. Worried about the harm to the academic program that this turnover was causing, the board asked the state education association to investigate the problem.

Attempts to obtain strong administrative leadership obviously had failed. In a three-month period in 1964, for example, the board records showed that fourteen persons were interviewed for the superintendency—excluding informal interviews or written communications. The salary was reasonably attractive and above that paid by comparable schools in the area.

The department of educational administration at the University of Nebraska proposed the coadministrator arrangement, with two men performing the functions of the superintendency, each on a half-time basis. Both persons were also able to carry nine semester hours of graduate work during each semester.

Participants were selected by the department from persons who had (1) qualified to pursue a doctor's degree in the department, (2) had not fulfilled the residency requirement, and (3) could complete

From *Nation's Schools*, March, 1967, pp. 150 ff. Reprinted by permission. Copyright 1967 by McGraw-Hill, Chicago. All rights reserved.

remaining requirements in two years on a part-time basis. The persons selected were recommended to the board of education of the participating school, which in turn set salaries and offered contracts.

The first coadministrator contracted was designated as superintendent and the other as assistant superintendent. The two men shared the salary which had been agreed upon for a full-time administrator with the senior person receiving the larger share.

The first coadministrator was employed for one year only and in this time completed the requirements for the Six-Year Professional Certificate. To provide continuity all subsequent persons were employed with a two-year understanding. Under this staggered turnover system, the assistant became superintendent the second year, receiving the responsibilities and larger salary.

To avoid overlap, duties were divided. The senior coadministrator had major responsibility for all items which were considered budgetary and financial, supervision of the elementary school, transportation services, the hot lunch program, custodial services, maintenance, and dealings with the board. The assistant superintendent was largely responsible for procurement of supplies and equipment, supervision of the secondary school, guidance services, student affairs, and federal programs. Times of responsibility were staggered so each person assumed the total responsibility in the absence of the other. Whenever possible and desirable, responsibility was shared, as in the case of staffing the school. Through co-ordinated effort, persons were interviewed and contracted by either or both administrators.

The first year of the experiment the coadministrators faced essentially the same problems as a full-time administrator would in the identical situation. The two major problems first to face the experimenters were the formulation of a budget from scanty information and the selecting of a staff.

The budget was a battle

Although there was some skepticism, the experiment appeared well accepted from the beginning. Not all persons were in favor but no particular problem developed solely because of the uniqueness of the situation. In fact, many took pride in participating and in having a connection with the university. Perhaps the most positive result was that the community, staff, and students had confidence in the administrators and in their ability because of this identification with the state university.

The first year of the experiment each administrator was responsible for one-half of each school day, with one available in the morning and the other in the afternoon. During the second semester the periods of responsibility were reversed, but in each case the changeover came during the noon hour.

The second year a variation was attempted from the previous plan for periods of responsibility. All was the same except that on two days each week only one administrator would arrive at school and remain all day while the other spent the entire day on studies. These were never consecutive days. Tuesday and Thursday were used first semester and Tuesday and Friday the next. The long weekend was particularly helpful during the time doctoral research was being written. Although there was some overlap and duplication of effort, this was held to a minimum and both plans mentioned proved successful. The administrators spent more time at the school than was expected or scheduled.

Another advantage in the second year of the experiment (1965–66) was the added assistance of a teaching principal. All previous full-time superintendents had such persons, but not the first co-administrators.

Among the needed ingredients to make such a program possible and successful are (1) a school needing competent administration, (2) a preparing institution willing to co-operate, and (3) two qualified administrators willing to sacrifice. A fourth and most important requirement is a board of education with ability, foresight, and a willingness to experiment.

Briefly, we feel coadministration can do the following:

1. Provide competent administration for small schools unable to obtain and retain a qualified full-time superintendent;
2. Provide worthy and needed internship experience;
3. Provide communication between the preparing institution and the field;
4. Provide financial assistance for deserving graduate students;
5. Maintain desirable relations with, and receive acceptability by, the concerned board of education, the degree-granting institution, and the state department of education;
6. Provide continuity and direction in the total school program;
7. Provide leadership in desirable district reorganization.

28. Home-School-Community Relations

THE farmer looked up from his work and called out to the passing boy.

"How do you like your new teacher, Jimmy?"

"Swell! School's great this year," replied Jimmy as he hurried toward school on his bicycle.

Thus the child—strategic bearer of good or bad tidings—is the key person in any school public relations program. Then come the parent, the teacher, the school board, the superintendent, and the board of education. These individuals are the first and foremost allies of education, and it is through them that the public at large gains its news and views of the schools.

Now it is of questionable ethics, and certainly not sound practice, for the child to be exploited by making him an agent of propaganda for the school system. To be sure, through the school paper, radio broadcasts, and other activities . . . the child naturally becomes an indispensable "aide-de-camp" of the public relations program; but for the most part, his role in publicizing and interpreting education should be spontaneous and casual. The boy or girl who enjoys school life, likes the teachers and principal, and feels that he or she is engaging in worthwhile pursuits cannot help promoting education to the public at large.

From the marts of merchandising comes the profound advice that to sell one must have something worthwhile to sell, and indeed, the better the product the easier the salesmanship! While just "selling the school" is no longer considered the goal of public relations,[1] this counsel from the business world has an implication which educators

From *The County Superintendent of Schools in the United States, 1950* (National Education Association, 1950), 146–50. Reprinted by permission.

[1] National Education Association, Department of Elementary School Principals, "The Public and the Elementary School" (Twenty-Eighth Yearbook, Washington, D.C., The Department, 1949), 11.

cannot afford to overlook: we must develop a school system which places the welfare of the whole child first and which makes the hours spent in school by all children happy and profitable ones. Exposed to such a system and endowed as he should be with a free spirit and an alert mind, the American child—with neither coaching nor coaxing —will unconsciously "sell" education to the community.

But children are human and the human species has at times quaint quirks of personality. Therefore, once in a while, even in the best systems of education, the child will convey to his parents and adult friends a false interpretation of what is happening in school. This is especially true of those children who are incapable of fitting the fantasy dreamed up by ambitious parents and who consequently seek alibis for lack of educational achievement by unjustifiably pointing out shortcomings in the teachers and schools.

Over-protective parents often have an abnormal love for their children and therefore are prone to believe childish accusations. But the alert educator realizes that in this love lies the salient solution to the child-parent problem of public relations. For the more a parent loves his child, the more concerned he is with the child's schooling; and once this parent understands that the school, also, is sincerely interested in and wants to help the child, he will usually co-operate and lend a hand in the ever-unfinished task of teaching.

How can teachers and parents get to know and understand each other better? Through participation of the teacher in community activities such as service clubs, church organizations, and through school affairs such as the after-school tea, the PTA, the holiday exercise, and the "open house." Better understanding can also be achieved through an improved system of reporting pupil progress. Many schools have learned that the formal report card, even when "doctored up" with modern devices, is at best a cold and distant appraisal of the child. To remedy this situation they have instituted a system of private conferences with parents which, though a heavy drain on the teacher's time, pays dividends to the child, the parent, and the school. And where this technique fails to bring out the parents, there is always the last and probably best technique of all: the home call.

In education there is no substitute for personal contact between parent and teacher. This is the "open sesame" for success in teaching and progress in school improvement.

However, to make personal relationships most effective, the teacher must like children and people in general and must be well informed on educational psychology, methods, and objectives. In addition, he must understand the needs and resources of the community and know about the financial problem of the school system. The latter, in particular, is often neglected by teachers; and in many cases the fault here lies not in the teacher himself so much as in the administrator. All too often superintendents and principals fail to take teachers into their confidence regarding the everlasting and sometimes crucial problems of financial support for education. This can have tragic results, for the teacher has numerous contacts with the public in both a professional and personal capacity and can play an important part in correcting faults as well as disseminating accurate information relative to the needs and philosophy of the school system.

An often neglected means of achieving constructive parent-teacher co-operation is in the field of curriculum development. While most school systems now have committees working on continuous development of the curriculum, too few see the need and advantage of bringing lay people into this important phase of educational improvement. This is a mistake, for parents, businessmen and laborers, are all vitally interested in what is being taught in our schools and can lend valuable assistance to curriculum committees. In the process of working democratically with professional educators these laymen acquire a new understanding and appreciation for education.

In a number of counties lay people are playing a significant role in this once restricted field of curriculum reorganization. An example of this is the booklet for parents of pre-school children published each year by Waukesha County, Wisconsin. Called "Looking Forward to School Days," this booklet was originally written and is yearly revised by a committee of parents and teachers assisted by the county superintendent's staff, the county nurse, and the county psychiatrist. It is distributed in the spring to parents of pre-school children and used by primary teachers as a guide for group and individual conferences with parents, and has proved to be eminently worthwhile from the standpoint of public relations and educational practice.

As time goes on, a well-conceived and democratically guided teacher-layman curriculum project can expand its field of interest beyond the usual deliberations over core curriculum, subject matter, and child development and take on special problems such as building needs, school financing, community betterment, and state and federal school legislation.

The public relations program depends to a great extent upon the willingness of the teacher to accept a position of leadership in school and community life. To do so, he should not be overburdened with too many classes and pupils and should receive an adequate salary.

The disgruntled and unhappy teacher is respected by no one and has little constructive influence; but the sincere and conscientious teacher—both after and during school hours—is an asset to the school and community. Such a teacher realizes that even a casual conversation with the grocer has educational significance and that in his classroom are thirty little reporters ready and anxious to carry home the news to a willing audience of adults who will relay that news to every corner of the community. It is a truism that a school system can at times rise or fall because of the acts or attitudes of a single instructor of youth. Obviously, there is no substitute for a good teacher.

The county superintendent can plant the seed and guide the growth of almost every phase of the public relations program. He can be especially helpful to the teacher in relationships with pupils, parents, and public at large. If the superintendent is informed on modern education—and not to have this information is inexcusable—he practices, as well as preaches, democratic administration and takes teachers into his confidence on issues and policies. This is done through friendly calls and personal conferences, a teacher advisory committee, a schoolmasters' club, handbooks, bulletins, letters. In Bergen County, New Jersey, for example, the superintendent counsels with teachers both as individuals and in groups and issues a monthly bulletin which stresses ways in which school people can interpret the school to the public. In addition to encouraging teachers and furnishing them with factual information about policies and problems, this bulletin gives helpful hints on how to interview parents, how to correspond with patrons, how to handle telephone calls, and other techniques of public relations.

"Men learn by precept and example," says the philosopher, and this is advice to which the superintendent of schools should lend an ear. He and his immediate staff are constantly in contact with parents and the public and in this capacity have an obligation to set an example for teachers and principals.

There was a time when the county superintendent (a) devoted his energy to politics and spouted platitudes as his casual contribution to education, or (b) scorned the people and with pedantic superiority boasted that "he'd stand on his record," or (c) appointed a publicity man and forgot all about the school's patrons. That day is now over and should have gone out with the hickory stick! The modern superintendent must be an efficient administrator, a sincere student of trends and methods, and "sparkplug" of the public relations program.

Part Four. **Strategies and Innovations**

Introduction to Part Four

"GOOD" rural schools cost money, but no community can afford the social costs of "bad" schools. The costs for inadequate rural schools are measured in terms of items such as welfare payments, juvenile delinquency, and racism. It takes a considerable amount of courage for some rural communities to evaluate their school programs and then map out priorities and strategies for improvement. A major problem is the adaptation of curricula to meet the current needs of rural pupils and their communities. An improved quality of instruction requires additional funds, dedicated staff, and ideas to innovate.

Rural schools are characterized by acute financial problems. Special types of facilities are sometimes needed, and the need for new buildings is one of the most urgent problems now facing all school districts, rural and urban. The shortage of school facilities and buildings in rural areas is due largely to the reorganization of school districts and the inability of small districts to finance long-term capital expenditures. State and federal funds have become an important source of revenue for rural schools. However, only a few states have accepted responsibility for adequately assisting in the financing of high-cost small schools. In some instances, when local funds are not sufficient, the federal government has provided monies for compensatory education programs.

Slow rate of change

If—as we have stressed throughout this book—we are to understand the problems of rural schools, we must understand the forces affecting their communities. Rural communities throughout the nation are being influenced by the forces of change. Change tends to produce anxiety; it threatens security, creates problems, and requires adjustments. Since much that rural students learn in school is applicable to their home life, members of rural communities are not merely resisting changes in school but are also resisting changes in the home.

Regardless of its program, its budget, or its leadership, the school is a community institution.

School improvement is more than a matter of reorganization and additional financing or a collection of buildings; it is improved teacher, administrator, and student relationships. The rural school's place in the community frequently is more than educational. Sometimes the school's athletic events provide the only leisure-time activities for children and adults. This, then, is another reason rural school patrons may resist changes in their school programs—especially if the change will result in the loss of school identity with the community.

In most rural communities there is a sense of school loyalty, especially in athletics. Often teams consist of a wide age range. For instance, a graduate of a rural school in Oklahoma took pride in the fact that he played on the junior high basketball team when he was in the third grade. Rural school teachers notice that their students have the ability to improvise and play with almost anything. In most schools there is not an extensive amount of playground equipment but, as one teacher commented, "They just pick up a stick and imagine it to be something else." Rural children find ways to have fun. Administrators must find ways to improve the curricula. In some instances, this requires consolidation.

Consolidation   Consolidation, eliminating or combining several small schools into larger schools, is an issue with many sides. In the past thirty years, several states have reorganized school districts in order to achieve consolidation. The major purpose of all reorganization in rural areas has been the formation of rural school districts with sufficient enrollment to justify and afford an expanded program of education.

Those who support consolidation raise many important issues. It is difficult for small schools to offer an adequate curriculum, to recruit the best teachers, and to afford modern facilities. A large school does offer the possibility of more money, better facilities and staff, and curriculum diversity. But this is not always true. Certainly a school does not automatically improve simply by increasing its size. There is ample evidence to allow us to conclude that not only can a small school be just as good as a large one, but the advantages found in a small school may be enough to cause students to prefer it over a large school. One thing seems to be clear: small schools will be with us for many more decades.

The fact that the small school will be with us for a while longer need not be discouraging. Once we realize the advantages, the thought of their continued existence is exhilarating. Many rural students feel a greater sense of personal identification than urban students. Their class sizes are small, allowing them to receive a greater amount of individual attention. They have a greater opportunity to participate in co-curricular activities and, in some instances, to excel in competitive activities. Unlike their urban counterparts, they are less likely to feel like IBM cards—punched, stapled, mutilated, and filed. *Place for innovation*

The small school is an ideal testing place for new educational theories; it can be a laboratory for innovators. Actually, the task of improving small schools may be easier than that of improving larger schools. Because of their size most small districts are able to quickly revise class schedules. Similar changes are more expensive in big city schools that have to resort to computers for system-wide changes. In order to improve rural schools so that quality education can be achieved, much more innovation is needed.

Experimentation is the key to rural school development. Innovators must be employed and encouraged, and their innovations should be carefully considered. Various projects—the Catskill Area Project, the Rocky Mountain Area Project, the Western States Small Schools Project, the Oregon Small Schools Project, the Upper Midwest Small Schools Project, the Texas Small Schools Project, and others—have continually shown that small schools need not adopt large-school policies in order to improve. However, the innovations required to move a small school from where it is to where it should and can be is seldom the matter of minor adjustments in teaching procedures. But in most instances, what is needed is an almost completely new instructional design.

When devising methods and strategies for change, educators usually fail to remember that a small, rural school is not a large, urban school. The former should not be considered as a miniature of the latter. Too many educators are hung up on the idea that biggest means best. This hampers adoption of learning and practicing procedures which are appropriate to individual small schools. Of course, many educational practices that work well in urban schools will be appropriate for rural schools and vice versa.

The following are some of the more effective practices: activities which allow students to proceed at their own pace; team teaching where two or three teachers with various specialties share classes, *Promising practices* enabling students to have the benefits of many teachers' skills; using teacher aides, which frees teachers from clerical tasks; multiple class teaching, in which two or more related fields are taught at once; and shared services, where several schools share supplies, teachers, and equipment. A few of the more progressive schools have shifted to flexible scheduling and modified self-instruction so that learning is student-centered instead of teacher-centered.

In regard to the use of technical equipment, the most popular seem to be tape recorders, slide projectors, and films. The tape recorder is a useful instrument for both students and teachers. The teacher can record lectures to be listened to by one class while she offers help to another. Students can replay tapes in order to clear up major points of an assignment or to actually hear themselves talk. Slide projectors and films can be used to clarify points that the teacher is not sure of or to acquaint the students with things that they otherwise would not see or know about. Although television is used extensively as an educative device in urban schools, it is of much less importance in rural schools.

In some small schools, maximum use is made of technical equipment. For instance in Springfield, Vermont, a nongraded rural high school gave students five weeks out of the classroom for the purpose of obtaining trade skills. Each student was given tape recorded lectures, slides, and a projector, all to keep them up with preprogrammed lessons. Teachers became research organizers, consultants, and tutors when help was needed. Thus the students learned from textbooks, programmed instruction, home assignments, and cooperative trade experiences. The classes, therefore, were self-instructed, and often turned into consultation sessions. Achievement tests were given at the end of each assignment.

In several places, amplified long-distance telephone systems have been used to provide small schools with courses they normally could not offer. In western Colorado, a Western State College history professor has simultaneously taught history to five different rural classes in this manner. On the day following each half-hour lecture, the professor held a half-hour question-answer period for the classes. Unlike the television, the teacher on the telephone talks back to students, answering their questions.

Some rural districts have set up regional purchasing services, allowing schools to purchase services at a price their district can afford. These services are in six categories: teacher services, administrative services, occupational services, special education services, pupil personnel services, and miscellaneous services. Shared teachers are of great benefit in this and any other program. Another form of sharing is found in data processing centers. Regional centers are used to take census, keep attendance records, do class scheduling, score tests, fill out report cards, and handle the payroll. There is a small amount of computer-assisted instruction available to rural high school students.

In some communities, high school students attend a vocational school for half-day sessions; the other half of the day is spent in their regular high school where they take the academic subjects needed for graduation. Vocational schools offer instruction in nursing, agriculture, child care, electronics, drafting, etc. By pooling teacher resources, some rural districts are also able to provide programs for gifted students. Finally, sharing regional or district resources has allowed small schools to have psychological and social work services on a limited basis.

In addition to the above changes, some rural districts are securing help from universities and colleges in areas such as writing proposals for federal funds, in-service training for teachers and administrators, evaluation of new programs, and involving the community in school activities. Professors who respond to the rural school districts' pleas for help are finding that they too are learning some things.

One-teacher schools are still fairly neglected. Many are being consolidated with other one-teacher schools or into a larger system, but those that are not do not have the appeal to professors that the larger schools do. Most often, teachers must go it alone. A few teachers in one-teacher schools have done remarkable things to update their schools. They use tape recorders, film projectors, and some have even implemented ungraded systems. Most, however, offer an inferior quality of instruction.

Everyone connected with the rural school is involved in some aspect of curricula. Despite the isolated innovations that we have noted, most rural education is still rural-oriented. Vocational courses still reflect rural life: park and estate forestry, soil conservation, pollution control, veterinary service, landscaping, horticulture, and food processing. Of course, such courses are important to both urban and rural living, and if trained in these fields a person could get along well in either environment. Still, rural education tends to be weak in college preparatory courses. Lately, there is a growing feeling that there should be several courses of study evolving around agricultural education, college preparation, and other vocational training.

Yes, there have been significant changes in a few small school districts. But the over-all picture is not so encouraging. The continuing high unemployment and school drop-out rates are illustrations of the failure of rural schools to prepare their students for a productive life as adults. State and federal funds can help somewhat, but, ultimately, it may take irate parents committed to quality education in order for most rural schools to provide modern curricula.

Readings Albert Mitchell's article, "The Rural-Urban Dichotomy: A Problem for Teachers," stresses the need for rural teachers to abandon dual standards and prepare rural students for life in an urban nation. Rowen Stutz ("Strategies for Strengthening Small Schools") and Ovid Parody ("Big Ideas for Small Schools") suggest broad areas in which rural schools can be improved.

Thomas Leigh offers a vivid illustration of ways small schools can schedule time to permit more individualized instruction. His article, "Big Opportunities in Small Schools through Flexible-Modular Scheduling," illustrates how a big city program can be adjusted to solve a small school's problem.

If rural schools must provide vocational agriculture programs, they should be modern, updated courses. James Hamilton's article, "Guidelines for Developing Vocational Agriculture Programs for Youth with Special Needs" is timely.

Bob Taylor answered his own question, "Are Small High Schools Doing an Adequate Job of In-Service Education?" No, they are not. Lee Witters' article, "In-Service Education for the Smaller School's Faculty," begins where Taylor leaves off and offers suggestions for improved in-service programs.

John Waybright ("A Community Becomes Involved in Education") suggests ways to get optimum community involvement in the education process, while Jim Jackson's article, "Whatever Happened to the Little Red Schoolhouse?" clearly illustrates that small schools can be leaders in school improvement. In fact, they can teach big schools a few lessons in innovation.

29. The Rural-Urban Dichotomy: A Problem for Teachers

Albert Mitchell

TEACHERS, like other Americans, have become accustomed to thinking in terms of urban or rural, city or country, farms or factories, sidewalks or shaded country lanes. This dichotomous division of our society has become common in contemporary planning and writing, as well as in teaching. It is the purpose of this article to submit two questions for consideration. First, do teachers overemphasize the urban-rural divisions of Americans during classroom instruction? Second, how accurately do they present the existing differences between urban and rural life?

Certainly there is a historical basis for the classification of people as rural and urban or, to be more accurate, as agricultural and urban. In a country which makes a hobby out of American history, there is no need to elaborate on our agricultural heritage. America was once a nation of farmers.[1] Is it not now a nation of "urbanites?" The United States census indicates a dominance in urban population. It is true that the Bureau of the Census has classified only 69.9 per cent of the population as urban in 1960; however, only about 7 per cent of the population could actually be classified as farm people.[2] To look at this in another way, the Industrial Conference Board of New York reported that in September, 1965, only 6 per cent of the households in the United States were farm households.[3]

Thus, there is a residue of some 23 per cent of the population which is not urban and not agricultural and, for want of a better name, has been classified as rural-nonfarm. Nearly one out of every four per-

Overemphasis?

From *Journal of Geography*, Fall, 1967, pp. 60-62. Reprinted by permission.

[1] Henry J. Carman and Harry J. Syrett, *A History of the American People* (New York, Alfred A. Knopf, 1959), 254.

[2] U.S. Bureau of the Census, *U. S. Census of Population* (Washington, D.C., 1960), Vol. I.

[3] J. Frank Gaston (ed.), "Households in the United States," *Road Maps of Industry*, No. 1529 (New York, Industrial Conference Board of New York).

sons in the country belongs in this category and as a group they form the bulk of the population living outside of the cities and large towns. If it were true that rural-nonfarm people were agricultural in orientation, the rural-urban division could rightly be emphasized in the schools. However, it would seem that there is very little reason for believing that rural-nonfarm people are either agricultural or even rural in philosophy or outlook. Close investigation might well show that rural-nonfarm people hold the same types of jobs, live the same kind of lives, and are interested in the same things as urban people. In fact, it may well be that what we still find is an urban population living in the country. If this is true, it represents a fundamental change from a century ago when the city was urban and the country was agricultural.

An excellent example of this change in outlook and orientation occurs in Farmington, Maine. In the latter half of the nineteenth century a divergence of interest became apparent among the citizens of Farmington. The inhabitants of the village wanted fire protection and a public water supply but the agricultural element of the area was very much opposed to paying for services which it would use very little if at all. Thus a Village Corporation, including only the built-up area of the village, was formed in 1860 to provide the above services separate from the New England town government.[4] The corporation later expanded its services to include such items as street lights and local police protection.

This separation of Farmington into urban and agricultural segments lasted until the middle of the present century. In the past few years the agricultural nature of the area around Farmington has changed to the point where it no longer deserves its name. One result of this change is that most of the outlying population has become rural-nonfarm in nature. At the same time the interests of this nonfarm group have apparently become very much like those of the village population. As a result the functions of the Village Corporation have been assumed one by one by the town government and the corporation is now reduced to the ownership of a water company which it does not operate. Does the development in recent years of many regional planning boards to replace city planning boards reflect the same fundamental change described for Farmington?

Thus, instead of a rough 70-30 per cent division of the population into urban and rural people, is the division roughly 95 per cent urban

4 Francis Gould Butler, *A History of Farmington*, (Farmington, Press of Knowlton, McLeary and Co., 1885), 203.

and only 5 per cent rural? If this is true, schools are in danger of reaching the same stage in regard to rural life that many have reached in teaching about the Eskimo. There may be as many as twenty-five thousand Eskimos in North America, but they often receive more classroom time than all of Canada.

Should urban and rural people take a point from the ecumenical movement and emphasize what they have in common rather than what divides them? Part of the problem arises in the confusion of the form with the functions of rural and urban existence. In terms of form there is a tremendous difference between the skyscrapers of New York and the collection of stores, banks, and gas stations that characterize Farmington. This difference in form is equally true for the suburban sprawl of southern Connecticut and the new homes outside of Farmington. However, the function in each case seems to be essentially the same. In other words, there is little difference in kind of services between the country crossroads and the large city; there is only a difference in size and complexity. It appears that this same concept applies equally to residential function. The rural-non-farm home is remarkably like the urban home in purpose and activity. There is certainly a valid reason for distinguishing between urban functions and agricultural functions, but there seems little reason, in the broad sense, to distinguish between urban and rural. Even in distinguishing between urban and agricultural functions there is a real danger of exaggerating the differences between urban and agricultural life. The modern successful farmer sits at a desk and uses a calculator instead of wearing overalls and driving a horse. His wife shops in the nearest city and his children go to college. How much alike is it possible to become?

The second question follows from the first, namely "How accurately does the teaching in our schools present the existing difference between urban and rural life?" Aside from the considerable difference from school system to school system and even from classroom to classroom, it is probably accurate to say that in general teachers do a very poor job of presenting the true picture. There are a number of reasons for this. First, many teachers remember in a nostalgic manner how it used to be on "grandfather's farm." They reflect in their teaching and thinking how it used to be and not how it is. The very rapid manner in which rural areas have become like urban areas plays a part here. Edward Higbee points out that there has been an

Unrealistic instruction?

agricultural revolution since World War II which has vastly altered rural life.[5] Teachers should be acutely aware of this.

The rapid change is creating a great reserve of obsolescent books in the same way that it has created teachers with obsolescent ideas. Do current textbooks reflect accurately the difference between urban and agricultural life? One of the more common descriptions encountered in this type of book is of a one-man dairy farm with twenty cows. This is a great improvement over what was available a few years ago, but at the present many students are being introduced to an excellent example of the kind of agricultural life which is rapidly disappearing, if not already extinct. Twenty-five years ago, twenty-cow dairy farms were common, but even then they were going out of business. How accurate is instruction about urban and rural life when agricultural life of the 1940s is presented?

Outside the social studies area the situation is worse. A survey of reading textbooks used in the primary grades makes apparent a frequent reference to "grandfather's farm" There is the kindly old grandfather who has one cow, one horse, one chicken, and a goat, all with names. Preschool children receive a steady diet of this stereotyped subsistence farm which would be representative of the colonial period. This is suitable teaching how things *were*, but it would seem more important to teach how things *are*. It seems unreasonable to teach inaccurate concepts to young people because instructors are fond of those concepts.

The significance of the above questions and their tentative answers will be found with individual teachers and how they view the rural-urban dichotomy. Whatever that view may be, students should be taught to distinguish accurately between urban and rural life. This end might be accomplished through the use of modern materials and current ideas.

[5] Edward Higbee, *Farms and Farmers in an Urban Age* (New York, The Twentieth Century Fund, 1963).

30. Strategies for Strengthening Small Schools

Rowen C. Stutz

I will start with a brief analysis of certain commonly proposed and somewhat time-honored solutions to the problems of small schools so that these will not be cluttering the scene as we talk about some new and somewhat divergent approaches to helping small schools respond to 1967 demands for quality.

First, let's take care of the most commonly proposed solution—elimi- **Consolidation** nate the small school through school district reorganization and school consolidation. It must be conceded that this approach does eliminate duplication of staff and facilities and promotes more efficient school operation. The broader tax base provided by extending school district boundaries is an essential step in the long road to small school improvement. However, it must be honestly admitted that *increasing the size of a school does not automatically result in improved instruction.* Also in many sections of our country the population is so sparse that greatly enlarging the area of a school district or a school attendance area does not appreciably increase school enrollment. In Nevada, for example, where school district reorganization has reduced the total number of districts to seventeen, some of these districts are as large as some eastern states, yet these districts will enroll fewer than two hundred students in high school. The elementary school will probably have fewer than one teacher per grade. Students may spend long hours riding one way to attend school. There is a limit to how far children can be transported and therefore a limit to how far schools can be consolidated to make larger attendance centers.

Another proposed solution that has been used in foreign countries **Public** but has not gained much acceptance here in America is providing **boarding schools**

From the *North Central Association Quarterly*, Fall, 1967, pp. 196–99. Reprinted by permission.

245

for public boarding schools. The rationale of this proposal, of course, is that you would thus be able to bring together enough children to make an economically feasible unit.

The boarding school has failed to gain acceptance in the West for various reasons. First, the diversified unit with children at boarding schools is contrary to presently accepted rural traditions. Secondly, many of the students are needed on the farm or ranch to do chores morning and evening, as well as on weekends.

The economic savings and problems overcome by daily transportation would be replaced in the boarding school by costs of food, dormitories, and twenty-four-hour supervision responsibilities.

Increased financing A third proposal has partially been implemented in many states where small isolated schools exist. It involves spending more money for education in these schools. Thus in some states there are special appropriations because of small size and remote location. The difficulty with this proposed approach is that money alone will not solve the problems and so it is not too surprising that even some of those few rural schools that are endowed with considerable financial resources are still not providing too well for the education of their students.

Consolidation, boarding schools, and additional finance represent the three most commonly advocated means of getting at the problem of small schools. And consolidation and additional finance represent to date most of the small school improvement efforts throughout the country.

Small schools need unique approaches What *directions* then should our small school improvement efforts take? Can those schools which, because of location or community resistance, must remain small, at least for several years, offer quality education in an age that is demanding so much more of all schools? The answer must be yes. And it is this assumption that has prompted and guided the Catskill Area Project, the Rocky Mountain Area Project, the Upper Midwest Small School Project, the Western States Small Schools Project, the Oregon Small School Project, the Texas Small Schools Project, the Southern States Small Schools Project, and many other efforts that are not as well known as these.

It is significant that each of these projects has concluded that small school improvement is not predicated upon the adoption of successful large school practices. Rather, there is common agreement that there needs to be invented a new kind of educational program uniquely suited to the small school and its setting.

The innovations required to move the small school from where it is to where it should and can be are not limited to minor adjustments in teaching procedures. What is needed is an almost completely new instructional design for small schools. Few of the arrangements that will work effectively in a large high school will be practical or will prove effective in the small schools mainly because of differences in size and location.

New instructional design required

1. We need to invent new ways of organizing the small school for instruction.
2. Through remodeling and new construction, the physical facilities needed to do the job should be designed and provided.
3. We need to learn and practice those instructional procedures that are appropriate to small groups that still contain the full range of student diversity and reorganize the curriculum so appropriate learning opportunities are provided each student.
4. We will need to invent some new ways of providing the diverse kind of staff and staffing patterns that is needed—shared staff, staff by telephone, tape, TV, etc.
5. A different kind of training program for teachers that will effectively retrain present staffs and prepare teachers for service in small schools will need to be devised. This will involve a different content and different ways of involving teachers in training activities.
6. The resources available to the small school need to be reassessed and some imaginative ways of utilizing them for learning need to be invented. Also ways of bringing to the small school instructional resources not normally available to it need to be developed.

As I suggested before, these kinds of unique approaches to schooling will not likely be developed in a very usable way in larger schools nor in the laboratory schools springing up around the country. If they are developed, and they must be, they will be invented by those who work in small schools and by using the small school as the laboratory. We need to help outstanding educational thinkers become acquainted with small school problems so they can be helpful to us as consultants. We have been using the Goodlads, Allens, Passows, Brickells, and the Frank Browns extensively in our project and they are acquiring considerable insight and skill as consultants to small school improvement efforts.

In some ways the task of improving small schools is easier than that of improving programs in larger schools.

For example, we think the small school has several advantages as a suitable experimental laboratory, including:

Small schools are good laboratories

1. Easy access to the minds of administrative and instructional personnel.
2. Flexibility for adjusting the structure of the school to accommodate field-testing activities.
3. Ease of demonstrating for dissemination.

The obvious disadvantage of size of sample can be partly offset by replication in several schools. This adds the additional feature of variety of situations and personnel.

The small school has great potential for field-testing new ideas in education. The ease with which change can be made in a small-school situation permits an immediacy of implementation and evaluation not available in schools with large enrollments and complex structures. Small schools are good laboratories for instructional innovation. So, while there are problems unique to the small school situation which need to be solved if these schools are to meet the current challenges in education, the program designs to get at these problems and the field testing of these designs can also make an important contribution to the general cause of instructional innovation.

Small school improvement is also very challenging. These schools are mostly located in small communities. Small communities have tended to create a kind of a defense mechanism against outside forces that would cause changes in the community life. This defensiveness arises out of some illusions about the small community. Most small communities view themselves as warm hospitable places to live, as places where people can really learn the elements of success, as the last real stronghold of democracy and grass roots control of public affairs, and as places where there is the highest level of local autonomy and independence.

As I said, these are illusions and it is doubtful that these virtues of the small rural town really exist in 1967 if in fact they ever did to the degree we thought they did. In order to maintain these illusions about the small towns, its residents have had to develop some modes of adjustment which have become serious roadblocks to change. These I have borrowed from a summary of research findings by Vidich and Bensman entitled *Small Town in Mass Society* (Doubleday, 1960).

ROADBLOCKS TO CHANGE

A. The repression of inconvenient facts—facts which tend to reveal the problems of small communities and small schools are so uncomfortable that we have tended to pretend they don't exist.
B. The falsification of memory and the substitution of goals.
C. The maintenance of some illusions and the surrender of others.
  "When a sufficient number of people surrender their hopes

and aspirations in a given direction, the psychological and social character of the town is reconstituted and it is at this point that the linkage between social and economic forces and the personal fate of individuals take on a social character."

D. Mutual reinforcement of the public ideology.

"There is silent recognition among members of the community that facts and ideas which are disturbing to the accepted system of illusions are not to be verbalized except perhaps, as we have noted, in connection with one's enemies. Instead, the social mores of the small town at every opportunity demand that only those facts and ideas which support the dreamwork of everyday life are to be verbalized and selected out for emphasis and repetition."

As a result there exists in many small communities a glaring paradox. Farmers, loggers, ranchers have been forced to improve their methods or go out of business and so we see the application in these enterprises of the latest scientific technology. But the agrarian community has been singularly resistant to experimentation and planned change in their community institutions. Libraries, schools, community centers, and the communities themselves show many signs of neglect and little signs of the imaginative use of modern technological developments.

Because the small community is so close to its school and because school practices in a small community are so highly exposed, it is virtually impossible to effect changes in the small school and have them last without a fairly high degree of community understanding and support. Also, because faculty members are so integrally a part of the community and have easy access to community attitudes, the entire faculty needs to understand and support proposed changes. One dissident faculty member can easily foul up an otherwise successful innovation.

We in Western States Small Schools Project have found through the careful analysis of our successes and failures in attempting to get small schools to change that there are four important requirements that must be met if any innovation is going to have a chance to succeed and if, after it has proven itself, it is going to last. The four requisites are: *Requisites for innovation*

1. *Gaining commitment to a new set of goals.* Individuals and social systems tend to function to maintain the integrity of institutionalized value systems. The tendency is to resist pressures to change important values.

2. *Producing environmental conditions and mobilizing the re-*

sources necessary to the attainment of new goals. Because a school exists in and is dependent for support upon a situation that is external to it, the success of an innovation will depend to a considerable degree upon the ability to mobilize the resources and support of the community, school district, or state for the attainment of a given set of goals. Superintendents must be committed.

3. *Changing the value system and retraining the staff.* Innovation is not likely to survive unless there is a strong staff commitment to the change, at least on the part of those teachers involved. Where innovations have failed, the weak point has usually been human rather than theoretical. It appears that the capacity, energy, and commitment of the teacher still are the crucial elements in effective instruction.

4. *Integrating the change with all other units of the system.* We can safely assume that the introduction of an innovation will disturb an equilibrium and that accommodations throughout the system will be necessary in order to create a new equilibrium. Many good instructional practices have been rejected because of failure to properly integrate them with other aspects of the program.

There is nothing startling about these four. But the important thing is—*all four of these problems must be solved* if an instructional improvement is to have quality and permanence. Leaving any one of them unsolved will doom even the best practices to be discarded and encourage even greater resistance to future efforts to improve practices.

The small school can respond successfully to the challenges of the last half of the twentieth century. But it can do so only because those who work with small schools catch a vision of what can and should be done. School accreditation associations can help by recognizing that the criteria for measuring quality programs in larger schools are not necessarily those that measure quality instruction in small schools. And willing to develop criteria that will assess the quality of instructional programs uniquely designed for the small school situations, they will evaluate small schools for accreditation using relevant criteria, and thus quit trying to make "small schools" look like little "large schools."

31. Big Ideas for Small Schools

Ovid F. Parody

THE old saying that the best things come in small packages is as out of date as high-button shoes when it comes to public high schools. It is widely acknowledged today that better services, facilities, and over-all opportunity for good education can be found in large high schools more often than in small ones. This is not to say that bigness is synonymous with excellence in a school; but difficulties in financing, staffing, and providing materials do tend to harass the small schools more than the larger ones.

The answer over the past thirty years has been to consolidate the scattered rural schools into large district schools. The students are gathered from farms, towns, and hamlets for miles around and transported to the large central school. There they enjoy the benefits of a large school such as an athletic field, a library, a lunchroom, a broad array of specialized classrooms and teachers.

Consolidation is not possible, however, for the vast number of little schools hidden away in inaccessible regions of the nation. Some are so isolated that their nearest neighboring school is a hundred miles away. Many communities are separated by mountains, rivers, valleys, or impassable roads. Rural schools in the frigid northern areas of the nation become so snowbound during many months that a bus could not possibly transport students to a district school.

Consequently there are still hundreds of small schools tucked away in remote areas. They face many special problems. Take, for instance, a school of under 150 high school students in which one teacher might teach the entire tenth grade in one room at one time.

John is an eager reader, stimulated by abstract ideas. He instigates discussions of the philosophy of government in his social studies class and compares rural and urban political action as he knows one and has read about the other. He is fortunate in that there are two or three

From *American Education*, (U.S. Office of Education, July, 1965), 1–3. Reprinted by permission.

251

members of the class who enjoy debate, and his teacher is well informed and a good moderator.

Jim, in the same class, is bewildered and soon bored by this. He may know as much as John knows about the interrelationships and human behavior they are talking about, but he has learned what he knows through acquaintance with the local politicians and through baseball and his observations of the reactions of the players to the rules.

Mary is interested up to a point, but John's vocabulary and generalizations are beyond her. She counts the time until chemistry class, regrets that it takes place only three times weekly, and stops listening.

Bill and three others are impatient for further work on yesterday's algebra problems. The three others want to understand them and Bill longs to explain; he is ready for trigonometry, if his teacher has time for it.

Matt is pleased that agriculture period will come today. He wants to talk about the possible purchase of a tractor for his family's farm. Harry too is pleased; he is concerned about a pullet disease threatening his barnyard.

Sally, who would like to be a writer, daydreams the time away until English class, which John may enjoy, Harry find soporific, and Matt infuriating because he doesn't read well.

Their teacher, however efficient, cannot do the job he is trying to do, and since he is a good teacher he knows it. His morale lowers, he thinks about the city schools and debating societies and next year.

How to bring better facilities to students in these out-of-the-way schools is a problem that has been puzzling educators for many years. Elibe Gann of the Colorado State Department of Education has called them the "necessarily existent" small schools. Edmund A. Ford, formerly with the U.S. Office of Education, has given the situation intensive study, and has coined the phrase "Rural Renaissance" for the improvement we now hope to bring to these schools.

Within the past eight years four major projects have been undertaken in widely separated sections of the country. In 1957 the Catskill Area Project in New York State, involving twenty-seven small secondary schools, and the Rocky Mountain Area Project with twenty-five schools, were begun. The Texas Small Schools Project started in 1960 and is still underway. In January of 1962 a much larger regional project including five states grew out of the Rocky Mountain Area Project and was launched with Ford Foundation funds granted for three and a half years.

Called the Western States Small Schools Project, it is comprised of Arizona, Colorado, Nevada, New Mexico, and Utah. These states know problems in common; they are all rural with some small schools at great distances from each other; their land is irregular and weather conditions extreme; and their sociological levels are widely divergent.

The Project Policy Board is made up of the chief state school officers from each of the five states, and Byron W. Hansford, Colorado's chief school officer, has been serving as chairman. Project directors have been appointed for each state. Participating schools are selected on these basic criteria:

—The schools must be small, isolated, or otherwise rural in character. Schools which might have consolidated but did not are not considered "necessary" small schools.
—Local administrative leadership and staff commitment are essential factors in the successful functioning of the project.
—Boards of education must demonstrate their ability to form constructive policy and their willingness to innovate.
—The Community must be acquainted with the goals and in agreement with the intentions of the program.
—Schools must explore new, modified, or unusual approaches. They must be free to experiment, without restrictive or obstructive regulations which might deny exploration of methods of improvement.

As safeguards, all project proposals must have the approval of the state department of education in which the project exists, and they must demonstrate through clear statements of plans for evaluation that sound principles will be employed in conducting research and controlling experimentation.

Separate states have added their own criteria. For example, they may require participating schools to co-operate with the colleges and universities, to include some elementary schools, to be willing to perpetuate the methods found to be of value, and to provide space and materials for the project.

The new methods and techniques introduced are often departures from the rigid and orthodox. Flexible scheduling, multiple classes, programmed self-instruction devices and texts, tapes, films, television, and telephone communication, correspondence courses, seminars, shared services, and teaching aids have been used when and where they are available and appropriate.

Flexible scheduling can replace the uncompromising rigidity of the division of the school day into exactly equal divisions and the enforcement of attendance in all classes. Why, more and more teachers and school administrators are asking, must every student spend the same amount of time in each subject? The conviction is growing that each student's school time could better be determined by his own needs, abilities, and rate of comprehension.

In the many small schools where one teacher has three or four classes in one room, electronic devices and other teaching aids can make the big difference. For instance, while John and his fellow debaters follow their premises to a logical conclusion, another group could be listening through earphones to a tape on history. It is hoped that a library of prepared and co-ordinated tapes can be built up for such purposes.

Programmed textbooks and teaching machines are being prepared on the principle of presentation of material step by careful step. Programed texts are, in effect, silent tutors. The student proceeds at his own rate, and if he is in error of judgment or calculation the text tells him so and he rectifies his mistake before going on to the next step. Questions are anticipated, and confusions clarified as they arise.

Small screens and easily operated projectors now make it possible to use films for small groups without interrupting other classroom activities. Such films are also used on television programs, and it may be that television will become the teaching assistant so woefully lacking in small schools at present. With co-ordination between the classroom teacher and the studio lecturer the possibilities of efficient team teaching are promising.

The amplified telephone conversation, allowing transmission of a lecture, followed by free questions from the audience direct to the source, has been used with success in project experiments. The opportunity to listen to a discussion of poetry by an acknowledged authority such as Clifton Fadiman and to ask him questions and receive his spontaneous answers is not one otherwise likely to come to students in isolated communities. Its very novelty can introduce a student to the pleasures of poetry, and such broadening of horizons is surely all to the good.

Correspondence courses developed by universities and supervised or monitored by teachers offer enlargement of scope and economy of precious teaching time.

The small school projects are already bearing fruit. Teachers and school administrators, as well as local and state educational leaders, are gaining valuable experience in the uses of new and imaginative techniques. Especially promising is the indication that the new techniques and methods, combined with modern teaching aids, may free teachers to give more time to discovering latent talents and developing individual abilities in students.

Many of the innovations employed in these projects are still under trial and scrutiny, and full appraisal and reports have not yet been published. It is known, however, that those involved have adhered to their intention to use free but measured experiment. They want to adhere to another of perhaps greater importance: that those methods found to be of value be perpetuated and facts on them be disseminated.

There is now hope that this intention may be realized and that many more small schools may be helped in similar endeavors. . . .

The new Elementary and Secondary Education Act is designed to achieve for the nation what the small school projects are achieving for the necessarily existent small school. We are seeing what can be done when additional resources are made available for release of creative imagination and professional know-how at state and local level.

Perhaps some of the big ideas from this rural renaissance will serve to spark a nationwide rebirth of American education.

32. Big Opportunities in Small Schools Through Flexible-Modular Scheduling

Thomas B. Leigh

SMALL schools have long been recognized as possessing certain innate advantages in the educational process. Small class size, individual attention, personal identification, and the opportunity to participate to a greater degree in extracurricular activities are among those to be listed. However, for many years small schools have also been recognized as possessing some very distinct limitations and disadvantages. Among these are restricted curricular offerings, single section offerings, restricted vocational training opportunities, interdisciplinary teaching assignments, and difficulties in teacher recruitment.

Julian High School in San Diego County, California, a school of 130 enrollment, is one of 110 small high schools with an enrollment of less than 350 in the state of California. Of these 110, 55 have an enrollment of less than 200 students. It has long recognized, as has the community, the distinct advantages of a small school as well as the restrictions seemingly imposed. The purpose of this article is to recount the steps and processes through which Julian Union High School went in its attempt to meet and solve the restrictions upon small schools. It is felt that most of the steps and procedures followed would be those which might be easily transferable to other districts in their attempts to face the same problems and that the same resources would be available in other districts which might be utilized.

Through the use of a Vocational Education Act Project a survey of vocational opportunities within San Diego County was instituted in the fall of 1965. For this purpose a countywide Vocational Advisory Committee was formed which included representatives from the State Employment Office, the Apprenticeship Training Program Farm Labor Office, and local business representatives. The needs identified by this committee, after a series of meetings, were establish-

From the *Journal of Secondary Education*, April, 1967, pp. 175–87. Reprinted by permission.

ment of terminal vocational programs in three areas—business, welding, and small engine repair.

In addition, a course to be titled Model Home would be offered at a future date. This program would involve building a small vacation type cottage on the school grounds by the students in the shop class and would include carpentry, sheet metal, plumbing, electrical work, etc., as well as involving the business education program in all of the business aspects such as ordering, processing of invoices and bills, cost accounting, etc. The home economics students would be involved in planning and decoration; the mechanical drawing class, in drawing up plans and specifications. This program would necessarily involve a large number of students and would then in essence become a core program involving almost all of the vocational education students in the school. However, it was felt that some ground work need be laid and thus this program should not be instituted until the fall of 1967.

Following the development of these recommendations, the problem then was faced of how to schedule such an ambitious program into an already restricted curriculum which was crowded with courses required to be taught for college entrance; to meet state requirements; and to meet local requirements. At that time the only vocational offerings were small engine repair, beginning and advanced agricultural science, general shop, and typing. Operating within the financial structure possible in our school district, the curricular structure was quite lopsided in favor of the 30 per cent of students who would be going on to four years of higher education. The 70 per cent who were not planning to do so were neglected in the number of course offerings were small engine repair, beginning and advanced agricul-needs identified by the faculty, board of trustees, and administration were in the areas of business, industrial arts, shop, and enrichment courses such as art, music, chorus, music appreciation, and arts and crafts.

The availability of ESEA money in February of 1966 permitted an expansion of the vocational education program for the second semester to include business machines, bookkeeping, business English, mechanical drawing, and two classes for girls—clothing and homemaking.

In addition, through the use of Elementary and Secondary Education Act funds, a curriculum study project was instituted during the second semester of the school year. The curriculum study project was directed toward examination of the feasibility of adoption of modular scheduling and was done through contract with Stanford School Scheduling System, Stanford University.

After a series of faculty meetings which outlined the above needs and parameters within our district, the information was supplied to the Stanford School Scheduling System which in turn developed a modular schedule including all of the elements outlined. This schedule was reviewed by the entire faculty and revised as necessary and resubmitted for a final run-off and scheduling.

The machine program thus developed resulted in no reduction in the total number of courses in the academic areas available to students during the high school career, but did increase the number of non-academic courses both in vocational and enrichment areas to a total of thirty-three or an increase of 364 per cent. This program, which included two or more sections in each course save one—New Photography—involved alternating schedules, such as offering world geography to all freshmen and sophomores and U.S. history to all juniors and seniors one year; then offering world history and civics to the same groups the next year. Over a four-year period, this would result in the availability of nearly one hundred courses to students enrolled in school.

During this period of time, meetings were also held and informational materials supplied to the community outlining the problems identified and the proposed means of their solution. Community response varied from skepticism to enthusiastic endorsement. Practically no objections were raised to the programming after the principles underlying it were explained.

One of the greatest areas of concern to parents, school board members, administrators, and teachers in the consideration of modular scheduling was that of unassigned time necessary to permit individual research and study as well as to permit individual assistance from teachers in the subject area. Ideally a 60 to 70 per cent loading of students and a 60 per cent loading of faculty were deemed desirable. The remaining time would be available for the above mentioned individual help, individual study, and consultation.

In May the district began efforts toward teacher recruitment. Previous experience had indicated that the more highly qualified teachers, being more in demand, would not be interested in a small school situation; and that difficulties in obtaining top-quality personnel might be encountered. As in the past, a number of applications were received from well qualified people and these people were invited to come in for interviews. Repeatedly the impression given by teachers at the inception of the interviews was that of polite interest. However, upon learning of the modular scheduling program and discussion of the opportunities and the challenges so presented, applicant response was highly enthusiastic and top-quality teachers were obtained with a surplus of such applicants for each position vacancy. Teacher recruitment and placement thus was no problem in comparison to difficulties experienced in previous years.

It was generally accepted that the level of responsibility the individual is able to assume is directly linked to the level of his interest. For example, if the level of responsibility were measured by observing a person digging a ditch, one might assume this person to be highly irresponsible because of poor performance of the task. However, if the same individual were interested in welding and assigned to a welding project, one might judge the same individual to be highly responsible. Therefore, we assumed that by scheduling students into areas of interest, much of irresponsible behavior previously exhibited would be very likely to disappear.

Experience in schools where modular scheduling has been in operation has shown that approximately 95 per cent of the students are able to assume the full amount of responsibility offered them. The remaining 5 per cent have been scheduled individually for each module of the day in order that they may have no free time. Thus, the 95 per cent are not being penalized academically in order to control the minority 5 per cent.

Based on this experience, all students were left free at the inception of the program to use their unscheduled time at their discretion. Provisions were made, however, to schedule these students into additional classes and/or some type of restrictive environment if they proved themselves unable to handle the responsibility. As might be expected, the first few weeks gave rise to several problems of student behavior and conduct. However, the number of incidents was considerably less than had been predicted. Interestingly enough, some students tentatively identified as potential problems fell into the routine quite readily with no difficulties whatsoever.

Student, parent, and faculty reaction from the inception of the program has been quite good. No serious problems have arisen and morale within the school has been exceptionally high in comparison to previous years. Some basic assumptions were made at the beginning of the program. These were: 1) all teachers were experienced in the techniques of large group instruction, inasmuch as it is the primary method used in traditional systems; 2) small group instruction is a new technique to be learned and developed by all teachers and, therefore, should receive primary attention in the in-service training program; 3) individual research should receive early attention in order that the students may be guided in the use of free time, as well as teachers guided in development of techniques for making and following through assignments or work to be conducted during these periods; 4) students will evidence responsibility in areas in which they are interested. Therefore, it is highly desirable at an early point in time to identify these areas of interest for each student and to pursue them as rapidly as a student is able. These assumptions were the ones around which the weekly in-service training meetings were built and to which particular emphasis was to be given.

From the beginning of the implementation phase, these meetings were held to discuss the problems of modular scheduling. Problems discussed are those brought up by the faculty concerning the implementation of the program and are discussed in a small group situation in order that not only may the problems, feelings, opinions of the various faculty members be shared, but also that they may gain experience in small group dynamics which can be carried back into the classroom.

Attention is also given during these in-service meetings to methods and means by which students may be encouraged to use their individual research times to best advantage. The type of assignments which teachers should make are also subject to a considerable amount of discussion and to exchange of ideas. Teacher reaction to these in-service training periods was highly enthusiastic and it is felt that much good is being accomplished.

Legal requirements dictated that a teacher must be in attendance at all times with students. Thus, the original plan to leave the multipurpose room open as a student union during the entire day had to be abandoned. The multi-purpose room was closed for nine of the fifteen modules of the day and teachers were assigned supervision duties during the periods in which the room was open. This problem, when explained to the students, created no adverse reaction and seemed to be very well received.

Modular scheduling in itself was deemed to have no magical qualities, but was merely a rearrangement of the use of time. The schedule permitted many advantages for students in meeting their individual needs and interests. Since the program does focus on the individual, another consideration came to the fore. This consideration was that of evaluation of the students' accomplishments and issuance of credits.

For many years our curricular structure has been in a lock step "serving of time" connotation. As has been aptly said, "How do you know when you have covered a course in English?"; the answer being, "It is June." The mere serving of a particular period of time to course objectives is regarded as archaic and some other means of evaluation was sought. Serious consideration was given to the question, "What do we expect a student to learn?"; or in other words, "What are our course objectives in each area?" The answer to this question by teachers was relatively specific. We expect certain basic concepts, skills, and attitudes to be evidenced. Further exploration of this question resulted in the establishment of performance criteria based on the individual teacher's expectation in the particular course.

Logically it followed that if these performance criteria could be expressed in some form, then the measurement might be made, and as the student demonstrated that he or she has met these standards, credit could be given for the individual course regardless of the amount of time spent.

Let us, for a moment, consider a simile—that of knowledge as a measurable liquid such as water—and we measure the student's "glass of knowledge" at the end of a particular period of time. Previously we have said that if this glass of knowledge is over 60 per cent full he receives a "D"; over 70 per cent full, a "C"; over 85 per cent full, a "B"; over 94 per cent full, then we can assume that he will not gain appreciably more from the course and, therefore, may be given credit and permitted to go on to another course.

To be more specific, let us examine a skills course such as typing. If performance criteria set up say that the skill developed should be that of forty words per minute at the end of the course, then a student who can type forty words a minute is given credit for Typing I, regardless of the amount of time taken to develop this skill. He is then permitted to go on to Typing II where the performance criteria might be sixty-five words a minute with certain other skills, such as laying out letters, typing of stencils, and similar activities. At the time he can demonstrate his ability to meet these criteria, he is given credit for Typing II and is permitted to go into an additional business education course if he so desires.

Similar performance criteria can be established for all other courses in the curricular structure. Thus, the student has been freed of lock step conformity to the curricular structure and has been permitted to go forward at his own speed in each course according to his abilities and interest. It is conceivable that a student might take a year and a half to complete the requirements of Typing I, or another student might be capable of completing the requirements of Typing I and Typing II in a one-year period, the focus then being on skills and abilities developed rather than the amount of time spent in the class being exposed to the skills and concepts.

To illustrate the actual operation of flexible-modular scheduling,

Fig. 1

SCHEDULE CARD

Name __Discipline Problem — Boy__   Grade __Soph.__

_____Average Ability — Low Motivation_____

	MONDAY	TUESDAY	WEDNESDAY	THURSDAY	FRIDAY
1	DRIVER ED.	DRIVER ED.	DRIVER ED.	DRIVER ED.	DRIVER ED.
2	DRIVER ED.	DRIVER ED.	DRIVER ED.	DRIVER ED.	DRIVER ED.
3	MATH TEACHER	ENGLISH TEACHER	MATH TEACHER	HISTORY TEACHER	MATH TEACHER
4	SHOP TEACHER	HISTORY TEACHER	ENGLISH TEACHER	MATH TEACHER	MATH TEACHER
5	BOYS P.E.	BOYS P.E.	BOYS P.E.	BOYS P.E.	BOYS P.E.
6	BOYS P.E.	BOYS P.E.	BOYS P.E.	BOYS P.E.	BOYS P.E.
7	ALGEBRA I	ALGEBRA I	WORLD HISTORY	ALGEBRA I	ENGLISH TEACHER
8	ALGEBRA I	ALGEBRA I	WORLD HISTORY	ALGEBRA I	HISTORY TEACHER
9	LUNCH	LUNCH	LUNCH	LUNCH	LUNCH
10	ARTS & CRAFTS	ORAL COM-MUNICATION	EARLY AMERICAN LIT.	ORAL COM-MUNICATION	SCIENCE TEACHER
11	HISTORY TEACHER	ORAL COM-MUNICATION	ARTS & CRAFTS	HISTORY TEACHER	ARTS & CRAFTS
12	ARTS & CRAFTS TEACHER	WORLD HISTORY	ARTS & CRAFTS	HISTORY TEACHER	ARTS & CRAFTS
13	HISTORY TEACHER	P.E. TEACHER	EARLY AMERICAN LIT.	ARTS & CRAFTS TEACHER	ARTS & CRAFTS TEACHER
14	ARTS & CRAFTS TEACHER	P.E. TEACHER	EARLY AMERICAN LIT.	ARTS & CRAFTS TEACHER	ARTS & CRAFTS TEACHER
15	SCIENCE TEACHER	SCIENCE TEACHER	SCIENCE TEACHER	SCIENCE TEACHER	SCIENCE TEACHER

six different schedules are included. These examples typify the individuality possible in this type of scheduling. At the foot of most schedules is a key showing the symbols representing various teachers. During the periods the student has independent study time, the symbols of the teachers available for individual instruction are shown on the student's schedule.

There is one factor not indicated on these schedules. This is the Materials Resource Center which is open from one half hour before

Fig. 2   SCHEDULE CARD

Name ___College Bound – Boy_____ Grade ___Senior_____

_____Above Average Ability – High Motivation_____

Excused from Physical Education because of Interscholastic Athletics

	MONDAY	TUESDAY	WEDNESDAY	THURSDAY	FRIDAY
1	⊗	√	ADV. MATH	ADV. COMP.	○ □
2		★ ⊗	ADV. MATH	JOURNALISM	○ □
3	CIVICS	PHYSICS	○ □ ★ ⊠	PHYSICS	○ □
4	CIVICS	PHYSICS	○ □⊠	PHYSICS	○ □
5	√ ○ □⊠	○ □⊠	× ○ □	ADV. COMP.	○ □⊠
6	√ ★	√ ○ □	× ○ □	ADV. COMP.	×
7	√ ○ □⊗ ★	MECH. DRAW.	× ○ □⊗ ★	MECH. DRAW.	○ □⊗ × √ ★
8	○ □ ⊗ ⊠√ ★	MECH. DRAW.	○ □⊗ ⊠ √	MECH. DRAW	√ ○ □× ⊠ ★
9	LUNCH	LUNCH	LUNCH	LUNCH	LUNCH
10	JOURNALISM	ADV. MATH	JOURNALISM	⊗ ⊠ √	JOURNALISM
11	JOURNALISM	CIVICS	JOURNALISM	EARLY ENG.LIT.	JOURNALISM
12	√ × ★	EARLY ENG.LIT.	PHYSICS	EARLY ENG.LIT.	PHYSICS
13	√ ○ □⊠		√	○ □	×
14	√ ⊠		√	○ □	×
15	√ × ○ □ ★ ⊗ ⊠	√ × ○ □ ★ ⊗ ⊠	√ × ○ □ ★ ⊗ ⊠	√ × ○ □ ★ ⊗ ⊠	√ × ○ □ ★ ⊗ ⊠

√ CIVICS   □ ADV. COMP.   ⊠ PHYSICS (Open Lab)
× MATH   ★ EARLY ENG. LIT.
○ JOURNALISM   ⊗ MECH. DRAW.

school to one and one half hours after school each day. Students may choose to do their independent study there.

As noted in Figure 1, this student—a discipline problem—has no independent study time. He is of average ability and low motivation and has indicated a desire to attend college after completing high school. His performance is below average and coupling this with his poor behavior, he is supplied with a schedule of directed study. It will be noted that of the seventy periods a week he is in class or in directed study, only two periods of directed study are not with teachers of his academic subjects.

The College-Bound Senior Boy, Figure 2, represents the opposite extreme in independent study time. This student has approximately

Fig. 3   SCHEDULE CARD

Name Vocational Arts — Girl   Grade Senior

_____ Average Ability — High Motivation _____

	MONDAY	TUESDAY	WEDNESDAY	THURSDAY	FRIDAY
1	DRAMA	DRAMA	DRAMA	x	DRAMA
2	DRAMA	○ x	DRAMA	★ ○ ⊗	DRAMA
3	GIRLS P.E.	GIRLS P.E.	GIRLS P.E.	GIRLS P.E.	GIRLS P.E.
4	GIRLS P.E.	GIRLS P.E.	GIRLS P.E.	GIRLS P.E.	GIRLS P.E.
5	★ ⊗ ○ √	OFFICE PRACTICE	★ ○ ⊗		★ ○ ⊗
6	SHORTHAND	SHORTHAND	SHORTHAND	SHORTHAND	SHORTHAND
7	SHORTHAND	BUSINESS LAW	SHORTHAND	BUSINESS LAW	SHORTHAND
8	★ ⊗ ○ □ √ x	BUSINESS LAW	□ x	BUSINESS LAW	□ x √ ★ ⊗ ○
9	LUNCH	LUNCH	LUNCH	LUNCH	LUNCH
10	★ ⊗ ○ □ √	□ √ ○ ★ ⊗	★ ○ ⊗ □ √	★ ○ ⊗ □ √	□ √ ○ ★ ⊗
11	INTERMEDIATE TYPING	CIVICS	OFFICE PRACTICE	INTERMEDIATE TYPING	OFFICE PRACTICE
12	INTERMEDIATE TYPING	★ ⊗ ○ □	OFFICE PRACTICE	INTERMEDIATE TYPING	OFFICE PRACTICE
13	√	CIVICS	√	CIVICS	
14	√	CIVICS	√	CIVICS	
15	√ x ○ ★ ⊗	√ x ○ ★ ⊗	√ x ○ ★ ⊗	√ x ○ ★ ⊗	√ x ○ ★ ⊗

√	CIVICS	★ BUSINESS LAW
x	DRAMA	⊗ INTERMEDIATE TYPING
○	OFFICE PRACTICE (Not in school office)	□ SHORTHAND

59 per cent of his time for independent study, but has ample time to seek individual instruction from his teachers. Because of interscholastic athletics, his physical education periods (the thirteenth and fourteenth periods daily) have been omitted and credit for P.E. is extended on the basis of athletic participation.

The vocational arts senior girl, Figure 3, has 38 per cent of her

Fig. 4   SCHEDULE CARD

Name___Vocational Arts — Boy_____ Grade___Junior_____

_____Low Ability — Low Motivation_____

Excused from Physical Education because of Interscholastic Athletics

	MONDAY	TUESDAY	WEDNESDAY	THURSDAY	FRIDAY
1	⊗	ADV. COMP.	⊗	ADV. COMP.	x ⊗
2		ADV. COMP.	⊗	○ ★	x ⊗
3	SPAN I	☐	SPAN I	SPAN I	SPAN I
4	SPAN I	√ x	SPAN I	SPAN I	SPAN I
5	√ x	EARLY ENGLISH LIT.	x	EARLY ENGLISH LIT.	x
6	√ ○ ★	EARLY ENGLISH LIT.	x ★	EARLY ENGLISH LIT.	★
7	(SPAN I) TEACHER	MECH. DRAW.	(SPAN I) TEACHER	MECH. DRAW.	√ x ○ ☐ ⊗
8	AG. ORIENTATION	MECH. DRAW.	AG. ORIENTATION	MECH. DRAW.	AG. ORIENTATION
9	LUNCH	LUNCH	LUNCH	LUNCH	LUNCH
10	SPAN I	MECH. DRAW.	(SPAN I) TEACHER	AG. ORIENTATION	√ ○ ★
11	√ ○	CIVICS		√ ★	⊗
12	√ ○	EARLY ENGLISH LIT.	x	x ★	x ⊗
13	WELDING	CIVICS	WELDING	CIVICS	WELDING
14	WELDING	CIVICS	WELDING	CIVICS	WELDING
15	√ x ○ ☐ ★ ⊗	√ x ○ ☐ ★ ⊗	√ x ○ ☐ ★ ⊗	√ x ○ ☐ ★ ⊗	√ x ○ ☐ ★ ⊗

√	CIVICS	★	WELDING & AG. ORIENTATION
x	ADV. COMP.	⊗	MECH, DRAW.
○	EARLY ENG. LIT	( )	DENOTES ADDITIONAL TIME SCHEDULED BY TEACHER
☐	SPANISH I		

time for independent study. In addition to the wide variety of business courses, a course in drama will be noted. In addition to business, other areas of interest are open to her. The Office Practice shown is not done in the school office, but in a model office in the business department. This model has a complete array of business machines and is set up and run in the fashion of a one- or two-girl office. During her independent study time, this girl elects to work in the school office assisting wherever possible.

The schedule shown in Figure 4, Vocational Arts Junior Boy, illustrates another feature of this form of scheduling. The Spanish I teacher has indicated this student needs invididual instruction outside of class and has arbitrarily selected the seventh period on Monday and Wednesday and the tenth period on Wednesday as the time this individual instruction will take place. Any teacher of any subject may schedule students for additional individual instruction. This additional time becomes a part of the student's schedule until such time as the teacher indicates there is no longer a need on the part of the student.

The College-Bound Sophomore Girl, Figure 5, has the lowest rate of independent study time of these samples during the first quarter. Her present rate is 26 per cent independent study time, after completing driver education it increases to 40 per cent, the figure originally sought in our curriculum planning. This student is of above average ability and is highly motivated. She is taking an additional course for enrichment—Instrumental Music.

Figure 6, Vocational Arts Freshman Boy, is typical of all freshmen, in that senior requirements permits only one elective course. This particular student is taking an additional course because his physical education credit is being earned through our athletic program. Also shown is the noncredit course of Orientation required of all freshman students. This student has 33 per cent independent study time which represents the average for his class.

In all sample schedules there are some common factors. All class meetings, except Orientation, which meet for a single period, are designated as large group meetings. That is, all students taking this course meet at this time, e.g., World History, when all eighty-three freshmen and sophomores are together. All classes scheduled for two or more successive periods are designated as small group instruction. This not only refers to reduced class size but also type of instruction (nonlecture) used. Small groups vary in size from drama with three students to world history with eighteen students, the vast majority of classes having between five and nine students.

Fig. 5

SCHEDULE CARD

Name___College-Bound — Girl_____ Grade___Soph._____

_____Above Average Ability — High Motivation_____

	MONDAY	TUESDAY	WEDNESDAY	THURSDAY	FRIDAY
1	GIRLS P.E.	GIRLS P.E.	GIRLS P.E.	GIRLS P.E.	GIRLS P.E.
2	GIRLS P.E.	GIRLS P.E.	GIRLS P.E.	GIRLS P.E.	GIRLS P.E.
3	x	BEGINNING TYPING	⋆ ⊗ ⊠ ☐	BEGINNING TYPING	x
4	☐ x	BEGINNING TYPING	☐	BEGINNING TYPING	x
5	√ ☐	☐ ⊠	x ☐	√	☐
6	DRIVER ED.	DRIVER ED.	DRIVER ED.	DRIVER ED.	DRIVER ED.
7	DRIVER ED.	DRIVER ED.	DRIVER ED.	DRIVER ED.	DRIVER ED.
8	○ ☐ √ ⋆ ⊗	INSTRUMENTAL MUSIC	GEOMETRY	INSTRUMENTAL MUSIC	√ ○ ☐ ⋆ ⊗
9	LUNCH	LUNCH	LUNCH	LUNCH	LUNCH
10	☐ √ ⋆ ⊗	ORAL COMMUNICATION	EARLY AMERICAN LIT.	ORAL COMMUNICATION	SPAN II
11	SPAN II	ORAL COMMUNICATION	SPAN II	SPAN II	SPAN II
12	SPAN II	WORLD HISTORY	SPAN II	SPAN II	SPAN II
13	GEOMETRY	GEOMETRY	EARLY AMERICAN LIT.	GEOMETRY	WORLD HISTORY
14	GEOMETRY	GEOMETRY	EARLY AMERICAN LIT.	GEOMETRY	WORLD HISTORY
15	√ x ○ ☐ ⋆ ⊗ ⊠	√ x ○ ☐ ⋆ ⊗ ⊠	√ x ○ ☐ ⋆ ⊗ ⊠	√ x ○ ☐ ⋆ ⊗ ⊠	√ x ○ ☐ ⋆ ⊗ ⊠

√	HISTORY	☐	TYPING	⊠	DRIVER ED.
x	GEOMETRY	⋆	ORAL COMMUNICATIONS		
○	SPANISH	⊗	EARLY AMERICAN LIT.		

In summary, through the use of flexible-modular scheduling those limitations and disadvantages of a small school have been largely overcome. The curricular offerings have been increased by well over 100 per cent. Students are able to have a choice of over one hundred courses during their four years in the high school. Single section offerings have been all but eliminated. The vocational educational

Fig. 6   SCHEDULE CARD

Name ___Vocational Arts — Boy_____ Grade___Frosh_____

_____Average Ability — Low Motivation_____

Instrumental Music lessons are scheduled as shown — Individual practice is
during study time.

	MONDAY	TUESDAY	WEDNESDAY	THURSDAY	FRIDAY
1	COMP.	GEN. MATH	COMP.	GEN. MATH.	GEN. MATH
2	COMP.	GEN. MATH	COMP.	GEN. MATH	GEN. MATH
3	GEN. SCIENCE	BASIC SHOP	BASIC SHOP	BASIC SHOP	GEN. MATH
4	GEN. SCIENCE	BASIC SHOP	x	BASIC SHOP	GEN. MATH
5	B.P.E.	B.P.E.	B.P.E.	B.P.E.	B.P.E.
6	B.P.E.	B.P.E.	B.P.E.	B.P.E.	B.P.E.
7	◯ ★ ☐ ⊗	INSTR. MUSIC	SUR. LIT.	INSTR. MUSIC	SUR. LIT.
8	x ◯ ★ ☐ ⊗	INSTR. MUSIC	SUR. LIT.	INSTR. MUSIC	SUR. LIT.
9	LUNCH	LUNCH	LUNCH	LUNCH	LUNCH
10	√ ☐ ⊗	x ◯ ★ ⊗	√ x ★ ⊗	★ ☐ ⊗	x ★ ⊗
11	GEN. MATH	SUR. LIT.	WORLD HISTORY	★ ⊗	WORLD HISTORY
12	COMP.	WORLD HISTORY	WORLD HISTORY	GEN. SCIENCE	WORLD HISTORY
13	x ◯ ★ ⊗	★	ORIENTATION	◯	√ x ★ ☐
14	x ⊗	★	x ★ ⊗	◯	√ x ★
15	√ x ◯ ★ ☐ ⊗	√ x ◯ ★ ☐ ⊗	√ x ◯ ★ ☐ ⊗	√ x ◯ ★ ☐ ⊗	√ x ◯ ★ ☐ ⊗

√ GEN. MATH   ★ SURVEY OF LITERATURE
x GEN. SCIENCE   ☐ BASIC SHOP
◯ COMPOSITION   ⊗ WORLD HISTORY

program offers terminal education in three fields with others to be
added in the near future. Inter-disciplinary teacher assignments have
been all but eliminated. All teachers, save one, are teaching in their
major field. Difficulties in teacher recruitment have not been evidenced. The establishment of performance criteria further frees the
student to pursue his individual interests at his own speed and permits

a further individualization of attention and instruction. Schedules are arranged to meet individual abilities and needs.

All of the advantages of the small school have been retained and in addition we are informed that our program now offers students a greater variety of courses and better vocational training opportunities than may be found in many schools of over fifteen hundred enrollment.

33. Guidelines for Developing Vocational Agriculture Programs for Youth with Special Needs

James B. Hamilton

WE often associate youth with special needs with the large metropolitan areas, the inner city, with specific depressed areas of the nation, or with various cultural segments of the population. It is seldom that we in agricultural education consider youth with special needs to be an important consideration for the conduct of programs in vocational agriculture.

Rural youth There are, however, substantial numbers of youth with special needs in rural areas. In the nonmetropolitan areas of Ohio one of every six boys in the ninth grade were identified as youth with special needs. This amounts to over five thousand rural, ninth-grade youth with special needs in one state alone.

Serving the educational needs of rural youth with special needs is a problem of considerable magnitude. While the responsibility for meeting the educational needs of these students does not automatically fall to vocational agriculture, vocational agriculture must assume its share of this responsibility by providing programs for those who desire and can profit from instruction in agriculture. It is our duty to develop vocational agriculture programs which are designed to prepare these students for employment in agriculture where there is a need and where there is student interest and ability commensurate with the occupation.

Characteristics of students Recommendations concerning vocational education programs to serve youth with special needs must take into consideration the characteristics and background of the students to be served. When compared with other ninth-grade students, those ninth-grade students identified as youth with special needs were found to have the following characteristics:

From *Agriculture Education Magazine*, September, 1968, pp. 74–75. Reprinted by permission.

270

—They were nearly a year older.
—They were from larger families.
—Their parents had completed fewer years of school.
—Their parents' level of occupation was lower.
—They were more likely to be living with only one parent.
—The head of their household was frequently not working.
—Their occupational and educational aspirations were much lower than other students.

When compared with other ninth-grade students, the ninth-grade students identified as youth with special needs were found to have the following educational experiences:

—Their reading level was two grades lower.
—Their intelligence quotient was lower.
—Their grades averaged one grade lower.
—They were absent from school twice as much.
—They participated in fewer school activities.
—They were usually enrolled in general or vocational curriculums.

The following guidelines are suggested for developing and conducting vocational agriculture programs for youth with special needs. **Suggested guidelines**

Identify the potential students early—before they enter high school. If the program is to be effective it must reach the youth with special needs before they drop out of school. The largest percentages of high school dropouts occur at the ninth and tenth grade levels; therefore, if vocational agriculture is to prepare these students for employment we must be prepared to begin no later than when they enroll in high school. Youth with special needs can be identified early in school with a fair degree of accuracy. Although several sets of criteria have been developed for the identification of the potential dropout, teachers, guidance counselors, and principals know best which students will not be likely to achieve success in the regular school program.

Provide vocational guidance and counseling in the junior high school years to assist youth with special needs in making realistic educational and occupational choices. Prevocational experiences of an exploratory nature directed toward the discovery and development of interest and abilities should play a vital role in such a guidance program.

The vocational program should be designed especially for the type of students to be enrolled. Traditionally programs of vocational agriculture have been designed for the average or above average student who has developed satisfactory communicative, computational, and social skills. Youth with special needs show a lack in these character-istics upon which we ordinarily expect to build in the traditional vocational agriculture program.

Direct the program toward preparation for existing agricultural occupations which are realistic in the light of the student's potential. For some of these students the vocational agriculture program may serve as the catalyst for renewed interest and motivation for greater educational attainment. For most youth with special needs, the vo-cational program must provide the vital link between formal educa-tion and full-time employment. There are many opportunities for employment in agriculture in occupations which do not require high levels of technical knowledge.

Gear academic courses to the interest and ability level of the student enrolled. School administrators indicated that this might best be accomplished through integration of courses such as English, mathe-matics, and social studies within the vocational program. That is, teach each of these subjects in relation to and as a part of the students' preparation for earning a living. Operation and maintenance man-uals, parts lists, catalogs, and tax returns could very well find use as teaching materials in these courses.

Incorporate work for wages as an integral part of the vocational agriculture program. The supervised occupational experience pro-gram has long been one of the most valuable aspects of vocational education, for it provides students the opportunity for reinforcement of learning by putting into practice what has been taught in the class-room. Many youth with special needs are from homes without a father or without a working father. For those students whose parents are employed, parents have relatively low occupational status. When we consider these characteristics of youth with special needs, then opportunities to earn money, opportunities for growth in responsi-bility, and opportunities for building self-confidence and esteem are also important aspects which should be provided through the oc-cupational experience program.

Employ teachers who have special training or interest and ability to work with youth with special needs. As in any educational pro-gram, the success of the program is dependent to a greater extent upon the individual teacher than upon any other single factor. The willing-ness, the desire, and an understanding of the unique problems of working with the underachiever will be essential on the part of the successful teacher of youth with special needs. He must be prepared to work with the less able student and with the socio-economically deprived.

Develop special teaching materials for use in vocational agriculture classes for youth with special needs. Teaching materials and learning activities should be planned to be consistent with the lower reading levels, abilities, and educational and occupational aspirations of these students. Teaching by demonstration and learning by doing should characterize much of this instruction.

34. Are Small High Schools Doing an Adequate Job of In-Service Education?

Bob L. Taylor

IN many cases small secondary schools are failing to provide even the most basic in-service education programs for their faculties. It is unfortunate that the small high schools which commonly have both the more inexperienced teachers and the more poorly prepared teachers should be found so lacking in this area. The argument is often presented that because of the limited size of their faculties, the small secondary schools do not need to employ in-service education practices with their staffs. The in-service objectives are supposedly accomplished through the close contacts of the faculty and administration without any of the formal procedures found in the larger schools. However, a recent survey with 1,162 teachers provided evidence that many rural secondary schools were not even providing the most elementary assistance for their teachers.

Does the size and level of the school influence the nature of the in-service education program provided for the teachers? This problem was studied by a check-list survey conducted with 1,162 teachers who were in the summer sections of an educational research course at Indiana University. While the questions were factual in nature, they reflected the individual teacher's knowledge of in-service practices in his school. Although the teachers came from twenty-nine different states, the majority (65 per cent) were from Indiana with midwestern and southern-eastern states being the home states for most of the "out-of-state" teachers. Analysis of the data provided some very interesting comparisons between large and small schools and elementary and secondary schools with respect to the surveyed practices.

In the analysis of the returns elementary schools with 400 or more pupils was taken as the dividing point between large and small grade schools, and secondary schools with 600 or more pupils was taken as the dividing point between large and small high schools. This was

From the *High School Journal*, April, 1964, pp. 297–300. Reprinted by permission.

done to divide the returns into four fairly equal groups; however, there was a preponderance of elementary teachers in the sample so that the breakdown of returns was: 21 per cent from teachers at small elementary schools; 41 per cent from teachers at large elementary schools; 16 per cent from teachers at small secondary schools; and 22 per cent from teachers at large secondary schools.

Table 1 gives the percentages of positive responses to each of the questions by size and grade level of school. The small secondary schools had the lowest percentages of positive responses to practically every question. The large elementary and secondary schools had very similar percentages of positive responses.

Table 2 gives the chi square values computed for the teachers' responses to the nine questions. These tests were done to determine if the four samples which were divided by grade level and size of school were from a homogeneous population. Notice that when the grade level of the school was held constant the large schools were very definitely favored in the responses. The chi square values comparing the small elementary schools and the large elementary schools and the chi square values comparing the small secondary schools and the large secondary schools were either significant or highly significant in fourteen out of eighteen comparisons. The large schools were reported to be using a significantly greater number of the selected practices.

When size of school was held constant and chi square values were computed for elementary and secondary levels, there were no signi-

Table 1. Percentage of Teachers Responding Positively
to Each Question by Grade Level and Size of School

Question	Elementary		Secondary	
	Small	Large	Small	Large
There is a teachers' work room or lounge in your school.	.55	.78	.51	.82
The school takes and makes available to teachers a collection of professional journals.	.60	.74	.48	.71
Your school system provides a professional library for teachers.	.43	.49	.28	.45
There are teachers' study groups on your faculty.	.45	.59	.46	.61
There is a teachers' bulletin board in your school.	.78	.87	.73	.84
There is a teachers' book club on your faculty.	.04	.08	.09	.13
There is a teachers' handbook for your school system.	.70	.83	.63	.81
Teachers' committees make textbook selections.	.81	.84	.71	.82
There is a teachers' curriculum committee in your school	.38	.55	.41	.59

Table 2. Chi Square Values Computed for the Responses
to the Nine Questions by the Four Groups of Teachers

Questions	Small Elementary to Large Elementary	Small Secondary to Large Secondary Schools	Large Elementary to Large Secondary Schools	Small Elementary to Small Secondary Schools
There is a teachers' workroom or lounge in your school.	41.6**	6.8*	.74	1.5
The school takes and makes available to teachers a collection of professional journals.	14.4**	23.0**	2.76**	.86
Your school system provides a professional library for teachers.	2.35	14.2**	10.6**	.97
There are teachers' study groups on your faculty.	14.18**	9.4*	.07	.10
There is a teachers' bulletin board in your school.	9.86**	8.4*	1.37	1.14
There is a teachers' book club on your faculty.	5.02	1.6	5.4	1.14
There is a teachers' handbook for your school system.	16.89**	18.7**	2.85	.66
Teachers' committees make textbook selections.	1.05	8.1*	5.9*	.34
There is a teachers' curriculum committee in your school.	18.27**	13.4**	.35	.81

*Significant at 5% level.   **Significant at 1% level.

ficant chi square values for the large elementary schools compared to the large secondary schools. However, in nine comparisons out of eighteen, the percentages given in Table 1 favored the small elementary schools over the small secondary schools. Furthermore, as shown in Table 2, in two of the nine comparisons there were significant chi square values favoring the small elementary schools over the small secondary schools. Also, a third chi square value (5.4) was significant at the 10 per cent level of confidence.

Considering the selected group of practices, it is questionable if any school should be without them, and it is particularly unfortunate that the small secondary schools which commonly have both the more inexperienced teachers and the more poorly prepared teachers should be using fewer of the selected in-service practices than the other schools. A good in-service teacher education program is the most needed here, and while the evidence collected in this study is of a limited nature, it strongly indicated that a very poor quality of in-service teacher education was being provided in these small secondary schools.

35. In-Service Education for The Smaller School's Faculty

Lee A. Witters

AS a part of the rapid changes which are taking place in teaching methodology, curriculum content, and American society as a whole, in-service education for teachers is especially needed today.

Midwestern states will undoubtedly educate many of their young people in medium-sized and small schools for many years to come, and there is a great need for in-service activities in these schools. A recent survey indicated that both teachers and administrators feel that the existing in-service programs of their schools are inadequate to meet their needs. These schools often suffer from lack of resources, from frequent staff turnover, and from lack of teacher contact with more than a few, if any, teachers in their own field.

Fortunately, the smaller schools have certain advantages which can serve as the foundation for their in-service programs. Teachers can provide more personal help and administrators can schedule special programs for large numbers of pupils. What in-service education practices may administrators and teachers in smaller schools find helpful? Some ideas are briefly described.

In providing the teacher help that is directly related to day-to-day instructional activities, workshops or seminars conducted throughout the year have the greatest potential for getting to the heart of in-service education. Teachers generally prefer this approach because it provides effective experiences to meet the most crucial educational problems, namely, motivating students, providing for individual differences, and identifying new approaches and innovations. Since the success of a workshop or seminar depends upon the degree to which teachers institute ideas gained from it into their teaching, the participants must have certain common problems and concerns, they must be *active learners*, and they must be involved in the planning and

Instructional problem workshops

From the *Minnesota Journal of Education*, November, 1967, pp. 14–15. Reprinted by permission.

277

conduct of such meetings. Probably a series of meetings based around some unifying theme would be most effective. A number of smaller schools have had successful workshops built around themes such as "Providing for Individual Differences" and developing such skills as critical thinking or creativity, or based upon books related to areas of teachers' concern. One example of such a book is *Preparing Instructional Objectives* by Robert Mager, Fearon Publishers, San Francisco, 1962. These workshops or seminars enable teachers to discuss and consider, then to try out their ideas, and then come back for further discussion and consideration. Immediateness of help received is the key to an effective workshop or seminar.

Self-evaluation
Many administrators and teachers have used the self-evaluation for a successful in-service experience in their school systems. The self-study technique meets certain criteria essential to good in-service education. The problems are meaningful to the staff; members of the staff have the opportunity to relate to one another; it develops mutual respect and creativeness among many staff members; and attention is given to the problem-solving process. The administrator is the motivator for self-evaluation and one of his first tasks is the selection of the evaluation design. Many designs may be used, including locally prepared ones, but most administrators contact the state department of education or the state's North Central Association for help. Many schools use "The Evaluative Criteria"; this is a thorough guide for self-study and hundreds of schools have contributed to the latest edition. A steering committee and work committees are organized to study each segment of the program of studies, the pupil activities program, the school services, the plant, the school staff and the administration, instruction and methods—all in relation to the philosophy and purposes of the school system. Usually a visiting committee from the state department is invited to examine the school system and to act as consultants, but the "self-study" by the faculty is really the most important part of the total evaluation process. The self-study permits the staff to grow professionally and to improve instruction because the teachers identify the strengths and weaknesses of the school program and have the opportunity to make professional judgments for new approaches to areas which need improvement.

Exchanging Ideas for Improvement
Smaller schools can use a number of ways to share good in-service practices. Means for exchanging ideas must be kept meaningful and pertinent to the local school, however. Visitations to and observations of other teachers at work are highly valued by teachers and adminis-

trators in the smaller school systems. Ideas may also be exchanged through casual contact in the corridor or lounge, or a small group of teachers with a common interest (e.g., all math teachers) could exchange some ideas and practices over a cup of coffee. Demonstrations and teaching clinics are often conducted by the local or county education association. Some systems join together and publish "know-how" or "tip" sheets in which teachers describe practices and methods. In planning ways to exchange ideas administrators and teachers need to consider time, facilities, human resources, and problems of communication.

The first year is often the key period in the professional growth of a teacher. One practice found successful in aiding the beginning teacher is the "buddy system," which involves assigning an experienced teacher—preferably one teaching the same subject or grade level, although this may not be possible in the small school—to work with the inexperienced teacher. However, only experienced teachers who want to take on such a responsibility should do so. Workshops for beginning teachers from a group of similar schools discussing mutual problems is another practice helpful to faculties of smaller schools. Extra supervision, or if possible, assigning teachers classes which they will most likely be able to handle, is a suggestion for aiding the beginner. Supervision for the beginning (or experienced) teacher can be a key part of any in-service program. Supervision must be a joint endeavor, however, and the teacher and supervisor need to decide together such things as how long a supervisory visit is to last, what the supervisor is to look for, how the observation is to be made, and of what a follow-up conference is to consist. Both work together to identify an aspect of the teaching-learning process and to experiment with plans for improvement of the teacher's performance relative to that process.

Provisions for beginning teachers

Taking additional college courses is a popular in-service experience for teachers in smaller school systems and may be more valuable to increasing teacher competency than preservice education, because of the opportunities for immediate application of professional knowledge to the teacher's classroom problems. Moreover, local school systems need to provide greater opportunities for teachers to attend professional conferences. Specialized groups of teachers (e.g., music, English, social studies) have state organizations and hold meetings during the year. Administrators should acquaint their teachers with local policies regarding released time and expense payments to such

Other in-service education

educational conferences. Administrators and teachers should not overlook the many sources available for improving their in-service activities. State departments of education usually provide consultive services, self-evaluation aid, curriculum materials, and the administration of federal funds that can help finance projects. Local and state education associations and extension divisions of colleges and universities often help local districts with workshops, seminars, and off-campus classes.

There are some outstanding in-service practices in medium and small schools, showing that not only are some teachers receiving valuable help, but that strong programs are possible. Local initiative is an ideal toward which to strive.

36. A Community Becomes Involved in Education

John Waybright

WHEN an entire community becomes concerned about education, the way to better schools is opened.

This seems to be the point of a study now underway in Page County under a $31,700 grant from Title III of the Elementary and Secondary Education Act.

"We have tried to involve every area of the population in this program," says study director Raymond Bodkin. "Our efforts have been rewarded with excellent co-operation on the part of those whose help we have solicited."

The study is aimed at a complete reorganization of the system and is designed as a pilot project to guide other small, isolated, rural school divisions across the nation.

Committees working in the study include representatives of industry, business, civic organizations, local government, housewives, and workers, in addition to professional educators and technical consultants.

The voice of classroom teachers sounds loudly in the preliminary investigations and concerned citizens have been given the chance to air their views.

The Title III study began in August, 1968, with approval of a study director by the county school board. Former county superintendent Wayne King and county director of federal programs Frank Cosby prepared the original grant application for the school board. It set up six main principles:

—The dropout has experienced more failure in the elementary school than those who do not drop out.
—Dropouts have records of poor attendance that is more aggravated than the nondropout.
—A significant number of the dropouts are from low-income families—those with under $3,000 annual income.

From the *Virginia Journal of Education*, April, 1969, pp. 17ff. Reprinted by permission.

—Dropouts can be identified in a significant way early in their educational life.

—The general level of intelligence of the dropout is not significantly different from the "normal" distribution.

A curriculum study found that the teacher is the key to curriculum development. His idea of what is to be taught, his ability to create interaction among the students, and his attitude about teaching and learning all become the curriculum once he moves into the classroom with his students, closes the door, and initiates the activity. The study indicates that:

—Too often the curriculum is fragmented and irrelevant.

—Teachers would like an understanding of curriculum that shows continuity.

—The textbook has too often been accepted as the curriculum.

—The present curriculum needs to include a greater offering for the vocational areas.

—Quoting a Social Science Committee—"Outlines of the framework of curricula are needed by all teachers."

—Curriculum development should be more adapted to the needs of youth as related to their three major concerns—personal worth, relationship to authority, and misconceptions and worries over sex.

Finding out what is being done in nearby areas, and the development of programs based upon reorganization to better meet the needs of all children within an educational program, have been considered.

Schools with vocational programs have been visited, and data gathered on the development of their programs. Schools that are doing specialized work at the elementary level have been studied.

Using this background of research, the study has fortified ideas expressed in the original grant application.

Innovations envisioned to overcome the problems include a new centrally-located senior high school with expanded facilities for vocational programs, greater choice in subject matter, and a broad cultural program for both students and adults. This new facility would allow the present two high schools to be converted to intermediate schools and free areas in the county's five elementary schools to accommodate a new kindergarten program.

The achievement of these educational aims will take more study, time, and money, but school officials realize that with an informed and concerned community the goals can be reached.

In the words of Page County school superintendent Jack Harner:

"This study has provided a unique opportunity for both educators and local citizens working together toward a common goal to take a long, hard look into the effectiveness of educational programs. . . .

"It is impossible to estimate the number of hours spent in research, group meetings, communications, individual consultation and just plain down-to-earth, good, hardnosed thinking since the project began.

"An attempt at the present time to predict the final outcome of this would appear somewhat conjectural. . . . It all seems to boil down to how well we want to insure our own future and that of our children and what we are willing to do to get this insurance."

The object of the Title III study was to design a new educational program to meet the needs of a small, isolated rural school division, such as Page County's. This would mean: *Summary— What's it all about?*

—Changing courses of study to help all students improve their chances for success in whatever fields they ultimately enter.
—Adding programs needed but not now available.
—Providing for new physical facilities—buildings and equipment.
—Increasing community interest and changing negative attitudes toward public education.

The study asked the help of the entire community in planning improvements. Committees have been named to include every segment of the population: professional educators, businessmen, industrial leaders, civic and governmental representatives, professional men, workers, housewives.

The study is to help not only Page County, but similar school systems throughout the nation.

The efforts have turned up significant facts about the county's educational system that strongly emphasize the need for changes. . . .

A major revision would change the present seven-year elementary and five-year secondary arrangement. Elementary grades would include a kindergarten. Intermediate grades in separate buildings would provide a bridge to senior high school grades.

Senior high school grades could be included as part of a cultural studies center at a new centrally-located facility. The center would be not just a high school, but a place where carefully-planned vocational, academic, and cultural programs would be offered to a large part of the population. It would be used not only during normal class hours from 8:30 to 3:30, but many hours each day and night for educational and cultural programs for both young and old.

The aim of the high school or secondary program would be a total education plan with a wide range of choices for students. The division between "academic" and "vocational" programs would be lessened. All education is—or should be—vocational. That is, it should prepare a student for his ultimate vocation—his economic, social, and cultural role in life. The Title III study has uncovered a need for adding programs or improving those now available. This would help reduce dropouts and better suit graduates to what they will be doing after they graduate. For some it will be college, others will seek further technical training, still others will be prepared to go into jobs already available in the community.

In elementary schools, the Title III study indicates need for basic changes in teaching methods and more specialized personnel to relieve teachers of clerical and other nonteaching duties. Even at lower levels, the programs would direct students towards "vocational" goals—their eventual roles in society—through careful guidance and evaluation methods.

The proposed senior high school-cultural center complex would be open to adult programs to increase educational and cultural opportunities for everyone in the county.

Parents participate Meetings will be planned for the students of each community to explain the development of the study, and to give parents an opportunity for questions and an exchange of ideas. In addition to radio, TV, and press coverage, an attractive brochure for every home explains the Title III school study on educational problems in Page County.

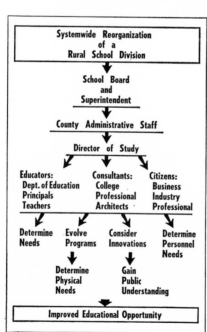

The funding of such programs as recommended and as a result of the study needs a complete understanding by all segments of the total community.

Continued research and study must be thorough. When such investigation has determined the cost of (1) facilities, (2) personnel, (3) equipment, (4) additional services, (5) consultants, (6) architects, and (7) developmental expenses, the sharing of the funding of the project will be determined. Recommendations made through the proper channels will then be based upon the determination of need, and the cost of providing for new programs.

When the school board has established priorities, and after the further study that is required, exact costs will then be determined. The continued involvement of education and a cross-section of all segments of the Page County citizenry will help to guide those charged with the responsibility of decision.

37. Whatever Happened to The Little Red Schoolhouse?

Jim Jackson

PUPILS at Okarche's new elementary school take off their shoes on rainy days before entering their classrooms. They're that impressed with their carpeting, and they want to keep it clean.

"I like our new school because it has air conditioning, and I like carpet, and I like the meals, and it's so pretty and so nice and I even feel like home," a breathless fourth grader wrote.

From first grade through sixth, the 130 pupils are happy with one of the newest and most modern education plants in Oklahoma. So are the eight teachers who moved into the building when classes opened August 25.

Arrel L. Reed, Okarche superintendent, said the school is "custom designed" to fill a list of requirements drawn up by teachers, the school board, and administrators.

Members of the Oklahoma City architecture firm of Locke, Smith and Wright had several sessions with teachers before the design was completed.

"They tried to build a building around our ideas," Reed said. "It's a little more functional than most, because the teachers had a hand in it, saying, 'This is what we want.' "

A $375,000 bond issue passed in May, 1968, financed the project for the 155-square-mile school district located half in Kingfisher County and half in Canadian County. The county line runs down the middle of Okarche's main street.

Triad Construction Co., Norman, built the 22,799-square-foot building at a contract price of $344,164.

"It's so nice it makes you wish you were back in school," a proud Okarche woman said of the new school.

"It couldn't be beat, I don't believe," said first grade teacher Mrs. Jean Hughes.

"The carpet makes all the difference in the world; you wouldn't believe the difference it makes," said Mrs. Golda Sanders, fifth grade teacher. "There's no scraping of desks and chairs. You don't hear anything but the talking."

Gene Luber, probably the only school maintenance supervisor in the state with a college degree, has high praise for the ease of house-keeping the new concept in school design provides.

Holder of a 1961 degree in horticulture from Oklahoma State University, Luber said cleaning carpets is one job, while cleaning tiled floors is three jobs. If the carpeting lasts five years—and it should last longer—it will pay for itself in savings on maintenance, he said.

Impressive as the gold, blue, green and coral carpeting is, it is but one of the innovations built into the new school. The classrooms, with one set aside for a kindergarten program expected to be added next year, are arranged in two groups of four, with restrooms and a storage and materials center located in the center of each quad.

Kindergarten, first, second, and third grades are in one quad; fourth, fifth, sixth, and special education are in another. Mrs. Rita Wilkerson teaches the new special education class for nine slow-learner pupils.

Each classroom has a reading nook, set apart from the classroom but open so the teacher can supervise both areas.

Chalkboards and tackboards go from floor to ceiling in a "child scale" concept making them the right height for any pupil.

The tackboards, brightly colored, account for a good portion of each room's walls. The remainder not covered by chalkboard is either wood paneling, brick or glass.

Each classroom overlooks either an outside, screened patio or a planting area in the skylight-brightened hallway. The hallways have terrazzo floors for heavier traffic than the carpeted classrooms.

The school's gymnasium serves also as the cafeteria, not only for elementary students but for junior and senior high students whose building is just two blocks east of the elementary school on the north-west side of Okarche.

Underneath the classrooms is a basement holding the heating–air conditioning plant, a choral music room, and gymnasium dressing rooms. Equipped with an outside entrance, the basement doubles as a storm shelter for the school and the community.

The school's clocks provide an automated system for start-and-stop air conditioning, heating, outside lighting and can even be set for weekends to warm or cool the classrooms before the pupils arrive Monday morning. Public address speakers are also part of the clock.

"It's a far cry from the little red schoolhouse," the superintendent said. He concedes he is still a little awed by all the quiet convenience of the new school.

Part Five. **Racial Integration in the Public Schools**

Introduction to Part Five

HORACE Mann described education as the great equalizer of the conditions of men—the balance wheel of the social machinery. The role of public education came into sharper focus on May 17, 1954, when the U.S. Supreme Court decided in the *Brown* case that racially segregated schools are not equal. The *Brown* decision touched off a chain of social events whose end we still cannot see. In this decision, the Supreme Court said that "separate but equal" school facilities required by law had resulted in depriving minority-group children of equal educational opportunities, as well as generating within them a feeling of inferiority. Such segregation, the Court concluded, deprived the plaintiffs of the equal protection of the laws guaranteed by the Fourteenth Amendment. Thus ended the fifty-eight-year legitimation of racially segregated public facilities and institutions as sanctioned in *Plessy* v. *Ferguson* (1896).

On May 31, 1955, the Supreme Court ordered "all deliberate speed" in obeying its earlier decision in the *Brown* case. However, the Supreme Court felt that school officials should assume the primary responsibility for abolishing segregated facilities, while the courts would decide whether the officials were acting in good faith and making a prompt and reasonable start toward compliance. No specific date was set for school districts to desegregate. As a result, "deliberate speed" for most school districts has been the equivalent of "slow speed" or "no speed." A conglomeration of laws, resolutions, and court cases in the seventeen Southern and Border states are illustrations of resistance to the *Brown* decision.

Compliance

The first efforts at enforcement of the Supreme Court's ruling were directed at overcoming the South's "massive resistance" to any school desegregation. In fact, most desegregation plans were designed to achieve minimum changes in the traditional pattern of total exclusion of black students from schools attended by white students. The princi-

291

pal devices employed against local resistance were pupil transfer privileges and the freedom of choice plans. Most school districts favored the freedom of choice plans. Contributing strongly to the gradual ascendency of the freedom of choice system and to the slow pace of desegregation was the decision handed down by federal Judge Parker in *Briggs* v. *Elliott* (1955):

> Nothing in the Constitution or in the decision of the Supreme Court takes away from the people freedom to choose the schools they attend. The Constitution, in other words, does not require integration. It merely forbids discrimination. It does not forbid such segregation as occurs as the result of voluntary action. It merely forbids the use of governmental power to enforce segregation.

From 1954 to 1964, the emphasis in school desegregation centered on determining what type of plans or systems would be sufficient to satisfy the various federal judges' orders that school officials make a reasonable start toward achieving desegregation. On July 2, 1964, after the most extended debate in congressional history, President Johnson signed into law "The Civil Rights Act of 1964" (Public Law No. 88-352). This law contained sections that represented the first federal school desegregation legislation. It authorized the federal government to take a major role in desegregating schools. The act contains two titles which have direct application to public school desegregation: Title IV, "Desegregation of Public Education," and Title VI, "Nondiscrimination in Federally Assisted Programs."

Following the enactment of the Civil Rights Act of 1964 and its implementation through the U.S. Department of Health, Education, and Welfare (HEW) Guidelines adopted under the authority of Title VI of that act, the courts began to shift their inquiries to the question of whether the proposed local desegregation programs would bring about full compliance with the *Brown* case principles. Titles IV and VI gave the federal government added leverage in demanding compliance.

Title IV seeks to facilitate the desegregation of schools in several ways. Specifically, the desegregation which the statute seeks is defined as the assignment of students without regard to race, color, or national origin but with the further expressed provision that it shall not mean the assignment of students to public schools in order to overcome racial imbalance. Under this title the U.S. Office of Education was authorized to:

1. Conduct a national survey to determine the availability of equal educational opportunity;
2. Provide technical assistance, upon request, to help states, political

subdivisions or school districts carry out school desegregation plans;

3. Arrange training institutes to prepare teachers and other school personnel to deal with desegregation problems;
4. Make grants enabling school boards to employ specialists for in-service training programs.

In addition, the attorney general was authorized to file civil suits seeking to compel desegregation of public schools, including public colleges. However, before filing such a suit the attorney general must have received a signed complaint from a pupil or his parents and must have determined that the complainant, according to standards set forth in the act, is unable to bring the action. The attorney general is also required to notify the school board and give it a reasonable period of time to correct the alleged condition before filing suit.

Under Title VI every federal agency which provides financial assistance through grants, loans, or contracts is required to eliminate discrimination on the grounds of race, color, or national origin in these programs. This title requires the following:

1. Elementary and secondary schools constructed, maintained and operated with federal funds have to admit children without regard to race, color, or national origin;
2. Schools for the deaf and the blind operated with federal funds have to serve the deaf and blind of any color;
3. Colleges and universities receiving funds for their general operation or for the construction of special facilities, such as research centers, have to admit students without discrimination.

The first guidelines for compliance with the 1964 law were not issued by HEW until 1965 and then primarily as a result of requests from Southern states wanting to know exactly how little they could change before facing possible termination of funds. Since then HEW has issued revised guidelines each year. Prior to 1968, little was done in the way of compliance or enforcement; HEW mainly concerned itself with the collection of paper statements of compliance or plans for desegregation. Their guidelines have been many and varied. *HEW guidelines*

1965
1. Desegregation of 4 grades by Fall, 1965
2. Desegregation of all grades by Fall, 1967
3. Two suggested methods:
   a. assignment on basis of geographic attendance zones
   b. freedom of choice

1966
1. Provisions for faculty and school staff desegregation

2. Free choice to be measured by percentage of student transfers
3. School districts made responsible for safe exercise of free choice
4. Administrators made responsible for end to dual system
5. Suggested:
   a. pairing Negro and white schools
   b. redrawing attendance zones on geographic non-practical basis

1967
1. Percentage system retained but doubling of actual percentages called for

1968
1. Declaration that end to discrimination requires positive action
2. If free choice fails to abolish dual system, it is to be done away with
3. Fall, 1969, set as last possible date to achieve full compliance
4. Guidelines apply to Northern school districts for the first time

Racial Isolation in the Public Schools, a report of the U.S. Commission on Civil Rights published in 1967, contains many pages of statistics which indicate that the rate of desegregation from 1964 to 1967 was negligible.[1] One survey, completed in the school year 1965–66 of the elementary school population of seventy-five cities in the U.S., showed that:

> The total elementary school enrollment for these 75 cities is 1.6 million Negro and 2.4 million white. Of the Negro school children, 1.2 million (75 per cent) are in 90–100 per cent Negro schools. . . . Of the white school children, 2.0 million (83 per cent) are in 90–100 per cent white schools.[2]

In 1965, almost 90 per cent of the school districts in the seventeen Southern and Border states had met the federal requirements of integrating at least four grades. What initially seems to be a high rate of compliance was in effect an indication of the token nature of the desegregation required by HEW. Because HEW was not applying its guidelines to the North, there are no figures available on the rate of compliance for that part of the country. However, figures in *Racial Isolation in the Public Schools* indicate that the position of the minority-group child in the North vis-a-vis attendance in mixed schools did not drastically differ from his counterpart in the South.

The so-called Coleman Report, *Equality of Educational Opportunity*, published in 1966 in accordance with the provisions of Section 402 of the Civil Rights Act of 1964, concluded that the majority of

---

[1] U.S. Commission on Civil Rights, *Racial Isolation in the Public Schools* (Washington, D.C., U.S. Government Printing Office, 1967).
[2] *Ibid.*, 5ff.

school children in America attended racially segregated schools, and Negroes were the most segregated of all minority-group children. The report also concluded that segregation was more publicized in the South but exists extensively in all other parts of the country. Finally, the same patterns of segregation of pupils also held true for teachers.[3] The situation is basically unchanged today. In terms of the 1964 law, HEW has been moving very slowly in Southern states and adhering to its traditional pattern of virtually ignoring the question of desegregation in the North.

In March, 1967, the Fifth Circuit Court of Appeals in *Stout* v. *Jefferson County Board of Education* ordered each state within the circuit to take all necessary affirmative action to bring about a "unitary school system in which there are no Negro schools and no white schools—just schools!" In October, 1967, the Supreme Court refused to review the order and the NAACP declared the Fifth Circuit ruling to be "the most influential school desegregation opinion since *Brown* v. *Topeka.*"[4] The significance of the decision lay in the legal sanction extended to HEW guidelines and further, in the judges' stated intent to investigate "freedom of choice" plans to determine their effectiveness.

It soon became very apparent that the freedom of choice plans had failed to produce integrated schools. Even when school officials tried to implement the plan, they were frustrated by the intimidation and coercion applied by various elements of the white community to dissuade blacks from electing to attend predominantly white schools. In such situations, the freedom of choice plan failed to work because no freedom of choice in fact existed.

Beyond freedom of choice

In 1968, the Supreme Court virtually eliminated freedom of choice as a workable method in achieving desegregation. The decision in *Green* v. *County School Board of New Kent County, Va.* clearly stated that freedom of choice plans were worthless if unable to effect rapid desegregation and should be discarded in favor of a more workable plan, i.e., geographic zoning plans resulting in mixed schools. Freedom of choice was cited as placing the burden of change on the black child and his parents who are "free" to choose to desegregate in the face of white pressure and violence.

The *Green* decision generated new congressional controversy, especially insofar as the degree of compliance was concerned. Some

3 James S. Coleman et al., *Equality of Educational Opportunity* (Washington, D.C., U.S. Government Printing Office, 1966).
4 Pat Watters, "Enforcing Civil Rights Laws," *Current*, 102 (December, 1968), 37.

congressmen believed the law of the land only required *desegregation* while others interpreted the Court's decision as a statement upholding the constitutionality of *integration*. The former condition is achieved by placing bodies together, while the latter condition requires significant interaction. The advent of the Nixon administration has served to obscure the issue even further. In his campaign for the presidency, Nixon advocated freedom of choice while insisting that the law does not require integration; he also made it clear he did not see busing as a legitimate means of achieving desegregation. On these issues he received unconditional support of many congressmen, including Richard Russell of Georgia, who said:

> While the Constitution prohibits segregation, it does not require integration. The busing of children to achieve racial balance would be an act to effect the integration of schools. In fact, if the bill were to compel it, it would be a violation because it would be handling the matter on the basis of race. The bill does not attempt to integrate the schools, but it does attempt to eliminate segregation in the school systems. . . . The fact that there is racial imbalance *per se* is not something which is unconstitutional.[5]

Busing, however, still remains the only available means to achieve desegregation in most school districts. This fact and the fear of many in Congress that the *Green* case did make integration a point of law led to the attachment of the Whitten Rider to the 1969 HEW Appropriations Act. The rider stated that federal funds cannot be used for busing, abolishing a school, or forcing students to attend a particular school to achieve racial balance. The acceptance of the Whitten Amendment has rather far reaching implications. The strong Northern support for the amendment shed doubt on the national commitment to integration and confirmed what many southerners have been saying for years: that Northern support for desegregation would diminish as the issue came closer to home.

In 1969, HEW stated that all but 352 of the 4,529 Southern public school districts were in *technical* compliance with the 1964 law. Technical compliance is underscored for there is a growing belief among observers of Deep South schools that no one knows the full extent of segregation.[6] HEW, the critics conclude, has played a numbers game with desegregation, making it difficult to judge progress or the lack of it.

It should be evident from this brief discussion that racial segrega-

---

[5] "Congress and Public School Racial Policy," *Congressional Digest*, 48 (February, 1969), 46.
[6] Henry Leiferman, "Southern Desegregation," *Atlantic*, 223 (February, 1969), 19.

tion rather than desegregation remains the predominant condition of American public schools. Charles Martin observed that the tokenism of desegregation has permitted the statistical use of a relatively small number of teachers and students to draw attention away from the vast majority who remain uninvolved and untouched.[7] But the problems go beyond segregation-desegregation-integration into the realm of *quality education* and *equality of education*. The minority-group child in this country has had almost no firsthand experience with either quality education or equality of education. In the North, as in the South, minority-group children attend overcrowded, segregated schools, whose physical facilities are likely to be old and dilapidated and whose teachers frequently are ill-prepared and insensitive to their plight.

Aware of segregated classrooms, faculty discrimination, and the transfer of public funds to private academies in 1970, President Nixon promised a prompt end to racial segregation in the public schools of the South. To do this, he stated that the Justice Department would accelerate its legal initiative by using mass law suits, and that the Internal Revenue Service would revoke the tax-exempt status of segregated private schools.

Promises for the seventies

However, it is easier to outline plans for ending school segregation than to effectively implement them. In Mississippi, for example, the National Association for the Advancement of Colored People (NAACP) Legal Defense and Educational Fund noted that fourteen of twenty-eight school districts reporting in 1970 had racially segregated classrooms within schools that the U.S. Office of Education had designated as being desegregated. During the same period, several school districts throughout the South were operating under court-approved desegregation plans that condoned all-black and all-white schools. Recently, numerous counties have set up segregated private academies in order to circumvent court orders to desegregate.

Neither segregationists nor integrationists have been pleased with the federal government's past efforts to end dual school systems in the South. Segregationists decry federal intrusion on their states' rights; while civil rights workers tend to adopt a wait-and-see attitude, fearing that current programs will fail to end school desegregation in the South. Ironically, it is quite possible that within a few years, most of the public schools in the South *will be* completely desegregated and the remaining defendants in school segregation court cases

---

[7] Charles E. Martin, "The Path to Integration," *American Education*, Vol. IV, No. 7 (September, 1968), 26.

will mainly represent school districts in other parts of the nation, especially the North.

The *Brown* decision and the support for the appellants by social scientists ("The Effects of Segregation and the Consequences of Desegregation: A Social Science Statement") give the reader a needed background into the reasons for and implications of the current commitment to school desegregation.

The negative reactions of many white southerners to the *Brown* decision are captured in Perry Morgan's article, "The Case for the White Southerner," and Margaret Long's article, "A Southern Student is Loyal to the Traditions of the Old South." Old patterns, especially patterns of racial subordination-superordination, are slow to change. Indeed it is difficult, if not impossible, for most segregationists to change their beliefs to conform to judicial decisions. But most, Morgan believes, will comply with the law of the land.

School desegregation affects all participants involved in the process. The mental strains and pleasures are sensitively captured in Robert Coles's article, "The Desegregation of Southern Schools: A Psychiatric Study." From Coles's article it is evident that desegregation can be accomplished with positive results if teachers work toward this goal. No, all children will not become friends, but this is also true in segregated schools. Tom Herman's article clearly illustrates that " 'Integrated' Schools in South Sometimes Keep Races Separated." For those who point accusing fingers at the South, G. W. Foster's article reminds them that "The North and West Have Problems, Too."

Many of the problems encountered in desegregating schools can, as shown in Bruce Rosen's article ("Quality Teaching and the Desegregation Workshop"), be overcome through in-service training. Finally, James Bash and Roger Long ("Public Relations in Desegregated Schools") suggest ways to involve the community in school desegregation efforts.

38. Brown v. Board of Education

THESE cases came to us from the States of Kansas, South Carolina, Virginia, and Delaware. They are premised on different facts and different local conditions, but a common legal question justifies their consideration together in this consolidated opinion.

In each of the cases, minors of the Negro race, through their legal representatives, seek the aid of the courts in obtaining admission to the public schools of their community on a nonsegregated basis. In each instance, they had been denied admission to schools attended by white children under laws requiring or permitting segregation according to race. This segregation was alleged to deprive the plaintiffs of the equal protection of the laws under the Fourteenth Amendment. In each of the cases other than the Delaware case, a three-judge federal district court denied relief of the plaintiffs on the so-called "separate but equal" doctrine announced by this Court in *Plessy* v. *Ferguson*, 163, US 537, 41 L ed 256, 16S ct 1138. Under that doctrine, equality of treatment is accorded when the races are provided substantially equal facilities, even though these facilities be separate. In the Delaware case, the Supreme Court of Delaware adhered to that doctrine, but ordered that the plaintiffs be admitted to the white schools because of their superiority to the Negro schools.

The plaintiffs contend that segregated public schools are not "equal" and cannot be made "equal," and that hence they are deprived of the equal protection of the laws. Because of the obvious importance of the question presented, the Court took jurisdiction. Argument was heard in the 1952 Term, and reargument was heard this term on certain questions propounded by the Court.

Reargument was largely devoted to the circumstances surrounding the adoption of the Fourteenth Amendment in 1868. It covered exhaustively consideration of the Amendment in Congress, ratification by the states, then-existing practices in racial segregation, and

From *Brown et al.* v. *Board Education of Topeka et al.,* 347 U.S. 483 (1954).

the views of proponents and opponents of the Amendment. This discussion and our own investigation convince us that, although these sources cast some light, it is not enough to resolve the problem with which we are faced. At best, they are inconclusive. The most avid proponents of the post-War Amendments undoubtedly intended them to remove all legal distinctions among "all persons born or naturalized in the United States." Their opponents, just as certainly, were antagonistic to both the letter and the spirit of the Amendments and wished them to have the most limited effect. What others in Congress and the state legislatures had in mind cannot be determined with any degree of certainty.

An additional reason for the inconclusive nature of the Amendment's history, with respect to segregated schools, is the status of public education at that time. In the South, the movement toward free common schools, supported by general taxation, had not yet taken hold. Education of white children was largely in the hands of private groups. Education of Negroes was almost nonexistent and practically all of the race were illiterate. In fact, any education of Negroes was forbidden by law in some states. Today, in contrast, many Negroes have achieved outstanding success in the arts and sciences as well as in the business and professional world. It is true that public school education at the time of the Amendment had advanced further in the North, but the effect of the Amendment on Northern states was generally ignored in the congressional debates. Even in the North, the conditions of public education did not approximate those existing today. The curriculum was usually rudimentary; ungraded schools were common in rural areas; the school term was but three months a year in many states; and compulsory school attendance was virtually unknown. As a consequence, it is not surprising that there should be so little in the history of the Fourteenth Amendment relating to its intended effect on public education.

In the first cases in this Court construing the Fourteenth Amendment decided shortly after its adoption, the Court interpreted it as proscribing all state-imposed discriminations against the Negro race. The doctrine of "separate but equal" did not make its appearance in this Court until 1896 in the case of *Plessy* v. *Ferguson* (US) *supra*, involving not education but transportation. American courts have since labored with the doctrine for over half a century. In this Court, there have been six cases involving the "separate but equal" doctrine in the field of public education. In *Cumming* v. *County Board of Education*, 175 US 528, 44 L ed 262, 20 S Ct 197, and *Gong Lum* v.

Rice, 275 US 78, 72 L ed 172, 48 S Ct 91, the validity of the doctrine itself was not challenged. In more recent cases, all on the graduate school level, inequality was found in that specific benefits enjoyed by white students were denied to Negro students of the same educational qualifications. Missouri ex. rel. *Gaines* v. *Canada*, 305 US 337, 83 L ed 208, 59 S Ct 232; *Sipuel* v. *University of Oklahoma*, 332 US 631, 92 L ed 247, 68 S Ct 299; *Sweatt* v. *Painter*, 339 US 629, 94 L ed 114, 70 S Ct 848; *McLaurin* v. *Oklahoma State Regents*, 339 US 637, 94 L ed 1149, 70 S Ct 851. In none of these cases was it necessary to re-examine the doctrine to grant relief to the Negro plaintiff. And in *Sweatt* v. *Painter* (US) *supra*, the Court expressly reserved decision on the question whether *Plessy* v. *Ferguson* should be held inapplicable to public education.

In the instant cases, that question is directly presented. Here unlike *Sweatt* v. *Painter*, there are findings below that the Negro and white schools involved have been equalized, or are being equalized, with respect to buildings, curricula, qualifications and salaries of teachers, and other "tangible" factors. Our decision, therefore, cannot turn on merely a comparison of these tangible factors in the Negro and white schools involved in each of the cases. We must look instead to the effect of segregation itself on public education.

In approaching this problem, we cannot turn the clock back to 1896 when *Plessy* v. *Ferguson* was written. We must consider public education in the light of its full development and its present place in American life throughout the Nation. Only in this way can it be determined if segregation in public schools deprives these plaintiffs of the equal protection of the laws.

Today, education is perhaps the most important function of state and local governments. Compulsory school attendance laws and the great expenditures for education both demonstrate our recognition of the importance of education to our democratic society. It is required in the performance of our most basic public responsibilities, even service in the armed forces. It is the very foundation of good citizenship. Today it is a principal instrument in awakening the child to cultural values, in preparing him for later professional training, and in helping him to adjust normally to his environment. In these days, it is doubtful that any child may reasonably be expected to succeed in life if he is denied the opportunity of an education. Such an opportunity, where the state has undertaken to provide it, is a right which must be made available to all on equal terms.

We come then to the question presented: Does segregation of children in public schools solely on the basis of race, even though the physical facilities and other "tangible" factors may be equal, deprive the children of the minority group of equal educational opportunities? We believe that it does.

In *Sweatt* v. *Painter* (US) *supra*, in finding that a segregated law school for Negroes could not provide them equal educational opportunities, this Court relied in large part on "those qualities which are incapable of objective measurement but which make for greatness in a law school." In *McLaurin* v. *Oklahoma State Regents*, 339 US 637, 94 L ed 1149, 70 S Ct 851, *supra*, the Court, in requiring that a Negro admitted to a white graduate school be treated like all other students, again resorted to intangible considerations: " . . . his ability to study, to engage in discussions and exchange views with other students, and, in general, to learn his profession." Such considerations apply with added force to children in grade and high schools. To separate them from others of similar age and qualifications solely because of their race generates a feeling of inferiority as to their status in the community that may affect their hearts and minds in a way unlikely ever to be undone. The effect of this separation on their educational opportunities was well stated by a finding in the Kansas case by a court which nevertheless felt compelled to rule against the Negro plaintiffs:

> Segregation of white and colored children in public schools had a detrimental effect upon the colored children. The impact is greater when it has the sanction of the law; for the policy of separating the races is usually interpreted as denoting the inferiority of the Negro group. A sense of inferiority affects the motivation of a child to learn. Segregation with the sanction of law, therefore, has a tendency to [retard] the educational and mental development of Negro children and to deprive them of some of the benefits they would receive in a racial[ly] integrated school system.

Whatever may have been the extent of psychological knowledge at the time of *Plessy* v. *Ferguson*, this finding is amply supported by modern authority. Any language in *Plessy* v. *Ferguson* contrary to this finding is rejected.

We conclude that in the field of public education the doctrine of "separate but equal" has no place. Separate educational facilities are inherently unequal. Therefore, we hold that the plaintiffs and others similarly situated for whom the actions have been brought are, by reason of the segregation complained of, deprived of the equal protection of the laws guaranteed by the Fourteenth Amendment. This disposition makes unnecessary any discussion whether such segregation also violates the Due Process Clause of the Fourteenth Amendment.

Because these are class actions, because of the wide applicability of this decision, and because of the great variety of local conditions, the formulation of decrees in these cases presents problems of considerable complexity. On reargument, the consideration of appropriate relief was necessarily subordinated to the primary question— the constitutionality of segregation in public education. We have now announced that such segregation is a denial of the equal protection of the laws. In order that we may have the full assistance of the parties in formulating decrees, the cases will be restored to the docket, and the parties are requested to present further argument on Questions 4 and 5 previously propounded by the Court for the reargument this Term. The Attorney General of the United States is again invited to participate. The attorneys general of the states requiring or permitting segregation in public education will also be permitted to appear as *amici curiae* upon request to do so by September 15, 1954, and submission of briefs by October 1, 1954.

It is so ordered.

39. The Effects of Segregation and the Consequences of Desegregation: A Social Science Statement

I

THE problem of the segregation of racial and ethnic groups constitutes one of the major problems facing the American people today. It seems desirable, therefore, to summarize the contributions which contemporary social science can make toward its resolution. There are, of course, moral and legal issues involved with respect to which the signers of the present statement cannot speak with any special authority and which must be taken into account in the solution of the problem. There are, however, also factual issues involved with respect to which certain conclusions seem to be justified on the basis of the available scientific evidence. It is with these issues only that this paper is concerned. Some of the issues have to do with the consequences of segregation, some with the problems of changing from segregated to unsegregated practices. These two groups of issues will be dealt with in separate sections below. It is necessary, first, however, to define and delimit the problem to be discussed.

Definitions

For purposes of the present statement, *segregation* refers to that restriction of opportunities for different types of associations between the members of one racial, religious, national or geographic origin, or linguistic group and those of other groups, which results from or is supported by the action of any official body or agency representing some branch of government. We are not here concerned with such segregation as arises from the free movements of individuals which are neither enforced nor supported by official bodies, nor with the segregation of criminals or of individuals with communicable diseases which aims at protecting society from those who might harm it.

Where the action takes place in a social milieu in which the groups

Appendix to Appellants' Briefs filed in the *School Segregation Cases* in the Supreme Court of the United States, October Term, 1952: *Brown* v. *Board of Education*, Topeka, Kansas, No. 8; *Briggs* v. *Elliott*, No. 101; *Davis* v. *School Board* of Prince Edward County, No. 191.

304

involved do not enjoy equal social status, the group that is of lesser social status will be referred to as the *segregated* group.

In dealing with the question of segregation, it must be recognized that these effects do not take place in a vacuum, but in a social context. The segregation of Negroes and of other groups in the United States takes place in a social milieu in which "race" prejudice and discrimination exist. It is questionable in the view of some students of the problem whether it is possible to have segregation without substantial discrimination. Myrdal[1] states: "Segregation . . . is financially possible and, indeed, a device of economy only as it is combined with substantial discrimination." The imbeddedness of segregation in such a context makes it difficult to disentangle the effects of segregation per se from the effects of the context. Similarly, it is difficult to disentangle the effects of segregation from the effects of a pattern of social disorganization commonly associated with it and reflected in high disease and mortality rates, crime and delinquency, poor housing, disrupted family life and general substantial living conditions. We shall, however, return to this problem after consideration of the observable effects of the total social complex in which segregation is a major component.

II

At the recent Mid-century White House Conference on Children and Youth, a fact-finding report on the effects of prejudice, discrimination, and segregation on the personality development of children was prepared as a basis for some of the deliberations.[2] This report brought together the available social science and psychological studies which were related to the problem of how racial and religious prejudices influenced the development of a healthy personality. It highlighted the fact that segregation, prejudices, and discriminations, and their social concomitants potentially damage the personality of all children—the children of the majority group in a somewhat different way than the more obviously damaged children of the minority group.

The report indicates that as minority group children learn the inferior status to which they are assigned—as they observe the fact that they are almost always segregated and kept apart from others who are treated with more respect by the society as a whole—they often react with feelings of inferiority and a sense of personal humili-

[1] G. Myrdal, *An American Dilemma*, 1944, p. 629.
[2] K. B. Clark, *Effect of Prejudice and Discrimination on Personality Development*, Fact Finding Report, Mid-Century White House Conference on Children and Youth, Children's Bureau, Federal Security Agency, 1950 (mimeographed).

ation. Many of them become confused about their own personal worth. On the one hand, like all other human beings they require a sense of personal dignity; on the other hand, almost nowhere in the larger society do they find their own dignity as human beings respected by others. Under these conditions, the minority group child is thrown into a conflict with regard to his feelings about himself and his group. He wonders whether his group and he himself are worthy of no more respect than they receive. This conflict and confusion leads to self-hatred and rejection of his own group.

The report goes on to point out that these children must find ways with which to cope with this conflict. Not every child, of course, reacts with the same patterns of behavior. The particular pattern depends upon many interrelated factors, among which are: the stability and quality of his family relations; the social and economic class to which he belongs; the cultural and educational background of his parents; the particular minority group to which he belongs; his personal characteristics, intelligence, special talents, and personality pattern.

Some children, usually of the lower socio-economic classes, may react by overt aggressions and hostility directed toward their own group or members of the dominant groups.[3] Antisocial and delinquent behavior may often be interpreted as reactions to these racial frustrations. These reactions are self-destructive in that the larger society not only punishes those who commit them, but often interprets such aggressive and antisocial behavior as justification for continuing prejudice and segregation.

Middle-class and upper-class minority group children are likely to react to their racial frustrations and conflicts by withdrawal and submissive behavior. Or, they may react with compensatory and rigid conformity to the prevailing middle-class values and standards and an aggressive determination to succeed in these terms in spite of the handicap of their minority status.

The report indicates that minority group children of all social and economic classes often react with a generally defeatist attitude and a lowering of personal ambitions. This, for example, is reflected in a lowering of pupil morale and a depression of the educational aspiration level among minority group children in segregated schools.

---

[3] M. Brenman, "The Relationship Between Minority Group Identification in A Group of Urban Middle Class Negro Girls," *J. Soc. Psychol.*, Vol. XI (1940), 171–97; "Minority Group Membership and Religious, Psychosexual and Social Patterns in A Group of Middle-Class Negro Girls," *J. Soc. Psychol.*, Vol. XII (1940), 179–96; "Urban Lower-Class Negro Girls," *Psychiatry*, Vol. VI (1943), 307–24; A. Davis, "The Socialization of the American Negro Child and Adolescent," *J. Negro Educ.*, Vol. VIII (1939), 264–75.

In producing such effects, segregated schools impair the ability of the child to profit from the educational opportunities provided him.

Many minority group children of all classes also tend to be hypersensitive and anxious about relations with the larger society. They tend to see hostility and rejection even in those areas where these might not actually exist.

The report concludes that while the range of individual differences among members of a rejected minority group is as wide as among other peoples, the evidence suggests that all of these children are unnecessarily encumbered in some ways by segregation and its concomitants.

With reference to the impact of segregation and its concomitants on children of the majority group, the report indicates that the effects are somewhat more obscure. Those children who learn the prejudices of our society are also being taught to gain personal status in an unrealistic and nonadaptive way. When comparing themselves to members of the minority group, they are not required to evaluate themselves in terms of the more basic standards of actual personal ability and achievement. The culture permits and, at times, encourages them to direct their feelings of hostility and aggression against whole groups of people the members of which are perceived as weaker than themselves. They often develop patterns of guilt feelings, rationalizations, and other mechanisms which they must use in an attempt to protect themselves from recognizing the essential injustice of their unrealistic fears and hatreds of minority groups.[4]

The report indicates further that confusion, conflict, moral cynicism, and disrespect for authority may arise in majority group children as a consequence of being taught the moral, religious, and democratic principles of the brotherhood of man and the importance of justice and fair play by the same persons and institutions who, in their support of racial segregation and related practices, seem to be acting in a prejudiced and discriminatory manner. Some individuals may attempt to resolve this conflict by intensifying their hostility toward the minority group. Others may react by guilt feelings which are not necessarily reflected in more humane attitudes toward the minority group. Still others react by developing an unwholesome, rigid, and uncritical idealization of all authority figures—their parents, strong political and economic leaders. As described in *The Authoritarian Personality*,[5] they despise the weak, while they ob-

---

4 T. W. Adorno et al., *The Authoritarian Personality*, 1951.
5 *Ibid.*

sequiously and unquestioningly conform to the demands of the strong whom they also, paradoxically, subconsciously hate.

With respect to the setting in which these difficulties develop, the report emphasized the role of the home, the school, and other social institutions. Studies[6] have shown that from the earliest school years children are not only aware of the status differences among different groups in the society but begin to react with the patterns described above.

Conclusions similar to those reached by the Mid-century White House Conference Report have been stated by other social scientists who have concerned themselves with this problem. The following are some examples of these conclusions:

Segregation imposes upon individuals a distorted sense of social reality.[7]

Segregation leads to a blockage in the communications and inter-action between the two groups. Such blockages tend to increase mutual suspicion, distrust, and hostility.[8]

Segregation not only perpetuates rigid stereotypes and reinforces negative attitudes toward members of the other group, but also leads to the development of a social climate within which violent outbreaks of racial tension are likely to occur.[9]

We return now to the question, deferred earlier, of what it is about the total society complex of which segregation is one feature that produces the effects described above—or, more precisely, to the question of whether we can justifiably conclude that, as only one feature of a complex social setting, segregation is in fact a significantly contributing factor to these effects.

To answer this question, it is necessary to bring to bear the general fund of psychological and sociological knowledge concerning the role of various environmental influences in producing feelings of inferiority, confusions in personal roles, various types of basic personality structures and the various forms of personal and social disorganization.

[6] K. B. Clark and M. P. Clark, "Emotional Factors in Racial Identification and Preference in Negro Children," *J. Negro Educ.*, Vol. XIX (1950), 341–50; "Racial Identification and Preference in Negro Children," *Readings in Social Psychology*, ed. by Newcomb and Hartley (1947); M. Radke, H. Trager, and H. Davis, "Social Perceptions and Attitudes of Children," *Genetic Psychol. Monog.*, Vol. XL (1949), 327–447; M. Radke and H. Trager, "Children's Perceptions of the Social Role of Negroes and Whites," *J. Psychol.*, Vol. XXIX (1950), 3–33.

[7] Ira Reid, "What Segregated Areas Mean" and T. Brameld, "Educational Cost," *Discrimination and National Welfare*, ed. by R. M. MacIver (1949).

[8] E. Frazier, *The Negro in the United States* (1949); D. Krech and R. S. Crutchfield, *Theory and Problems of Social Psychology* (1948); T. Newcomb, *Social Psychology* (1950).

[9] A. McClung Lee and N. D. Humphrey, *Race Riot* (1943).

On the basis of this general fund of knowledge, it seems likely that feelings of inferiority and doubts about personal worth are attributable to living in an underprivileged environment only insofar as the latter is itself perceived as an indicator of low social status and as a symbol of inferiority. In other words, one of the important determinants in producing feelings is the awareness of social status difference. While there are many other factors that serve as reminders of the differences in social status, there can be little doubt that the fact of enforced segregation is a major factor.[10]

This seems to be true for the following reasons among others: (1) because enforced segregation results from the decision of the majority group without the consent of the segregated and is commonly so perceived; and (2) because historically segregation patterns in the United States were developed on the assumption of the inferiority of the segregated.

In addition, enforced segregation gives official recognition and sanction to these other factors of the social complex, and thereby enhances the effects of the latter in creating the awareness of social status differences and feelings of inferiority.[11] The child who, for example, is compelled to attend a segregated school may be able to cope with ordinary expressions of prejudice by regarding the prejudiced person as evil or misguided; but he cannot readily cope with symbols of authority of the State—the school or the school board, in this instance—in the same manner. Given both the ordinary expression of prejudice and the school's policy of segregation, the former takes on greater force and seemingly becomes an official expression of the latter.

Not all of the psychological traits which are commonly observed in the social complex under discussion can be related so directly to the awareness of status differences—which in turn is, as we have already noted, materially contributed to by the practices of segregation. Thus, the low level of aspiration and defeatism so commonly observed in segregated groups is undoubtedly related to the level of self-evaluation; but it is also, in some measure, related among other things to one's expectations with regard to opportunities for making use of these achievements. Similarly, the hypersensitivity and anxiety displayed by many minority group children about their relations with the larger society probably reflects their awareness of status differences; but it may also be influenced by the relative absence of opportunities

---

10 Frazier, *The Negro in the United States*; Myrdal, *An American Dilemma.*
11 Reid, "What Segregated Areas Mean," *Discrimination and National Welfare.*

for equal status contact which would provide correctives for prevailing unrealistic stereotypes.

The preceding view is consistent with the opinion stated by a large majority (90 per cent) of social scientists who replied to a questionnaire concerning the probable effects of enforced segregation under conditions of equal facilities. This opinion was that, regardless of the facilities which are provided, enforced segregation is psychologically detrimental to the members of the segregated group.[12]

Similar considerations apply to the question of what features of the social complex of which segregation is a part contribute to the development of the traits which have been observed in majority group members. Some of these are probably quite closely related to the awareness of status differences, to which, as has already been pointed out, segregation makes a material contribution. Others have a more complicated relationship to the total social setting. Thus, the acquisition of an unrealistic basis for self-evaluation as a consequence of majority group membership probably reflects fairly closely the awareness of status differences. On the other hand, unrealistic fears and hatreds of minority groups, as in the case of the converse phenomenon among minority group members, are probably significantly influenced as well by the lack of opportunities for equal status contact.

With reference to the probable effects of segregation under conditions of equal facilities on majority group members, many of the social scientists who responded to the poll in the survey cited above felt that the evidence is less convincing than with regard to the probable effects of such segregation on minority group members.[13]

It may be noted that many of these social scientists supported their opinions on the effects of segregation on both majority and minority groups by reference to one or another or to several of the following four lines of published and unpublished evidence.[14] First, studies of children throw light on the relative priority of the awareness of status differentials and related factors as compared to the awareness of differences in facilities. On this basis, it is possible to infer some of the consequences of segregation as distinct from the influence of inequalities of facilities. Second, clinical studies and depth interviews throw light on genetic sources and causal sequences of various patterns of psychological reaction; and, again, certain inferences are possible with respect to the effects of segregation per se. Third, there

12 M. Deutscher, and I. Chein, "The Psychological Effects of Enforced Segregation: A Survey of Social Science Opinion," *J. Psychol.* Vol. XXVI (1948), 259–87.
13 *Ibid.*
14 I. Chein, "What Are the Psychological Effects of Segregation Under Conditions of Equal Facilities?," *International J. Opinion and Attitude Res.*, Vol. II (1949), 229–34.

actually are some relevant but relatively rare instances of segregation with equal or even superior facilities, as in the cases of certain Indian reservations. Fourth, since there are inequalities of facilities in racially and ethnically homogeneous groups, it is possible to infer the kinds of effects attributable to such inequalities in the absence of effects of segregation, and, by a kind of subtraction to estimate the effects of segregation per se in situations where one finds both segregation and unequal facilities.

III

Segregation is at present a social reality. Questions may be raised, therefore, as to what are the likely consequences of desegregation.

One such question asks whether the inclusion of an intellectually inferior group may jeopardize the education of the more intelligent group by lowering educational standards or damage the less intelligent group by placing it in a situation where it is at a marked competitive disadvantage. Behind this question is the assumption, which is examined below, that the presently segregated groups actually are inferior intellectually.

The available scientific evidence indicates that much, perhaps all, of the observable differences among various racial and national groups may be adequately explained in terms of environmental differences.[15] It has been found, for instance, that the differences between the average intelligence test scores of Negro and white children decrease, and the overlap of the distribution increases, proportionately to the number of years that the Negro children have lived in the North.[16] Related studies have shown that this change cannot be explained by the hypothesis of selective migration.[17] It seems clear, therefore, that fears based on the assumption of innate racial differences in intelligence are not well founded.

It may also be noted in passing that the argument regarding the intellectual inferiority of one group as compared to another is, as applied to schools, essentially an argument for homogeneous groupings of children by intelligence rather than by race. Since even those who believe that there are innate differences between Negroes and whites in America in average intelligence grant that considerable overlap between the two groups exists, it would follow that it may be expedient to group together the superior whites and Negroes, and average whites and Negroes, and so on. Actually, many educators

[15] O. Klineberg, *Characteristics of American Negro* (1945) and *Race Differences* (1936).
[16] O. Klineberg, *Negro Intelligence and Selective Migration* (1935).
[17] *Ibid.*

have come to doubt the wisdom of class groupings made homogeneous solely on the basis of intelligence.[18] Those who are opposed to such homogeneous grouping believe that this type of segregation, too, appears to create generalized feelings of inferiority in the child who attends a below average class, leads to undesirable emotional consequences in the education of the gifted child, and reduces learning opportunities which result from the interaction of individuals with varied gifts.

A second problem that comes up in an evaluation of the possible consequences of desegregation involves the question of whether segregation prevents or stimulates interracial tension and conflict and the corollary question of whether desegregation has one or the other effect.

The most direct evidence available on this problem comes from observations and systematic study of instances in which desegregation has occurred. Comprehensive reviews of such instances[19] clearly establish the fact that desegregation has been carried out successfully in a variety of situations although outbreaks of violence have been commonly predicted. Extensive desegregation has taken place without major incidents in the armed services in both Northern and Southern installations and involving officers and enlisted men from all parts of the country, including the South.[20] Similar changes have been noted in housing[21] and industry.[22] During the last war, many factories both in the North and South hired Negroes on a nonsegregated, non-

18 J. J. Brooks, "Interage Grouping on Trial—Continuous Learning," *Bulletin No. 87, Association for Childhood Education* (1951); R. H. Lane, "Teacher in Modern Elementary School" (1941); Educational Policies Commission of the National Education Association and the American Association of School Administration Report in *Education For All Americans* (published by N. E. A., 1948).

19 W. Delano, "Grade School Segregation: The Latest Attack on Racial Discrimination," *Yale Law Journal*, Vol. LXI, No. 5 (1952), 730–44; A. Rose, "The Influence of Legislation on Prejudice"; Chapter 53 in *Race Prejudice and Discrimination*, 1951; A. Rose, *Studies in Reduction of Prejudice* (Amer. Council on Race Relations, 1948).

20 E. W. Kenworthy, "The Case Against Army Segregation," *Annals of the American Academy of Political and Social Science*, Vol. CCLXXV (1951), 27–33; Lt. D. D. Nelson, *The Integration of the Negro in the U.S. Navy* (1951); "Opinions About Negro Infantry Platoons in White Companies in Several Divisions," *Information and Education Division, U.S. War Department Report No. B–157* (1945).

21 R. D. Conover, *Race Relations at Codornices Village, Berkeley-Albany, California: A Report of the Attempt to Break Down the Segregated Pattern on a Directly Managed Housing Project* (Housing and Home Finance Agency, Public Housing Administration, Region I, December, 1947 [mimeographed]); M. Deutsch and M. E. Collins, *Interracial Housing, A Psychological Study of A Social Experiment* (1951); E. Rutledge, *Integration of Racial Minorities in Public Housing Projects: A Guide for Local Housing Authorities on How to Do It* (Public Housing Administration, New York Field Office [mimeographed]).

22 R. D. Minard, "The Pattern of Race Relationships in the Pocahontas Coal Field," *J. Social Issues*, Vol. VIII (1952), 29–44; S. E. Southall, *Industry's Unfinished Business* (1951); G. L-P Weaver, *Negro Labor, A National Problem* (1941).

discriminatory basis. While a few strikes occurred, refusal by management and unions to yield quelled all strikes within a few days.[23]

Relevant to this general problem is a comprehensive study of urban race riots which found that race riots occurred in segregated neighborhoods, whereas there was no violence in sections of the city where the two races lived, worked, and attended school together.[24]

Under certain circumstances desegregation not only proceeds without major difficulties, but has been observed to lead to the emergence of more favorable attitudes and friendlier relations between races. Relevant studies may be cited with respect to housing,[25] employment,[26] the armed services[27] and merchant marine,[28] recreation agency,[29] and general community life.[30]

Much depends, however, on the circumstances under which members of previously segregated groups first come in contact with others in unsegregated situations. Available evidence suggests, first, that there is less likelihood of unfriendly relations when the change is simultaneously introduced into all units of a social institution to which it is applicable—e.g., all of the schools in a school system or all of the shops in a given factory.[31] When factories introduced Negroes in only some shops but not in others the prejudiced workers tended to classify the desegregated shops as inferior, "Negro work." Such objections were not raised when complete integration was introduced.

[23] Southall, *Industry's Unfinished Business;* Weaver, *Negro Labor, A National Problem.*

[24] Lee and Humphrey, *Race Riot;* A. McClung Lee, "Race Riots Aren't Necessary," *Public Affairs Pamphlets* (1945).

[25] Deutsch and Collins, *Interracial Housing, a Psychological Study of a Social Experiment;* R. K. Merton, P. S. West and M. Jahoda, *Social Fictions and Social Facts: the Dynamics of Race Relations in Hilltown* (Bureau of Applied Social Research, Columbia Univ., 1949 [mimeographed]); Rutledge, *Integration of Racial Minorities in Public Housing Projects;* D. M. Wilner, R. P. Walkley, and S. W. Cook, "Intergroup Contact and Ethnic Attitudes in Public Housing Projects," *J. Social Issues,* Vol. VIII (1952), 45–69.

[26] J. Harding, and R. Hogrefe, "Attitudes of White Department Store Employees Toward Negro Co-workers," *J. Social Issues,* Vol. VIII (1952), 19–28; Southall, *Industry's Unfinished Business;* Weaver, *Negro Labor, A National Problem.*

[27] Kenworthy, "The Case Against Army Segregation," 27–33; Nelson, *The Integration of the Negro in the U.S. Navy;* S. Stouffer et al., *The American Soldier* (1949), Vol. I, Chap. 19; G. Watson, *Action for Unity* (1947); "Opinions About Negro Infantry Platoons in White Companies in Several Divisions," *Information and Education Division, U.S. War Department, Report No. B-157* (1945).

[28] I. N. Brophy, "The Luxury of Anti-Negro Prejudice," *Public Opinion Quarterly,* Vol. IX (1946), 456–66 (Integration in Merchant Marine); Watson, *Action for Unity.*

[29] D. H. Williams, *The Effects of an Interracial Project upon the Attitudes of Negro and White Girls Within the Young Women's Christian Association* (unpublished M. A. thesis, Columbia University, 1934).

[30] J. P. Dean, *Situational Factors in Intergroup Relations: A Research Progress Report* (paper presented to American Sociological Society, Dec. 28, 1949 [mimeographed]); D. P. Irish, "Reactions of Residents of Boulder, Colorado, to the Introduction of Japanese Into the Community," *J. Social Issues,* Vol. VIII (1951), 10–17.

[31] Minard, "The Pattern of Race Relationships in the Pocahontas Coal Field," 29–44; Rutledge, *Integration of Racial Minorities in Public Housing Projects.*

The available evidence also suggests the importance of consistent and firm enforcement of the new policy by those in authority.[32] It indicates also the importance of such factors as: the absence of competition for a limited number of facilities or benefits;[33] the possibility of contacts which permit individuals to learn about one another as individuals;[34] and the possibility of equivalence of positions and functions among all of the participants within the unsegregated situation.[35] These conditions can generally be satisfied in a number of situations, as in the armed services, public housing developments, and public schools.

IV

The problem with which we have here attempted to deal is admittedly on the frontiers of scientific knowledge. Inevitably, there must be some differences of opinion among us concerning the conclusiveness of certain items of evidence, and concerning the particular choice of words and placement of emphasis in the preceding statement. We are nonetheless in agreement that this statement is substantially correct and justified by the evidence, and the differences among us, if any, are of a relatively minor order and would not materially influence the preceding conclusions.

[32] Deutsch and Collins, *Interracial Housing, a Psychological Study of a Social Experiment*; H. Feldman, "The Technique of Introducing Negroes into the Plant," *Personnel*, Vol. XIX (1942), 461–66; Rutledge, *Integration of Racial Minorities in Public Housing Projects*; Southall, *Industry's Unfinished Business*; Watson, *Action for Unity*.

[33] Lee and Humphrey, *Race Riot*; R. Williams, Jr., *The Reduction of Intergroup Tensions* (Social Science Research Council, New York, 1947); A. E. Windner, *White Attitudes Towards Negro-White Interaction in an Area of Changing Racial Composition* (paper delivered at the sixtieth annual meeting of the American Psychological Association, Washington, September, 1952).

[34] Wilner, Walkley, and Cook, "Intergroup Contact and Ethnic Attitudes in Public Housing Projects," 45–69.

[35] G. W. Allport and B. Kramer, "Some Roots of Prejudice," *J. Psychol.*, Vol. XXII (1946), 9–39; J. Watson, "Some Social and Psychological Situations Related to Change in Attitude," *Human Relations*, Vol. III (1950), 1.

40. The Case for the White Southerner

Perry Morgan

WHEN the good citizens of New Rochelle, New York, were accused last year of admitting Jim Crow to their schools, they denied it. When they were taken to court, they resisted. When the judge looked and saw old Jim sitting there plain as day and ordered his removal, a solid citizen of New Rochelle cried: "Nobody understands our situation."

New Rochelle is located in the Piety Belt that denounces racial discrimination and has it, too. The law is against it, but the majority of people are for it. Beginning in 1930, Judge Irving R. Kaufman found, the New Rochelle school board had confined Negro pupils exclusively to one school. This was the Lincoln School (presumably after Abraham Lincoln who signed the Emancipation Proclamation) from which transfers were denied even though all-white schools had twice as many vacant seats as children registered at Lincoln. Even after Judge Kaufman ordered Jim Crow expelled, a school board majority concocted a desegregation plan designed to sneak old Jim back into school by the side door. The judge, however, was adamant.

The Piety Belt is a varied land populated by people of good conscience. Their forefathers, according to much-loved myth, fought a war to free the slaves. And for the century since, by preachment and earnest exhortation, they have urged the white Southerner to conquer the evil in his heart and treat the Negro as a free and equal American. They have looked away to Dixie Land with fury and scorn and earnestly have hoped the downtrodden Negro would never doubt the constancy of their faith.

Abundance of precept, however, has been accompanied by a stringent shortage of example in the Piety Belt. Negroes migrating into the North early noted that, although the law was on their side, the people lacked some of the warmth and fellowship to which they were accustomed. "Up North," the saying sprang up, "they don't

From *Esquire*, January, 1962. Reprinted by permission. Copyright 1961 by Esquire, Inc.

care how high you get just so you don't get too close; down South, they don't care how close you get, just so you don't get too high." The point has not lost its sharpness.

The South has been given far too much credit for ingenuity in shaping the law to its own purposes. The Southern lawyer seeking to circumvent the Supreme Court decision really had to look no farther than Philadelphia to find the model for what in the South the Northern press sniffily defines as "token integration." According to a Public Affairs Committee study by Will Maslow and Richard Cohen, "more Negro children attend what are in fact segregated schools in the major cities of the North than attend officially segregated schools in urban areas of the South." Note the authors: "When Lieutenant Nellie Forbush, the Navy nurse in South Pacific, tells the world she hails from Little Rock, she is greeted from Maine to Madagascar with hoots, catcalls and other indigenous expressions of disapproval . . . yet Little Rock . . . has fewer Negroes than the South Side of Chicago. More significant, school segregation is as prevalent in that corner of Chicago as it is in the Arkansas Capital." So much for the soul of John Brown—in bivouac.

The non-Southerner naturally has ready excuses for this paradox. It is difficult to admit guilt. Having hidden his complicity in the crime of slavery for a century he cannot bring himself to face the fact now that the victim has caught up with him. His schools stagger from crisis to crisis under the weight of a vast influx of Negro children who lack the capacity to keep up with their white classmates. Achievement levels are dropping. The more affluent whites are fleeing. One school superintendent told *Look* Magazine's George B. Leonard, Jr., that a third of the children in his elementary schools may end up not only unemployed, but unemployable. But, as Leonard wrote, this is a shrouded crisis. Though Dr. James B. Conant has deplored the lack of statistics, school officials cannot publicly face the "delicate and complex matter of racial prejudice." Instead, "they cling to the vain old hope that racial prejudice will disappear if you pretend race does not exist."

So earnest is the innocent resident of the Piety Belt in his explanations that he forgets the white Southerner has heard them all before. In fact, he holds the patents on them. The Negro came to *him* on Yankee slave ships from the jungle. Yet in trying to shake the Northerner from his silly pretensions, *Look* indulged its own in a headline saying *"America's large cities are paying the grim price of a century of rural and Southern educational neglect."*

Southern neglect? God in heaven! By his standards of the time the

Northerner perhaps had excuse for visiting unmerciful vengeance upon the whites of the defeated Confederacy. But what of the freed man in whose name, and out of strategic necessity, the Civil War was given a sacred cause through Lincoln's Emancipation Proclamation? Leaving the freed man and the white man together in a pit of poverty, pain and ignorance, the victorious Northerner turned to a feast of prosperity whose cynicism sickened and dismayed Henry Adams and other sensitive souls.

On reflection, though, it is not quite accurate to say the North merely wrought ruin and departed. More precisely, with a host of exploiting devices, it leeched out of a destroyed region many of the pitiful resources left for its meager sustenance. Long before Franklin D. Roosevelt rediscovered America's own viciously exploited colony to the South, the Piety Belt was grieving for the downtrodden in faraway corners of the world.

The white Southerner and the Negro climbed out of the pit together, and unassisted. It was a long, grim and demeaning journey, and if it scarred the Negro it also scarred the white. For its part in the crime of slavery, as Gerald Johnson has written, the South has paid and paid and paid. It owes neither the North nor the world apologies for its stewardship of the human dilemma deposited on American shores three centuries ago. What qualifications the Negro now brings in support of his demand for full participation in the world's most difficult citizenship, he has from the white Southerner. If he goes North with an inferior education, he was given that by a white man who had never been able to afford adequate schools for his own children.

The Southerner has believed a lot of comforting bushwa about his own region—moonlight, magnolias, and all the rest. But having some little experience with the Negro problem, he is altogether disinclined to believe the North's nonsense too. He has observed that wherever the two races exist together in significant numbers—in London, Capetown or New Rochelle—walls are thrown up, and that when laws oppose, the walls somehow curve around the laws.

The case for the white Southerner is that he is a human being with a normal complement of virtues and vices. If he himself has been too much concerned with defending and vaunting his virtues, the North has been overly fascinated with condemning his vices. A Union officer made that point a century ago, as W. D. Workman has recalled, and so did Harriet Beecher Stowe when she got around to looking for herself.

Let the misunderstood citizen of affluent New Rochelle mark well this unique fact: twice in a hundred years the South has been forced to recast the laws, the mood and the mind of its people. In both cases, though it had no model for judgment, the nation decided to substitute revolutionary for evolutionary processes. The latter, to be sure, were still working injustices when the Supreme Court interrupted in 1954, but they had wrought profound changes too. The South at that point had begun rapidly to repair the spiritual and material ravages of a grim host of decades of poverty, ignorance, pain, disease, and economic exploitation. A growing middle class was bringing a new stability to political processes flawed and half-paralyzed by the racial factor. The region had begun to surmount the bleak, crippling pessimism that was the natural inheritance of the past and to take new and promising initiatives even in the field of race relations. Great strides had been taken in education, medicine, and agriculture. The fabled Southern female was slaving in field and factory, and sometimes both, to send sons and daughters to college and break once and for all the harsh grip of hoe and row. The winds of hope and progress, in sum, were quickening.

Then came May 17, 1954, and an historic decision concerned as much with conjectural foreign-policy needs for a purer national image as with the needs of the American Negro. Never before, not even in the Dred Scott case which wrecked the Court's power and prestige on the reefs of Northern outrage, had there issued a writ touching so profoundly and personally the lives of so many millions of individuals. Yet out of his profound innocence, the Northerner fully expected the South—by taking thought—to swallow swiftly its sociological medicine, cleanse the national conscience and miraculously reorder its ancient social rhythms.

Be it noted that the Court itself had no such expectations. Far less momentous writs of the Court had failed before to run beyond the narrow bounds of the District of Columbia. Less than two decades had passed since the Court had prevented its dismemberment by reversing—lock, stock, and barrel—its whole philosophy toward the New Deal.

The Court, nonetheless, had set out to make a social laboratory out of a vast region whose history had led, in Robert Penn Warren's phrase, to a massive "fear of abstraction—the instinctive fear that the massiveness of experience, the concreteness of life, will be violated." Now, suddenly, so far as the rank-and-file Southerner knew, the most fearful of all abstractions had been struck into the law of the land. Once again, the vast engine of the federal government that had ground his fathers down was to undertake a transformation of his and his children's lives. Once again, the national press would smoke with moral rebuke and condemnation. Already, the NAACP was promising to wrap up the whole revolution in a year or two and, as at least one NAACP official gave as his personal opinion, intermarriage certainly *was* one goal of the revolution.

If this travail would make the world love America more, the Southerner asked himself, what would it do to his children? The very essence of the Supreme Court decision was admission that in the mass the Negro was culturally inferior. And the white schools themselves, despite tax support proportionally greater than the national average, sorely needed strengthening. Thus it was that the most liberal Southerner—and the South has a strain of liberalism unsurpassed for courage and toughness—was forced to ponder earnestly when the learned and gentle William Polk asked: "If the Negro is entitled to lift himself by enforced association with the white man, why should not the white man be entitled to prevent himself from being pulled down by enforced association with the Negro?"

And there were other questions for the heart: What would happen to the virtues of that paternalism which had bound black and white together in a relationship that, however unprogressive, was often warmly human in its sharing? If the Southerner *knew* he did not understand the lesser figure in this bond, was it not frightening to be forced to comprehend that this friendly, agreeable, and sympathetic soul that jollied him and nursed his children was in reality a total stranger who changed vocabularies at quitting time?

Walter Lippmann once remarked that "all deliberate speed" in, say, Alabama might mean admission of Negro students to graduate schools of white universities by the tenth anniversary of the Court's ruling. Lippmann offered a piercing insight into the fantastic complexity of rejiggering human attitudes plus calm acceptance that wherever such engineering is attempted social turbulence, fear, and instability clog and distort the normal channels of social and political leadership. This, really, was not so strange a point—having been written down indelibly in blood and anguish throughout human history. But unhappily, American understanding that is capable of leaping an ocean often sinks midstream in the Potomac River.

As applied to Algeria, for example, the faithful reader of the *New York Times* and auditor of national television understands the difficulty very well. He sees clearly, for it has been movingly and expertly explained, why proud French generals, exquisitely mannered and magnificently educated, yielded to righteousness, insolence, and finally to armed rebellion against the great De Gaulle himself at a moment when the very existence of France seemed at stake. Nor can the literate Northerner have failed to understand why in the teeth of the furies and the face of inevitable defeat the French *colon* incessantly riots to retain a way of life that must—and will—go with the wind. The parallels, of course, cannot be drawn too closely, but it says something meaningful about the universal frailties of the human condition.

But, in fairness, the Southerner who would be understood must not overly complain about the myopia of the Northern eye as it skims swiftly over the iron segregation of its Negro ghettos to focus intently upon the South. For if the Supreme Court decisions created opportunities and even felt necessities for false prophecy and senseless doctrine in the South, the market also turned bullish in the North.

Hearken to that admirable and sincerely self-righteous senator from Illinois, Paul Douglas, regularly informing the South that it simply must throw off the palpable sins of segregation, get right with God and be born again in the image of the Americans for Democratic Action. Yes, verily, and let us not fret so much with the deliberateness of our speed. Keating of New York pats his foot. Ditto Javits and so also Clark of Pennsylvania and other evangelists of instant racial equality.

Let us not impute a lack of charity to these gentlemen. Indeed, they have the faith of their fathers. To befriend a recalcitrant South, they are ready at the drop of a hat to enact a force bill or to employ with federal monies sociological shepherds to lead the region to redemption. And though all this piety falls sweetly upon the ears of Harlem and South Chicago, with their balances of power and their largely separate and patently unequal schools, it would be idle to charge these gentlemen with insincerity. Moreover, it would be immaterial. The Ku Klux Klan has been full of thugs who wielded the whip with absolute—and terrible—sincerity. John Brown, sainted by the sages of Concord for exploits including the insane murder and mutilation of five nonslaveholders in one night, was the acme of sincerity.

In the light of this heritage, then, which later unconstitutionally forced the fateful Fourteenth Amendment upon the South, does not Paul Douglas' impatience begin to seem entirely reasonable? And, in fact, isn't it understandable if just a bit insane that the last Democratic National Convention would declare an intention to abolish *all* literacy tests for voting in order finally and fully to extend the franchise to the Negro in the South . . . even in those many places where, as stubborn fact has it, he outnumbers the white? The answer is yes, of course, if one is prepared to admit that in the light of the Southerner's entirely different heritage the nation in 1954 would have foreseen that Faubus' rabble would for a time drown out the never-stilled voices of hope, faith, and charity in the South. The answer is yes, if one is prepared, as the editors of the *New York Times* are not, to comprehend the resentment of Southerners when with merciless stupidity and frightening innocence "freedom riders" depart the ghettos and, with headlines and television cameras going on before, venture forth to tempt the violent boob from his lair.

Let us not turn so quickly away from this violent man, however, He, too, has a history. Perhaps he is kin to the tenant, Gudger, from whose barren, wasted life James Agee fashioned, in the 1930s, poignant prose for his *Let Us Now Praise Famous Men*:

"Gudger has no home, no land, no mule: none of the more important farming implements. He must get all of these of his landlord (who), for his share of the corn and cotton, also advances him rations money during four months of the year, March through June, and his fertilizer. Gudger pays him back with his labor and with the labor of his family. At the end of the season he pays him back further; with half his corn, with half his cottonseed. Out of his own half of these crops he also pays him back the rations money, plus interest, and his share of the fertilizer, plus interest, and such other debts, plus interest, as he may have incurred. What is left, once doctor bills and other debts have been deducted, is his year's earnings. . . ." Or perhaps this man screaming in the street was related to Ricketts who, with hope of good times, "went $400 into debt on a fine young pair of mules. One of the mules died before it had made its first crop; and the other died the year after; against his fear, amounting to full horror, of sinking to the half-crop level where nothing is owned, Ricketts went into debt for other, inferior mules; his cows went one by one into debts and desperate exchanges and by sickness; he got congestive chills; his wife got pellagra; a number of his children died; he got appendicitis and lay for days on end under the icecap; his wife's pellagra got into her brain; for ten consecutive years now, though they have lived on so little rations money and have turned nearly all their cottonseed money toward their debts, they have not cleared or had any hope of clearing a cent at the end of the year."

In all his variety from a Klansman plotting an atrocity to a school-board member secretly urging Negroes to apply for admission to the upper-class schools to the wan little interracial groups meeting in the church parlor, the white Southerner is a creature of a heritage that he can no more reject than a mother can reject her children. Splotched with evil, to be sure, that heritage also is compounded of triumphs of endurance, of courage, of selflessness that moved a world. Simply because it is gone does not mean it is forgotten or, indeed, could be forgotten. For if the "good Southerner" could break the bonds with the "bad Southerner" to whom he is bound irrevocably by ties of blood, religion, race, memory, myth, and love of land, where would he seek a new code of conduct? Not in the North, surely, for the Southerner knows in his bones what the historians know in fact: that the North has no moral credentials to preach in this matter, that whatever virtues that region may accidentally have earned by "freeing the slaves" was corrupted by a conscienceless "Reconstruction" of a freed man without freedom and a white man without hope or even youth. For the Negro there was no Jubilee-jubilo. For neither white nor black was there a Marshall Plan.

The Southerner's senses told him rightly he had no corner on the corrupting of the American dream. He knew that the zeal of the abolitionist was not the reflection of a higher Northern morality—that to the North there was also greed, cynicism, and calculation. He knew there was a reason that when the Supreme Court first came to the Fourteenth Amendment that charter of human freedom was converted to one of corporate privilege.

All this is remembered by the defeated as naturally as it is forgotten by the victorious. All this is the stubborn stuff of the barrier reef in the Potomac that keeps the white Northerner and Southerner forever strangers and prolongs the sterile ritual of finger-pointing that has woven both Paul Douglas and Orval Faubus into the sardonic and not-so-secret mirth of Negro intellectuals. Connoisseurs of that humor must await with relish the answer to the riddle: "What's the difference between a group of distressed Negroes being driven into a church by a white mob in Montgomery and another group being driven out of a church by a white mob in Chicago?" Only a dense literalist would torture that riddle with legalisms.

The legalisms remain, of course, and the white Southerner will make his peace with them. And though some of his number take secret pride in having been able with courage and statecraft to hew a path to compliance through a dense thicket of difficulties, he does not forget that the New Order requires most of the "poor white" Southerner who has been given least. He wonders, watching the flight to the suburbs and the proliferation of private pools, clubs, and schools, if the grand design of 1954 does not trend North and South toward integration of the impoverished. Knowing something of the Negro's own intense concern for shadings of color that can reject as "too dark" a baby offered for adoption, he ponders earnestly whether the sociologists in their toneless tracts have not assumed too much in their vaunted knowledge of human nature. He understands the Negro professional man's remark to Harry Ashmore that he can always get a contribution for the cause but never an apartment in a New York Jewish neighborhood. He admires the frankness of another successful Negro who, having come up from squalor by dint of great determination, found himself "too busy to practice sociology." He can simultaneously admire the courage of a young Negro sit-in demonstrator, detest the white louts profaning the Confederate flag, and wonder all the while whether the sit-ins will sabotage better job opportunities for Negroes. He is bound to wonder, too, if the Negro ever will turn from the faults of the white man's society to grapple with those grievous failings of his own that crowd the dockets of crime, disease, and illegitimacy. For as the North ceaselessly has reminded that white Southerner, there is a limit to the number of excuses to be found in deprivation.

Writing that, I see in my mind's eye a white woman with a fifth-grade education who, driven finally from the tyranny of the field, took a town job that paid $26 a month for sixteen hours a day in labor and transit, and who from this meager sum bought schoolbooks for three children; who, after washing their single sets of clothes at midnight, rose for work at 4 A.M. to leave biscuit dough in the oven and a stern note not to be late for school; who in all her life never bought unless she could pay and carries within her still a fierce independence that denies her pleasure from any gift, but who finds pleasure in giving. She is a Baptist who voted for Kennedy, but, may Myrdal forgive her, she is "prejudiced" against the Negro.

Not for the white Southerner is the sweet and innocent assurance of the slogan. No man knows better than he from mourning a dozen "New Souths" that died a-borning how swiftly the high rhetoric of progress can collapse into a wail and turn him back to the bleak rewards of the beloved and immemorial land.

He moves hesitantly, uncertainly into the New Order. Some of him dares to hope that this time a truly expanding economy will bathe both races in prosperity's magical sprays of tolerance. But he would also hope that some of the virtues of the old might be retained and perhaps even recognized beyond his borders: that in the new patterns the old civility and generosity and, yes, even the romanticism might find a cranny.

For if his fathers' dreams of a noble breed of learned men carried within itself a fatal flaw, was it otherwise so wild a dream? Was it one that a man—glimpsing it, as it were, in a smashed antique mirror—

could quite relinquish in an age when men move as ants beneath the edifice of the Great Machine?

The white Southerner will not fail his nation, nor himself. Out of the aged anguish and conflict of the human heart, the strongest of him will accommodate the pressures of the New Order into something comprehensible to the kin of Gudger and Ricketts and to the Negro who in the company of the white Southerner has at least learned to read the Declaration of Independence.

It may be true that the white Southerner could have done better in the past and that today he could move more swiftly to accommodate the New Order in the tangled skein of the old. Many of his own courageous prophets tell him so, and millions of his number are not averse to taking new paths laid out with care and reason. It may be, as this loyal son believes, that the grinding mills of the New Order will in time refine the South's great virtues into a new statecraft that will not suffer by comparison with the wisdom and vision of the old.

Certain it is that few beyond are equipped to judge the Southerner's stewardship of the human dilemma the North so long ignored, but soon must face.

The white Southerner fears not history's judgment so much as the misjudgments of the non-Southerner who, armored in innocence and shielded by mass anonymity, sometimes forgets that allegiance to high principle purchases neither wisdom nor political responsibility.

41. A Southern Student Is Loyal to The Traditions of the Old South

Margaret Long

OXFORD, MISS.—The harsh and hating faces of young Southerners photographed in troubled scenes of the desegregating Deep South have shocked and baffled most other Americans, among them, indeed, many rational and peaceable people in Dixie. To investigate the ideas and feelings that fire many of these boys and girls I made a mission to Mississippi, the state where segregationist sentiment is most intense. Here I found many attractive and voluble youngsters eager to proclaim white superiority, Southern culture, and Negro contentment. These high-school and college boys and girls exhibited a common innocence of the Negro movement, which they believe is fomented by outsiders and Communists. (The NAACP, the only civil-rights organization most of them know, seems to them a blend of both.) They also showed intense emotions of both affection and revulsion toward Negroes.

The sweetly mannered young people I talked to seemed most of all gripped by a poignant loyalty to the precarious present and the easy past of the white South, a fealty uncorrupted by alien facts and ideas from beyond the tight and turbulent little world of Mississippi.

From here, the common ground fell away into varying attitudes, ranging from the valiant "Never!" of one Delta boy who would "die for" segregation, to the "It's coming" of several others and the pained confusion of a seventeen-year-old girl who thought, "It's *awful* Nigras can't come to our *churches*."

The Confederate dedication of one eighteen-year-old probably best expressed the adamant segregationist mood typical of many young people of the Deep South. He was Don Barrett, a Phi Delta Theta pledge at the University of Mississippi at Oxford, who answered questions at word-tumbling length, his replies replete with nice, old-fashioned "Yes'ms" and "No'ms." His forebears came to Mississippi from Virginia and South Carolina, and his great-grand-

From the *New York Times*, November, 1963. Reprinted by permission.

325

mother, he said, gave eighty thousand dollars that she had hidden away to the Confederate Army after her plantation, Newstead, was used by Grant as headquarters during the Vicksburg campaign and then was sacked and ruined.

"She turned it over, lock, stock, and barrel," he said, his round, rosy face glowing and his eyes dark with love. "That's the kind of heritage I come from—and I'm proud of it."

Young Barrett's more immediate heritage includes a pleasant childhood of play in backyard pecan-tree houses, fishing and hunting, adoration of a beautiful mother (she was beauty queen in high school, at Millsaps College in Jackson, and at Ole Miss) and a trusting attachment to his energetic and commanding father. ("He's got more sense in a minute than I've got in three weeks. He's the wisdom I draw on.") He also exhibits the usual masculine pleasure in two little sisters and pride tinged perhaps with rivalry, in an older brother, Pat, Jr., who is taking psychology at Millsaps and planning to study law at Ole Miss.

"Yes, of course, I used to play with Negro children," he said. "We quit, well, we quit when . . . when we both realized the difference, and they went their way and I went mine. You may be surprised that our next-door neighbors were Nigras. They lived catty-corner across the street from us . . . the nearest neighbors."

Mr. Barrett spoke ardently of the good Negroes and his affection for them and their profound loyalty to him and his. He smiled quickly and radiantly at the memory of these ancient felicities. Dora, who cooks and cleans up, is "a young 43"—like his mother. They were born on the same day and exchange birthday presents. Allie Mae, a registered nurse by correspondence course, "respected by the white community and venerated by the Negro community," nursed Don when he was born and promised his grandmother "she'd always take care of Sara," his mother. Allie Mae visits frequently in Miss Sara's bedroom and on the phone. Amelia, older, cooks on Sunday, and Pecolia, he confided with a flash of delight, "is making me a quilt." There are several Negro hands on his father's cattle farms who are also life-long familiars at the Barrett house in Lexington.

Lexington is the seat of Holmes County, seven miles in the hills at the edge of the Delta, "the heart of Mississippi and the citadel of Southern rights," with "stark nekkid bluffs looking out to the Mississippi River." It is to him the most beautiful place in the world, a rich center of farming which produces the best crops and "the best people, too." The citadel of Holmes County has 19,600 Negro citizens and 7,000 whites.

"I feel, as do most of the white population of the South, that the Negro is inherently unequal," Barrett said. "Now they say it's lack of opportunity, cause and result, the reason men first took fire and light of learning, that the Nigras never had the need in Africa because they could just pluck the fruit of the woods and all, and sustain life on that. But you can't say they didn't get learning and civilization because of the easy climate, because they've got a range of all climates and mountains and jungles. They came into contact with the Saracens in North Africa. And Alexander the Great and they never did catch the light of learning, nobody in the region. If they hadn't been taken over by the white man. . . .

"Well, where they're not, they're still eating each other," he said, his voice vibrant with triumph and disgust.

"But the white South has taken the Neegra, fed, clothed, taught them how to speak and wear clothes and taught him Christianity. Still, look at 'em, their illegitimacy rate!"

Mr. Barrett was at such polite pains to say the respectful Southern "Nigra" and never to lapse into the easy and offensive "nigger," and I was so vigilant with my proper and hard-learned "Negro," that we quite rattled one another. Once, in the heat of exchange, he said "Neegra" and again, "Neeger," and I once wildly pronounced it "Nigroo," to our mutual dismay. But we both behaved well upon these lapses, quite as if they had not occurred, and proceeded as nice as you please.

"In my opinion," he said, "the South made its biggest mistake— because they hated to do it out of our love and affection for the Nigras —but our mistake is in talking states' rights instead of anthropology.

"The moderates [and here Barrett used the term as it is widely understood in Mississippi, as equivalent to Communists or other enemies of order and freedom], prophets of gloom and doom, say it's coming—we gotta accept it. I think if the Nigra is able to live on an equal footing after the troops leave, then we are wrong—wrong when we say the Nigra is not capable.

"Yes'm, I expect there'll have to be an occupation before there'll be integration in Mississippi, and the Kennedy twins are ruthless enough to do it without batting an eye if they're re-elected. It would probably be the most tragic thing that could happen to our beloved state. But afterward, when the troops leave. . . ." Here he explained that white resistance to the troops would be so adamant that upon their despairing withdrawal, "everything would be just like before, only the poor Nigras would lose all the friendship and goodwill they had."

Barrett's uncle is a cotton planter and head of the Citizens' Council in Lexington and his father is a founder. Don himself is "a sort of honorary member" because he "wanted to give [his] $5," though he is under the usually accepted age. Contemplating the possibility of Negro political control in the Delta through its 65 to 70 per cent Negro majority—"although it would *never* happen"— Barrett said such a regime "without white man's control would be chaos."

"If we turned politics over to them, we'd have another Congo. It's not wild like that under the patient, restraining hand of the white man, when they behave reasonably well.

"Do anything to us? I don't think so, no'm. I don't believe the Nigras, if they got control, would have any reason to hurt people who have nurtured and cared for them, but it would be chaos. Yes, out of their incompetence. The economy would collapse, and it would be like Reconstruction. You remember the Nigras in power in Reconstruction were voting themselves carriages and all kind of luxuries. It wouldn't be out of malice—they're a kindly people—but out of inability to run things. The Southern code of hospitality, gentleness, kindness—they've learned it and accepted it. . . .

"If the majority of Nigras with the vote there"—this was in reference to Charles City County, Virginia—"haven't taken over, it's because they haven't got the initiative. But look at Memphis. Nigras are 32 per cent of the electorate. They're beginning to control politics, and Memphis is beginning to look like a dirty Northern city," he said in another spurt of disgust.

Barret is also apprehensive about treatment of white women under black domination. "If the social system is thrown out of kilter, as moderates would do, there would be more danger than there is now under the patient hand of white leadership. I would certainly take up arms to protect our women. To me there is nothing more wonderful than a Southern lady. Gosh! It's really undefinable. But she's cultured, genteel, intelligent, beautiful—usually beautiful, anyway."

In defense of the social and economic system, Barrett would not eat with a Negro, or call one Mr. or Mrs. or Miss, because "it's not socially acceptable, it's not done—any more than I'd cut more than one piece of steak at a time or tuck my napkin under my chin."

Nor would he betray his manners for distinguished Negroes or for different customs in other places. In Milwaukee, where he visited an aunt and "a wonderful Yankee uncle—the only good Yankee I know," he did not desist from giving his bus seat to standing ladies, in the Mississippi way, just because it was not the usual practice in Wisconsin.

As for celebrated and accomplished Negroes, Barrett says, "more power to 'em." He cited "Gaston in Birmingham"—a millionaire Negro banker and property owner. "You can see he obviously has a very high IQ, is well-mannered and a fine man, I'm sure. Well, it's just a combination of genes that worked out that way. But the chances are one in five thousand that his children would be like that."

There are "exceptional" Negroes in Lexington, who own stores, cafes, and funeral businesses, but no professionals. "We are courteous and treat them with the respect due their education," he explained. "There's none of this pushing around or 'Get outa my way' for them in stores or anywhere—or for the lowest field hand either."

Barrett scoffs at the outsiders' notion that it's deprivation and "brutality" which makes Negroes migrate from the South.

"That's ridiculous. It's economic. The Negro definitely was necessary to farming twenty years ago. My uncle owns a plantation where he had sixty families chopping cotton, borrowing money, depending on him—you know, old-style sharecropping. Ten of the fifteen left live there now because they love my uncle and they depend on him, although he just needs five of 'em. But he gives them Saturday night spending money and everything and he could say, 'Fred, go up the hill and kill me a big snake,' or 'go cut off your head,' and Fred would do it.

"They don't help *him*. They're an economic liability. He supports ten families out of love and loyalty. He's a fine fellow, president of the Tchula Citizens' Council. The others left because they had to sell their small farms—with mechanization, the Nigras can't make a profit on a little farm—and had no place to live. Now you just see old grandfathers and little bitty children, pickaninnies. The young ones have gone to Chicago.

"My girl, I talked to her on the phone and this horrible thing had happened. Houston was dead. Houston drove their tractor and she just loved him. Mr. Foose's father—that's his name, Mary's father, Mr. Foose—and Houston's father were always on the place together. Houston's father had worked for Mr. Foose's father all that time, and they loved him.

"The Citizens' Council, Mr. Foose is a leader in it, is not like the Ku Klux Klan. We hate violence. But we are determined to keep our way of life," he declared with rapidly rising fervor. "Nobody can take it away from us, and I would die for it. I wouldn't do anything foolish, but we will not give up.

"People say Nigras are catching up—that's wonderful—but that's no justification for social change in 1963 for what might happen in five hundred or thousand years."

Barrett is not much disturbed by the current Mississippi Negro drive to write in fifteen or twenty thousand Negro protest votes for Aaron Henry, state NAACP president, for governor, and the Rev. Ed King, a young, white civil-rights devotee, for lieutenant-governor, and to draw two hundred thousand disfranchised Negro votes in a straw election for Henry. Nor does he share outside dismay at intimidation of Negro voting aspirants—random violence, arrests of demonstrators, eviction of would-be voters from jobs and property, and a few killings.

"Federal right to vote? No, the Constitution gives the states the right to say who shall vote and who shall not. There's no such thing as the right to vote. It's a privilege, earned only after qualifications set up by the state have been met. Instead of reducing voting requirements, we ought to make them more strict. I believe in the poll tax. Our two dollar poll tax goes straight to the schools, white and colored.

"I don't think there's any harm in a few qualified Negroes voting. But you can't open the floodgates. I don't condone violence, but the state has the right of police power to protect the health, morals, and general welfare of the people. And when feelings are running high and the spark is there, they could set off a riot.

"I think the police were right in Greenwood and Jackson [scenes of summer disorders and mass arrests of Negroes seeking the vote and other civil rights]. And about these peaceful grievances, they should not trespass on private property."

Barrett went—"defending my state; no, not that, either, as an observer"—to the University of Mississippi upon the entrance of James Meredith to the university. He drove to Oxford with a friend, without his father's permission.

"I was close enough to the marshals to see what was happening," he related. "Some of the boys were armed, and one man was standing by the Y building shooting out street lights with a .22 rifle. The students were jeering and sneering and occasionally tossing a cigarette butt at the marshals. All of a sudden, McShane [Chief U.S. Marshal James Joseph McShane] said, 'Gas 'em!' and from a clear blue sky, a patrolman got hit in the head, from behind, and knocked down by a marshal throwing tear gas—that metal case hit him.

"Barnett [Gov. Ross Barnett] made a mistake. That Sunday, if he'd issued a call to white males of Mississippi to stand firm at the gate, why, you'd have seen six hundred thousand men mustered at the gate. I know all of Holmes County would have come, except a couple of scalawags.

"I didn't attack the marshals, and I was not armed, it was not my place to. But if Governor Barnett had called the Citizens' Councils and other responsible citizens, and had said, 'Come, it is Armageddon, get your gun,—well, I certainly *would*. Yes, ma'am!

"Oxford seemed to me a nightmare. I felt I was not in the United States, but in Budapest or a Warsaw ghetto. If that was American, action, then God save us."

If whites and Negroes attend schools together, he wonders "what's to keep little white Mary from bringing home little black Johnny from school some day, and that leads to mixed dating and mixed marriages."

Would either of his sisters grow up to choose a Negro husband? "Heavenly days, no! But girls who haven't had the upbringing would if we change the social order."

He considers Cleve McDowell, the Negro recently expelled from the University of Mississippi for carrying a gun, as "more dangerous than Meredith. The way he behaved, like I've heard people say, 'he's a good Nigra, he just wants an education.' And that would lead to acceptance. He behaved like a nigger, he would open doors, he had good manners and he scuffed his feet and held his head down. So, he could be the leak in the dike, and then the dams burst.

"Of course, Meredith was the most segregated Nigra in the United States. He was ignored. Yes." (He laughed in appreciation of the placard rhymes which appeared on the campus: "Ignore the Nigger with Vigor" and "Nigger-free in '63") "Ole Miss has never really been integrated."

Barrett was "not much impressed" by the Negro March on Washington. "It wasn't any different from what I see Saturday night in Lexington when they come to town to get drunk and cut up, except they're happier in Lexington." He smiled here at the remembered spectacle of Lexington police warning the tipsy Fred, "Now, Fred, how many times I got to tell you?" and at Fred's shuffling, laughing promise to stay sober.

He described Negro pleasure in government " 'modities"—the surplus foods that they get on welfare—and the willingness of "many, many, many" simply to collect relief and " 'modities" rather than work. All the Negroes on the Barrett place "get real butter and cheese" from the welfare, and "we use oleo."

Barrett, a 96-average student in high school and on a scholarship at Ole Miss, would vote for Governor Barnett, "the most courageous leader of our time," for "dictator or anything." He is now more proud of being a Mississippian than an American, and laments our "federal power, a crushing force, a rampage," under which we're "no longer the land of the free." He also deplores foreign policy which, with the United Nations, "is destroying the only pro-West governments in Africa. Katanga and the Union of South Africa, we stab them in the back."

He takes a grisly view of federal aid to states and localities. His story is "not original," but he compares federal aid to the starving hunter who whacked off part of his famished dog's tail, ate off the meat, and threw the bone to the beast. Whereupon the "whimpering dog," like recipients of federal aid, gratefully "licked the hunter's hand."

For all his lordly and loving attachment to Negro friends, Barrett sees an eventual solution in the departure of all Negroes for the North "to live on welfare," since the planters and automated land no longer need them. He also believes the Delta will be "forever agrarian," though partly industrialized with small, imported industries employing whites in a prosperous blend of his beloved old way of life and new Yankee paychecks.

This, then, is the romantic tradition and reactionary passion with which the young segregationists of a dwindling old South face the nonviolent Negro revolution. In love with the life long gone, they stand embattled, fighting change with talk of old times, planter-rulers and good servants happy in subjection.

42. The Desegregation of Southern Schools: A Psychiatric Study

Robert Coles

IT is fairly obvious that Negro children are doing things which are new and not always approved. Tension and fear often surround them from the weeks before they enter school through the months of their stay. Their families are under considerable anxiety about them, and about their own lives and jobs. When they are in school they may experience rejection, isolation, or insult. They live under what physicians would consider to be highly stressful circumstances, and their adjustment to these strains is of considerable medical interest.

Those Negro children who initiate court-ordered desegregation in the South are likely to be different from their peers on several accounts. Their very selection often recommends them as more intelligent or without emotional disorders which are grossly visible. While some cities allow open transfers on the basis of geographical location, many cities, particularly in the first years, consider and assign children on the basis of evaluation by tests and interviews, and thus initial selection occurs at this point. But, a closer look at these children and their families reveals that they are highly motivated, determined, or willing to endure possible or probable pain for goals which are important to them. Furthermore, there are secondary gains for them as well as fears and troubles, because they may be honored and respected in their own community, and given considerable attention and support. Finally, they will often emphasize to a white person that ostracism and epithets are not new to them: they have been endured for a long time, and, therefore, can be sustained as each of them has managed, in his own way over many years, to sustain many similar situations.

It certainly is true that the pressures which these children must meet are different only in degree rather than kind, and that this makes

From *The Desegregation of Southern Schools: A Psychiatric Study*, (Anti-Defamation League of B'Nai B'rith, July, 1953), 4–19. Reprinted by permission.

them, on the whole, less vulnerable, in the sense that they have learned from their earliest years techniques and methods of dealing with their position in society and its consequences for them in their daily lives. For them to enter a desegregated school may be hard, but it offers them certain hopes and opportunities for work, for assertion of self, which contrast with other moments that may have seemed to them not only hard but also futile and less fulfilling.

Each of them has his or her own life and own personality, and each of them will engage with the problems of desegregation in different ways. Doctors know that just as there are categories of diseases, there are also individual expressions and anomalies to all of them. Desegregation will vary in itself from city to city, and within any city from neighborhood to neighborhood. In the same school, each Negro child may be not only an individual, and different in that sense from others, but may elicit from white children varying reactions and responses. The irony of human existence is often revealed in striking examples, which upset all the expectations of experience and knowledge.

For instance, in Atlanta the Negro girl who was most liked by her classmates and teachers, who, of all the transfer students in Atlanta, had the highest grades, who was in the school located in the most genteel and "liberal" section of the city where acceptance of desegregation was considered most likely and its implementation least hazardous, had to return to her old Negro high school after three months. She was suffering from insomnia, depression, and cumulative fatigue; her collapse may have been precipitated by the stresses of desegregation, and slowly cleared after her departure from them, but cannot be separated from personal and family problems which simply did not allow her to remain in good mental and physical health in such a crisis. As in war, and as in disaster, a crisis will reveal hidden weaknesses as well as show unexpected strengths, and these both are often hard to predict in advance.

One child may score high in intelligence tests, may be polite and neatly dressed, but also may come from a home with many tensions below the surface, and may under stress, respond with nervous overactivity, withdrawal from friends, or severe bodily evidence of anxiety, such as gastric disorders or migraine. Another child may be somewhat dull and of dubious sociability, but may draw in tough times upon a sense of humor or a relaxed disposition which may not be attractive or ingratiating to others, but may be quite resilient and enduring.

During a school year one can see among these children all of the medical and psychiatric responses to fear and anxiety. One child may lose his appetite, another may become sarcastic and have nightmares. Lethargy may develop, or excessive studying may mark the apprehension common to both. At the same time one sees responses of earnest and effective work, new gifts of industry and patience, and evidence of stubborn determination which surprises parents and, in retrospect, even the child. Each child's case history would describe a balance of defenses against emotional pain, and some exhaustion under it, as well as behavior which shows an attempt to challenge and surmount it.

The majority do indeed survive. Certainly in Atlanta and New Orleans only one child has really succumbed to emotional illness. These children illustrate once again the paradox of what health is. During the war it was noted in England that given a fairly stable home environment and reasonably good mental and physical health, children can sustain bombing, military disaster, and all the trials of such times with remarkable ability.[1] On the other hand, every psychiatrist knows that mental illness can strike the most fortunate few who will never worry about desegregation or war. The roots of most mental illness probably lie in the early life of the child, his relationships with his parents, and his inheritance, and less likely in specific incidents in a school or playground unless these draw upon existing disorders or difficulties. Of course, sustained terror and threats can cause any mind to disintegrate, but this is not what these children in Atlanta or New Orleans have experienced.

What is important to stress here is the observation that their admission to white schools in the South and their attendance in them is stressful but not incapacitating. Their inner thoughts and feelings are of interest to social scientists, as well as to anyone concerned with how human beings get along and live with themselves and one another. But it is also important and relevant to point out that these children manifestly have been promoted and graduated, and this reveals something both of them and the nature of the stress. They draw upon reserves of home and friends and hobbies. They receive hurtful looks and words, and some of them have walked through angry crowds outside and silent reproach or noisy jeers inside. How-

---

[1] Anna Freud's work in this regard is historic. All interested in how much children can sustain, and under what conditions they are liable to develop emotional disorders, might well read her small but deeply moving and profound *War and Children* (New York, International University Press, 1944). Of additional interest are some studies of children under the stresses of such disasters as tornadoes (in Vickburg, Miss., 1953) or floods (Río Grande). These are available as publications of the National Academy of Sciences–National Research Council, 2101 Constitution Avenue, Washington 25, D.C., under the listing of their *Disaster Study Series*.

ever, they also spend long hours at work in school, and they may receive friendship there, too. Indeed, so long as the school continues to function, most of their time will be spent in learning and studying.

If they are young, as in New Orleans, they will play with white children naturally and with no hindrance from them. At the height of tension in that city the few white children and the Negro children went through streets of abuse, but had no trouble with one another in the school itself. In Atlanta there may be less ease and spontaneity for these older, high school children, part from fear or hatred and part from a natural consequence of awkward, silent adolescence; but in high schools children are in class most of the time, and this restricts opportunities for embarrassment or worse. One Negro boy in Atlanta summarized the feelings of most when he said, "It was rough at times, but I learned a lot and met some nice people, and I think they got to know us a little and we got to know them, too." A little girl in New Orleans can draw similar thoughts about her own identity as a Negro, and how she plays at school with white children even though, at six, she carefully knows her color, her special problems associated with it, and her special condition of attendance in a desegregated school.

White children   When Southern schools desegregate, the cameras and news reports concentrate most of their attention upon the Negro children, unless, as in New Orleans in 1960, there is a boycott attempted by whites, in which case some white families may be more harassed than the Negroes. But in every school where Negro children enter, white children are there, and they have ears and eyes, memories and ideas, beliefs and feelings. Knowledge about the adjustment of white children to this new moment in their lives and history is no less important, and, in many future situations may be decidedly helpful.

It is, again, a commonplace, but one to be remembered, that each white child will be different, coming from parents with differing backgrounds and traditions, jobs and experiences and themselves differing in intelligence and in emotional qualities like sympathy, empathy, readiness to obey, or quickness to rebel. Whatever his personal nature and family story, he lives in a society which is changing before his very eyes, and with him as a participant. Young children of even the earliest years notice colors as they notice forms and shapes and all those things, people, and events which make up a world which they are increasingly able to comprehend. By the time a child enters school he may have many ideas about racial identity, and can begin to draw them more readily than talk about them. It is a mistake to think that young children are unaware of racial differences, or many other differences and phenomena around them. They hear, and they store memories of instructions, prohibitions, affections, and rewards. They also, in the first few grades, are at an age when they live more in the moment, more in the present of action and deeds, things to do and wishes to live out and play out. Later, as they get older, they will plan more, think more, hesitate, and control themselves in increasing nearness to and preparation for the adult world. Not that they will necessarily as adolescents accept the world of their parents, because the nature of youth is to question and disagree, sift and sort, accept and discard in the sure recognition that each generation has its own truth, its own hopes, fears, and promises. And so we see high school children naturally going through all the struggles of growing up, the doubts, silences, and outbursts which express what it is to feel one's body stretch and, hopefully one's mind challenged.

Thus, it is in this context of human development that we may look at what happens to white children under desegregation. We must distinguish between an attitude, or custom, and a passionate involvement. We must differentiate between an annoyance and a phobia which masks fear, with intense avoidance of things or hatred of animals or people. People like and dislike, choose and reject all the time. We get to the psychopathological when we see the consuming and possessive quality of an irrational love or hate which defies common sense or reality. Every day, doctors must separate the wide spectrum of behavior which is called "normal" from those distortions and panics of human beings which seem so strange and which signify so much unhappiness and fear.

Among the young white children in New Orleans, our remembrances about the nature of childhood and personality development will clarify our observations. Even under the worst situations outside, the children in the schools managed well together. Those white children who remained in the desegregated Frantz school in New Orleans thoroughly enjoyed the increased attention of their teachers, the excitement around them. They often urged their more timid or justifiably frightened parents to keep them in school. In 1961 one of the white children who returned to the almost totally boycotted Frantz school told a little colored girl that she would not play with her because her mother had forbidden this, and then, a few minutes later, did just that.

One hears this over and over from children who obey *both* their parents and their own natural inclinations of age and whim, by saying words which are ideas to them, to know, and to be remembered, and yet by also doing the deeds which the moments in the playground or classroom suggest. Of course, a child of five, or fifteen for that matter, may develop a true phobia about Negroes, just as he may about dogs or heights or certain foods. The child has been taught to associate extreme danger and hurt or harm with dark skin. The fear may reflect other problems in the life of the child, or may simply represent the transmission of charged and intense feelings from parent to child. In order for these parental feelings to affect the behavior of children in elementary school, however, they must derive from more than ordinary habit, or casual inclination. White parents may often be opposed to desegregation, but they consistently note that their children in the desegregated elementary schools get along easily in those schools, and the very few who don't come from homes which make such a stand a matter of virtual life and death for the child. Such children, burdened with fright, will usually avoid the Negro child rather than bother him. They are a very small minority even in a white community whose sentiments may very much be segregationist.

As the children grow and enter high schools like the four desegregated ones in Atlanta, another picture emerges. Early ideas about racial identity, carefully drawn but quickly forgotten amid play and fun, now return, with their associations and lessons, to a child who grapples with new ideas and feelings, many of them conflicting and contradictory. Some begin to adopt their parents' ideas and some begin to reject them. As we talk with these children over the school year, we see that they fall under three large groups in their behavior and thinking about their new Negro classmates. A small number are immediately friendly and disposed to welcome them. By far the largest number are quizzical, annoyed, or would say that they don't want them or don't really care. A third group, small but articulate, are very much opposed to them and angrily willing to express their feelings in word or act which separate themselves from the quietly disapproving or careless majority.

We are struck by the continuing discrepancy between fretful dislike and passionate hatred, by the separate consequences of these two for action and thought. Annoyances shift from time to time, from object to object, but depend on such matters as this: on what feelings he brings to the school before the Negro child comes there about race and its meaning, and on the origin of these feelings. It is important here to emphasize again the development of their behavior and feelings as seen over a year's time with respect to the school and class situation. We know that every mind has its own style of ideas and actions and we know that skin color has a wide variety of real and symbolic meanings to people. But, how does all this affect the white child once desegregation is a reality for him? How does he come to grips with his life, his traditions, and these changes?

None of the white children seen have suffered any medical or psychiatric damage during the past year. Regardless of their views they have all continued in school and graduated or been promoted. Apart from the usual colds and an occasional laceration from football there were no medical problems; and no breakdown in ability to work and study and get along with friends and teachers could be noted. Their parents described their general physical and mental status as "normal" or "O.K." at the end of the year just as they had at the beginning of the year. The Negro children had not caused illness of body or mind observable to either themselves, their friends, their family, or a physician and psychiatrist.

Doctors have learned that even their sickest patients, some near coma or death, will notice and respond to their environment, will react to changes, visits, and messages. In psychiatry this holds, as in the rest of medicine. The most distant and disturbed or even disoriented patient will notice events around him, notice people and hear what they say, watch what they do. These people and their actions will, of course, have to sustain the filtration of a mind not well, a mind which can distort the world and cause it to splinter in prismatic fragmentation. In some way, however, in some fashion, at some level, regardless of how inaccurately and mistakenly, actions and words by people are felt and absorbed by their neighbors, by other people at hand.

What, therefore, the white child senses and feels in a desegregated classroom will depend on the Negro child in that room, the particular white child, and how he sees the particular Negro child, and, most important, what *actually happens*, in the room, between the Negro child and his white classmates and teachers. What one sees after some months is the slow development of discretion and selection in the white child, the breakdown of quick and total vision and the beginning of particular vision based on daily experience. In weekly meetings one can hear even the most segregationist-minded child describe the different personalities and mannerisms of the several Negro children. One can hear them described by their faces, actions, clothes, traits. This is a kind of learning common to everyone, and represents the ability of any mind to see some of the various shapes of things and kind of behavior around it. One can also notice after a while that none of these children, in one way or another, is insensitive to what happens at his side. If a Negro child is hurt, his white friend will be upset, his white neighbor who would vote to keep him out of the school notices, and his white enemy observes and reacts to it, too.

Illustrations abound. Tapes can be brought to life and the impact and private ripples of response to any specific event can be heard from the different children. Someone throws something at a Negro child in a class. The Negro child may laugh it off, cry about it, get angry, get a headache or stomach ache, as consequence fight with his brother at home in delayed reaction to his inability to fight with the person in the classroom, get depressed, study intensely to make up in hard and driven work and achievement for the ignominy of the incident. A white child may see the same occurrence and sympathize with the Negro child, feel sorry for him, get angry at the person who did the deed, laugh nervously, laugh with pleasure, feel like doing the same thing, get angry at the Negro child for being in the room, say that the child deserves whatever happens because he has no right to be there, argue about the Negro child and what should be done following such events.

Over a year's time these individual responses take on the configuration of attitudes. As they congeal, they reflect changes and resistances to change, and it is often hard to predict which person will feel which way at the end of the year. A classroom is in many ways a temporary family. Children learn in it, but they also have to get along with their brothers and sisters in it, as well as their parent-teacher. When a child is isolated or feels bad, many others notice this. They notice this apart from their political or social views, and sometimes even in spite of them. For these views are abstract and often not tied to people as concrete as classmates. *How* one notices will vary. You can notice by fellowship and pity and tender identification. You can notice by guilt and anger, by wishing to get rid of the source of pain or shame or embarrassment. You can notice by hate and rage, by angry denunciation which often may reflect inner, unknown anxiety, fear, or even guilt.

White and Negro children together There are definite patterns to the way Negro and white children get along in the schools of the South which desegregate. These will depend upon the age of the child, the nature of the school and its neighborhood, the specific climate both within the school and in the city, and, of course, the children involved. Cities differ, and districts within them also. Police may perform differently, papers vary in their messages, and community leaders are not all the same. In talking about how individual children manage we cannot ignore the world in which they live.

Together at six is not like being together at sixteen, regardless of all the other factors. Young children of the two races play together and work together even though they have heard many remarks at home which might discourage this. A game means more to a child than an idea at this age. When they get into junior high and high school, this will change, as, indeed, will many other kinds of behavior, apart from the racial problem; then one sees both friendliness and antagonisms expressed in the ideas and activities which characterize teenagers. One sees changes in these ideas and activities, too. You can hear old ideas of suspicion and distrust, contempt and disdain, give way to personal knowledge. This happened with two of our openly segregationist children in Atlanta, and has been reported by others in their white friends.

In the school in Atlanta where social and economic conditions were poorest, with people worried about jobs, income, security of home, and place in society, the two Negro girls went through a year of continued silence, isolation, occasional insult of word and even deed. When one of them was ready to graduate she felt that she had no friends at all, and could really talk to no one, though all year she had reported that many would talk to her furtively in cloak rooms or empty corridors. White children had, at the same time, reported her difficult times, and their own fears of talking with her, despite their impulses of sympathy, curiosity, or friendliness. Adolescents worry deeply about what others think because they are so unsure of what they themselves think, or who they are. Each fears the ostracism of the other, because each trembles at himself and with himself in those uncertain years. On the last day of school the Negro girl was approached by over fifteen classmates who asked her whether they might autograph her year book. She was afraid, as the first child asked, because she felt that it might be a means of attack and insult rather than an expression of good will. Any Negro child has her own angers and distrust, and must come to terms with them, too. Many cannot accept friendliness out of long years of their fate. But Martha offered her book, and some of the comments speak for themselves:

"Martha, I don't know how you've felt this year, but I'm sure there have been times of loneliness and frustration. Surely you realize that ways you have been tested at times are not personal but merely instances of a gigantic, universal, social problem. I have known you to be a quiet girl with courageous dignity. Best wishes . . . "

Another said: "Martha, I have admired your great courage in your great decision. I'm sure you've been subjected to much unpleasantness, but you've met it in a most gracious way."

Again: "Dear Martha, . . . as you said in English class one day some of us can't express how we really feel toward you, but I would like to take this opportunity . . . ."

A girl wrote: "Dear Martha, . . . I know that since I, too, am a new senior I have had my troubles. I only hope that you will forgive those of us who have been mean and ugly . . . ."

A boy wrote: "Martha, I cannot tell you how much I admire your courage and determination. After you had finished that little talk in English, in my eyes you were 'nine feet tall.' "

Finally: "Dear Martha . . . I'm sorry not to have been able to get to know you better, but that is just the way it turned out . . . . I guess that you can understand why I haven't become better acquainted with you. But I personally think that I have missed a great opportunity."

It seems that one cannot predict until the last minute has departed how these children will get along.

There are no easy rules in human behavior, and there seems to be no easy way of evaluating the different schools and different cities. It is obvious that a city where the Negro and white communities get along well and with equality will offer the best hope for a quiet transition. The rural, Appalachian towns in North Carolina seemed to bear this out. Certainly in Burnsville the high schools showed the fullest harmony and spontaneity among the colored and white children, which the principals felt to be a reflection of communal ease in racial relations.

In Atlanta, the best situation from the point of view of both Negro and white students—that is, that situation which both groups felt to be least tense and most nearly normal—prevailed in neither the two schools located in what are often called "marginal areas" (racially changing neighborhoods with relatively low income), nor in the school belonging to the wealthy area. It occurred in a school in a middle-class region which drew upon a more diverse religious and ethnic population, and which had high standards of teaching corresponding to the high ambitions of the parents for their children. In this school real friendships developed between the two Negroes and their white classmates, and the Negroes became less guarded and cautiously aloof. It is dangerous to generalize, but there certainly can be an unnatural strain in transferring one or two very poor Negro children to a wealthy suburban school where, at first, class differences are as confusing as those of skin to both parties.

During the year Negro children get their satisfactions from simple survival, from survival with good performance, and from signs of welcome and friendship which may come their way. During the year the white child may slowly begin to recognize the Negro child and speak with him, or steadfastly avoid him. All of the white children whom we saw who favored desegregation were nevertheless inhibited in their words and deeds during the school year. They repeatedly said that they were afraid to talk with Negro children at certain times or in certain public places such as the cafeteria or crowded corridors. Such was the case particularly in the first months in all the schools, and, in two of the schools, all year. The Negro students felt that many of their classmates were sympathetic or curious about the Negroes, but afraid to reveal any relationship with them because of fear of ridicule or rejection. All attributed the sources of such potential animosity to vague elements—"a few who are noisy," or "a lot of the kids," or "enough people to make it uncomfortable." Many increasingly saw themselves victimized more by their own anxiety than by what others did or might do. At this point they usually initiated the kinds of friendly exchanges which they had denied themselves earlier out of apprehension.

Among the segregationist children several changed their minds over the year, all attributing this change to what had happened at school, to noticing and getting to know a particular Negro child, to thinking about the problem because they were part of a desegregated school, to responding to their friends and their ideas and examples and influences. These children still had considerable trouble in talking with the Negro children, even after their feelings had changed, describing themselves as being shy, feeling awkward or uneasy, or, in one case, guilty. The following excerpt from a taped interview describes very clearly what happened to one boy, a senior in one of the four schools in Atlanta. It was made in April, 1962, the first year of desegregation then nearing its end.

I've really changed a lot of my ideas. You can't help having respect for them, the way they've gone through the year so well. They're nice kids, that's what you find out after a while. They speak well, and are more intelligent than a lot of my friends. You have to understand how we've grown up. They were slaves to us, I mean even after the Civil War. . . . I was taught to expect them to do anything I wanted at home . . . They belonged in the kitchen, or fixing your socks . . . that's the way you grow up and that's what most of us expect . . . and then we're told that they're supposed to go to school with us. . . My daddy nearly died. . . . Mom told him he'd get a stroke if he didn't stop it. . . . I sneered a few times the first few weeks, but I just couldn't keep it up, and I felt kind of bad and sorry for them. I used to get nervous when I'd see them eating alone. I wondered how I'd have felt if I were in their shoes. . . . Next thing I knew I was quiet when some of my friends were calling them all the old names. . . . I felt that I never again would look at them the way I did last September and before. . . . I can't really describe any time or episode . . . no, it was just a kind of gradual feeling. . . . I argue with my parents. . . . My mother is pretty good on the subject, she can change her mind, but my father is impossible to talk with. . . . My brother and I agree that he's probably going to be in a desegregated school in a few years. . . . It'll be easier for him. . . . I still argue with my friends, they laugh at me, call me a damn "nigger lover." . . . They sit and have a time planning what they'll do to make things rough for them, but never do them . . . never do much but mutter something under their breath in the corridor. . . . Teachers won't let them get away with anything "wise." . . . they'll insult one of them, then call them up in the evening and joke with them about going out on a date. . . . I can't figure this out.

This is a record of obvious emotional change, based on new kinds of human contact. It can and does happen. It also can fail to happen. Three children have clearly and consistently indicated their strong dislike of Negroes, of their presence in the white schools, of their presence in any situation not traditionally accepted as for them. Their attitudes were essentially the same at the end of a year of desegregation, in one case expressed even more strongly and angrily. At some other moment their stories, their feelings and fears must be told. We can only mention here the chief themes which come again and again: that Negroes will lower standards; that they are dirty and diseased; that they are like animals; that they are not like white people, inferior, less intelligent, born and made to serve. Themes of betrayal, of being cheated and hurt come to their minds and words. Two of these children experience physical revulsion when near a Negro; "like dirt being rubbed on you," one told me, and they try to avoid them with great care and obvious show. One is less afraid of them than provoked, and is more concerned with expressing his anger, showing them that he can taunt and tease them. It may be a psychiatric interest that they show a kind of sensitivity and concern for the Negro children, and some guilt and anxiety about their own behavior and thoughts, and that this can be ascertained by listening over long periods of time to them, to their words and associations, to their account of their feelings, to their dreams and stories and jokes and deeds.

Nor do some Negro children lack strong feelings about whites, feelings of hatred, feelings often remarkably similar to those encountered by them from hostile whites. A Negro boy told us: "I hate them, all of them, and when I can help it, I try to stay clear of them. They cause trouble whenever they can, and they're the ones who are dirty. . . . I'm here to claim this school, because it's as much ours as theirs. . . . They're going to have to learn to live with us, and they'd better learn it, because they need us. I mean, they need our help to civilize them. . . . They're like savages, that's what whites are like, savages."

Psychiatrists know that sometimes people express affection with anger, their interests or curiosity with sarcasm and distance, their shame and guilt with rage and hatred. But such knowledge must be very carefully translated into the practical problems of the school, the classroom, and the teachers. Let us turn to them now.

In the South teachers will not be immune from natural curiosity and surprise when a custom of long duration changes. As human beings they will have many and different views, perhaps conflicting views and feelings. The rhyme or reason to what one sees in the several towns and cities can only be seen in just this: that what happens is highly individual, and will depend on the local situations, the local school within a school system, the particular problem at hand, the nature of the white and colored children, who they are, how they generally get along, what has happened to them in the past and, finally, upon their teachers, and principals, what they do or do not do, and their view of their role in this new situation. *Teachers and classrooms*

In a sense, issues and developments like this put to test the very nature of education, the very profession of teaching, the very role of the school in the life of the city or town. All professions struggle with the balance, and occasional tension in that balance, between the private man with his own personality and emotions, hopes and doubts, and the more public man of the profession or job, with all its special needs and requirements which seem to have a life of their own, apart from that of the individual. In moments like those facing the South today, there will inevitably be challenges to this balance in public officials, in lawyers and judges, and in school officials and teachers. New accommodations seem to be needed, and there will be strains as these are made. We cannot expect that an issue like that of school desegregation, so charged with meaning and symbolism to so many, could leave teachers unaffected or uninterested.

It is a fact of the past few years that schools plagued by crowds, boycotts, and even violence have, with occasional forced interruptions, continued to function. In New Orleans the two schools there persisted even though one of them had only the three Negro children in attendance, and, in effect, was more abandoned than desegregated. Teachers there were subjected to heavy pressures to boycott these schools, and their problems were often the same as those of the white parents. Many of them were opposed to desegregation, some very strongly, others with less fervor. But they were also teachers, and loyal to their job, their principal, the decisions of their school board. What happened was that the schools remained open, if underpopulated, and the teachers taught.

Several of them have described the development of a kind of school spirit which emerged from a position of beleaguered isolation and experience of attack. Songs like "Frantz School Will Survive" were sung, and a kind of small family feeling developed. "Divided loyalties" would describe much of the situation, and a kind of adherhence in the end to professional responsibilities and obligations. What was described by one teacher was, "I didn't like it, but I also couldn't walk out on my job. That would be unthinkable." This view has been described by many teachers themselves coming to terms with the problem as citizens, some favorable, some opposed, many in doubt, conflict, and ambivalence. But one could also sense in them a deep sense of professional integrity, of identity as teachers which transcended their private feelings about race. The children felt this, too. We heard few criticisms from white or Negro children about their teachers, few complaints of hurtful action or expression. This was one of the subjects which seemed to unite all the children, black and white, integrationist and segregationist. (In some cases, teachers not emotionally able to cope with a desegregated classroom have been permitted to take other assignments.)

Those who have taught under these new conditions describe interesting things about themselves and their classes. They will talk about their own nervousness, their own early uncertainties and fears, and their own curiosity about these Negro children, and how they will get along. Many of them went through, during the year, the kinds of re-evaluations and re-assessments which can come only from actual human contact and experience. For many it is as much a year of finding out and observing as of teaching. Like the white children, they are meeting Negroes in a new context, and many new perceptions may come to them, and must be assimilated in their minds. Teachers will describe their own estimates of the Negro children, their own likes and dislikes of them as individuals and as a group distinct from white people. They will describe the early silence and tension, the developing patterns of behavior, the onset of problems and dilemmas, the ways that the year ended, and their estimates of how the year's experience went for them as well as the children.

Needless to say, reports like these will vary from teacher to teacher, from situation to situation, as will their classroom behavior and their feelings and beliefs. Many teachers have been very sympathetic and kindly to the Negro children, and have attempted to convey this to them, and to white children also in some hope that they will be influenced. Others have felt more distant, and unwilling or unable to do more than teach in fine impartiality or neutrality. A few have had to deal with serious disciplinary problems, when teenagers in Atlanta have thrown objects or marked school property with unfriendly words of chalk and pencil. Then there develop questions of school clubs and activities, athletics and newspapers, all the various groupings and actions which revolve around the school, even if not part of formal teaching and studying. A high school in America is much more than a place where children learn. Even an elementary school is more than that. In New Orleans there were problems about whether the Negro mothers would come to the parent-teacher meetings, the school parties at Easter or Christmas, or help, as parents do, in school plays or celebrations. In Atlanta similar problems about the Negro parents had to be faced, and, also, the more complex ones about whether a Negro boy or girl could belong to a school club, or go to a game, work on the paper, or go to a dance.

By the time one is in the second year of close scrutiny of these matters, and has traveled from city to city for comparative purposes, one begins to see how many of the solutions to these problems come about. Like the very nature of our American school system, they are not decided uniformly or by wide ranging administrative fiats.

Indeed, all the paradoxes of man's nature can be seen in the landscape of these Southern schools. So much seems to come from whim, fancy, sudden impulse, as well as from careful planning and calculation. Hard times in New Orleans' streets stood side by side with easy times in the school (the crowds outside the school were largely *not* the mothers of the school children, anyway). In Atlanta no Negro parents appeared at a parent-teacher meeting which expected them, while in another district they attended with no trouble. Their own initiative decided the issue. In the two schools where the Negro children had the easier time, they avoided dances, advised in this course by principals aware of possible difficulties. Yet, in another school, where there had been much less friendliness among the children, the Negroes, perhaps propelled by their own dissatisfactions and loneliness, decided to go to a dance. Their principal allowed this to happen, and the event turned out quite well. One city, where there has been no trouble, hesitates about club membership, while another, more harassed, simply assumed that certain extracurricular activities go with attendance itself, even in the midst of desegregation. The patterns are almost as numerous as the numbers of schools.

The philosophy and desires of the teacher cannot be underestimated. It is fairly obvious that a teacher can set many standards and establish many kinds of climates. Some teachers have felt that their work should be pursued with no concern for what happens to the children emotionally, with little active involvement in the way the children of both races get along. "They're in the school, I'll teach them . . . if there's disorder in the class, I'll stop that . . . but that's as far as I'll go." Other teachers are very much concerned with how their students get along with one another, and are aware of how much they can facilitate this with a word here, a deed there. The references made by Martha's white classmates to the English class, as quoted earlier, illustrate very graphically what one teacher did, and how much this affected so many children.

There had been much silence, and a few were heckling her while the majority sat by nervously and anxiously. The teacher, sensing this, simply asked Martha, suddenly, and with no advance notice, to tell the class how she felt about her several months' "stay" at the school. Martha did, in her quiet, plain and simple manner, and she was heard. What we had been hearing from some of the white children during some of the episodes of teasing, of throwing paper and pennies, was their own anxiety and disapproval of this and their sense of helplessness in the face of what they felt to be intimidation. Two events helped change this. One was the teacher's action in allowing Martha to talk, which helped Martha, and helped mobilize the sentiments of these white children. The other was when Martha and her friend, Rosalyn, the other Negro girl, reached the point where they started resisting by reporting incidents, and, also, speaking out their determination to defend themselves from attack if necessary. Many white children had reached the point of intervening themselves, so upset were they. They were relieved by this firmness on the part of the Negro children, and the combination of resistance by the Negroes, rather than quiet and daily passive acceptance of insults, with action from the teachers and principal, stopped the grosser episodes of molesting behavior.

There can be no doubt that teachers can allow things to go on, and often prevent them from occurring. Teachers recognize that their continuing task is to encourage those parts of the person which want to learn, study, co-operate in class, contribute to the school community; and to discourage those inevitable parts of any person which tend to discourage education, co-operative effort, and individual acquisition of information and skills. The noisy, unco-operative child, the emotionally disturbed child, the defiant child, the extremely shy child who cannot communicate or will not share, the arrogant genius, and the shy retarded child, all these are but variations in the school population, daily variations, daily challenges, requiring daily decisions affecting the welfare of both these special cases and the rest of their mates. The entire school's children will be influenced by the way these particular children behave, and by the way they are handled by their teachers, and allowed to be treated by others.

It would seem that once the Negro child enters the schools, he would also require the kinds of thought and preparation which traditionally are accorded such unusual or special cases. A desegregated classroom in many Southern cities in this period is a specially challenging one to the educational profession. The level of educational achievement may well vary with the skills of the teachers in handling some of the problems of human encounter before them.

43. "Integrated" Schools in South Sometimes Keep Races Separated

Tom Herman

DeKALB, Miss.—DeKalb High School, once all white, is now "fully integrated, that's for sure," says E. G. Palmer, Kemper County superintendent of education.

Except for one thing. The whites go to school with whites and the blacks go to school with blacks.

The 108 blacks at DeKalb High, all tenth graders, attend all-black classes in a wing of the red brick school building separate from the 190 whites. The blacks ride to and from school in buses driven by blacks, eat lunch only with blacks and do their homework in an all-black study hall. Black teachers teach only black children. White teachers teach whites.

"I can't tell you how humiliating this feels," says Miss Vera Kirkland, a black tenth grade biology teacher. "The school separates us from whites so carefully that we hardly ever see one except if we peek out our classroom windows."

This is integration, DeKalb-style, and it suits county officials just fine. Integrating the school building but segregating the classrooms, they say, "complies" with a recent U.S. Court of Appeals order to desegregate and at the same time alleviates the fears of white segregationists tempted to withdraw their children from the public schools. Kemper County has 2,100 Negro and 800 white school children. "If we ever tried to put those Negroes in with the whites, do you think the whites would stay for a minute?" Mr. Palmer asks. "Of course not. Most of them would flee to the private school down the road."

Leaving school   Mr. Palmer may be right. Already, 424 white children formerly in the school system have been yanked out by parents opposed to even Kemper County's segregated version of integration. Integration advocates freely admit integration of classrooms might lead to the kind of massive pullout by whites that Mr. Palmer warns against. But

From the *Wall Street Journal*, May 15, 1970. Reprinted by permission.

they're convinced that the makeshift private schools set up by segregationists wouldn't last long and that whites would eventually return to the public schools.

As men like Melvyn Leventhal see it, the Kemper County school system "is clearly segregated and is in contempt of a court order." Mr. Leventhal is a Jackson, Miss., lawyer for the Legal Defense Fund, which is filing suit next week against the county. Mr. Leventhal's chances in court are considered excellent; in a recent ruling the U.S. Court of Appeals in New Orleans told a Louisiana school district it must integrate classrooms as well as school buildings.

Meanwhile, in Kemper County and dozens of other places across the South, race relations authorities are finding a proliferation of recently "integrated" schools in which blacks and whites attend separate classes. The tactic has attracted especially wide acceptance in Mississippi, where earlier this year federal courts ordered a final end to segregation in thirty-three school districts. Integrationists fear that unless it is snuffed out quickly such desegregation without classroom integration will spread to hundreds of Southern school districts.

Even with the New Orleans court order to give them cheer, civil rights strategists worry that eliminating segregated classes in integrated schools may be difficult. Many school boards maintain they put all blacks in the same classroom not because of race but because of ability differences. (Several schools have tried to back that contention by devising ability tests for all pupils to take. That can backfire. In some instances, poor whites have flunked such tests while bright blacks have done well.) *Hard to combat*

Other school boards argue they can't integrate classrooms because the black pupils are too far behind their white peers in their studies—a claim that is often true where Negro students have for years attended poorly staffed and inadequately equipped segregated schools.

Civil rights advocates say it's hard to police all the school districts across the South to make sure they aren't quietly segregating classes. And to date, such policing has been left to private groups. The Nixon administration, relying more on persuasion than force, has yet to file any suits to insure integrated classrooms, even though the Justice Department says it has received "a pretty fair number" of complaints since January from teachers, parents, and students concerning segregated classes.

David Norman, deputy assistant attorney general of the Justice Department's civil rights division, says, "So far we haven't completed our *The administration's position* review of any cases. To the extent that we find unlawful segregation, we will correct it." But Mr. Norman won't define "unlawful segregation" and says the department might condone classroom segregation where it "could be shown to be purely for educational purposes."

Such governmental inaction distresses civil rights groups, which don't have the manpower or funds to do a thorough job of monitoring school districts themselves. "So far, the Justice Department has been terrible," says George M. Strickler Jr., an attorney with the Lawyers Constitutional Defense Committee. "They've sat on their hands all spring while many supposedly integrated schools were segregating their classrooms. I can name ten examples in Louisiana off the top of my head," he says.

"I'm afraid this semester is lost," laments Mr. Leventhal of the Legal Defense Fund, which is bringing the suit against classroom segregation in Kemper County and won the earlier suit against a Louisiana school district. "All we can do is file suits over the summer and hope that the courts will enjoin school districts from segregating classrooms next fall. The Justice Department has been tragic. We used to be partners in the integration fight and we aren't anymore. Every time I phone someone in the Justice Department for help, I feel this new tension in the air."

Civil rights observers worry that segregated classrooms worsen race relations. "I think this situation is even worse than segregated schools," says Frances Pauley, civil rights specialist for the Department of Health, Education and Welfare. Class segregation in an integrated school, Mrs. Pauley believes, is "worse for the black child because he can see from his classroom window that he is being discriminated against. In the past, at least he wasn't exposed to the indignity of watching the discrimination."

HEW has the power to cut off federal funds to districts that don't comply with court-ordered integration, but under the Nixon administration civil rights enforcement has been largely moved from HEW to the Justice Department and fund cut-offs have been avoided in favor of court action.

A look at Kemper County indicates that segregated classrooms can indeed heat up racial tensions. At DeKalb High, nearly all the 108 blacks recently staged a mass walkout. The students marched about a mile across the tiny town (two square miles in area, population about 1,100) to the all-black school, Whisenton High. They complained they were "second-class citizens" at DeKalb High and would rather be with their fellow blacks on an equal footing.

The black students returned to DeKalb High, but the grumbling can still be heard inside and outside the school. One student says, "We want to have classes with the whites or be kept in a separate building. We've had enough of being in the same building but being kept apart like animals."

Black teachers feel the same way. "In the old days, at least we didn't have to watch the whites ignore us," says Mrs. Thelma Jean Kirkland, an English teacher (and a relative of Miss Kirkland, the biology teacher). "Now it hurts." She adds: "I know that integration would work if only the white parents would let their children give it a try."

Superintendent Palmer doesn't agree. "Integration won't work in a county where nearly 75 per cent of your school children are non-white," he says, "Hasn't it been your experience that the whites flee when the black school child population is over 30 per cent?"

Integration advocates are depending not only on the Legal Defense Fund's coming suit but also on an HEW plan that would require Kemper County to integrate grades ten through twelve by next fall. The county school board, however, is likely to ask for a court modification of the plan, and, some legal observers say, may win a ruling that once again requires only tenth grade integration for the time being. (The court earlier this year okayed the county's request for integration of only one grade after the school board pleaded it couldn't possibly integrate three grades in one stroke.)

DeKalb High's black teachers have no doubts the county will ask the court for relief from the HEW proposal, and they're bitter about that. "If nobody applies any force to the school board, things will be the same two hundred years from now as they are today," says Miss Kirkland, the black biology teacher.

The determined opposition by black students and teachers here has the backing of some of DeKalb's adult Negroes. Willie McIntosh, a 1962 graduate of Whisenton High who now owns a gasoline station, says the current state of affairs "is making the Negro children madder than they've ever been. It's intolerable. They know integration can work if only the adults will get out of the way. And they're right."

But most of the county's Negroes—about seventy-five hundred compared with about five thousand whites—are remaining silent. One possible reason: Many live and work on white-owned farms and are therefore dependent upon a white-controlled economy that is far from booming. The town of DeKalb, the county seat, has only one bank, one cafe, no movie theaters, a police force of three, an old, one-story city hall, a few gas stations, several Protestant churches, and the schools. The center of town, as in most small Southern towns, is the dark and dingy county courthouse.

The town's most famous resident is U.S. Senator John Stennis. The senator is also a major reason the county school board feels reasonably confident in resisting classroom integration. "I understand some of our school board members have talked with the senator," says one local merchant. He claims that "The senator's going to try like hell to make Nixon understand the Negroes ought to stay in their place."

In Washington yesterday, a spokesman for Senator Stennis said the senator has made no such approach. "However," the spokesman added, "I'm sure the senator has tried to make the president realize that desegregation so far has been much too massive and that the North and South ought to be treated equally."

Should the courts strike down segregated classrooms all across the South, segregationists have yet another resort: segregated desks within integrated classrooms. An official of the National Education Association says, "We've received several reports of classrooms where the whites sit on one side of the room separated from the blacks by several rows of empty desks. The teachers speak directly to the white students, with their backs to the blacks."

Integration advocates say that tactic would be no problem. Explains one: "If we get the black kids into the classrooms with the whites, we've won the battle. The white kids aren't like their parents, and they'll eventually start to mingle with the blacks. Segregated desks won't last for long because the kids are too much in tune with modern times."

44. The North and West Have Problems, Too

G. W. Foster, Jr.

BY the beginning of 1963, the attack on public school segregation had become nationwide. In more than sixty communities of the North and West there were active and organized pressures for desegregation programs.

The drive in the North and West differs in many respects from the efforts which continue in the South. The problems are different. So are the tactics, the demands, and—inevitably—the legal issues raised when conflict ripens into court action.

In the years after the 1954 Supreme Court decision in the school segregation cases national attention focused largely upon the South. There the attack was against a whole legal structure which compelled segregation. Negroes, insisting that state officials must be color-blind, sought removal of racial classifications and demanded reorganization of schools without regard to race.

By the 1960s a drive developed against what is called "de facto" segregation in the public schools of the North and West. De facto segregation does not result from any formal, legal classifications based on race. Rather, it arises from the effect of residential segregation upon patterns of neighborhood school attendance districts.

The problems raised by de facto segregation are more sophisticated and more subtle, and they stem from complex causes. The Negro fortunate enough to find housing in predominantly white neighborhoods usually has little difficulty in obtaining access to schools that serve those areas. Most Negroes in the North and West, however, live in crowded urban slum areas that racially are almost or entirely homogeneous. Even those with resources adequate to acquire housing elsewhere encounter private discrimination that discourages and often prevents their escape from segregated neighborhoods. Still more

From the *Saturday Review*, April 20, 1963. Reprinted by permission. Copyright by the Saturday Review, Inc.

Negroes, caught by discrimination in employment and having few developed skills, simply lack the resources to escape.

School officials, accused of being responsible for de facto segregation in the schools, usually counter by insisting that residential patterns and not racial bias on their part produced the result. An attorney representing Negroes who commenced judicial action against Philadelphia school officials gave his answer to that position:

> The position of the board is that it does not consider race at all in the operation of the school system, either in setting boundaries or in administrative practices. This is not enough. The board cannot be color-blind. It is the affirmative responsibility of the board to work toward integration. Every choice which may arise in making decisions about school matters must be made in such a way as to accomplish results leading to the integration goal.

This concept of color-consciousness marks a sharp break, tactically and legally, with the thrust of school desegregation efforts in the South. It poses for many educators troublesome questions in attempting to provide adequate education for academically and culturally handicapped children in slum schools. And finally, the demand for color-consciousness raises some serious legal questions of constitutional proportion.

Assignment by race was of course the historic basis for the dual school systems of the South. Outside the South, school assignment is typically based on geography. The school system is divided into a single set of zones and each child is initially assigned to the school in his zone of residence. Frequently some provision exists for attending school outside the zone of residence, either by permitting transfer under specified conditions or by allowing a free choice of any uncrowded school in the system. A few communities do little or no zoning and simply permit a choice among all or some of the schools in the district.

The predominant pattern, however, involves geographic zoning with rather stringent restrictions against transfer or attendance outside the zone of residence. Often this is referred to as a "neighborhood" school pattern, although there is much variation in defining the characteristics of the neighborhood. The school in a particular "neighborhood" may be large or small and it may be located near the center, or close to the edge, of the area it serves.

The neighborhood school is particularly characteristic of the organization of elementary schools in urban areas. There, with younger children involved, concern is felt for having the schools close at hand and available along safe routes which avoid major traffic problems.

In more sparsely populated areas the neighborhood concept tends to break down. Buses are then provided to bring children in from greater distances, and convenience in fixing bus routes may be a major factor in determining the attendance area of a school.

At the level of secondary schools the neighborhood concept tends to be somewhat less important. These schools are generally larger and serve more extensive geographic areas. Where a high school does not offer a comprehensive curriculum, but instead is specialized and offers either a vocational or college preparatory curriculum, it may serve quite a large area of the community. In communities with two or more high schools the student populations in each are derived from a group of "feeder" elementary schools and thus a high school acquires the population characteristics of the "feeder" schools.

A neighborhood school—however defined—reflects the economic, social, cultural, and racial characteristics of the area served. Since most Negroes in the North and West live in densely populated, racially homogeneous slum areas, the schools available to them are largely or entirely segregated. Negro discontent, then, grows largely out of the problems of these slum schools.

Slum schools have traditionally had their problems. Poverty, squalid and congested housing, and social and economic discrimination combine to produce higher rates of adult crime, juvenile delinquency, general disorder, and disease. Yet the successive waves of white immigrants who once filled the slums in time found ways to escape into the white mainstream of America. The fact that escape was possible supplied motivation for many who finally succeeded in getting away.

A great fraction of the slum dwellers in the 1960s however, are not white and they face additional handicaps which stem from their race and the peculiar problems of thier cultural isolation from the whites. Oriental minorities, principally on the West Coast, with more stable family organization, higher levels of motivation, and tighter self-discipline, are steadily finding it easier to become assimilated into the community at large. But the Spanish-speaking Puerto Ricans and Mexicans and the English-speaking American Negroes, burdened after centuries of slavery and peonage with far greater rates of family disorganization and illegitimacy, and lower levels of motivation and discipline, are still finding it difficult to escape.

Many Negroes in the North and West are recent immigrants from the South and they bring with them the inherited educational and social handicaps of their rural Southern background. Hoped-for employment does not always materialize and the combination of job discrimination and their own limited skills relegate them generally to the lowest-paying jobs, or, worse yet, to chronic unemployment.

Other school problems grow out of housing. Population densities in areas occupied by Negroes in the cities of the North and West rise sharply above the levels in the same neighborhoods when earlier occupied by whites. Schools become overcrowded and in many instances operate on double shifts, providing each child with only a half-day of education. Elsewhere in the community, school populations drop in older white neighborhoods because the children have grown up and left. The result is that there are often empty classrooms and smaller classes in many white sections of a city and overcrowded and sometimes double-shift classes in others which are all or largely Negro.

Still other difficulties grow out of employment barriers faced by minority groups. Racial discrimination, particularly by many of the skilled craft unions, seriously affects vocational training programs. Pupils, seeing few prospects for employment after being specially trained for it, shun vocational programs. And job discrimination generally contributes to higher rates of dropping school altogether since there is little incentive to acquire an education when it cannot be gainfully used.

The problem of obtaining an adequate supply of interested and competent teachers for the overcrowded slum schools also haunts school administrators. A Baltimore school official admitted the use of some eleven hundred uncertified elementary teachers, largely in the slum schools, during the 1961–62 school year. On Manhattan in the same year more than one-third of the teachers newly appointed to the schools rejected their assignments and looked for jobs elsewhere.

The hesitation of many teachers to serve in slum schools grows out of a variety of causes. Most teachers, middle class in aspiration if not in fact, are under many pressures which direct them away from teaching in culturally disadvantaged schools. Schools of education generally train teachers on the assumption that "a child is a child"—and use the middle-class white child as the model to be taught. As a result many teachers are but little equipped to deal with the distinctive problems of communication barriers, economic deprivation, and social and cultural disadvantages of children in depressed-area schools. This, and factors of teacher aspiration to work in the "better" schools close to where the teacher lives, create attitudes which minimize the desire or willingness to teach in the slum schools.

Physical facilities in the slum school, too, are often inferior. Many buildings tend to be old and the pressures from excessive enrollments add further burdens on the physical plant and the educational program. Major programs to rehabilitate and enlarge facilities in crowded slum areas are to be found in most large cities today. Too often, however, it has remained true that the demands for additional classrooms have continued to outrun the rising supply.

The slum schools, then, are handicapped in many serious ways and protests on behalf of those forced to attend them can commonly be grounded on objections that they furnish inadequate educational opportunities. Since the troubles are often linked with segregation as well, many of the protests take the form of demands for increased integration.

The demands for school integration in the North and West have taken a variety of forms depending upon the particular situation on which attention focused. Understandably, some of the demands have been inconsistent with one another. At New Rochelle, for example, Negroes won a court order permitting free transfer from a largely Negro elementary school to predominantly white schools elsewhere in the city. A year later, groups at Philadelphia were opposing a free transfer policy on the ground that it permitted too many whites to run away from schools in which Negroes were enrolled.

Protests against segregation in schools around the periphery of Negro neighborhoods generally suggested one or more of three alternatives:

1) *Rezoning of attendance areas.* In some instances, it has been possible to show that school officials have apparently zoned schools to "contain" Negroes once they moved into a particular neighborhood. In other instances, zone lines remained unchanged from the days that whites occupied the entire area. In both these situations it is occasionally possible to show that existing zone lines may reasonably be changed to promote integration. Thus, it has been insisted that school authorities have a duty to rezone whether the resulting segregation has been the project of intentional board policy or merely a refusal to deal with the changing character of the neighborhoods involved.

2) *The Princeton Plan.* Another suggestion, taken from a plan installed at Princeton, New Jersey, in 1948, calls for reclassification of schools to handle fewer grades and thus serve larger geographic areas. This is accomplished by pairing two adjacent schools both of which cover grades from, say, kindergarten through the sixth. On reclassification, one of the "sister" schools handles all pupils in both

attendance areas from kindergarten through third grade and the other school serves both areas for grades four through six. By doubling the geographic area of each school it is occasionally possible to promote integration around the edges of segregated neighborhoods.

3) *Location of new school facilities.* The location of new facilities, either to replace over-age buildings or to handle the needs of increased enrollments, has frequently provoked much controversy. Obviously, the location of facilities can have substantial shortrun effects upon the racial composition of a school.

These suggestions for promoting integration along boundaries between segregated neighborhoods often have only temporary effect. Boundaries between racial groups tend to be unstable, holding only where freeways, rivers, or railroad tracks block expansion. Elsewhere the segregated areas expand, sometimes abetted by "blockbusting" techniques of unscrupulous realtors who panic whites into moving out as Negroes begin to move in. Integrated schools in these areas frequently become segregated again in relatively brief periods of time.

For schools deeper within segregated neighborhoods, other plans are suggested. Rezoning or reclassification of schools in these cases produces no change because of the homogeneous neighborhood patterns. In such situations the proposals involve moving some of the children out to uncrowded, predominantly white schools elsewhere in the city. Occasionally, protests have led to complete abandonment of a school, with resulting reassignment of all pupils to less segregated schools in other areas. The demands for transfers out of segregated areas are frequently coupled with insistence that bus service be provided without charge.

These open enrollment and free transfer policies merely scratch the surface. They provide means of escape for relatively small numbers of minority-group children who are strongly enough motivated to seek transfer. Most children, however, are left behind in congested, segregated schools.

To alleviate congestion, the urban school systems are busy with vast programs of new construction. Because of the high costs of acquiring additional land, much of this is going on at the sites of existing schools. Some systems—Chicago and Philadelphia are examples—are also using so-called mobile-unit classrooms, carried to a site on a trailer. These units are attractive and air conditioned, but in Chicago particularly many Negroes regard them as symbols of a settled intent on the part of school officials to preserve segregation.

And indeed, new school construction in segregated areas is increasingly coming under fire everywhere because of its failure to mitigate the effects of residential segregation.

There is broad agreement among educators that a policy of providing integrated experience for all children is a desirable objective if equality of educational opportunity is to be achieved. From this point on, however, there is real dispute among them over how much weight integration should be given in shaping school organization and educational practices.

Even in desegregated schools there are wide differences in classroom organization and teaching methods. These grow primarily out of the problem of dealing with differences in motivation, ability, and achievement among children at the same grade level. Most school systems make some efforts to group children according to one or more of these characteristics. In some instances, achievement grouping occurs within the classroom, with the teacher devoting attention to each group in turn. In other instances, achievement groups are isolated in separate classrooms. Less frequently, no achievement grouping is attempted and the entire class is considered as a heterogeneous unit.

The cultural deficiencies and poorer educational backgrounds among minority-group children tend to separate them at one end of the grouping scale. This means that many wind up in the "slow" group within the classroom or off in a separate classroom by themselves. There is much disagreement over the extent of damage which this kind of isolation does to social adjustment and ability to learn.

Some, placing greatest weight on the damage done by isolation, argue that properly trained teachers can handle heterogeneous classes without grouping. Others disagree, laying stress on the need to expand the horizons of the gifted child and to protect slow learners from situations in which the goals are beyond their reach.

The same sorts of differences grow out of discussing what to do about children in segregated schools. Those who strongly support policies of open enrollment and free transfer stress the value of an integrated education. They are met, however, by others who argue on behalf of strengthening the neighborhood school. The case for the neighborhood school is supported by a wide range of arguments.

Experimental programs in a number of school systems have produced striking results in upgrading the performance levels of disadvantaged children. A feature common to many of these is a concern for the child not only during the school day but in his neighborhood and his home. Social workers, school psychologists, and teachers deal with families and others with whom the child associates. Special efforts are made to enlist those around the child to encourage and support him in seeking an education. The child himself is placed in situations designed to expand his horizons and motivate him to set his own sights higher. The Banneker Group program at St. Louis and the Higher Horizons project in New York are notable examples of such endeavors. The "Great Cities" project sponsored by the Fund for the Advancement of Education has also launched experimental programs in a number of cities designed to improve educational opportunities for deprived children.

An interesting program at Hunter College in New York attacks the problems of segregated and culturally deprived schools on another front, that of training teachers for the job. This, a voluntary program open to education majors while still at the undergraduate level, places them in slum schools for their practice teaching.

Attacks are being made on still other fronts, among them on the kind of teaching materials furnished children in depressed-area schools. Beginning with the "Look, look, look. See, see, see" elementary readers, the conventional teaching materials describe a white, middle-class world which is as foreign to that of the slum child as the back of the moon. He never sees himself in that world and cannot see himself becoming part of it. In a few places, Detroit and New York among them, efforts are being made to create teaching materials that give the disadvantaged child a chance to identify himself and see a way to goals beyond anything he or his family ever experienced.

The disagreements among educators suggest that there is much to be learned before any specific program can be imposed with much more than a hunch that it would be better than some competing alternative. Whether or not open enrollment or free transfer programs are adopted, most children will remain in their neighborhood schools. And the neighborhood schools in depressed areas will require much more understanding and attention before many of the children in them can acquire the skills, confidence, and motivation that will be needed to move into middle-class status.

Indeed, programs to increase integration by siphoning off some small fraction of these children through open enrollment and free transfer mechanisms create other problems. Placing the child in a school far removed from his home environment makes it virtually impossible for the school to work closely with his family and neighborhood problems. Again, as happened in New Rochelle during the 1961–62 school year, if the child is too far out of step with the motivation and achievement of the other children in the school to which he transfers, the result can be a humiliating failure for the disadvantaged youngster and a hardening of attitudes against him among those who make the grade and see him fail.

There are questions, too, about the effects of open enrollment on the children who remain behind in the neighborhood schools. The children who transfer are likely to be the more strongly motivated, better achievers. Their absence only makes it more difficult to create good neighborhood schools with a wide range of goals to spur everyone along more rapidly.

The concept that public officials should become conscious of race —provided they do so benignly—represents a substantial departure from the position long asserted by and on behalf of Negroes in their fight against racial restrictions. They have fought for, and won in a number of states, legislation that prohibits keeping public records by race. They have insisted that colleges and universities not require photographs as a condition to admission and that job applications contain no reference to race.

Indeed, the principal argument advanced in the Supreme Court in the cases which led to the school segregation decision of 1954 was that classifications based on race have no place in public education. "That the Constitution is color-blind is our dedicated belief," reads a key sentence in the brief submitted to the court on behalf of the Negro plaintiffs in the school segregation cases.

Yet the basic issue before the Supreme Court in 1954 was quite different from the question whether state officials could take racial considerations benignly into account. The question at that time was whether states could require separation of public schools by race in view of the obligation under the Fourteenth Amendment to provide all persons "equal protection of the laws." The court's answer was that public school segregation could not be required. "Separate educational facilities are inherently unequal," the court held. Neither then nor later did the court speak specifically to the question whether the Constitution required public officials to be color-blind, although the concept of color blindness was implied in a series of cryptic decisions which the court handed down thereafter that invalidated laws requiring segregation of parks, buses, restaurants, and the like.

Many questions remain to be decided in determining how far and in what manner state authority may—or perhaps must—constitutionally take race into account in shaping public policy.

It was abundantly clear by the beginning of 1963 that the process of doing away with the dual school systems in the South has endlessly taken racial considerations into account. Everyone involved in the process has done so—the community at large, school officials, even the courts. The patterns and practices of school operation have to be understood before solutions can be worked out. In this respect the actions of public authority are not color-blind.

It is also reasonably clear that, while racial considerations can be taken into account, they cannot be used invidiously against any racial group. Thus, school zone lines cannot be gerrymandered to contain Negroes. And even with racial considerations not in the picture, substantial questions of equal protection are raised by claims of serious overcrowding or that schools are badly deficient in physical plant, quality of teaching, or curricular offerings. Where any such questions develop, the Constitution probably affords a basis for judicial relief.

Other questions, however, are more difficult. As long as private discrimination produces residential segregation, it will affect the racial composition of the schools themselves. The state, whether it likes it or not, must take the community as it finds it. Since segregation cannot under the circumstances be erased, racial considerations must be taken into account. What is needed, it seems, is some flexibility of choice among reasonable educational alternatives to avoid placing any group at a disadvantage because of its race.

Where it can be shown that the practices of school authorities operate purposely to place Negroes at a racial disadvantage, judicial relief can be expected. There are, however, difficult and delicate problems in fixing the constitutional line that measures the extent to which judicial relief may be forthcoming. Several illustrations suffice to make the point. San Francisco closed down a junior high school after protests that its student population would be 60 per cent Negro. Was this a "separate"—or "segregated"—and hence "unequal" school in the sense that the Constitution would require judicial action to put it out of business or to require alteration of its racial composition? Or was the action merely one which the political processes of the community are free to take—or not take? Again, it has been suggested that Negroes may be entitled to compensatory educational benefits because of damage done by past practices of racial segregation. It hardly seems constitutionally possible that the state can establish a compensatory program exclusively for Negroes and bar similarly handicapped whites who attend the same school.

Yet the controversy over de facto segregation in the schools of the North and West is reaching the federal courts under a wide range of claimed constitutional deprivations. The most celebrated case thus far came out of New Rochelle, New York, where the court found that school board practices more than a decade earlier caused the development of a segregated elementary school. This produced a court order permitting pupils in that school to transfer to any uncrowded school in the district. Cases like this one, which produce findings of intentional segregation practices, manifestly demonstrate a need for some corrective action. The far harder question is that of determining what kind of relief is appropriate; a number of Negro children in New Rochelle suffered serious setbacks when they transferred to classes maintaining higher academic standards.

For wholly understandable reasons, Negroes continue to insist that school authorities have the duty to mitigate the effects of residential segregation. The farthest reach of judicial language on this point came from the case in Hempstead, Long Island, in April, 1962. The school board moved to dismiss the case before trial on the ground that residential patterns, not school board practices, produced the school segregation. The court denied the motion to dismiss, indicating the board had an obligation to mitigate the effects of segregation, whatever its cause. The board's obligation, the court said, could be discharged either by doing something to relieve segregation or by "a conclusive demonstration that no circumstantially possible effort can effect any significant mitigation." Thus, where the Hempstead case departed from earlier cases was in the court's insistence that the state, in operating its school, has a constitutional obligation to mitigate the effects of private discrimination.

So far as the drive against school segregation in the North and West insists that school authorities become benignly color-conscious, it raises many questions still to be resolved. In a great many situations public authority is not, and cannot be, color-blind. The earlier insistence by Negroes that the Constitution required the state to be color-blind seems clearly inconsistent with the minimum need of the state at least to be sufficiently color-conscious to make sure that invidious racial discrimination is not being practiced in its name.

The courts, too, in passing on claims of racial discrimination, have to take race into account. That the Fourteenth Amendment requires judicial relief against intentional segregation of public schools has been settled. Whether the courts are required by the Constitution to insist upon maximum integration where segregation is attributable to private discrimination is another question. Particularly is it another question in light of the deep differences among educators about methods for overcoming social, cultural, and educational disadvantages suffered by those isolated from the mainstream of American life.

Merely that judicial action may not be available to compel maximum integration, however, does not suggest that the state cannot experiment with such educational programs. Nor does it suggest any impropriety in having Negroes and others make political demands for these things. It does suggest that there are certain questions which must be addressed to the political processes of the community and state rather than to the courts. And where state legislation requires affirmative integration programs, courts could be looked to for enforcement of the statutes; but judicial action in such cases would flow from legislation rather than from the federal Constitution.

Manifestly, public education has a great burden to discharge in helping disadvantaged children develop their abilities to the fullest extent possible. But public education seems hardly equipped to carry the whole load of mitigating and ending all the disadvantages minority groups suffer from private discrimination. Other efforts, both public and private, must continue on many fronts if America is to make good on its constitutional commitment to equality for all its people. Fortunately, more and more Americans are aware of this. And while much more effort is still required, significant changes are taking place in lessening job discrimination, in breaking up patterns of housing discrimination, and in generally providing more and more reasons for hope among the nation's minority groups that they can share our democratic ideals on equal terms.

45. Quality Teaching and the Desegregation Workshop

Bruce Rosen

WHILE educators and self-appointed "experts" in all areas of the United States are busily trying to improve the quality of instruction in our schools, some of the poorest teaching today is being done where the best possible teaching is an absolute necessity. I have reference to the teaching in the workshops, institutes, and seminars being held across the United States to prepare teachers and administrators for the problems they may expect to encounter in desegregated schools and classrooms. Unfortunately, too many of these workshops, whether in universities and colleges or in school districts, have followed a pattern that can only be described as violative of the principles of good teaching.

It is a truism that most of us teach as we are taught and not as we are taught to teach. Thus, when we have institutes designed to provide the information and, more important, the *skills* required in the newly integrated classroom, workshops must be developed to provide the types of experiences teachers need and which they, in turn, can provide for their students. To be specific, aside from the simple fact of requiring that the institutes be desegregated, a wide variety of experiences in desegregated environments should be provided. At the present time, most of these institutes and workshops rely in large part on four basic procedures: first, the use of experts; second, lectures; third, discussion groups; and fourth, films and other ancillary activities.

No one will dispute the value of having an expert on some aspect of school desegregation work with the teachers. Too often, however, reliance is placed on an acknowledged expert who is given a very general topic and flown in for the day to give a one-hour presentation. Instead of working *with* he lectures *at* the teachers and, if time permits, perhaps works briefly with one or two discussion groups. The

From the *Journal of Teacher Education*, Winter, 1967, pp. 491–94. Reprinted by permission.

367

great weakness in this procedure is that it is impossible for the experts to correlate their material and remarks, and since many of the presentations vary drastically from the topic assigned, the institutes oftentimes lack any semblance of orderly continuity. Further, many of the specialists feel that their only responsibility to the institute is to present their paper; they will only reluctantly, if at all, work with discussion groups or go beyond their formal presentation. Also, more often than not, they are selected, not because of the relationship of their topics, but because they happen to be available on a particular day at a particular time and are able to make a presentation. In many instances, therefore, more than one paper is presented on the same day. All this, of course, further hampers continuity in many of the desegregation workshops.

The use of lectures as a teaching technique has long been recognized as one of the weakest forms of education available. Lectures do have a place, albeit a severely restricted one, but in too many institutes and workshops, they have constituted the most important part of the program. Usually, there is a minimum of one lecture per day, and in some cases, as many as three or four. They are often completely unrelated to one another and consequently do not make for continuity in the workshop. In most cases, the guest speaker does not provide materials relevant to his presentation nor make copies of his speech available. (The discussion groups and the question-and-answer sessions following the lectures would obviously be more meaningful if the participants had copies of the speech or other materials to which the speaker made reference.)

The third technique is the discussion group. In education circles, it is considered gauche to say anything negative about discussion groups; nonetheless, there are many who feel that it is time we took a serious look at them. First, it is necessary to distinguish the discussion group from the buzz session, which has no goal in mind and merely uses the topic as presented for a general kicking-off point. To expect anything more than a general clearing of the air from a buzz group is to overestimate the effectiveness, and even the purpose, of this technique. On the other hand, discussion groups usually have a leader and are more structured. If this is the case, structure should generally be one of two types: either it should be based on a long-term topic which will be discussed by subtopics on a day-to-day basis, or it should be based on the lecture usually given prior to the discussion group. In an ideal situation, where the lectures and the general topics are correlated and continuous, both of these values can be realized.

The greatest failures with discussion groups seem to fall into two categories: First, when the discussion group leaders are inexperienced, they either use the discussion as a forum for the presentation of their own views, or they lack the ability to guide and control the flow of discussion, thus permitting a form of intellectual anarchy. The second type of failure is found in the relationship of the consultant to the discussion group. Since he is usually one and the same, the consultant is changed as often as the lecturer, and very often the group is so overwhelmed or awed by having a distinguished speaker in its midst that discussion dries up and the participants all turn to the guest for words of wisdom. Few men are able to remain quiet when a respectful group asks for their opinion, and thus guest lecturers and consultants often wind up lecturing rather than serving as resource persons.

The fourth phase of these institutes that is subject to criticism is the ancillary activities, which usually take the form of bibliographies, films, tape recordings, and field trips. In most cases, these are not integrated into the program and consequently serve only to provide a rest period for some of the workshop participants or fodder for their folders. Bibliographies are often too long, unannotated, and contain outdated materials. Tape recordings are difficult to listen to even under the best of circumstances, and films are too often totally irrelevant to the topics being discussed. A field trip in a comfortable air-conditioned bus with closed windows and a guide can hardly be expected to bring home to the participants the hard realities of slum life. A short tour through a Negro school in which pupils and teachers are dressed in their Sunday best can hardly prove to be of any great educational worth.

Implicit in all the foregoing criticisms are a number of alternative courses of action that might be suggested concerning the planning of workshops.

1. Since it is to deal with problems of desegregation the teachers will face and, to some degree, prepare them for those faced by students, the program should utilize the experiences of participants in previous desegregation activities; specifically, this means that it should be planned in large part by the participants. Such questions as Gertrude Noar raises in her new book *The Teacher and Integration* will probably be raised by many of the teachers: "How can I control them?" "Where shall I put them?" "How can I make them learn?" "Should I use separate groups?" etc. It is imperative to structure a workshop around the problems that the teachers feel are important.

Not only should the participants of the workshop take an active part in the planning, but during this earliest stage, teachers and students who have been involved in the process of desegregation should be used as consultants to help the participants define the questions considered to be most important and separate out those that experience has shown to be irrelevant. A good mixture of old hands at desegregation, to serve as discussion group leaders or resource persons, and teachers new to the area would easily lend itself to such techniques as role playing, in which Negro and white teachers might try playing the role of a teacher (or student or administrator) of another color.

2. The second suggestion for improving the workshops is to maintain a high degree of continuity. In the light of previous experience, this would mean that consultants be brought in on a long-term rather than a short-term basis. An expert who is with the institute or workshop for an extended period of time is of considerably more value than short-term consultants in terms of providing continuity and serving as a continuous source of information.

3. More emphasis should be placed upon the realities of the situation than upon the theoretical dimensions. Consultants should be sought who can provide precise information and detailed guidance for the teacher in the classroom. This is in no way meant to negate or disparage the value of the theory, for good practice is always an outgrowth of good theory. Nonetheless, in these workshops, greater emphasis should be given to the relationship between theory and practice, to techniques such as role playing, and to the case histories of teachers who have successfully dealt with integration as well as of those who have been unsuccessful.

Within this context, teachers who have actually worked in desegregated classrooms, urban and rural, North and South, should serve as consultants and as explicators for the case histories. Students, too, need to be involved, and the contributions of panels and of interviews with children in desegregated schools should not be ignored. Further, with the availability of audio-visual and mass-media techniques for bringing relevant materials into the workshop, there is no reason why classroom observation should not be provided either in the traditional sense or through the use of video tapes or films of desegregated classrooms. If either video tapes or films are used, they can be stopped, analyzed, rerun, or used in a variety of other ways that can elicit discussion of solutions.

4. In the area of readings, there are a great many bibliographies and lists of materials that can be handed out. Unfortunately, in most

institutes, those running the program feel that the handing out of reading lists is in itself sufficient and that in some mystical manner participants will acquire all of the significant literature as part of their frame of reference. This is, of course, not the case; and since the participants do need to read the materials, a planned reading program, using short annotated reading lists that parallel the discussions and the experiences provided, would seem to be a relevant and important dimension of any desegregation institute. Some readings, too, should be required prior to the first formal workshop meetings, thus giving participants a common source of materials to draw upon.

Films and field trips should be used in the same way. It would cut down on the misuse of both of these techniques if those who put them into the program would first ask themselves, "Why am I using this film?" "Why are we taking this field trip?" "Is it really relevant, or does it provide part of the continuity of the program?" "Am I using the best possible film?" "Is this the best possible way to set up this field trip to accomplish our purposes?" Unfortunately, these questions too often remain unasked, and films and field trips are slapped into the workshops with no regard for rationale or the continuity of the program.

5. The final suggestion for the improvement of these programs is that they should in all cases have a built-in follow-up. If the workshop ends without this, one fails to provide for the *continuing* human relations education of his teachers (a process barely begun in an initial institute), as well as failing to provide for new teachers coming into the system. There is a great need for a follow-up that will take the form of continued discussions with the teachers over a long period of time, as well as for regular observation of classrooms in the district. Through observation by other teachers within the same district (a technique not usually employed) or teachers from other districts where desegregation has successfully occurred, followed by discussion, analysis, and criticism in a threat-free environment, plans can be made for a continuous program and an ongoing evaluation of the desegregation activities maintained. A record of all speeches, observations, and relevant discussions should, of course, be kept for reference purposes. It is only through such observation and participation that teachers in a given district will learn how better to desegregate, and indeed *integrate*, education within their own district. Thus workshops should have no end: they should be ongoing and continuous, and *funds should be provided so that the program can be maintained as long as the need exists.*

46. Public Relations in Desegregated Schools

James H. Bash and Roger L. Long

SCHOOL desegregation is not a problem of the school alone; the community itself is very deeply involved. Orderly desegregation can be accomplished more easily through the joint efforts of school and community organizations which involve many members of the community. If the principal makes use of the community resources available, referring individual requests for assistance to the appropriate organizations, he may build better relationships in both the school and community.

The principal should undertake a vigorous program to develop and maintain genuine understanding. An effective school public information program is continuous; it is positive; and it is honest in its intent and execution. The principal seeks to supply every citizen with clear information and a better understanding of the work of the school.

In a desegregation situation, he will want to determine some of these factors:

What are the values of the community concerning desegregation? How deeply imbedded are interracial prejudice and hostility? What specifically can the school do in promoting desegregation without causing offense to the community? What problems has school desegregation caused in the community? What can be done to reduce tensions? Should the school play the chief role in desegregating the community, and what roles should other agencies and groups play? To what extent do the attitudes of community groups and agencies toward the school reflect the same objectives as those of the school? What unified action has been attempted in the past, or is possible in the future? Who are the persons, within and outside the formal

From "School and Community," *Effective Administration in Desegregated Schools* (Phi Delta Kappa, 1969), 57–64. Reprinted by permission.

organization of the community, who "get things done"? How can they be utilized?

Principals, responding to a questionnaire, were asked to rank community groups in terms of the degree of assistance they provided the school in desegregation. Two-thirds rated parents as either first or second, and over half ranked the PTA first, second, or third. Scored on a basis of 12 points for each first-place ranking, 11 for second place, etc., the composite ranking was: Parents, 804; Parent-Teacher Association, 670; Civic Organizations, 471; News Media, 470; Status Leaders, 462; Informal Power Structure, 442; Formal Power Structure, 421; Ministerial Association, 388; Police Department, 377; Welfare Department, 354; Juvenile Court, 222.

Parents. What do parents fear from desegregation? White parents may be resentful of the large number of Negroes when the school ratio increases. They may ask what is happening in such areas as academic standards and social activities as a result of Negro pupils and Negro teachers being present. Disagreements among students before desegregation are dismissed with "boys will be boys"; after desegregation, the same situation becomes a racial incident.

Negro parents want the same benefits from life for their children that white parents have received for their children. Parents of any underprivileged group of children see the school as the chief hope; they want to help but do not know how. Negro parents do not have the same questions to ask as the middle-class white, or they may not ask questions at all. The chief concern of Negro parents is to make the child mentally comfortable and secure within the desegregated school. They want the child to participate in activities, but they feel that white people should initiate the first friendly action because of prior domination in this realm.

There is no one simple recipe for working with either Negro or white parents. Getting both to work together is an even more difficult problem. The initiation of interaction belongs to white persons because they generally are accepted already in the mainstream of American life.

Many parents, regardless of race, do not feel comfortable in school situations. Negative parental attitudes, including fear or distrust of school personnel, mean anxiety for the child. To break down many of these negative attitudes, natural acceptance and noncritical feelings toward parents and children must be demonstrated. Even if the clothing or the background and ideals are not to the liking of the typical middle-class principal (Negro or white), genuine interest in the person as an individual is essential to the child's welfare.

Informal meetings with a parent can be held in the home of the parent or at school. Meetings at school should be in a small conference room rather than a classroom. Sitting beside the parent rather than putting oneself above him or across a desk is best.

The principal must not talk down to parents, but should tell in simple, easy-to-understand terms how the child is doing and why he thinks the child is doing as he is. Realistic suggestions for improvement should be provided. Frankness is essential. Any evasive tactic will be interpreted as being deceitful, especially by those accustomed to not trusting white people. Parents should be given a chance to "sound off," but the administrator should not argue with parents. He should control facial expressions of disapproval and avoid showing surprise or anger. A parent should never be given cause to feel embarrassed about his own background or educational shortcomings.

Parent-Teacher Association. Several principals told of PTA activities pointed toward improvement of community relations. Panels of leaders from schools, churches, courts, city governments, police departments, and other parts of the community discussed human relations and respect for authority. Audiences were encouraged to ask questions. Name cards in front of panel members facilitated communication. Negro parents were involved as committee members and PTA officers, and working together on a common project increased understanding and acceptance.

Civic Organizations. Principals who reported on their own experiences advised using civic organizations as a "base of operation" to talk to small groups of students; provide leadership to special interest groups; provide speakers and sponsor special activities; conduct special learning activities to demonstrate interest; assist teachers by better acquainting them with the community; conduct community surveys to provide information for student guidance; co-operate with the school in providing supervised activities; sponsor clubs and advanced study groups over a wide range of interests; and enlist assistance for school-sponsored programs. Many principals also have sought the support of informal leaders as advisory committee members or as a sounding board for community opinions.

Police and Courts. Principals reported that co-operation from police departments and juvenile courts was found essential to supervision of students before and after school hours, and that police never hesitated to assist at athletic events, dances, and special events. Police and court officials, especially in cities, spent long hours conferring with school personnel and students to solve discipline problems and overcome racial tensions.

News Media. The principal should provide the news media with information by means of interview, personal discussions, phone inquiries, and news releases, keeping his statements and releases clear and concise and remembering press deadlines. He can expect editing by the press for purposes of spacing and clarification. Many principals surveyed on desegregation experiences commended the newspapers highly for emphasizing positive aspects of the school situation.

Part Six. **If We Fail**

Introduction to Part Six

THROUGH the eyes of American children we can look at America and see an endless series of beautiful and ugly ironies. For these children, reared in an affluent society reflecting a technological now-you-see-it world, there are few places to hide either our humanity or our inhumanity. From the inner regions of radio, television, and newspaper medias, they are socialized in a nation being torn apart by wars, riots, social-economic deprivations, and racism. Of course, they also see heart transplants, moon flights, and humanitarian projects.

No other generation of young people has been so widely exposed to the totality of the nation and the world they live in. Interestingly, past generations were more concerned with such activities as attending two movies a week, swallowing goldfish, crowding into telephone booths, and winning dance marathons. They were generations committed to "doing their own thing." Today's children are becoming increasingly more concerned with environmental and social pollution.

We have become a mass communication and rapid transportation society whose technology has stripped us naked and revealed our hatred, violence, and social concerns. It is these and other conditions which cause some writers to conclude that *the primary need of all children is to learn to accept themselves and to have respect for themselves and others.* In Part Three, Susan Rucker summarized this goal in terms of her students:

> If I could just leave them . . . alone and know that they wouldn't hate so much, and that hate wouldn't ooze from every pore to the point that they have to hit and crush somebody's face. If I could teach them to respect each other. . . . I want very badly to do that for them and to do that for me.

Lessons
children
learn There is a grotesque image of ourselves which we pass on from generation to generation. In many ways, we are a people of little love. In short, our humaneness has not kept pace with our technology. If American children are to become more humane, it is not likely that most adults can teach them. Rural and urban children are taught to master the skills needed to hate, segregate, and kill, instead of those needed to love, integrate, and heal.

Most parents, for example, use the words "acceptance," "love," and "brotherhood" in such limited ways until they exclude people who do not look like, think like, or smell like them. This myopic view of humanity allows parents to teach their children to call other children "niggers," "dagos," "honkies," "wet backs," "poor white trash," and a multitude of other derogatory names. For those who say that names do not hurt people, we caution them that names hurt like the very dickens. Accordingly, we could paraphrase a popular chant: "Sticks and stones can break my bones/And names can hurt my ego." Children listening to and observing adults soon discover that whites are taught to hate blacks, blacks are taught to hate whites, and Indians and Mexicans are taught to hate both blacks and whites. In addition, children see that individuals claiming to be religious frequently are the most avid haters.

Some writers state that Americans are the most efficient and hypocritical segregationists in the world. As a nation, we have a society based on the ideology of equality but communities based on the actions of inequality. As a nation, we have been able to place men successfully on the moon but have failed to place together successfully in the same school white and nonwhite children who live only a few blocks apart. A growing number of social critics express the belief that in terms of social-scientific knowledge we could eradicate most social inequalities but we lack the collective will to do so.

Children watch adults and learn how to kill. The fact that some people brag about America never losing a war attests to our international skill at killing. The fact that each day thousands of Americans are killing other Americans attests to our national skill at killing. No part of our society is immune from killing: we do it in the inner city, we do it in the outer city, and we do it on the farm; we do it to the poor and we do it to the affluent. We use killing as the central theme in movies and cartoons. Thus children are taught "thou shalt not kill" but see social dramas in which people are rewarded for killing. To be sure, we teach what we live.

The youth of the late 1960s saw that Malcolm X and Martin Luther King, Jr., had to lose their lives before some people would call them "men": They also noted that the dove of peace was sleeping in the sands of Vietnam. During this same period, most Americans shut their ears to the cries of the poor. However, the deaths of John and Robert Kennedy caused some people to say that too many citizens had died from assassins' bullets. Unfortunately, then and now the mountain of racial prejudice still stands. Therefore a major domestic question continues to go unanswered: How many more years can black, brown, and red Americans exist before they are allowed to be free? And if children of today grow up to be like their parents, that answer will continue to blow in the harsh, cold winds of racial segregation and discrimination.

The concern for producing humane children is but a reflection of W. E. B. DuBois' dream as expressed in his classic, *The Souls of Black Folk*: <small>Producing humane children</small>

> Teach thinkers to think,—a needed knowledge in a day of loose and careless logic; and they whose lot is gravest must have the carefulest training to think aright. . . . Teach the workers to work and the thinkers to think; make carpenters of carpenters, and philosophers of philosophers, and fops of fools. Nor can we pause here. We are training not isolated men but a living group of men,—nay, a group within a group. And the final product of our training must be neither a psychologist nor a brickmason, but a man. And to make men, we must have ideals, broad, pure, and inspiring ends of living. . . .[1]

As we have noted in earlier sections, a number of studies have shown that children from low-income families make lower scores on standardized achievement tests and are retarded in grade placement more often than their affluent counterparts. As poor children grow older, their academic performance levels frequently decrease. Furthermore, they drop out of school in larger numbers than higher status children (This is so even when allowance is made for differences associated with sex, race, parents' education, and rural-urban residence.) Within this depressing picture are the encouraging summaries of preschool and early school programs which offer great possibilities for improving the educational levels of low-achievers. Unfortunately, there are too few preschool and early school programs in rural school districts.

Dropouts face increased difficulties finding employment or, if employed, securing better jobs. Children from poverty-stricken families who remain in school and want to attend college, or post–high-school vocational institutions lack the needed financial resources

1 W. E. B. DuBois, *The Souls of Black Folk* (New York, Fawcett, 1961), 72.

and, in most cases, academic achievement levels. Clearly, many of the poor never reach their full potential because of inadequate financial resources and educational retardation. It is not merely individuals but the nation that is the loser for lack of full academic development of the poor.

Home and school failures

Although the school must accept much of the blame for our educational failures, a large share also goes to the home. A significant correlation has been observed between school achievement and (1) the education of the parents, (2) the level of occupation of the parents, (3) the number of children in the family, and (4) marital status of the parents. Furthermore, measured intelligence tends to increase with a decreasing number of siblings and a decreasing frequency of unmarried parents.[2] This latter condition is important because the level of developed intelligence does, to a great extent, reflect how much difficulty the student will have in mastering the work he is given at school.

The major factor influencing a child's achievement in school is the preparation he receives from his home. The quality of communication in the lower-class home differs significantly from communication in the middle-class home. Middle-class children are "talked to" more frequently by adults and encouraged to talk among themselves. While the middle-class child is taught to be aggressive verbally, the lower-class child is taught to be aggressive physically. In fact, lower-class children usually learn to talk later in their childhood than do middle-class children. Thus the child who is poorly equipped with language skills has little chance to succeed in school where success is based on language competency.

There is a conflict of values between the lower-class home and the school. The aggressive behavior which is so prevalent in the lower-class home is not encouraged or sanctioned in the classroom. The lower-class child is, therefore, expected to behave in ways contradictory to those he has developed. Nor is the lower-class child adequately prepared to work hard, study on his own initiative, and delay gratifications. This conflict of values triggers aggressive behavior. The child is not rebelling against the school as much as he is trying to maintain some semblance of psychological equilibrium.

The poor living conditions of the lower-class child affect his success in school. Poor housing and health habits lead to illness which in

2 Robert Green, Louis J. Hofman, and Robert F. Morgan, "Some Effects of Deprivation on Intelligence, Achievement and Cognitive Growth", *Journal of Negro Education*, Vol. XXXVI (Winter, 1967), 7.

turn leads to absenteeism from school. The number of days a child is absent from school correlates closely with his achievement. Physiological disabilities observed in urban children are also found in rural children.

Studies, though sparse, indicate that nutritional deficiencies lead to a loss of energy, lack of ability to concentrate, loss of self-control, and increased irritability. Volunteers for starvation experiments, for example, have found it difficult to concentrate on reading or to maintain their usual social relations because excessive food imagery interrupts their normal thinking patterns.[3]

For a variety of reasons, the lower-class child has little chance to succeed in his school work or to behave in any way other than with aggression or rebellion. In addition, the child who is hungry or in ill health will concentrate almost totally on meeting that physiological need. Only after physiological needs are met, along with psychological needs for safety and love, can a child begin to excel in school.

Most lower-class homes are dominated by females. Many lower-class mothers never marry the fathers of their children; others marry but are deserted by their husbands. Adding to this condition is the fact that most welfare laws encourage fathers to desert so their families can receive the financial help denied as long as he is present. Because of the female-dominated home, boys, and especially Negro boys, rebel against their female teachers. Seldom is this rebellion against her as a teacher but against her as a female.

For the low-achiever, school tends to be anything but an institution of academic enlightenment. The low-achieving child is expected to measure up to the level of achievement of the "good" students. His low level of achievement and negative self-image make improbable this adjustment.

In a sense, school "competition" becomes a daily punishment for those of lesser ability. Repeated frustration in competitive situations produces a tensional state which makes large demands on the child's emotional balance and may alter his proper relationship with companions, teachers, and parents.[4]

A series of school failures can lead to frustration. Repeated frustration can lead to anger. Not all angry students drop out of school. Some stay in and become disruptive students. Few become good

---

[3] Joan I. Roberts (ed.), *School Children in the Urban Slum* (New York, The Free Press, 1967), 12.
[4] Robert D. Strom, "Family Influences on School Failure", in Joe L. Frost and Glen R. Hawkes (eds.), *The Disadvantaged Child* (Boston, Houghton Mifflin, 1966), 381.

students. Some become rebels, picking up the call for White Power, Black Power, Brown Power, or Red Power. They set out to destroy "the System."

The challenge To date, only a few rural students have adopted the physical confrontation tactics characteristic of alienated urban youth. They have, however, shown the same degree of disillusionment with the American Dream. Each year, it becomes increasingly more difficult to convince rural youth to commit themselves to goals such as integration, equality of educational opportunity, and the Protestant work ethic.

It may be that as more rural communities undergo urbanization, their residents will adopt the violent protest tactics of urban militants. On the other hand, it is also quite possible that increased alienation will not lead to physical aggression but, instead, greater isolation and withdrawal. While it seems too late to reverse the negative trends set in motion in large urban areas, there is still time for rural communities to prove that equal educational opportunity and quality education can apply to all rural people.

Schools and other institutions are slowly undergoing changes in rural communities. Unfortunately, community attitudes are changing at a much slower pace. For example, rural people vehemently resist racial desegregation while accelerating their efforts to update school buildings and curricula. In addition, poor people of all colors are being rejected by their affluent neighbors.

We need few additional studies of ineffective school personnel and more studies of effective personnel. Even more pressing, we need fewer "talk" conferences and more people actively involved in the process of constructive change. If we fail to improve the quality of instruction in rural schools, our student failures will grow up, marry, and multiply: educational failures increase at a geometric rate. The little red schoolhouses may be disappearing but the people controlling those schools are far from becoming extinct.

Readings Horace Aubertine's article, "The Rural Student Speaks Out," summarizes the positive and negative aspects of rural schools. Failure to improve rural schools will result in the continuing talent drain that is spelling the doom of many rural communities. In addition, failure to desegregate the schools will result in widening the racial gap described by Donald Matthews and James Prothro in "Living Together as Strangers."

But the racial gap is not merely a black-white issue. Susan Hunsinger (" 'Militant' Navaho Wants to Preserve an Old Nation") and

Richard Beene ("Mexican-Americans Weary of 'Hyphenated' Status") point out the alienation found among Indians and Mexican-Americans. While both Red Power and Brown Power are nonviolent movements, younger Indians and Mexican-Americans (Chicanos) are not immune to violence. If pushed long enough and hard enough, people will physically fight back.

Paul Good's article, "To Live in Freedom, To Die a Timely Death," illustrates that poor people of all colors are trapped in rural poverty. This article makes a dramatic appeal for Americans to hurry and finish "the creation of a society where all citizens may walk in dignity, eat a wholesome diet, sleep in a decent house, live in economic and social freedom, and finally die a timely death unhurried by malnutrition and the lack of adequate medical services." If we fail our nation will die an untimely death.

47. The Rural Student Speaks Out

Horace E. Aubertine

THE consolidation movement continues to reduce the number of small, rural schools, but in the plains and mountain regions of our nation the combining of school districts is not always feasible. Rural communities are satisfied with the advantages the small school offers, although acknowledging that improvements could be made in some areas of education. Funds for the new buildings, books and buses which consolidation would require are lacking, and the rural resident does not favor possible tax increases. Moreover, if schools were consolidated the more remotely located student would spend unduly long hours traveling. His participation in extracurricular activities, a major feature of the rural school, would be limited; consequently, his isolation would be increased. These are reasons to consider the rural school as a continuing part of the educational picture.

Curiosity led me to seek student judgment of the advantages and disadvantages of a rural high school education. I was able to secure thirty-five volunteer college students who had attended rural high schools enrolling three hundred students or fewer. The states of Montana, New Mexico, Colorado, Nebraska, and Kansas were represented in the study. All but two of the thirty-five respondents had attended high school during the 1960s and were commenting upon current circumstances; however, the two older participants made essentially the same statements. Each person spoke into a tape recorder in private. The question was left open-ended: No specific areas of concern were mentioned. However, all focused their view upon personal relationships, participation in athletics and extracurricular activities, close contact with teachers, range of curricula, availability of resource materials and facilities, competition and challenge within the classroom, and quality of teaching.

Almost all the students praised the cohesive personal relationships

From the *Phi Delta Kappan*, June, 1969, pp. 592–94. Reprinted by permission.

possible in the rural schools, stating that "You learn to get along and work with people other than your friends. If you don't learn this in high school it will be a hard thing to learn later." "In a smaller school you can function as a group, not as a few individuals or as a clique. ... [It is] easier to live, to identify with and understand society, and to be a better American." In schools where cliques did exist it was noted that they interacted and in schools composed of mixed ethnic populations students developed greater insight into the situation of minority groups. On the negative side, two students expressed a desire for a wider range of contact with others and a greater choice of friends.

Those who had attended both urban and rural high schools confirmed that in the smaller school community they were more aware of a sense of personal value and felt more socially fulfilled and accepted. One stated that in the urban school "shy students just stayed introverts most of the time, due to large classes giving no opportunity or encouragement to bring themselves out." Furthermore, urban students separate during the day, whereas in the rural school they usually stay together, know each other better, and feel more at ease. This was noted as one of the outstanding differences between large and small school classes by a boy who attended sixteen different elementary and high schools.

General participation in athletics and extracurricular activities was a point of pride among the small-school students and all agreed it strengthened the bonds of the group. Their dependence upon one another for success in common enterprises brings a sense of achievement rarely found in the larger school, where only top students take part in extracurricular activities and only top athletes represent the school in sports. One student stated that the rural pupil willing to take on the responsibility matures faster than the urban pupil who cannot participate so freely, but at the same time it is easy to take on too many activities and fall behind in school work. All students, freshmen as well as seniors, are expected to expend a great deal of effort in extracurricular endeavors. Sometimes activities provide too ready a reason to leave the classroom and excuse slips from administrators or organization sponsors are seldom questioned by teachers.

In the main, the students participating in the study are convinced that the rural school environment is ideally suited to social interaction, the establishment of self-identity, and the development of character traits of value. They also voiced almost unanimous approval of the close association they enjoyed with faculty members. The smaller-sized class is conducive to personal contact between student and teacher; they are active together in general activities and frequently the teacher is a family friend as well.

In academic matters this close relationship can be faulted, as a teacher who has instructed a pupil for a period of several years tends to take improvement for granted. Also, those students assessed as academically able seem slated to receive top grades as a matter of course, while those viewed as average or below in scholastic ability sometimes are not encouraged to advance beyond these arbitrary limits. Furthermore, although many respondents noted the advantage of individual instruction made possible by the smaller-sized class, most agreed there was a dearth of advance instruction for the student who wished to work on special projects. Many teachers were not competent enough in subject matter to supervise special studies or were burdened with time-consuming extracurricular duties.

Furthermore, seldom are there enough funds to permit employment of a greater number of qualified teachers in order to offer a more diversified curriculum. Accredited rural schools offer the "basics" and most of my respondents believed themselves to be as well prepared in this realm as students from urban schools; however, many commented upon the desirability of enlargement and enrichment of English and social studies programs and the addition of business and language courses. Many rural schools are making an effort to expand the science program, but generally basic courses in chemistry, biology, physics, and mathematics are not offered or are not taught by competent science teachers. As a result, students are often allowed to study texts or perform experiments on their own or with a minimum of supervision. One student recalled that "teaching myself out of the chemistry book was not quite the way I wanted to learn chemistry, but it didn't concern me that much. However, when enrolled in the university as an engineering student, I found in my first quarter in chemistry that it made a great deal of difference. I am presently an art student and am quite happy; perhaps engineering wasn't my stick after all, but I do feel inadequate preparation in high school had a part in my change of majors."

A narrow high school curriculum can constrict a student's choice of major in college or an inadequate background can handicap him in competition, perhaps forcing him to seek other academic pastures. Those who manage to overcome poor preparation experience a period of academic struggle, not made easier by involvement with social adjustment to the larger college population.

As college students, those interviewed tend to stress high school curricula in terms of college preparation, but consideration should be given to those graduates of rural schools whose formal education terminates with completion of the twelfth grade and for whom greater range in the programs mentioned above would be equally pertinent and profitable.

Limitations in curriculum are more unfortunate when material resources are lacking and when competition and challenge within the classroom is not evident. Incomplete school and town libraries bind the student to the textbook, which in many cases is not intended to serve as a sole source of information. When specialized, advanced courses are not available and special study materials are not provided, the student is confined to the classroom situation and the more gifted find it a simple matter to stay at the top of the class. Courses of study are structured to serve the needs of the class majority rather than to expand with the interest of the able and ambitious and stimulate them to pursue further study. Furthermore, there is a gap between the scholar and the average student which very few in the latter category attempt to close. One student said that work which earned her an "A" would have been evaluated at "B" level in a larger school where more students would have challenged her for the top mark. Another commented that this lack of competition deprives all concerned, as both superior and average pupils would profit from competition. It also was observed that the top student suffers from a side effect: He does not have to learn to study to maintain a position of scholastic honor, a shortcoming some found to be a serious handicap upon entering college.

The majority regretted the lack of scholastic rivalry during the high school years; having previously praised the spirit of competition in nonacademic activities, the students' concern lay in the failure of cohorts to carry this attitude into the classroom. I would suggest that the failure lies at least in part with teachers who do not quicken the classroom tempo and motivate students to fulfill their academic potential. Teachers failed to perform well in other areas too; most of the respondents were not impressed with the quality of teaching in their rural schools.

Many rural school districts contend with geographical isolation, narrowness of curricula, poor classroom and laboratory facilities, and restricted funds for salaries. These factors combined with community rigidity on academic matters, restriction of the teacher to the textbook, and unwillingness of many school boards or principals to support teachers on matters of discipline cause a high rate of turnover. The better teachers can secure jobs in districts not faced with such drawbacks. One student stated that newer, more enthusiastic teachers will "buck the system," but most respondents took note that such teachers come to the rural district primarily for experience and soon move away. As another said, "Quality instruction is to be had in the rural school if you happen to be there at the same time as the good teachers." Often left in the wake of departing teachers is a staff composed of some who are weak in subject matter, some who hold no degree at all, and others trained in inferior institutions. Many are employed under the tenure system and have grown too old to function adequately as teachers. Sometimes women teachers are available because their husbands work in the locality. Be they good or bad teachers, they are there. One respondent mentioned that several teachers in her school were farmers who taught in the winter as a "sort of hobby."

A related problem is that the teachers are not prepared to give good counseling service. Since rural school budgets rarely permit employment of full-time counselors, it falls to the teachers to be adept in personal counseling and to have extensive information about requirements and offerings of various colleges and universities. Many respondents commented on the limitations of counseling services and one person expressed the view that there would have been fewer dropouts in her school and more graduates continuing into college if judicious counseling had been offered.

Limited curriculum, poor resource materials, and inadequate counseling are problems in the rural school, but the major disadvantage, in the opinion of the graduates of the system, is the poor quality of teaching. It would be difficult or impossible for each small school district to correct the circumstances that cause teacher turnover, yet consolidation presents difficulties of its own, as previously noted. However, it would be possible for several small school districts covering an area of perhaps several hundred square miles to join together to create a regional center composed of five or six teachers who would be specialists in their major fields. These teachers would travel among the schools, supplementing formal instruction and providing counseling services as well. Each school would set aside time blocks during which the visiting teachers would handle advanced instruction or give direction to individual study projects, present "special interest" material, and counsel teachers as well, in order to help the pupils realize their full potential. These teachers would arrange for teacher exchanges among the schools with the idea of offering once a week (or more often) music, language, or business and vocational instruction. This group should be knowledgeable about available resource

materials and special aids and could arrange for occasional guest
speakers to come into the area. Also, the regional teachers could
arrange for students in outlying districts to take periodic trips to the
best-equipped school in the co-operative area and could arrange for
use of its facilities.

Such a regional group could be started with private foundation
funds, "seed money," and could be paid for in future years with combined funds from the participating schools, thus distributing the
burden of payment. State or federal agencies could augment the
budget as well in cases where districts could not afford to contribute
toward the employment of such a group. In order to remain aloof
from adverse community conditions which affect the locally based
teacher, this special team would be responsible to the state department
of education, an administrative agency serving all of the co-operating
schools, rather than to local school administrators.

The rural citizen's decline in political representation has lessened
his ability to exert influence with state or federal agencies for funds
to make improvements in education. It is left to prominent persons in
the field of education to strive for more equitable distribution of
resources, material and human, between the urban and the rural
school. Every effort should be made to raise the quality of teaching in
the rural school, so that this system with its multiplicity of advantages
can be maintained in the future.

Many of the rural students I interviewed are in teacher training, and
some have expressed a desire to return to teach in their home communities. Here is one possibility of upgrading instruction through the
recruitment and development of a pool of teachers on the basis of
ability, rural upbringing, and interest in teaching in a rural environment.

There is an acute need to bring rural education into a balanced
qualitative relationship with its urban counterpart, and this equalizing
process must be based upon greater allocation of state and federal
funds to the rural schools. But equally important is the need for
imaginative and efficient use of funds allocated to rural educational
improvement. The creation of a pool of trained teachers aware of the
uniqueness of the problems and needs of rural communities is the
final touch to any positive movement toward rural educational renaissance.

Economists contend that education is one means of developing
human capital which, properly invested, leads ultimately to raising a
society's standard of living. It would seem appropriate to redirect
some of our human capital back to the rural communities for reinvest-

ment. If this could be done, it would help reverse the impoverishing effects of the talent drain. It would improve the quality of rural instruction and ultimately raise the standard of living in rural areas.

48. Living Together as Strangers

Donald R. Matthews and James W. Prothro

THE prospects for major changes in white racial attitudes seem to be fairly good only if we take a long-range view. But Negro leaders have made it abundantly clear that they are unwilling to wait for slow processes gradually to erode segregation. "We want our freedom *now*; we want it *all*; we want it *here*." The words are those of the Reverend Martin Luther King; the sentiments they express are shared by most black southerners. The South must somehow ameliorate—if not "solve"—its racial problems *before* the millennium has arrived, *before* the hearts and minds of most white men have been won to the cause of equality.

If this sort of accommodation is to be made, southerners must first realize the depth and extent of their differences. Knowledge of the conflicting views that divide southerners along racial lines seems a necessary if not sufficient condition for coping with these differences through democratic political processes.

How well aware are white and Negro southerners of the differences that divide the races on the question of segregation? Most non-southerners would probably assume that neither race could exist in the midst of such strongly divergent opinions without being aware of their existence. And they might be joined by social scientists: survey data have revealed a reasonable measure of success among citizens who were asked to estimate the position of various groups on questions that divide the groups less sharply and about which they have less intense opinions.

But other findings leave open the possibility that southerners might actually be ill informed about their differences. In the first place, communication crosses caste lines in a highly imperfect fashion; hence, one or both races may receive inaccurate impressions of the preferences of the other. In the second place, selective perception, through which an individual's perceptions of the views of others are

From *Negroes and the New Southern Politics*. Reprinted by permission of Harcourt Brace Jovanovich, Inc., Copyright 1966 by Harcourt Brace Jovanovich, Inc.

influenced by his own values, may lead to a distortion of the information that is communicated. These are mutually reinforcing phenomena in public opinion, and southern race relations is a ripe field for the operation of both.

Table 1 indicates that, regardless of the overwhelming preference of Negroes for integration and of whites for strict segregation, neither group can correctly estimate the views of the other. Although both races are misinformed, the estimates of whites are much more inaccurate than those of Negroes. Only 22 per cent of the whites recognize that most Negroes favor integration, but 47 per cent of the Negroes recognize that most whites favor segregation. The greater inaccuracy of whites can also be seen by comparing the proportion of whites who say that "less than half" or "practically none" of the Negroes prefer integration with the proportion of Negroes who perceive equally small numbers of whites as favoring segregation. Such grossly inaccurate estimates occur among whites at twice the rate at which they occur among Negroes. The greater frequency of "don't know" responses among whites than among Negroes is a more direct expression of the relative lack of information among whites.

The great inaccuracy of whites in estimating the views of Negroes is not surprising. Inaccurate information about the views of the subordinate group may be considered one of the prices the superordinate group must pay for a repressive social system. Or, rather than viewing misinformation as a liability, one could say that the communication process permits the dominant group the luxury of ignorance about the wishes of those who are dominated. The percentage of Negroes who favor integration actually exceeds the percentage of whites who favor strict segregation. But the communication of Negro views is blocked in various ways. In almost all forms of activity in the South, Negroes are required by law to behave in conformity to segregationist values, whatever their opinions. Negroes in some localities may be afraid to express their dissatisfactions. In some cases, behavioral conformity may not be enough; white employers may elicit assurances from their Negro employees that they prefer segregation. Although the pressures from the dominant white majority have not succeeded in molding Negro opinions, then, they have succeeded in inducing many Negroes to refrain from expressing those opinions—or even to express contrary opinions—in contacts with local whites.

Southern Negroes, on the other hand, live under a system of segregation that is a constant institutional reminder of the segregationist beliefs of the white majority. Local police and judges stand ready to correct any misperceptions on which Negroes begin to act. How, then, can we explain the fact that only a minority of southern Negroes—

albeit a very large minority—recognize that most southern whites favor strict segregation? The answer must lie in selective perception. Their personal preference for integration must lead southern Negroes to underestimate the degree of white hostility to integration, despite the conspicuous evidence to the contrary.

Selective perception characterizes whites as well, as Table 2 demonstrates. White integrationists are three times more likely than segregationists and twice as likely as those in between to perceive correctly the portion of Negroes favoring integration. White integrationists are better able to perceive Negro preferences, not necessarily because they are better informed but because they hold the same preferences.

The opinions of Negroes similarly tend to influence their estimates of the other race's preferences, although to a less extreme degree. Over half the Negro segregationists recognize that all or most whites also prefer segregation, whereas somewhat less than half of the Negro integrationists make such an accurate estimate. But this contrast (53 per cent to 47.5 per cent) is not nearly so great as that between white integrationists and white segregationists (50 per cent to 18 per cent). Just as the pattern of communication in the South leaves the superordinate group as a whole less informed about the other race's aspirations, so does it permit them greater freedom to project their own views to others.

From the Negro's vantage point, however, the preferences of whites are less ambiguous. The harsh realities of segregation set bounds that usually leave little room for selective perception; the more severe the repression, the more narrow the limits of misperception. Thus the Negroes in Piedmont County—the least segregated and most "liberal" of the counties we studied in detail—have the least accurate picture of white attitudes in their area; only 43 per cent realize that most local whites prefer segregation. In Bright Leaf and Crayfish these figures are 53 and 58 per cent, respectively. And in Camellia County, which has a long, bitter, and largely abortive experience in racial protest, 73 per cent of the Negroes are realistically aware of the structure of white attitudes.

Although each race in the South is surprisingly ignorant of the other's point of view, the failure of southern whites to realize how discontented their Negro neighbors are is a more serious stumbling block to racial accommodation. Even in the midst of sit-ins, boycotts, and freedom rides, a majority of southern whites did not realize in 1961 that Negroes were bitterly unhappy about segregation. Let us examine the 22 per cent of southern whites who did recognize deepseated Negro resentment then. Are their characteristics such as to suggest early recognition by other whites of the nature of Negro demands?

To begin with, we must face the possibility that correct information on Negro attitudes is simply one manifestation of a generally superior level of information. When we analyze the results of our political-information test with the racial views of the respondents held constant, we find that general political information has no relation to awareness of Negro racial attitudes.[1] Among the strict segregationists, those who are ignorant of Negro preferences actually have slightly higher information scores than those who are aware of Negro attitudes. Among the moderates, the difference is reversed, but in both cases the differences are minute. Although we may expect modern modes of mass communication to raise the general information level of southern whites, then, such an improvement will apparently have no direct effect on white perceptions of Negro attitudes.[2]

When we look at the level of formal schooling rather than at the level of political information, the sense of stability in white misperceptions is even stronger. Table 3 reveals that, with white racial views held constant, more education makes no contribution at all to greater white awareness of Negro attitudes. Indeed, for strict segregationists there is a slight decrease in awareness as education goes up, and for moderates, a fairly sizable decrease. The assumption that white perceptions of Negro demands might be changed more quickly than white attitudes gets no support from these findings.

If white ignorance of Negro attitudes does not stem directly from lack of information or education, perhaps it results simply from lack of contact with Negroes. The most common form of close contact between whites and Negroes in the South is in an employer-employee relationship, but contact with Negroes as employees is associated with a lower level of awareness of Negro attitudes when we compare whites with the same racial attitudes. Because the employer-employee relationship places the Negro in the familiar role of subordination, such white contact with Negro employees seems to reinforce inaccurate views of Negro attitudes.

Contact with Negroes as fellow shoppers is probably the type of association in the contemporary South most nearly akin to contact

---

[1] The mean number of questions answered correctly by each group of southern whites was: Strict segregationists aware of Negro attitudes, 4.4; strict segregationists unaware, 4.5; moderates aware, 5.2; moderates unaware, 4.9; integrationists aware, 5.3. Too few integrationists were unaware to permit computing a mean score for this group.

[2] Although exposure to the mass media of communications does tend to weaken white commitment to segregation, it does *not* contribute to an awareness of Negro views. The percentage of whites "aware" of Negro racial attitudes varies thus according to the number of media they are regularly exposed to: none or 1, 23 per cent; 2, 17 per cent; 3, 25 per cent; 4, 21 per cent.

in the use of integrated public facilities. But, again, whites with a given racial attitude are less likely to be aware of Negro attitudes if they report contacts with Negroes as fellow shoppers than if they report no such contacts.[3]

Like education and information, contact with Negroes does not contribute directly to white awareness of Negro attitudes. The effect of travel and of military service on white awareness, when preference is controlled, is similarly nonexistent or unimpressive. Ironically, each of these factors *does* contribute directly to more moderate or integrationist sentiment. Contrary to our expectations, white misperceptions of Negro preferences may be harder to change than white attitudes themselves.

The general conditions under which whites may become aware of Negro attitudes are suggested by the contrast in awareness between whites in the Deep South and Whites in the Peripheral South. This is the only variable we have examined in this chapter that serves, in clear independence of white preferences, to increase awareness of Negro preferences. Among strict segregationists, 32 per cent in the Peripheral South compared to 22 per cent in the Deep South realize that Negroes prefer integration (see Table 4). And the difference between moderates in the two subregions is slightly greater. The Peripheral South contains a much larger proportion of moderates and integrationists than the Deep South does, but these are differences between people with the same personal preferences.

The greater ability of whites in the Peripheral South to recognize the preference of most Negroes for integration appears to be supported by three factors, all of which are important for the future race relations and politics of the region.

First, more of the Negroes in the Peripheral South than in the Deep South actually do prefer integration. The difference is not great (68 per cent to 60 per cent), but it is large enough for us to say that the actual situation in the Peripheral South should call forth more white estimates that most Negroes prefer integration. Despite this difference, the fact remains that most Negroes, even in the Deep South, are integrationists.

A second factor underlying the subregional difference in awareness is that Negroes in the Peripheral South are more articulate about their opinions. With more Negroes voting, sometimes supported by active and efficient political organizations, and with public and private expressions of discontent over segregation, the muting effects of the

---

[3] For a more detailed analysis of the importance of different kinds of contact on racial attitudes, see John Orbell, "Social Protest and Social Structure: Southern Negro College Student Participation in the Protest Movement" (Ph.D. dissertation, University of North Carolina, 1965).

Deep South's pressures for conformity are decreased. Even whites who are appalled at Negro demands may be forced at least to recognize that the demands exist.

Finally, the whites in the Peripheral South are not nearly so close to consensus on segregation as are those in the Deep South. With a large minority of fellow whites rejecting strict segregation, even the strongest segregationist may be forced to recognize that Negroes must also reject segregation.

Thus, in a county like Crayfish, the local whites are almost entirely ignorant of Negro racial attitudes—only 8 per cent of the whites there realize that most of the local Negroes are integrationists! In Camellia County, which actually contains a smaller proportion of Negro integrationists than Crayfish but where the Negroes are more aggressive, articulate, and active, and where they have the support of a minority of whites, 28 per cent of the whites have a reasonably accurate picture of Negro aspirations and goals. In Piedmont County, where white integrationists and moderates are more numerous than in Camellia and where the Negroes are more effectively organized, 38 per cent of the whites are adequately aware of Negro attitudes. But only in Bright Leaf County, of those we studied in detail, did a majority (63 per cent) of the whites correctly assess Negro attitudes, and there only because a majority of the Negroes preferred what the whites wanted them to—segregation.

Despite all the southern whites' talk about understanding "our niggers," and all the southern Negroes' stories about knowing "our white folks," the two races truly are "living together as strangers." *This situation is getting worse, not better.* In 1961, 22 per cent of whites had a reasonably accurate view of predominant Negro racial attitudes; over three years later they could do no better. Indeed, they did a little bit worse (21 per cent). In the meantime, however, a burst of optimism seems to have swept the Negro communities of the South. In 1961, 21 per cent of the Negroes believed that "all" southern whites favored "strict segregation"; in 1964, only 4 per cent of them did. In 1961, 26 per cent of the Negroes interviewed said that "most" southern whites were segregationists; three years later 14 per cent of them did. As southern Negroes gain power and concessions in the region, as the federal government intervenes in the racial struggle more and more strenuously on their behalf, harsher days were almost impossible—except for white people.

So long as this mutual underestimation of the seriousness of the conflict persists, the new biracial brand of southern politics promises to be a dangerous version of blind man's bluff.

Table 1. Southern white and Negro estimates of the other race's attitudes on segregation and integration

Estimated Number of White Strict Segre-gationists or of Negro Integrationists	Negro Estimates of White Opinion	White Estimates of Negro Opinion
All	21%	4%
Most	26	18
About half	21	21
Less than half	20	39
Practically none	0	1
Don't know, refusal, no members of other race in area	12	17
TOTAL	100%	100%
N	615	685

Table 2. Percentage of southern whites and Negroes aware of other race's attitudes on segregation and integration, by racial attitude

Respondent's Racial Attitude	Negro Awareness of White Opinion		White Awareness of Negro Opinion	
Strict segregation	53%	(94)	18%	(443)
Something in between	44	(89)	25	(194)
Integration	48	(400)	50	(44)

NOTE: The percentages in the first column indicate the portion of Negroes with a given racial attitude who say that "all" or "most" whites favor strict segregation; the second-column percentages indicate the proportion of whites with a given racial attitude who say that "all" or "most" Negroes favor integration.

Table 3. Percentage of white southerners aware* of Negro racial attitudes, by racial attitude and education

White Racial Attitudes	White Education		
	Low	Medium	High
Strict segregation	29%	29%	27%
In between	45	41	37
Integration	**	**	89
N	173	134	111

*The view that "all" or "most" Negroes favor integration is counted as "aware"; the view that "less than half" or "practically none" favor integration is scored as incorrect. Other responses—"about half," "don't know"—and failures to respond are excluded from this and subsequent tabulations related to white awareness of Negro racial attitudes.
**Too few cases for figuring percentage.

Table 4. Percentage of white southerners aware of Negro racial attitudes, by racial attitude and subregion of residence

Racial Attitudes of Whites	Subregion of Respondent's Residence	
	Deep South	Peripheral South
Strict segregation	22%	32%
In between	31	42
Integration	—	88
N	105	315

49. "Militant" Navaho Wants to Preserve an Old Nation

Susan Hunsinger

WHEN people ask him, "Do you want to integrate?" Michael Benson, a young "militant" from the nation's largest remaining Indian reservation in Shiprock, New Mexico, says, "No."

Mr. Benson is not just an American, but a "Native American." He hopes, not that his people can carve out a new nation within a nation, but that they can preserve one.

He denies it's a question of racism. "It's just a natural characteristic of a tribal people to want to remain together. Even the anthropologists say so."

He left the reservation at age sixteen after attending schools run by the Bureau of Indian Affairs and Catholic missionaries. For the last two years he has attended prep school in Lenox, Massachusetts, with the aid of a scholarship and the Organization of Native American Students.

Next fall he will enter Wesleyan University in Middletown, Connecticut, in a special Indian affairs program. "I'll be the first in my line to go to college," he says. "My mother made it through high school."

Michael Benson feels no special affinity for the urban East. "Being here is sort of like being in a foreign country for me." He adds that he has "lost out on a lot of Navaho vocabulary."

But the experience has sharpened his sense of Navaho identity. "It's strange, but I never thought much about being a Navaho until I left the reservation to be among white people. Now I evaluate every action they (the whites) make from this perspective: will it help us remain a people or will it help destroy us?"

The white man's acts of destruction toward the Indian, says Mr. Benson, have sometimes been subtle; they are part of a policy of paternalism and condescension that began when "we signed the Treaty of 1868 and agreed to be friendly."

The paternalistic policies have resulted in Indian submissiveness. "The people aren't brave anymore," according to Mr. Benson. They send their children off to a boarding school run by the Bureau of Indian Affairs starting in the second grade. The children receive free food and clothing, but they pay a price.

"At the BIA school we were not allowed to speak Navaho. The teachers expected the kids to raise their hands high in competition the way middle-class white students would, while that's not the Navaho way."

Nor was there much respect at the school for native religion.

"When we registered at school, we were asked, 'What religion are you—Protestant, Catholic, or Mormon?' We were not given the choice of Navaho, which most of us really are. So we just picked one of the alternatives, and ended up attending a Protestant or Catholic church, regularly, rather automatically, even though our parents might be medicine men."

The children don't adjust easily. "At the BIA school I set the record for running away. I ran away eight times the first year," he said.

While the parents do not like to send their children away from home so young, they apparently have neither the will nor the power to press for change. "It's like everything else," he added, "it's sort of accepted, and it's unhealthy."

Yet there are some stirrings for change. Mr. Benson has joined an Indian activist movement. "I call it an activist movement. It is militant, though only in comparison with the past. A few Indians are no longer afraid to question or to shout at a priest, a BIA official, or a reservation superintendent. Of course, some of the tribal officials object, for they have long become accustomed to co-operating with the BIA."

The activism he describes is elementary: its purpose is to "activate" a once proud people. And that activism "is not of the rock-throwing variety," but "to prepare them to help themselves."

Mr. Benson sympathizes with all revolutionary movements, whether "it be the Brown Berets, Cesar Chavez' farmworkers, or the Black Panthers."

"But," he adds, "Indians can't be like that. We can't speak of guns or liberation. We are too few in number (six hundred thousand Indians compared to twenty million blacks) and too practical."

In the Indian activist movement, he says, there are no militant spokesmen who stand out. Nor is there a distinctive rhetoric. "When I read the Black Panther paper, the language sort of makes me laugh. Some Indians talk that way too—in symbols and of liberation. They call our movement 'The United Native Front' (to parallel the Panthers' United Front against Fascism). But most Indians feel alien to that sort of talk."

While he can do without the rhetoric, he thinks the revolution is essential. "We simply have different goals, and, to some extent, different tactics."

He distinguishes the goals of young Indian activists from those of "American" youth: "The American youth revolution is a reflection of a luxury problem. Most young people just want to change a way of life, a system of morals. But we're defending our way of life. The American youth revolution is vague, abstract. They ask the question, 'Who am I?' But Indian activists are just trying to wake people up to what they have as a people."

The goals of the Indian revolution, as Mr. Benson sees them, are fairly simple. He wants to strip away the white paternalism which has reduced his people to submission, and to allow the Navahos to survive as a tribal people in a technological society.

"That isn't to say that we have to retain all the old dilapidated houses, but we don't have to have the factories. . . . We shouldn't bring the New York and smog atmosphere to the reservation. . . . The land is all we have. . . ."

Specifically, he thinks it's all right for people to work, perhaps on a seasonal basis, in factories in the city. But the reservation should be preserved as a place to return to, a place to raise families.

And he thinks his people, left to themselves, can do a lot to increase the economic return from the reservation itself. "If we had more and improved irrigation projects we could advance without bringing in the factories." The people should also take control of the reservation trading posts where they purchase food, clothing, and other staples. Presently these are operated almost entirely by white traders, licensed by the Bureau of Indian Affairs.

"Anglos ask what they can do to help," he says "Well, the answer is not to swarm to the reservation. From the American people we would like their money and their moral support."

Navahos are beginning to organize their own antipoverty efforts. This summer Mr. Benson will be part of an all-Navaho investigation of the reservation trading posts, which are suspected of charging unjustifiably high prices. His job is sponsored by the Southwestern

Indian Development, composed of Navahos ages seventeen to thirty-five.

Last August this group held what it claims as the first reservation-directed protest against the Bureau of Indian Affairs. "You might say we invaded the office of the tribal chairman and the area director of the BIA. We just expressed our general discontent with BIA policies."

He hopes that this kind of nonviolent demonstration, together with investigatory findings, will help arouse his people to channel their frustrations into constructive action.

50. Mexican-Americans Weary of "Hyphenated" Status

Richard Beene

LUPE Chavez squinted in the New Mexico sun at the dirt road, stagnant drainage ditch, and ramshackle homes that she and her children know so well.

A breeze came to life. Puffs of dust and the stench of sewage drifted toward her.

She shook her head in disgust and a black strand of hair fell across her face. "I know one thing," she said. "I don't want to live this way all my life."

Lupe, 26, had voiced softly the same thought expressed by a growing number of her fellow Mexican-Americans throughout the Southwest, who are shouting they are fed up with being second-class citizens and demanding Brown Power.

There are an estimated five million Mexican-Americans in the vast Southwest. Poverty war officials, researchers, and Mexican-American leaders say Lupe's plight is a way of life for most of her race.

Lupe lives in one of Albuquerque's poorest *barrios* (neighborhoods). Outdoor toilets and wood stoves are common. Houses are a slapped-together jumble of boards, tin, and cement.

For Lupe and her three dust-streaked little boys, virtually every meal is the same: Beans, rice, "meat when you can afford it," surplus peanut butter, flour tortillas.

Like Lupe, about 80 per cent of the "Chicanos," as they often call themselves, live in the cities, with the heaviest concentrations in Los Angeles and San Antonio, Texas, "the Mexican-American capitals."

Their problems are countless, but the biggest is lack of education. The average Mexican-American has just eight years of schooling, compared to twelve for Anglo-Americans. Only the American Indian is said to be farther down on the education scale.

Witnesses told a U.S. Civil Rights Commission hearing that most

From the *Kansas City Star*, August 17, 1969. An Associated Press article. Reprinted by permission.

Chicanos automatically assume that they won't be able to attend college. "From the very beginning," said one high school senior, tears filling her eyes, "we're taught that this is an impossible dream."

Dr. Leo Grebler of the University of California at Los Angeles, who directed a lengthy survey of Mexican-Americans, blames the high drop-out rate in the group on school systems that he says alienate the Chicano while concentrating on white pupils.

Until recently, he said, "Mexican-American pupils often were placed in one room," and were promoted to the next grade "simply to get rid of them."

A common complaint is that Mexican-Americans are forced into vocational classes and that school systems promote shop courses for Chicanos rather than upgrade the curriculum.

Texas State Representative Joe Bernal, a former teacher, charges that vocational classes for Mexican-Americans in his state are grossly inferior. "They graduate from high school making bookends," he says, "but they don't have a salable skill."

The root of Mexican-American problems, however, goes deeper than poverty or lack of education. It's a matter of the Chicano winning acceptance, more than mere token recognition, from his fellow Americans—whom he calls Anglos—while still maintaining his own identity as a Mexican-American.

Chicanos want to erase the stereotyped image of the lazy Mexican taking an endless siesta, which they say is perpetuated by Anglo-dominated movies, television shows, and commercials.

Their human dignity is at stake because of attitudes like that of one Angelo businessman who smirked: "These Mexicans, they don't need much. Give them a sack of beans and they can live for a month on them."

For many years past persons who bore Spanish surnames were subject to discrimination and lack of acceptance in areas of the Southwest. While this has diminished considerably, it is a fact that less than six years ago in Crystal City, Texas, 70 per cent of the residents were Mexican-American but had no representation at city hall.

Anglo political machinery had controlled the town for twenty years. An intensive voter organization campaign turned the tables.

Until a few months ago Chicanos weren't allowed in Tahoka, Texas, barber shops and in a Marlin, Texas, swimming pool. In both cases, the recently formed Mexican-American Legal Defense Fund of San Antonio applied pressure and won desegregation.

From early childhood, the Mexican-American is faced with choosing between two cultures and trying to strike a happy medium between the two.

Fellow Chicanos tell him that if he rejects Mexican-American culture and identifies with that of the Anglo, "he may be considered a traitor to his own ethnic group," says Dr. Manuel Ramirez, a Rice University psychology professor.

Still another message, Ramirez says, comes from teachers, employers, or Anglo friends "who tell him that if he doesn't reject the Mexican-American culture, then he will be unable to reap the educational benefits of the Anglo society."

While many think the Brown Power push was sparked by the Negro upheaval, the majority of the Mexican-Americans contacted in an Associated Press survey of the five-state Southwest say they want no part of the violence that has permeated the Negro cause.

There are indications that the Chicano does not want to join hands with the Negro. Mexican-American leaders say time and again that their problems, culture and even their grievances are different from those of the blacks.

California leaders of the Brown Berets, an activist Chicano youth organization, say they have not aligned themselves with the Negroes —but that they have signed "nonaggression pacts" with militant black factions to avoid clashes between the two groups.

Notably in Texas and California, the young adult Mexican-Americans are more impatient than any other age group. It is they who have popularized the term, "Chicano" (a derivative of "Mexicano.")

Some of the younger people warn of violence if the *gringo* (white racist) establishment doesn't change its views toward the Chicano.

They say they're tired of being "hyphenated Americans" and no longer want to "imitate the white man" or become "Anglocized" to succeed in life.

Within the last two years, Mexican-American youngsters have staged unprecedented high school demonstrations in Los Angeles, Denver, San Antonio, and South Texas to protest "Anglo-oriented" school systems and to focus national attention on the Brown movement—what they call *La Revolucion*.

A look at Mexican-American conditions in the Southwest indicates why a prominent Mexican-American minister, the Reverend Roger Granados, told a San Antonio audience that "as a people, we have come a long way to nowhere."

In Texas' Lower Río Grande Valley, eight members of the Refugio Martinez family live in a Mexican-American *colonia* (unincorporated community) on fifty-five dollars a week. Until recently, their home had been a huge moving van trailer and they still cook their meals there. The strain of living shows in Mrs. Martinez' face. Her eyes are weary and her forehead is stitched with wrinkles. Her hair is more gray than black. She is only forty-three.

Deep inside the Texas Gulf coast city of Corpus Christi, in the *barrios* that the tourists never see, there is a saying among Chicanos:

"The only way a family can get out of debt here is for their son to get killed in Vietnam, so they can collect on his insurance policy."

Take a walk in the sun-bathed rows of an Arizona onion patch not far from Phoenix. As many as six hundred men and women are at work in one field, husband and wife often side-by-side. Their bodies become a blur of motion as they squat and bend and pull green onions from the soil, shake them until the dirt falls free, twist a rubber band around them, throw them in a pile, squat, bend, pull, shake, twist, throw—on and on for hours.

The workers say they each earn about fifty dollars a week this way.

Almost without fail in the Southwest, wherever there is a large concentration of Spanish-surnamed people there is an organization dedicated to the betterment of the Chicanos, this nation's second largest minority.

Among the best known are the American GI Forum and League of United Latin-American Citizens (LULAC), which were founded years ago.

But young Mexican-Americans say such groups have worked too quietly and too patiently and that their progress has been far too slow. The young people speak of fiery leaders like Reies Lopes Tijerina of New Mexico and Corky Gonzales of Colorado and say these men, at least, have brought the Chicano problems to light.

Tijerina, 42, who with his followers has laid claim to six hundred thousand acres of Northern New Mexico, says an Anglo "conspiracy" is keeping the Spanish-surnamed down.

Tijerina's cause is based on claims to old Spanish land grants. But he has broadened his approach, calling for unity among the Spanish-speaking throughout the Southwest. "Our god is our language, our blood!" he cries.

Inside a battered, former Baptist church in Denver, former boxer Corky Gonzales, forty-one, boasts that he can put together a protest march "at the drop of a hat."

He and members of his Crusade for Justice were among those staging a Mexican-American demonstration at a Denver high school earlier this year. Violence broke out between young Chicanos and police. Gonzales and about twenty-five other protesters were arrested.

The mustached, self-styled poet and civil rights leader tells of plans for walkouts "in every school where there's a Mexican-American child" on September 16, Mexico's independence day.

Popping into public view within the last two years have been young Chicano groups such as the Brown Berets in California and the Mexican-American Youth Organization (MAYO) in Texas.

David Sanchez, a handsome, clean-cut young man of twenty, is the founder and "prime minister" of the Berets, headquartered in predominantly Mexican-American East Los Angeles.

Sanchez says the Berets have twenty-six chapters in California, Texas, and other states as far east as Michigan. Their aim, he says, is to achieve unity among the Chicanos and "restore the dignity in our people."

The Berets are often described as militant, but Sanchez asserts they don't advocate violence—"we never have"—but at the same time, he adds, they are not opposed to violence as a means of self-defense.

The Texas counterpart to the Brown Berets is MAYO, whose trademarks have become serape jackets and clenched brown fists raised in defiance of the Anglo "establishment."

MAYO recently announced a formal alliance with Corky Gonzales' Crusade for Justice to further unify Mexican-Americans.

MAYO leaders have said that as a last resort they may be forced to eliminate racist gringos by killing them. But in private these same leaders admit they have to issue such militant statements to get the Anglo's attention and make him more aware of Mexican-American problems.

Like the Brown Berets, MAYO spokesmen say they would resort to violence only in self-defense.

MAYO leaders talk of plans to fight the Chicano problem non-violently through politics, education, and the establishment of Chicano-owned businesses.

The San Antonio-based group was financed indirectly by the Ford Foundation until Representative Henry B. Gonzalez (D-Tex.) criticized the foundation for doing so. He accused MAYO of spreading racial unrest in Texas, which was denied.

The MAYO chieftain, Mario Compean, twenty-eight, said MAYO cut its ties with the foundation after Ford officials asked the group to refrain from political activity.

Gonzalez says MAYO has absolutely no support from the Mexican-American community in general. MAYO denies this allegation also. However, Compean lost heavily in a recent election of representatives for the poor on San Antonio's chief poverty war agency. Perhaps the central symbol to thousands in the Brown Power movement is the United Farm Workers organizing committee, headed by softspoken, sad-faced Cesar Chavez—who once fasted twenty-five days to dramatize his dedication to nonviolence.

Often working from bed in his Delano, California, home because of a back ailment, Chavez, forty-two, has organized hundreds of grape pickers in California, and his cause has gained supporters ranging from senators to religious groups.

Manuel Chavez, Cesar's brother, has been laying the groundwork for union activities in Arizona. Manuel designed the bold black eagle on the blazing red flag that has become the emblem of the farm union and young Chicano groups throughout the Southwest as well. Antonio Orendain, one of Cesar's key men, has been busy at groundwork union activities in the Río Grande Valley of Texas.

Yet to be answered is the question of violence. Older Mexican-Americans state flatly there will be no widespread violence from this ethnic group. The younger Chicanos aren't so sure.

"To deny myself the use of violence would be like forming a union without being able to strike," said one young Mexican-American at U.C.L.A. "I'll tell you one thing. If it does come to violence, we won't be destroying our own homes."

In the Anglo communities, private industry has made some effort to alleviate the condition of the Mexican-American.

Ling-Temco-Vought Aerospace corporation of Dallas sent a mobile classroom to the Río Grande Valley to train 684 Mexican-Americans. After completing their training, the men and their families were moved to the Dallas area for permanent jobs with L.-T.-V. The project has been called an outstanding success.

The Technical-Vocational Institute in Albuquerque has had similar success since it opened just four years ago. Students range in age from eighteen to sixty-one at this publicly supported school, where tuition is only five dollars. Training is offered in more than a dozen fields, such as electronics and drafting.

In Phoenix, the Southwest Council of La Raza is channeling $630,000 in Ford Foundation funds to various Mexican-American groups for such programs as community development and voter registration.

But Vincente Ximenes, chief of the federal Equal Employment Opportunity Commission, complains bitterly that no one can "convince the establishment that Mexican-Americans are really there."

Ximenes has called for a ten-year, billion-dollar-a-year program that would improve education systems that now "produce a preponderant number of angry high school Mexican-American dropouts and a pitiful number of college graduates."

Educators say one of the biggest barriers the Mexican-American faces is the English language, particularly in Texas, which has thousands of first- and second-generation immigrants from Mexico.

Typically, a Chicano child starts the first grade knowing no English at all.

In the past, teachers punished youngsters for speaking Spanish in the classroom and even on the playground. It was officially barred from school in some areas, except in language courses. Texas repealed state public school laws to this effect only this year.

Five years ago the San Antonio school district, like others in the Southwest, launched a bilingual education project in elementary schools.

"Years ago you couldn't utter one word of Spanish in the schools and you got to thinking your language is no good so you yourself are no good," recalled Nick Garza, former principal at one of the bilingual project schools in San Antonio.

51. To Live in Freedom, To Die a Timely Death

Paul Good

THE end of the hearing does not insure the beginning of change. Change comes hard anywhere when race relations, with their economic, social, and psychological complexities, are the issue. This is especially apparent in rural Alabama where traditions that limit life for some men are a way of life for others. Old forms block the way of new visions. Racial myths and economic realities combine to thwart black aspirations and to make whites uneasy warders of despair.

If the testimony at the two hearings ten years apart proves anything it is that the federal government *can* be the prime instrument of change. Whether it *will* be an instrument of significant change is uncertain, the evidence mixed. C. Erskine Smith, a white lawyer from Birmingham and Chairman of the Alabama State Advisory Committee to the U.S. Commission on Civil Rights, brings an analytical eye and compassionate mind to the plight of poor black citizens in his state. He speaks as a member of an old and respected Alabama family, and as a contemporary observer disciplined by law to avoid hyperbole. He says:

> . . . the federal programs which are designed to aid the poor have had little impact on the black poor of rural Alabama. These people, who have had their hopes raised again and again as they were told of many federal programs which were supposedly written with them in mind, find that in reality they were empty promises and a cruel hoax.

Mr. Smith says that Community Action programs too often are controlled by that ubiquitous exploiter of the poor, the power structure. He finds that " . . . the only antipoverty programs which offer any real promise are those which are funded directly from Washington and have by-passed the local CAP." Even Washington fails where

From *Cycle to Nowhere* (United States Commission on Civil Rights, 1968), 45–51. Reprinted by permission.

education is concerned. According to Mr. Smith, all the HEW guidelines and directives have not appreciably changed black education from its habitual state—segregated and inferior. The latest HEW pledge of an integrated Alabama school system by 1969-70 at the latest draws this comment:

> . . . the black people of Alabama don't believe these words and they told us so in countless meetings across this state. We say it is a serious thing when people have lost faith in their government.

He sees improvement in registration and voting despite an inadequate federal presence with examiners sent to only twelve counties. But gains are under continuous pressure from the forces of recidivism.

"The 'rules of the game' are being changed constantly to maintain white supremacy," he tells the hearing which receives testimony of filing fees jumping 900 per cent when Negroes seek to become candidates. "Fear is still a formidable enemy and the lack of economic security leads to the lack of effective use of the franchise, which contributes to the lack of economic security."

Mr. Smith feels there is better administration of justice and a reduced incidence of violence against civil rights workers in Alabama. But the number of workers is also reduced sharply in comparison to the force that worked in the violent days a few years back, and he warns that "if there were an increase in direct confrontations there would be an increase in acts of violence. The Civil Rights Act of 1968," Mr. Smith continues, "should be of some value in this area, if it is vigorously enforced by federal authorities."

Federal enforcement of equal job opportunity laws is so lax that he calls this an era of "paper compliance." Mr. Smith and his Advisory Committee find "little evidence of really affirmative action on the part of employers to recruit, train, and employ Negroes." The record in agriculture, he reports, is similarly dismal.

"We are convinced," Mr. Smith concludes, "that the problem of the rural poor cannot be solved by patching up existing regulations. We think new structures and new personnel who are sympathetic to the needs of the people are needed, along with new programs."

Rev. Kenneth L. Buford lives in Macon County, home of Tuskegee Institute, and he is Alabama state field director for the NAACP. Neither radical nor reluctant to press for equal rights, Rev. Buford testified at the first Montgomery hearing in 1958. Ten years later he is asked what major changes have taken place in the state since then and the veteran of thirty years in the civil rights movement replies: "I would say some improvements have been made. I hesitate to use the word 'progress' but I would say that there has been some improvement."

Rev. Buford's own Macon County probably has seen more progress or improvements than any other. But it is unique in being able to draw on Tuskegee's staff and students, and on black employees in a large Veterans Administration hospital for political activists economically independent of whites. Improvements in the black community have centered around the political process. Even before the Voting Rights Act of 1965, federal court orders opened the way for the county's four-to-one Negro majority to vote and hold office (Rev. Buford himself was registered under court order after a white registrar decided he was not "intelligent enough" to be an Alabama voter). Black men on the Board of Revenue have meant paved streets in Negro neighborhoods historically served by dirt roads, muddy or dusty depending on the season. There are local government salaries shared by black residents where such paychecks used to be a white monopoly. There is even the first Negro sheriff in the South since Reconstruction, Lucius Amerson, who says he considers himself "an American first, and a man second, and a Negro third." Whites did not easily accept the notion of law in the form of a gun on a black man's hip, a badge on a black breast. But Amerson handled things with a forceful, confident cool.

"I don't know what is so different about my being sheriff than a sheriff in Mississippi," he says. "Other than I don't beat up folks."

But the racial millenium has not reached Macon County. Even there, the grip of racism is tenacious on affairs public and private. Some white churches still close doors in the face of blacks come to worship. Black farmers, like the witness Hosea Guice, still must fight white-dominated officialdom to get what is theirs by right under Agriculture Department programs. Whites control the board of trustees at all-black Tuskegee and the Institute has experienced the kind of student revolts occurring at Howard and Columbia universities. Militant black youth regard the pace of progress in Alabama as rank gradualism and the election of one black sheriff as irrelevant when measured against the scope of extralegal white actions that render the black franchise impotent throughout most of the state. Student Leon Kennedy is fired with suspicions about the white man who has profited through racism and he tells the hearing that he mistrusts both the man and the capacity of his system to reform itself.

"He has all kinds of tricks to use against our people," young Kennedy says:

Like you've got these people up here right now believing that the Commission is going to do something about this problem. And that is not going to happen. You cannot make a law and expect that law to be followed. The laws have been broken for years and years. . . . You cannot just in one day pass a law in Congress and expect every-body in the United States to follow that law. And you cannot have a marshal at every white man's door in Greenville, Alabama. . . . You can't have a marshal at every mill where a black man wants to be hired. And if you get discriminated against or shot dead tonight, who are you going to call? The Commission?

Bitter experience leads to bitter conclusions. Kennedy has grown up black in Alabama and he says:

People . . . are tired, very, very tired of all of this trickery up and down. And something is going to come out of it one way or the other. Give us half of the country . . . or put us out of the country. Or kill us all.

But for all the bitterness that eighteen years of Alabama living has produced in him, he does not want to uproot himself.

"I want to live in the South," he says. "The tropical area, the heat, geographical location and everything. I just dig the South, period."

So do a lot of older black Alabamians. It is a constant theme in all the testimony. Bernard Shambray whose dreams of becoming a weaver were rudely awakened once tried emigrating to New York to work. But he soon returned to Alabama.

"I guess I'm just a country boy," he says. "I really liked the country life rather than the city life."

Roy Thomas, evicted from his Sumter County farm after a life-time there, was offered a chance to go North by a nephew.

"He said people in the North were just as bad as the weather," Mr. Thomas recalls. "So I didn't think I wanted to get mixed up in that."

Willie Smith, demoted from staff sergeant to "boy" on his return to Alabama from the service, tried Chicago briefly. Neither he nor his Alabama-born wife was impressed.

"If things were changed, I would love living here," Mrs. Smith says. "Because living in Chicago, or when I was in New York, they are so crowded there. And I like to live in a house to myself, where I could have a big yard for my children to play in. I would prefer living here in Alabama where I could have a lot of air, fresh air, and a big house to myself."

"Actually, I don't think I liked Chicago," her husband testifies. "It seemed to be—well, it is too fast for me . . . everybody from here is up there. . . . I know more people in Chicago than I do at home since I been back home because all my friends and classmates—I can't think of but one classmate that is here now that graduated from high school with me."

It is eloquent, if wistful, testimony to the greatest migration of modern times, the movement of black from South to North, more than three million people in twenty-five years. But the hearing destroys the fiction that the North is seen as a Promised Land by black people eager to leave their Southland. The human truth permits no such Northern conceit. Home in the South, for all its poverty and exploitation, contains a familiar ambience, a link to past generations, the feel of belonging to the land despite white assertion that black exists there only through white sufferance. To go North means to exchange known country graces for the alien squalor of a ghetto with its dangers and disillusions. The ghetto is a last resort, an undependable refuge from the intolerable social and economic oppression, and families driven to it do not carry great expectations in their Southern baggage, only small hope. The poverty cycle that has betrayed them in Alabama or Georgia too often continues that betrayal in New York or Illinois. The West Side of Chicago works no magic to undo the years of slack education in Bellamy, a Greenville broompusher is not transformed into a computer specialist on establishing residence in Bedford-Stuyvesant. No "place" can revitalize bodies run down beyond their years or make a shining receptacle of minds that have become rusty buckets. Children are dropped into the tough new world of the ghetto, a world often physically brutal and spiritually barren. Some become the living stuff of riot, others drift for the rest of their lives in urban backwaters never touched by those ongoing currents of modern American life. Their personal tragedies are unrecorded. But contemporary history is writing large the price society pays for their failure.

Faced with the Northern alternative, it does not take much to induce some black people to trick it out in Alabama. Lewis Black is director of the Rural Advancement Project for the Alabama Council on Human Relations. The title is cumbersome but the thrust of the Project is not encumbered by titular or theoretical burdens. It simply tries to help those who are struggling against severe odds to live decently in Alabama. A handful of credit unions, quilting bees, and tiny co-operatives have been formed with little or no help from local or federal agencies.

Mr. Black says:

> ... the awareness of the services that these people can receive from these agencies has been systematically kept from these people because

of this bureaucracy. Everything comes through the same power structure folks. And when I say power structure folks it may be the banker, or it might be the person who is FHA supervisor, it might be the mayor of the town or it could be the judge, or city councilmen.

Mr. Black's obvious love is co-operatives and he draws a nice distinction between them and the usual business enterprise.

"When you set up corporations," he says, "the main emphasis is put on money, the capital outlay that people have. But when you set up a co-operative, the main emphasis is put on people."

People like the thirty-eight ladies from Hale and Greene counties who had been fifteen dollars and twenty dollars a week domestics, cleaning up after white people and watching white children while their own watched each other. Instead of fleeing north or continuing their domestic indenture, they formed the Greene-Hale Sewing Co-operative, a cottage industry. It holds no lucrative government contracts like Dan River and it does not subsist on federal loans. Starting with nothing, the co-op has survived through determination and a few hundred occasional dollars from concerned private agencies like the Southern Regional Council, American Friends, and the Sharecroppers Fund.

"We gave written proposals to several agencies and foundations," Mr. Black reports. "And the only thing that we have received from them is that they are just considering, that they are looking into it. But it is difficult for real—when I say 'real' I mean low-income people —to get money from government agencies because people have got to see some feasibility there on a project before they put money into it. So these ladies have to start somewhere to show that they have the skills and the techniques to show this thing as being feasible."

They are showing their thing. The co-op that once measured output in two or three garments a day now counts production in the hundreds. A few Northern contracts have been obtained. Nobody is getting rich, it is slow going economically but "the main emphasis is put on people." People are being trained so that someday, even should the co-op fail, they will come away with a skill that can keep them out of a white family's kitchen. If Alabama industry will hire them.

Here and there the commission unearths cause for cautious optimism. There is the Dixie Shoe Corporation in Eufaula that has been fully integrated since it began operations five years ago. Rural blacks and whites were trained together under federal programs and today some make as much as three dollars an hour. Plant manager Harold Becker's testimony is a rebuttal to those who have excused job discrimination on the grounds that ill-educated field hands can't qualify for factory employment. He says that those hired were "farmers, peanut farmers, cotton farmers, regular farmers." Did they have trouble adjusting to a nonsegregated industrial setting?

"None whatsoever," says Mr. Becker.

If a small company named Dixie can put a crimp in the poverty cycle, large corporations could help to break it. One searches for evidence of corporate commitment and does not find it. Instead, there is tokenism in black hiring, evasion of legal responsibilities, and sometimes behavior that seems to make neither good sense nor good business. For example, MacMillan-Bloedel, Inc., prevented Wilcox County from getting a five-million-dollar federal grant to build an access bridge to its plant because it failed to sign a standard nondiscrimination pledge. MacMillan-Bloedel had already been the beneficiary of a tax-exempt seventy-million-dollar bond issue floated by Wilcox County to induce the company to erect pulp and plywood facilities there. A river had to be crossed to enable employees to reach the plant. The Federal Economic Development Administration offered the five million dollars if the job pledge were signed, and even Wilcox County (long a vigorous opponent of civil rights activity) was agreeable. But MacMillan-Bloedel was not. The company viewed the pledge as an abridgement of its hiring prerogatives with industrial relations manager Horace Hamby, Jr., explaining that his firm wants to hire "without any assistance or without any artificial restraints or interference." Hiring thusly, it has no Negro clerical help and no Negro supervisors although it is in partnership with a government contractor, United Fruit, supplying it with banana box material. The State of Alabama, which cannot find money for child welfare, found five million dollars for the bridge. Under law, of course, Mac-Millan-Bloedel is expected to comply with antidiscrimination law no matter who pays for the span. But the company will cross that bridge when it comes to it.

So the record of the hearing goes, the body of testimony negative, the weight of statistics oppressive. But if the record is filled with failure, it is also a receptacle of passionate commitment by some black men and white men that failure is not irrevocable. The Poor People's Campaign planned by the late Dr. Martin Luther King, Jr., was getting underway as the Montgomery testimony accumulated. Hosea Williams, one of Dr. King's lieutenants in the Southern Christian Leadership Conference, came to tell it like it was and what it must be.

   . . . the society or the system has overplayed one part of the Scriptures. That which reads, "You are your brother's keeper." And poor people have been kept so long that we are not able to keep ourselves. And we are asking for an opportunity to keep ourselves, to break that cycle of poverty, to break that cycle of illiteracy, to break that cycle of illegitimacy, to break that cycle of crime.

There are jailhouses that are filled with black men and poor whites in this nation. Not because they are black or poor white, but mainly because the father of that home does not make enough money to buy that boy decent clothes and give him a little spending change. So he falls out of school being ashamed of his run-over shoes or his ragged pants, and then he starts stealing from the five-and-dime store, stealing from the grocery store. He ends up robbing, he ends up lying and thieving and cheating, he ends up in a life of crime—good minds that could be productive, minds that might find the cure for cancer, minds that might find the cure for cardiac and other dreadful diseases.

We are not saying in our Poor People's Campaign that the Rockefellers and the Kennedys and the Fords should not be millionaires. But we are certainly saying that while there are millionaires, we must not have the Buttermilk Bottoms in Atlanta, Georgia; we must not have the Watts in Los Angeles; we must not have the West Sides of Chicago or the Harlems of New York. . . . Because we feel in this country God has blessed it and there is enough resources in this country that every woman ought to be able to get prenatal care. Every woman, if she so desires, ought to be able to stay home and raise her children rather than being driven out by a vicious, obsolete economic system every morning to leave her little children at home to raise themselves and she has to go over into other folks' homes and raise their children.

The woman cannot stay home, thereby the man has no comfort to come home to. . . . And the men, both black and white, are forced to work for such menial wages, they are forced to come up and be reared with such kind of education until they have to be Uncle Toms all day long just to keep a raggedy job, to keep a roof over their head and some food in their family's belly. And not being able to be men all day, they come home at night and they scold their wives, or they beat their children to prove themselves—which is one of the innate desires of mankind—to be men.

Williams, one of those overrun by mounted possemen on Selma's Edmund Pettus Bridge in 1965 and sojourner in Black Belt hamlets cartographers overlook, sums up what the campaign is all about.

Our Poor People's Campaign is a nonviolent program designed to help every man in this country find himself, love, understand, and respect himself. This is why a lot of people resort to violence and they resort to looting and they resort to burning and they resort to what we call the welfare system—because they have no respect for themselves, they are not allowed to understand themselves, particularly in the black community. Now all our program is designed to do is that every man in this country can get a job, one that he finds fulfillment and creativity in. . . . Our Poor People's Campaign is designed so that poor people in the South will understand this land is our land, and there's no such thing as a freedom land in a New York City or Chicago. . . . And we ask America, particularly in the absence of the Moses of our time, to please adhere to what we are calling for— a nonviolent, nationwide massive struggle to save America from burning herself to death, from looting herself to death.

Struggle inevitably involves upheaval and disruption—upheaval of old assumptions that time cloaks in the authority of natural law, disruption of ways of life so pleasantly familiar and rewarding to some men that they equate privilege with natural right. Many men of good will were affronted by the activism of the early civil rights movement, even as the current campaigns in Alabama and elsewhere raise the protest of "Too much, too fast" from those who have always had enough. Commission Vice Chairman Eugene Patterson, editor of the *Atlanta Constitution,* says of Mr. Williams after he has finished:

He has spoken from his heart. And he has spoken as a man, and he has spoken responsibly and he has spoken to us as whites. Through the years, history shows that all of us have stayed just a little bit behind what was happening. I as a newspaper man, know this especially well . . . because what I have said is public record. But at the death of Dr. King I looked back over these twelve years to this city of Montgomery and I recognize that the bus boycott, which at the time disordered my society and disturbed me, had led—now in looking back, I recognize now it led me to see a man lead his children onto a bus and sit where he pleased. And I am glad.

And when the sit-ins came to my city, they disordered my life and they disordered my city's life and they disturbed my peace and I was not altogether approving. In looking back I am a little ashamed and appalled that I ever made it necessary for a Negro father to take his children into a restaurant and fear anything, fear to drive down a highway and find a place where he could feed his child. I take no pride in that ever having been the case in my life. And the Freedom Rides disturbed me and I denounced them editorially from time to time. But I now, looking back, am a little ashamed that I ever sat in a waiting room while other men sat with their children in a separate waiting room.

And so all I want this record to show . . . is that things do change, times do move, and men do learn. And for the nonviolence that Dr. King preached and that Mr. Williams has echoed here tonight, I suggest that this Nation should be profoundly thankful and should take up that hand of friendship and move forward together as men, as Americans.

When the last witness has been heard, the camera lights extinguished, and the steno machine stilled, a question hangs in the hearing room: Will anything come from all the words and the emotions behind them? The question applies not only to Alabama but to every state where people hunger for bread and thirst for justice. The nation can no longer plead ignorance of need. The commission and private groups in scores of similar hearings have shown what is wrong and indicated what must be done to set things right. And now it is up to the national will to answer the question articulated in Montgomery. An affirmative answer involves nothing less than an American commitment envisioned by attorney Erskine Smith when he testified:

> ... the creation of a society where all citizens may walk in dignity, eat a wholesome diet, sleep in a decent house, live in economic and social freedom, and finally to die a timely death unhurried by malnutrition and the lack of adequate medical services.
>
> It is not very much to ask.
> It will be everything to refuse.

Index